The NOLO *News*—

Our free magazine devoted to everyday legal & consumer issues

To thank you for sending in the postage-paid feedback card in the back of this book, you'll receive a free two-year subscription to the **NOLO** *News*—our quarterly magazine of legal, small business and consumer information. With each issue you get updates on important legal changes that affect you, helpful articles on everyday law, answers to your legal questions in Auntie Nolo's advice column, a complete Nolo catalog and, of course, our famous lawyer jokes.

Legal information online—24 hours a day

Get instant access to the legal information you need 24 hours a day.

Visit a Nolo online self-help law center and you'll find:

- hundreds of helpful articles on a wide variety of topics
- selected chapters from Nolo books
- online seminars with our lawyer authors and other experts
- downloadable demos of Nolo software
- frequently asked questons about key legal issues
- our complete catalog and online ordering info
- our ever popular lawyer jokes and more.

Here's how to find us:

America Online Just use the key word Nolo.

On the **Internet** our World Wide Web address (URL) is: http://www.nolo.com.

Prodigy/CompuServe Use the Web Browsers on CompuServe or Prodigy to access Nolo's Web site on the Internet.

MAD AT YOUR LAWYER ?

by Attorney Tanya Starnes

with Arthur G. White and Jennifer A. Becker

NOLO PRESS ⚖ BERKELEY

Using a Self-Help Law Book

...and accurate information in this book. But laws and ...ubject to differing interpretations. If you want legal ...er. If you use this book, it's your responsibility to make sure that the facts and general advice contained in it are applicable to your situation.

Keeping Up to Date

To keep its books up to date, Nolo Press issues new printings and new editions periodically. New printings reflect minor legal changes and technical corrections. New editions contain major legal changes, major text additions or major reorganizations. To find out if a later printing or edition of any Nolo book is available, call Nolo Press at 510-549-1976 or check the catalog in the *Nolo News*, our quarterly publication.

To stay current, follow the "Update" service in the *Nolo News*. You can get a free two-year subscription by sending us the registration card in the back of the book. In another effort to help you use Nolo's latest materials, we offer a 25% discount off the purchase of the new edition of your Nolo book if you turn in the cover of an earlier edition. (See the "Recycle Offer" in the back of this book.) This book was last revised in: September 1996.

First Edition	SEPTEMBER 1996
Editors	ROBIN LEONARD & RALPH WARNER
Illustrations	MARI STEIN
Cover Design	TONI IHARA
Book Design	TERRI HEARSH
Index	SUSAN CORNELL
Proofreading	ROBERT WELLS
Printing	CONSOLIDATED PRINTERS, INC.

Starnes, Tanya, 1953-
    Mad at your lawyer / by Tanya Starnes with Arthur G. White and Jennifer A. Becker. -- 1st ed.
      p. cm.
    Includes index.
    ISBN 0-87337-326-X
    1. Attorney and client--United States--Popular works. 2. Lawyers--United States--Fees--Popular works. 3. Lawyers--Malpratice--United States--Popular works. I. White, Aruther G., 1948- .
II. Becker, Jennifer A., 1959- . III. Title.
KF311.Z9S73 1996
340'.023'73--dc20   96-27640
                                               CIP

For information on bulk purchases or corporate premium sales, please contact the Special Sales Department. For academic sales or textbook adoptions, ask for Academic Sales. Call 800-955-4775 or write to Nolo Press, Inc., 950 Parker Street, Berkeley, CA 94710.

Dedication

To Martina, my partner in all things, who makes me laugh.

Author's Note

Writing this book was a collaborative effort. The two lawyers with whom I have practiced for many years wrote substantial portions of the book and contributed to it in many other ways. The material on attorneys' fees and much of the material on conflicts of interest were primarily written by Arthur G. White. The material on disciplinary matters (Chapter 8) and trust accounts was primarily written by Jennifer A. Becker. This book is the result of years of our close collaboration, working together to develop a law practice in which we primarily sue other lawyers. Without their hard work on both the book and in our law practice, the book would not have happened.

Acknowledgments

My heartfelt thanks to the following people:

Martina Reaves, communicator extraordinaire, who made substantial contributions to Chapter 2, always knows what to say, and has spent countless hours polishing my language and demeanor.

Robin Leonard, a brilliant editor, who wrote significant portions of Chapter 11, who made me think I was doing a good job, even when I wasn't, whose kindness, hard work and reassurances enabled me to complete this book and who made it come alive. **Jake Warner**, who asked me to write this book, shared his creative genius and never-ending editorial enthusiasm, and has had more patience than one could ever ask. **Steve Elias**, who read this manuscript from cover to cover, offered many creative suggestions, and didn't ask me to start over.

My clients who have inspired me to do good work, especially **Mollie Katzen, Teresa Menzel, Donna Rosenthal, Zachary Solomon, Jim Hennefer, Mary Ann Wilton** and **Lorene Lake**. **Dan Mancinelli** was even willing to let me conduct legal experiments on his case so I could use them in this book.

My colleagues, friends and frequent adversaries at Long & Levit, including **Ron Mallen** (the original guru of legal malpractice), **Joe McMonigle, Howard Garfield** and **John Hook**, all of whom got me started in the legal malpractice business and who have kept me going in more ways than one. **Wanda Ginner**, C.P.A. par excellence, who has a special gift to make numbers make sense and who is always willing to answer my questions. **Donald Steedman** from the State Bar of California, who shared his knowledge and insight about lawyer disciplinary matters.

Terri Hearsh and **Toni Ihara**, for the layout and design. **Susan Cornell**, who offered many kind words of encouragement as she retyped draft after draft. **Stan Jacobson** at Nolo, who did everything that no one else would do.

Judy B. Reaves, for her exuberance and for being the light of every Thursday, and for reading the manuscript from cover to cover. **Pam Wolpa**, for being a great assistant, who juggles ten balls in the air at once, while making sure deadlines are calendared, pleadings are filed, the right lawyer is in the right courthouse with the right file at the right time, five copies of the exhibits are in the trial binders, the jury instructions are ready, everyone is happy, the 50-state chart is ready for Nolo, the iced tea is made, and "Pam, would you hold my calls?"

Judith Daar, who collected information from every state bar in the country. **Lila Booth**, who made many last-minute phone calls, taught me everything I know about computers and has brought years of good cheer. **Donna Dobkin**, who took care of business while I was in the library. **Laura Stevens**, the best employment lawyer in Northern California, who is always willing to share her knowledge and experience.

Cooper, my daily inspiration, who let me take time off part-time from being a mom. I promise now we'll play tennis, read more books, go to the movies, and I'll start cooking dinner again!

My mother, whose strength and iron will I must have inherited, who taught me to know myself, speak my mind, enjoy what I do and who was the perfect mother for me. **My father**, whose never-ending effort to teach me right from wrong is remarkable, who helped me through school even when he didn't like what I was learning, who has a happy, easygoing nature and is always willing to play dominoes. **My sister**, who has a heart the size of Texas and makes everything fun.

Suzanne Mounts, my first teacher of trial practice skills, who showed me that getting ready for trial can be exhilarating, that you can get a case dismissed if a witness doesn't show up, and how to bag out on a vacation if something better comes along. **Sandra Shapiro**, trial lawyer par excellence, who offered fashion advice when I needed it most and who taught me how to cross-examine a witness. **Linda Krieger**, my conscientious law professor friend, who is always willing to answer my obscure legal questions about civil procedure.

My loyal friends, **Billie Middleton**, **Anita Hayward**, **Jenny Grogan**, **Marjorie Cox** and **Nancy Rhoda**, who have been extraordinarily good-natured about my dropping out of sight to work on this book. **Bonnie Ng**, **Paul Kramer** and **Perry Kramer**, for being the greatest neighbors in the world, for feeding my family like royalty and for picking up more slack than anyone could ever ask.

Jan Goodman, principal with principles, for her wisdom and guidance.

TABLE OF CONTENTS

4 CONFLICTS OF INTERESTS— IF YOUR LAWYER ISN'T LOYAL TO YOU

5 FIRING YOUR LAWYER

6 GETTING YOUR FILE

7 FEE DISPUTES AND FEE ARBITRATION

8 FILING A COMPLAINT WITH YOUR LAWYER DISCIPLINE AGENCY

9 SUING YOUR FORMER LAWYER

10 Taking Action Against the Lawyer for the Other Side

11 Help Beyond the Book

Index

INTRODUCTION

You've picked up this book because you're mad at, miffed with or disappointed in the person you hired to do legal work for you. You thought your lawyer would work diligently and professionally on your problem, but you have learned otherwise. The cause for your dissatisfaction may be any of the following:

- You haven't spoken to your lawyer in months, and none of your calls have been returned or your letters answered.
- Your lawyer forgot to attend a deposition or court hearing, leaving you feeling both scared and abandoned.
- You have learned that your lawyer is a close friend of the opposing lawyer—or worse, the opposing party—in your case.
- You have received a bill for far more than you agreed to or believe your lawyer is fairly entitled to.
- You believe your lawyer's work is incompetent and that, as a result, your interests or rights have been jeopardized.

If you have a complaint with an attorney, you're probably well aware that you're not alone. Thousands of people each year file complaints with state bar associations or sue lawyers—and these people represent just the tip of the iceberg of disatisfaction. According to a survey done by *Consumer Reports* magazine, an estimated 25% of all clients who hire lawyers to handle adversarial matters are somewhat, very or completely dissatisfied with their lawyer's work. (See *Consumer Reports*, February 1996.) Specific *Consumer Reports* findings are in the table below:

Nature of Dissatisfaction	Percent Dissatisfied in Adversarial Cases	Percent Dissatisfied in Nonadversarial Cases
Lawyer didn't expedite the resolution of the case.	32%	13%
Lawyer didn't keep the client informed.	27%	12%
Lawyer overcharged.	27%	13%
Lawyer didn't protect the client's rights and financial interests.	25%	9%
Lawyer didn't promptly return phone calls.	22%	8%
Lawyer didn't pay adequate attention to the case.	21%	7%
Lawyer didn't disclose costs up front.	20%	12%
Lawyer didn't explain how long process might take.	15%	6%
Lawyer didn't accurately predict outcome.	15%	3%

This book gives you the tools to confront your lawyer and take other action if you face any of these or other situations. No longer must you feel helpless when you're mad at your lawyer.

ICONS TO HELP YOU ALONG

 The "fast track" arrow alerts you that you can skip some material that isn't relevant to your situation.

 The "caution" icon warns you of potential problems.

 This icon refers you to helpful books or other resources for further information.

 The "tip" icon gives you hints on dealing with special situations.

Chapter 1

Is This Book for You?

Section A of this chapter defines the general kinds of problems people have with their lawyers and focuses on the specific solutions. Section B gives you real-life problems and directs you to the chapters of the book where you'll find more information.

A. A Roadmap to Problem Solving When You're Mad at Your Lawyer

Most problems that people have with their lawyers fall into four basic categories: communications problems, incompetence (malpractice) problems, ethical problems (when your lawyer doesn't represent you with undivided loyalty) and fee problems. Furthermore, it's rare that you will have just one problem—more likely, your problems will fall into two or more categories.

Communications problems. Communications problems can cause you to think you have a bad lawyer when you don't or that your lawyer is doing a bad job when she isn't. If your lawyer provided you with a basic description of your legal matter, and lets you know what problems to expect, how they'll be handled and when things will happen, you will be on the right track to having a good relationship with your lawyer—and to making sure that your legal matter is handled properly. Knowing how to talk and listen to your lawyer are the first steps toward minimizing problems with your lawyer.

Competence problems. If your lawyer makes a mistake in handling your legal matter that no reasonable attorney would have made and you were damaged by it, it is called malpractice. The mistake can be a failure to do something the lawyer should have done, such as filing a lawsuit on time, or doing something the lawyer should not have done, such as representing a business in bankruptcy while representing an investor negotiating to buy the business. This book will help you figure out if you have a malpractice claim and if so, what you can do about it.

Ethical problems. Each state has ethical laws which define standards of lawyer behavior. The most common rules look something like the following:

- Lawyers must represent their clients with undivided loyalty.
- Lawyers must keep their clients' confidences.
- Lawyers must represent their clients competently.
- Lawyers must represent their clients within the bounds of the law.
- Lawyers must not put their personal interests ahead of those of their clients.

Each state has a lawyer discipline agency which is supposed to enforce these rules. If a lawyer violates a rule, the agency can impose monetary fines, require the lawyer to make "restitution" (such as pay back stolen money), suspend a lawyer's license to practice law for a period of months or years, or disbar the attorney.

Fee problems. No matter how you pay your lawyer—by the hour, as a percentage of your recovery, or a combination of the two—what you want most is a lawyer who has common sense and will be fair. This isn't easy to find. You don't want your $15,000 legal problem worked to death so that you'll owe $25,000 in lawyer fees. Similarly, it doesn't seem fair to pay half of your $1 million recovery for your catastrophic injury to a lawyer who settled your case with a phone call.

If you pay by the hour, you don't pay according to how much time it should take to do a task—you pay according to how much time the lawyer actually spends doing it. Smart lawyers are not always fast workers, efficient or organized. Fast lawyers are not always smart. Keep in mind that a lawyer who charges $100 per hour can cost you more than a lawyer who charges $300 per hour to handle the same matter.

How much lawyers charge varies a lot. This makes it difficult to comparison shop based upon price. Given that no lawyer is cheap, it is unlikely that you will have a fee problem with your lawyer if you have good communication, your lawyer does a good job handling your legal problem, you and your lawyer treat each other fairly and exercise common sense, and your lawyer depends upon referrals from satisfied clients.

There are several possible solutions to your lawyer problems. Depending upon your problem, you may decide to pursue any of the following:

Work on improving communications. Make sure you aren't expecting too much from your lawyer, your expectations are realistic and you have done your part to give your lawyer what she needs.

Educate yourself about your legal problem. Read your file in your lawyer's office, go to the courthouse and look at your case file, talk to your lawyer about your case, conduct your own legal research to educate yourself and consider consulting with another lawyer for a second opinion.

Get your file. If your case is still going on, ask your lawyer to send you copies of everything— all correspondence and everything filed with the court or recorded with a government agency. This will help you keep up with what is and isn't happening in your case and will be important to show to another lawyer if you want to get a second opinion. If you've already ended your relationship with your lawyer, you need your file pronto to make sure all deadlines are met, to take any corrective steps to repair mistakes made by your prior lawyer and to get or keep the case or legal matter moving towards completion.

Get an opinion from a second lawyer. The more you can tell and show a second lawyer about your case, the better he will be able to advise you about whether your case is being handled correctly or make suggestions about what might be done differently. Keep in mind that no two lawyers handle a case exactly the same way and that a second opinion is usually a cursory review, not a comprehensive analysis. Nevertheless, second opinions are relatively inexpensive (an hour or two of a lawyer's time spent talking to you plus any time spent reviewing papers) and often very valuable.

Waive any conflict of interest. A conflict of interest exists if a lawyer may have to put her own interests or the interests of another client ahead of your interests. Your lawyer might ask you to waive a conflict if the only other option is to not represent you. If you are asked to waive a conflict, you must understand the nature of the conflict, how it could affect your case, why you should waive it, what it will cost you if you don't and whether the conflict is a mere possibility, a likelihood or actually exists.

Fire your lawyer. It's your absolute right to fire your lawyer at any time for any reason, but it can be expensive because any new lawyer will need time (that you may have to pay for) to get up to speed. It is probably a good idea if your lawyer is doing a bad job or if your relationship with your lawyer is intolerable. Still, proceed cautiously.

Understand how you are being charged. If you've agreed to pay your lawyer a contingency fee, be sure you know how the fee is calculated.

Compare your fee agreement to an accounting (breakdown of expenses) your lawyer gives you. If your lawyer doesn't give you one, ask. If you are paying by the hour, make sure your lawyer is charging you as agreed. Because your lawyer wrote your fee agreement, insist that ambiguities be resolved in your favor.

Refuse to pay your bill. You may not have to pay your lawyer if she quit representing you on the eve of trial, violated ethical rules or charged you fees considered "unconscionable" (outrageous). If your lawyer charged you for two lawyers to do the same thing, or charged an amount for compulsively and unnecessarily organizing files, insist that the bill be reduced to a reasonable sum.

File a complaint with your state's lawyer discipline agency. The kinds of complaints that the agency is most likely to take action on relate to a lawyer's failure to pay settlement proceeds, failure to return phone calls or communicate with you for an extended period of time, failure to show up in court, failure to do the work he was paid to do, criminal conduct or drug or alcohol abuse. Although you may not be happy with the pace at which the agency moves, the vigor with which it prosecutes your complaint or the agency's minimal communication with you, it is still important to report a legal skunk. Many agencies wait until they have several similar complaints about a particular attorney before taking action.

Sue for malpractice. If you were damaged by the way your lawyer handled your case, consider suing for malpractice. It is not an easy task, as you must prove two things: that your lawyer messed up and that you would have won the case (the "underlying action") had she not messed up. Put differently, it's not enough to show that your lawyer made a mistake—you must show that the mistake caused you financial losses which you would have collected if your lawyer had handled your case properly in the first place.

A common defense raised by attorneys sued for malpractice is that the client waited too long to sue. If you want to sue for legal malpractice, you'll want to file it as quickly as possible.

Legal malpractice cases are expensive to pursue. You should know what to expect before you start. For example, you'll want to know if you will be able to collect from the lawyer if you win. Does the lawyer have malpractice insurance? If not, does the lawyer have assets which will be available to pay your claim?

B. Real-Life Situations—Why People Get Mad at Their Lawyers

This section discusses many of the common reasons people become dissatisfied with their lawyers and directs you to the chapter and section of the book where your problem is discussed in more depth.

1. Communications Problems

If your lawyer is ignoring you or your case, you need to get your lawyer's attention and find out what is being done to move your legal matter towards completion. If something doesn't seem quite right, it probably isn't. Talk to your

lawyer, a friend, a financial advisor or a trusted colleague until you get a handle on what's bothering you. If your lawyer does something or asks you something that seems inappropriate or makes you feel uncomfortable, don't ignore it. It may be a warning sign that trouble is brewing.

a. Your Lawyer Isn't Returning Your Phone Calls or Otherwise Communicating With You

A lawyer's failure to return phone calls is the single most common complaint against attorneys, and it's a sign of possible trouble. You need to know why your lawyer is not returning your phone calls. Your lawyer may be busy, rude, sick, procrastinating or simply avoiding you because she believes you are too demanding. It's also possible a disaster may have befallen your case and your lawyer may be avoiding the unpleasant task of telling you. Or maybe you have become a low priority because you haven't paid your bill.

Do you have a remedy? You'll want to work on improving communications. If you can't get anywhere, you may want to get an opinion from a second attorney and consider firing your lawyer. If some disaster has befallen your case, consider suing for malpractice.

How can this book help? Read Chapter 2, *Communications Problems With Your Lawyer*, Chapter 5, *Firing Your Lawyer*, Chapter 6, *Getting Your File*, and if you think your lawyer committed malpractice, Chapter 9, *Suing Your Former Lawyer*.

b. Your Lawyer Doesn't Seem to Be Working on Your Case

If you haven't heard from your lawyer in a long time, don't know what is happening in your case and don't know when—or if—things are scheduled to happen, warning signs should be flying. It's possible that your lawyer is a good worker but a poor communicator, but more likely, mold is growing on your abandoned file.

Do you have a remedy? You need more information to know what's going on. But the longer your lawyer doesn't do work, the more likely it will become malpractice. You should act quickly to see that your case is properly handled, and get another lawyer if necessary.

How can this book help? Read Chapter 2, *Communications Problems With Your Lawyer*, Chapter 5, *Firing Your Lawyer* and Chapter 6, *How to Get Your File*.

c. Your Lawyer Is Friends With the Lawyer for the Other Side

At a social or sports event—perhaps on the tennis court or golf course—you saw your lawyer socializing with the lawyer for your adversary. You feel wronged. Why didn't your lawyer at least disclose this friendship? What, if anything, should you do to reassure yourself that your interests will not be jeopardized?

Do you have a remedy? Not necessarily. Your lawyer is entitled to be friends with other lawyers, including the one who represents your opponent. But if the friendship causes your lawyer to not represent your interests with undivided loyalty, she is probably guilty of a conflict of interest.

How can this book help? Read Chapter 2, *Communications Problems With Your Lawyer* and Chapter 4, *Conflicts of Interests*.

d. Your Lawyer Wants to Change the Fee Agreement

Your lawyer's proposal that fees be computed differently can be unsettling, but sometimes this is a good idea. For example, if you have a contingency fee agreement and your lawyer proposes changing it to an hourly fee agreement, you may suspect that your case is going poorly and that, reflecting this, your lawyer is trying to collect from you. But don't jump to conclusions until you get more information. It may be that your lawyer is proposing a change that will benefit you—for example, if a case is likely to settle quickly, an hourly fee agreement would be better and fairer as far as you are concerned.

Do you have a remedy? If you were not advised by your lawyer to obtain an opinion from a second lawyer before agreeing to the new agreement, your lawyer's advice to you to change the agreement is probably a conflict of interest and therefore malpractice.

How can this book help? Chapter 3, *Fee Arrangements*, describes what makes a good fee agreement. Chapter 7, *Fee Disputes and Fee Arbitration*, provides examples of what can go wrong and suggestions for how to resolve problems. Chapter 4, *Conflicts of Interests*, explains why you should be careful when doing business with your lawyer.

2. Litigation Problems

Most lawyers who handle litigation matters (lawsuits) have busy, hectic schedules. They make mistakes, forget to do things and get scheduled to be in two—or more—places at once. Court rules differ among courts, and complying with court rules is a lawyer's nightmare. Litigation lawyers spend a lot of time trying to fix mistakes, many of which cannot be corrected. Too frequently, litigation lawyers make hurried decisions, wait until the last minute to do things, take too many cases, take cases they don't know how to handle, fail to do adequate research, ignore clients and make promises they can't keep. If your lawyer takes the "putting out fires" approach to the practice of law, you need to light a fire your lawyer can't ignore or find a lawyer who will pay attention to your case.

a. Your Case Was Thrown Out of Court Because Your Lawyer Did Poor Work

You may not learn that your case has been thrown out of court until quite a while after it happens. And you may not find out from your lawyer. Even if your lawyer does tell you, you'll almost never hear an admission of fault. Most likely, your lawyer will blame the problem on the judge, or you'll be given a hard-to-understand technical excuse.

While there are a number of reasons why a case can be dropped or dismissed by a court, such drastic action is often an indication that your lawyer may have done shoddy work or missed an important deadline.

Do you have a remedy? If the dismissal was due to your lawyer's poor work or missing a deadline, your lawyer has committed malpractice. Your lawyer is responsible for whatever money you could have won. The difficulty will be in proving what you could have won and that you would have been able to collect it.

How can this book help? Read Chapter 9, *Suing Your Former Lawyer*.

b. Your Lawyer Didn't Show Up in Court

If your lawyer doesn't show up for the trial or to argue at a hearing without a very good excuse, your case may be dropped from the court's schedule or thrown out altogether, meaning it will be placed in legal limbo until something is done to resurrect it. At the very least, the fact that your lawyer has missed an important date is a sign that your case may be in poor hands.

Do you have a remedy? Yes—there is a legal solution to your problem which you may want to pursue unless you, your lawyer or a new lawyer does something to save your case before it's too late.

How can this book help? Read Chapter 9, *Suing Your Former Lawyer*, and Chapter 8, *Filing a Complaint With Your Lawyer Discipline Agency*.

c. Your Lawyer Didn't File Your Lawsuit on Time

If you want to sue someone, you usually have a limited amount of time (called the statute of limitations) to get your lawsuit on file at the courthouse. When a lawyer fails to file a case within that time, other lawyers often refer to this as having "blown the statute." This is one of the most obvious and damaging mistakes a lawyer can make.

Do you have a remedy? Yes. If the attorney clearly agreed to handle your case or advise you about your options, he or she is responsible for whatever money you could have won. The difficulty will be in proving what you could have won and that you would have been able to collect it.

How can this book help? Read Chapter 9, *Suing Your Former Lawyer*.

d. Your Lawyer Didn't Tell You About All Possible Outcomes

It is important that your lawyer tell you about all possible outcomes in your case. For example, when you sue someone who has injured you, the possible outcomes are somewhat limited—you may settle the case (for either a lot or a little amount of money) or, if you go to trial, you may win (again, a lot or a little amount of money) or lose. But not all cases are so straightforward. For example, if you file a motion against your child's other parent to increase child support, your lawyer should tell you that the court might:

- grant your motion
- deny your motion and maintain the status quo
- deny your motion and *decrease* the support you receive, or
- change custody and order you to pay support.

You could be in for a real shock if you are not told of all possible outcomes.

Do you have a remedy? If your lawyer fails to tell you about a possible outcome, which then occurs and leaves you totally shocked, you may have a successful malpractice lawsuit. Two substantial difficulties, however, will be proving what your lawyer did or did not tell you and proving your damages.

How can this book help? Read Chapter 9, *Suing Your Former Lawyer*, and Chapter 7, *Fee Disputes and Fee Arbitration*.

e. Your Lawyer Forced You to Settle Your Case

Clients often feel wronged when their lawyer pressures them to settle their case on terms the client believes are unfair or inadequate. This occurs most often in divorce and personal injury cases, when a lawyer threatens to withdraw shortly before a trial or other key event if the client won't accept a settlement offer.

Do you have a remedy? Not necessarily, unless the case was worth substantially more than you received in the settlement. Even so, the lawyer will probably argue that you wanted to accept the settlement rather than risking a lower recovery in a trial.

How can this book help? Read Chapter 9, *Suing Your Former Lawyer*. Other chapters which may be helpful are:

- Chapter 2, *Communications Problems With Your Lawyer*
- Chapter 4, *Conflicts of Interests*, and
- Chapter 7, *Fee Disputes and Fee Arbitration*.

f. Your Lawyer Said Your Case Was Worth Six Figures and Then Insisted You Settle for Peanuts

Clients are justifiably upset when a lawyer who has implied or promised spectacular results suddenly cools off and suggests dismissing their case or accepting a small settlement. Sometimes new facts or a change in the law justify the lawyer's change of position, but a lawyer's rapid loss of enthusiasm can also indicate a fundamental problem with her performance. It is also possible that your lawyer is being snowed over by the other side—that is, they present a low settlement offer, sound convincing and your lazy lawyer simply accepts their interpretation of the facts or law without doing his own research.

Do you have a remedy? Maybe. If your lawyer initially gave you an inflated value of your case, that is not malpractice—but it may be a sign of poor communication. If your lawyer didn't properly prepare your case and, as a result, the value of your case decreased, that is malpractice.

How can this book help? Read Chapter 2, *Communications Problems With Your Lawyer*, Chapter 5, *Firing Your Lawyer*, Chapter 6, *How to Get Your File* and Chapter 9, *Suing Your Former Lawyer*.

g. Your Lawyer Settled Your Case Without Your Authorization

Start by understanding that your lawyer must have your consent to settle your case. If you give it, you should be clearly told what you are agreeing to and what the future implications of your agreement are. If you believe your attorney has settled your case without your fully informed consent, you have a serious problem.

Do you have a remedy? Yes, this is probably malpractice if you can prove that the settlement your lawyer entered into was for less than your case was worth. It may also provide the basis for disciplinary action with the lawyer regulatory agency.

How can this book help? Read Chapter 2, *Communications Problems With Your Lawyer*, Chapter 8, *Filing a Complaint With Your Lawyer Discipline Agency* and Chapter 9, *Suing Your Former Lawyer*.

h. Your Lawyer Included a Provision in Your Settlement or Other Document Barring You From Suing for Malpractice

A lawyer can't ethically or legally put a clause in your settlement or fee agreement stating that you are prohibited from suing him in the future. If he tries to do this, it constitutes a serious breach of his professional duty to you. More important, it is also a strong clue that he may have mishandled the case. Note, however, that a lawyer can put a clause in the fee agreement that you must go to mediation because court is always an option after mediation, and that he can include a binding arbitration clause regarding fee disputes.

Do you have a remedy? Possibly. It is certainly a breach of your lawyer's duty to put her interests above yours—and a conflict of interest. It is also a clue that she may have mishandled the case. You should get your file from your lawyer and get a second opinion on your case.

How can this book help? Read Chapter 4, *Conflicts of Interests*, Chapter 6, *How to Get Your File*, Chapter 8, *Filing a Complaint With Your Lawyer Discipline Agency* and Chapter 9, *Suing Your Former Lawyer*.

i. Your Lawyer Rejected a Settlement Offer and You Lost (or Got Less) in the Trial

Lawyers are often asked to make educated predictions as to what is likely to happen in court. Because they are not blessed with the power to see the future, sometimes they guess wrong. Understandably, this can be disturbing in a situation where you reject a settlement offer (and you instead tried the case) because of your lawyer's optimism, only to achieve a worse result in court.

Do you have a remedy? Generally speaking, it is not wrong for a lawyer to make a bad guess, as long as the lawyer told you of the offer and rejected it with your consent. There is an exception to this general rule, however. It would be malpractice if your lawyer told you to reject a settlement offer in a situation in which no reasonable attorney would have advised a client to reject an identical or similar offer. For example, if you suffered a broken wrist in an automobile accident which healed without any residual problems, you had no lost wages and medical bills of $3,000, and the person who hit you had $50,000 of insurance, no reasonable lawyer would tell you to reject a settlement offer of $50,000 unless something indicated that the person who hit you did so on purpose.

How can this book help? To understand why this is generally not malpractice, read Chapter 9, *Suing Your Former Lawyer*.

j. Your Lawyer Sued the Wrong Person or Entity

That a lawyer failed to sue the right person or entity is a very common complaint clients make. Examples include the following:

- real estate cases when your lawyer doesn't include one of the brokers or title or escrow companies in the lawsuit
- personal injury cases when your lawyer doesn't sue the government for maintaining a dangerous intersection or road condition, and
- medical malpractice cases where your lawyer sues the surgeon who operated on you but not the hospital or the pathologist.

Do you have a remedy? Maybe. When you file a lawsuit, everyone possibly responsible for your damages should be included as a defendant and failing to do so is malpractice on the part of your lawyer. Otherwise, the people you do sue will point their fingers at the people you didn't sue and claim that it is those people's fault. (Lawyers call this the "empty chair" defense.) If someone you did not include in your lawsuit was found partially or totally at fault and you are unable to recover 100% of your damages, then you would have a malpractice case.

How can this book help? Read Chapter 9, *Suing Your Former Lawyer*.

k. You Disagree With How Your Lawyer Divided the Settlement Check

In contingency fee arrangements, your lawyer gets paid a percentage of your recovery only if you win money from the other side. The check is sent to your attorney, who deducts costs (such as court filing fees) and his percentage, and then you get what's left. In cases where court and medical costs are high, you may get far less than you expected. Clients are understandably confused and disappointed when the money is divided and they end up with little or nothing.

Do you have a remedy? It depends on what happened to the money. Your lawyer owes you a duty to account for how the funds were divided. If the lawyer misappropriated funds (stole your money), you have a malpractice case and grounds for filing a complaint with your state lawyer discipline agency. If the lawyer didn't steal your money, you may have simply received a hard lesson in how our legal system often rewards professionals more than victims.

How can this book help? Chapter 3, *Fee Arrangements*, explains how contingency fee settlements should be divided and will help you figure out whether or not your lawyer took a fair share. Chapter 7, *Fee Disputes and Fee Arbitration*, explains how to fight your lawyer if the arrangement is unfair or illegal. It also helps explain your lawyer's ethical obligations regarding money held in trust. And if your lawyer has stolen your money or breached an ethical duty concerning money held in trust, see Chapter 8, *Filing a Complaint With Your Lawyer Discipline Agency*. (You'll probably also want to report the lawyer to the local police.)

l. Your Lawyer Miscomputed the Fee on Your Personal Injury Case

As explained just above, in contingency fee cases, your lawyer will deduct costs and his fee for the recovery check before sending you your share. Usually, your lawyer does not personally prepare the accounting of how the recovery will be distributed. Most of the time, it is office personnel who figure out what medical bills, court expenses and legal fees should be paid and how much you'll end up with. Mistakes happen. Get an itemized accounting of what costs are being charged to you and how the fees are calculated.

Compare the accounting to the fee agreement you signed with your lawyer.

Do you have a remedy? Probably. If, according to your fee agreement, your lawyer kept too much and paid you too little, you are entitled to what you are really owed.

How can this book help? Read Chapter 3, *Fee Arrangements* and Chapter 7, *Fee Disputes and Fee Arbitration*.

m. Your Lawyer Handled Your Workers' Compensation Case, But Didn't Tell You About a Third Party Claim

In general, workers' compensation claims are brought against an employer. In many cases, you can also sue someone other than your employer (a "third party") for your injuries—such as the builder of the defective item that caused your injury. This lawsuit would be in addition to your workers' compensation claim and often you can recover more in a third-party lawsuit than in a workers' compensation claim. Lawyers who work in this area should alert you to the possibility of any third-party claims.

Do you have a remedy? If your lawyer doesn't flag the possibility of a third-party claim, you have the basis for a valid suit. But understand that many workers' compensation attorneys limit their practice to workers' compensation claims only and do not handle third-party claims. In this situation, your workers' compensation lawyer should tell you about any third-party claim you have and advise you to get another lawyer to handle it.

How can this book help? Read Chapter 9, *Suing Your Former Lawyer*.

n. Your Lawyer Didn't File Your Appeal on Time

After a trial, you have a short period of time—often as few as 30 days—to file an appeal. The same is true if you want to reject a nonbinding arbitration award and request a trial instead. You will be understandably furious if your lawyer fails to follow your instructions to appeal on time, with the result that your case is effectively over.

Do you have a remedy? Yes, unless you told your lawyer not to pursue the case further. But even if you said to appeal or reject the arbitration award and your lawyer screwed up—clearly malpractice—the legal road ahead of you is still rocky. To win a malpractice lawsuit, you will need to show that if your lawyer had filed the appeal on time, you would have won the case and you would have been able to collect your judgment.

How can this book help? Read Chapter 9, *Suing Your Former Lawyer*.

o. You Paid Your Lawyer a Ton of Money and Then She Quit Your Case

Your lawyer said you had a great case and encouraged you to sink your last $40,000 into it, with the prospect that if you won, you'd recover $200,000. But about the time you paid her all you had, she lost interest in your case and withdrew. Now you have an unfinished case and no lawyer.

Do you have a remedy? You need more facts to determine whether you have a remedy against the lawyer. It depends on your fee agreement, the guarantees the attorney gave you, the history of how the case was handled and the reason for the withdrawal. You will want to get the opinion of a second lawyer.

How can this book help? Several chapters may be helpful:

- Chapter 4, *Conflicts of Interests*, if the lawyer withdrew because of a conflict of interest she should have foreseen. Withdrawing under such conditions might entitle you to a refund of the fees you've paid.
- Chapter 3, *Fee Arrangements*, and Chapter 7, *Fee Disputes and Fee Arbitration*, can help you assess if your fee agreement was legitimate and what to do if it was not.
- Chapter 8, *Filing a Complaint With Your Lawyer Discipline Agency*, can help you decide whether or not to file a complaint with your state lawyer discipline agency.
- Chapter 9, *Suing Your Former Lawyer*, can help you figure out whether or not your lawyer committed malpractice.

p. Your Trial Is Coming Up and Your Lawyer Wants to Withdraw

You are in trouble if your lawyer wants to quit a few days or even weeks before a trial or other important event is scheduled to occur in your case. Another lawyer probably won't take over unless he believes you can get a postponement (continuance). You can object in court to your first lawyer's request to withdraw, but your objection may not be granted. You may be witnessing the legal death of your case unless you can get another lawyer fast or feel confident that you can represent yourself.

Do you have a remedy? If your lawyer has been diligently working on your case and has lost confidence in it—or you have not paid your bills—you probably don't have a legal remedy. This is especially true if she has kept you informed of her weakening opinion of your case.

But if your lawyer has not prepared your case for trial or let you know of her doubts, her precipitous withdrawal may be malpractice, especially if she leaves you in the lurch on the eve of your trial and you can't get a postponement or new attorney. Your claim against the attorney could include the cost of postponing your case until you were able to get a new lawyer. In addition, your lawyer may be violating your state ethical rules and her duty to you by quitting at the last minute.

How can this book help? Read Chapter 2, *Communications Problems With Your Lawyer*, Chapter 6, *How to Get Your File*, Chapter 8, *Filing a Complaint With Your Lawyer Discipline Agency* and Chapter 9, *Suing Your Former Lawyer*.

q. Your Lawyer Won't Return Your File

A lawyer may refuse to return your file when you want the lawyer off your case, but you haven't paid your bill or other costs. Even though the lawyer may be ignoring your case— or even hate it—she may still insist that you pay up before she'll turn over your file.

Do you have a remedy? Yes. Without question, you are entitled to your file. In addition, if your lawyer's refusal to turn over your case led you to lose your case, you may have a malpractice claim against the first lawyer.

How can this book help? Read Chapter 6, *How to Get Your File* and Chapter 9, *Suing Your Former Lawyer.*

r. Your Lawyer Didn't Investigate Your Case or Conduct Discovery

Sometimes in personal injury or other cases where a lawyer is paid a percentage of your recovery only if you win, and is expected to advance litigation costs (primarily for gathering evidence) out of his own pocket, the lawyer simply won't do it, with the result that your case is improperly prepared.

Do you have a remedy? Yes, but to prevail against the lawyer in a malpractice lawsuit, you will have to prove that the lawyer's neglect caused you to lose a case you would otherwise have won.

How can this book help? Read Chapter 9, *Suing Your Former Lawyer.*

s. Your Lawyer Failed to Call Important Witnesses at the Trial

The outcome of your case could be seriously affected if your lawyer does not have an important witness testify at the trial or is precluded from doing so because he has not arranged to have the witness present, or notified the lawyer for the other side that the witness will testify.

Do you have a remedy? Yes, but you will have to prove how the outcome of your case would have been affected by the missing witness's testimony. This means you will have to prove both your lawyer's neglect and that you would have won the case if the witness had testified.

How can this book help? Read Chapter 9, *Suing Your Former Lawyer.*

t. Your Lawyer Didn't Call an Expert Witness

Certain types of cases—including medical malpractice, legal malpractice and cases where the value of major asset is in dispute—rely on the testimony of an expert in a field. For example, in most cases, only a heart surgeon is qualified to testify that another heart surgeon screwed up. You could lose a good case if:

- your lawyer does not retain the proper expert witness
- your lawyer was precluded from using an expert witness because she didn't give the witness's name to the other side (lawyers usually must exchange their list of expert witnesses before a trial), or
- the judge ruled that a proposed expert witness was not qualified to testify.

Do you have a remedy? Yes, but to win a malpractice suit against your lawyer, you will have to prove not only that your lawyer was negligent, but also that the negligence was the reason you lost. This is done by a retrial of the case, with the new testimony added, as part of the malpractice trial.

How can this book help? Read Chapter 9, *Suing Your Former Lawyer.*

u. After You Lost Your Case, Your Lawyer Told You That You Had to Pay the Other Side's Attorney's Fees

In a few types of cases, you might be required to pay the other side's lawyer's fees if you lose. This is most common in contract disputes and business disputes, where a clause in the contract specifically says that attorney's fees will be awarded to the prevailing party in a lawsuit. It is also possible that a state or federal law requires the losing party to pay the other lawyer's fees. But one thing is sure: If you are faced with the possibility of having to pay the other lawyer if you lose, your lawyer should make this clear in advance of your pursuing the case (if you're the plaintiff) or vigorously defending it (if you're the defendant).

Do you have a remedy? If you were not advised of the risk of having to pay attorney's fees to the other side, you may have a successful malpractice suit. To win, you would have to show how your case would have turned out differently if you had been told. For example, if you can prove you would have accepted the settlement offer and not had to pay attorney's fees, you might prevail.

How can this book help? Read Chapter 9, *Suing Your Former Lawyer* and Chapter 2, *Communications Problems With Your Lawyer*.

v. Your Lawyer Is Suing You for Failing to Pay Fees

Insurance companies tell me that an attorney suing for his fee is the number one action that triggers a client to sue for malpractice. If you have been refusing to pay your lawyer because you believe he messed up your case, you may have reason to join this club.

Do you have a remedy? Yes, in that you can dispute your attorney's claim. Reasons for doing this would be that your lawyer committed malpractice or breached a state ethical rule.

How can this book help? Chapter 3, *Fee Arrangements*, can help you determine whether or not your fee agreement was fair. Chapter 7, *Fee Disputes and Fee Arbitration*, tells you what you can do if it wasn't. Chapter 9, *Suing Your Former Lawyer*, shows how to evaluate a malpractice claim.

w. Your Lawyer Died and Your Case Was Dismissed Because No One Took Over

If your lawyer practiced in a law firm, another lawyer in the firm should take over your case. Contact the firm and find out who is responsible for handling your case. On the other hand, if your lawyer practiced alone, your state's lawyer regulatory agency should have appointed an attorney to at least notify you that your lawyer died and that you need to obtain a new one. In some situations, you may be given the name, address and phone number of a lawyer who has taken over your lawyer's cases or a list of lawyers who may be willing to take on your case.

Do you have a remedy? Maybe. When a lawyer dies, many problems can be corrected, because courts will usually find that his death was a justifiable excuse for inaction. You should be given enough time to find a new lawyer and catch up. But some problems—such as the deadline to file a case—a court cannot fix or overlook. If your case was harmed or ruined, you may have a claim against the attorney's estate. (If the attorney had malpractice insurance, it might cover your claim.) Also contact the lawyer regulatory agency to find out if another attorney was appointed to take over your case and failed to take prompt action. If so, you may have a malpractice claim against that attorney.

How can this book help? Read Chapter 6, *How to Get Your File* and Chapter 9, *Suing Your Former Lawyer*.

x. A Court Fined (Sanctioned) Your Lawyer

Courts impose fines and other penalties (called "sanctions") against attorneys with increasing frequency in an effort to curb abuses within the legal system. If your attorney is sanctioned, it should be a warning to you that she may be handling your case poorly.

Do you have a remedy? Not necessarily, but the fact that a judge has penalized your lawyer may be an indication that she is not doing a good job. It's important for you to talk to your lawyer and find out her story as to why she was sanctioned. You may also want a second attorney to look at your file and give you an opinion about the sanctions and your case.

How can this book help? Read Chapter 2, *Communications Problems With Your Attorney* and Chapter 6, *How to Get Your File*.

y. Your First Lawyer Made a Mistake— Your Second Lawyer Tried to Fix It But Messed Up Too, and It's Too Late to Sue the First Lawyer

When consulted about a legal mess, a second lawyer will often try to fix a problem caused by your original lawyer instead of suing the first lawyer for malpractice. But what happens if while the second lawyer is unsuccessfully fiddling around, the time limit for suing the first attorney runs out?

Do you have a remedy? Yes. You have a case for malpractice against the second lawyer for not advising you to file a timely lawsuit against the first lawyer.

How can this book help? Read Chapter 9, *Suing Your Former Lawyer*.

3. Problems With Divorce Lawyers

Increasingly, lawyers who practice family law specialize in that area. They must be familiar with tax laws, property laws, pension laws, support laws and bankruptcy and debt laws. A huge percentage of client complaints are about divorce lawyers. Divorce clients are emotionally vulnerable and often unsophisticated consumers of legal services, their divorce being their only experience with a lawyer or the legal system.

Common complaints are that divorce lawyers charge too much, don't properly value the assets, agree to unfair settlements, settle for too little or too much support, don't take threats from the other side seriously, fail to consider the tax consequences of a settlement and make unwanted sexual advances, often coupled with a suggestion of a fee reduction. When a lawyer represents both the husband and wife, or drafted a premarital agreement, a client often comes away feeling that the lawyer failed to represent the client with "undivided loyalty."

a. Your Divorce Lawyer Wants Most of Your Property Settlement for His Fee

Too often, a divorce lawyer being paid by the hour will run up a bill so huge that it eats up

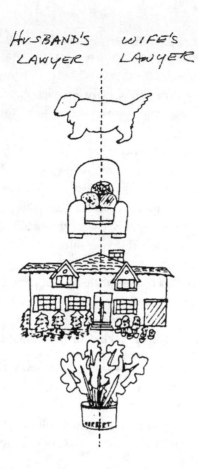

HUSBAND'S LAWYER   WIFE'S LAWYER

into accepting a settlement so you can pay her bill. Furthermore, your lawyer is on very shaky ground if she recommends that you pursue a legal position that is not likely to succeed and costs a bundle of extra money.

How can this book help? Read the following chapters:

- Chapter 4, *Conflicts of Interests*
- Chapter 7, *Fee Disputes and Fee Arbitration*
- Chapter 8, *Filing a Complaint With Your Lawyer Discipline Agency,* and
- Chapter 9, *Suing Your Former Lawyer.*

b. Your Divorce Lawyer Didn't Freeze Accounts and Your Spouse Took Your Money

In most situations where a divorce is hotly contested, your lawyer should take sensible steps to prevent your ex-spouse from absconding with or spending your joint money. Restraining orders to freeze access to marital bank accounts are easy to get. They are often issued by courts in divorce cases as a matter of course. But an order freezing a bank account or a brokerage account is only a piece of paper. Once your lawyer obtains the restraining order, she must also serve it on (deliver it to) the bank or financial institution in order to actually freeze the account.

Do you have a remedy? If your divorce lawyer fails to tie up marital accounts and your soon-to-be ex-spouse cleans them out, there is a good chance that you have grounds for a malpractice lawsuit against your lawyer.

How can this book help? Read Chapter 9, *Suing Your Former Lawyer.*

most of your share of the property settlement in your divorce. It may just be that your lawyer did a lot of good work on a hard case and your assets weren't all that valuable. But it's also possible that your lawyer and ex-spouse's lawyer unnecessarily dragged your case out until all your money was used up.

Do you have a remedy? Whether or not you are being overcharged is a complicated question, as you might guess. What you can to do about it is also far from simple. But one thing is sure: It's wrong for a lawyer to pressure you

c. Your Divorce Lawyer Accepted Your Spouse's Incorrect Value of a Major Asset

Sometimes, when a lawyer accepts the value claimed by the other side for a house, business, artwork or other asset, her own client comes up short and the spouse who keeps the asset gets it for a small fraction of what it is worth. It's the lawyer's job to be sure that assets are valued fairly, which often means having them independently appraised.

Do you have a remedy? Your lawyer's failure to hire appraisers to value all major marital assets (or failure to advise you of the risk of not doing so) means you have been shortchanged and may have grounds to recover what you are out from your lawyer. But, in proving your case, you will have to reopen the entire settlement. This includes having all of the marital assets and debts valued as of the date of your trial or settlement. If it turns out you received your appropriate share (one-half, in most states), you probably won't win your claim against your lawyer even if a major asset was substantially undervalued. Besides, the cost to reevaluate your assets may cost more in lawyers' fees than you lost.

How can this book help? Read Chapter 9, *Suing Your Former Lawyer*.

d. In Your Divorce, You Received a Portion of Your Ex-Spouse's Retirement Plan, But Now the Plan Administrator Won't Pay You

To receive pension benefits from an ex-spouse's pension plan, you usually need a court order called a QDRO (qualified domestic relations order) identifying your interest in the plan and specifying how you are to be paid. QDROs are very technical and must be drafted with precision. If your lawyer fails to do this, the administrator of the pension plan may refuse to pay you what you believe to be your share.

Do you have a remedy? If the attorney handling your divorce did not follow the proper procedure or advise you about obtaining a QDRO, you may have a claim against the attorney for either the value of the lost benefits or the cost of securing your interest in the retirement plan.

How can this book help? Read Chapter 9, *Suing Your Former Lawyer*.

e. Your Lawyer is Making Sexual Advances

This situation can arise in all types of cases, but is a complaint frequently heard from clients going through divorce. It is often coupled with the client having an outstanding bill which the lawyer might waive in exchange for the client saying "yes."

Do you have a remedy? Yes. It is a breach of the lawyer's fiduciary duty—that is, the duty of utmost loyalty. It is also malpractice because a sexual relationship is likely to impair the lawyer's ability to be objective and represent you competently. Furthermore, in a divorce case, it could have a direct financial impact on your right to receive alimony or have custody of your children.

How can this book help? Read Chapter 4. *Conflicts of Interests*, Chapter 8, *Filing a Complaint With Your Lawyer Discipline Agency* and Chapter 9, *Suing Your Former Lawyer*.

4. Problems With Bankruptcy Lawyers

Bankruptcy law has its own set of rules, with which most lawyers aren't familiar, unless they do a lot of bankruptcy work. Lawyers often get lost in the quagmire of legal technicalities and have many claims made against them for representing clients with conflicting interests.

a. Your Bankruptcy Lawyer Forgot to List a Debt in Your Papers

In general, only debts listed on bankruptcy papers will be eliminated (discharged) in bankruptcy. If a lawyer overlooks one or more of your debts he either knew about or should have known about, his mistake will mean you'll still owe the creditor if the creditor doesn't otherwise learn of your bankruptcy case.

Do you have a remedy? If the debt is one that could have been discharged in bankruptcy had your lawyer prepared your case properly, chances are good you can recover the amount of the debt from your lawyer in a malpractice case.

How can this book help? Read Chapter 9, *Suing Your Former Lawyer*.

b. Your Bankruptcy Lawyer Filed Your Case Too Soon and a Debt Wasn't Discharged

Bankruptcy rules are precise. You may be able to discharge certain debts only if your timing in filing your papers is correct. For example, a student loan generally cannot be eliminated in bankruptcy unless your payments first became due more than seven years ago (plus any time

you were in deferment or forbearance). If you file too early, the debt won't be discharged. Lawyers are supposed to know the rules.

Do you have a remedy? If your lawyer makes a mistake through ignorance of bankruptcy rules, you have the basis of a successful malpractice case.

How can this book help? Read Chapter 9, *Suing Your Former Lawyer*.

c. Your Bankruptcy Lawyer Got Your Debt Wiped Out, But Didn't Get the Lien Extinguished

It's fairly common for a debt to be secured by the equity in your house—for example, someone sues you, gets a judgment and records the judgment as a lien against your property. Those kinds of liens can often be wiped out completely in bankruptcy without you having to pay a cent. It may come as a shock to you, however, if you were told that the debt was wiped out in bankruptcy, only to have the lien show up when you are in escrow to sell your house.

Do you have a remedy? Yes. The amount you are entitled to recover from the attorney would be the reasonable cost of getting the lien removed. This may be as simple as sending a copy of the bankruptcy discharge to the creditor who recorded the lien and demanding that it be removed. In some cases, however, it may require filing a motion (a request) to the bankruptcy court to reopen your case and then filing papers requesting that the lien be removed.

How can this book help? Read Chapter 9, *Suing Your Former Lawyer*.

5. Problems With Estate Planning and Probate Lawyers

Estate planning and probate lawyers must be familiar with laws pertaining to drafting and proving (probating) wills, trusts, taxes, property and the environment. Many are not. Clients often complain of the following:

- failures to comply with time limitations, particularly those required by tax laws
- representing parties with conflicting interests, and
- lawyer self-dealing—the lawyer who prepares the will is a beneficiary.

a. A Lawyer Erred in Drafting a Friend's or Relative's Estate Plan; You Didn't Get Property You Were Supposed to or You Had to Pay Significant Taxes

A common error lawyers make is drafting a will leaving property to a particular person, but then doing—or failing to do—something else, meaning the bequest can't take place. This might involve a lawyer overlooking the fact that according to a preexisting contract or a joint tenancy deed, property willed to you would actually go to someone else. Another common mistake is when a lawyer drafts a trust for a person to minimize the beneficiaries' estate tax bill, but never transfers the property to the trust. When the person dies, the property passes outside of the trust and the beneficiaries have to pay additional estate taxes.

Do you have a remedy? In both of these examples and in estate planning generally, if the lawyer failed to use the ordinary skills of a lawyer who works in this field, you have the basis for a valid malpractice lawsuit against the lawyer.

How can this book help? Read Chapter 9, *Suing Your Former Lawyer*. (Although the lawyer isn't technically "your" lawyer, the information applies equally.)

b. Your Lawyer Didn't File an Estate Tax Return on Time

When a person dies, the IRS may be entitled to estate taxes, and in many cases, an estate tax return must be filed.

Do you have a remedy? If the lawyer didn't do it and was supposed to, or didn't tell the executor or administrator of the estate to do so, the estate beneficiaries hit with the tax bill may have grounds to sue the lawyer for malpractice. It is not malpractice if the executor or administrator had been told to file the return but did not.

How can this book help? Read Chapter 9, *Suing Your Former Lawyer*.

6. Problems With Business Lawyers

Common errors made by business lawyers include:

- failing to file documents necessary to protect a secured interest in property in the event of a default
- drafting errors, such as omitting something which was agreed upon
- drafting an agreement with an illegal provision, such as charging an illegal rate of interest, and

• representing a partnership or corporation and a party with an interest in conflict to the business.

a. The Lawyer Who Advises Your Partnership Is Representing Your Partner in Your Breakup

You feel betrayed. Not only is your small business partnership breaking up because you and one or more of the other owners are having a dispute, but you have just learned that the lawyer you have worked with for years—your lawyer—has agreed to represent one of the other owners.

Do you have a remedy? Probably, because this is a breach of the lawyer's fiduciary duty—that is, her duty of utmost loyalty to you as well as to the other principals in the business.

How can this book help? Read Chapter 4. *Conflicts of Interests*, Chapter 8, *Filing a Complaint With Your Lawyer Discipline Agency* and Chapter 9, *Suing Your Former Lawyer*.

b. Your Lawyer Didn't Get Adequate Security for the Promissory Note When You Sold Your Business

You sell all or part of a business, and agree to accept some cash and a promissory note for the rest of the sales price, secured by the equity in the buyer's house. Assume that the buyer fails to pay and you suddenly learn you can't get at the security for the promissory note because your lawyer made a mistake—for example, drafted the document improperly or failed to record it.

Do you have a remedy? Probably yes. If the lawyer was negotiating the terms of the sale, she should be liable for the results of her negligence.

How can this book help? Read Chapter 9, *Suing Your Former Lawyer*.

C. Maybe the Lawyer Who Messed Up Wasn't Your Lawyer After All— When There Isn't a Lawyer-Client Relationship

In general, you cannot sue someone else's lawyer for malpractice. You can sue a lawyer for malpractice only if the lawyer was providing services to you or for your benefit. The lawyer must owe a "duty" to you. Usually, this means you can only sue the lawyer you hired. You generally can't sue the lawyer who represented the other side for escalating the litigation, refusing to engage in settlement discussions or bad lawyering. (You may be able to sue the lawyer for some things, however. See Chapter 10.) Nor can you sue your friend's lawyer for mishandling your friend's legal matter, even if you paid the bill. If anyone sues the lawyer, it would have to be your friend.

1. Casual Conversation at a Cocktail Party

It is rare that a lawyer with whom you conversed at a party or another informal setting owes you any duty. Before a lawyer can be responsible to you for giving bad advice, you and the lawyer must have established a lawyer-client relationship. Usually, a lawyer-client relationship is established by an engagement letter, a fee agreement or the payment for services. It may be that such a relationship developed during a cocktail party, but you will have a hard time proving it. The lawyer either will not remember talking to you or will describe the conversation as you simply telling her your legal tales of woe. The lawyer will deny that she gave you any advice; at most, she'll admit that she may have made a suggestion, but it was not intended as advice.

2. Consulting a Lawyer-Coach

Representing yourself and using a lawyer as a coach may have saved you a lot in legal fees—assuming you found a lawyer willing do this. Most lawyers won't act as a coach because they are worried that you will hold them responsible for any mistakes, even when they have incomplete information. If you want to sue someone who acted as a lawyer-coach, pull out any agreement you signed and read it carefully.

If it clearly states who is responsible for what, the lawyer may have a solid defense to any lawsuit you file. Your agreement probably states that you are responsible for the overall handling of the case and that the lawyer is responsible only for giving you accurate advice about certain specified matters—and nothing else. You'll have a hard time suing and claiming that the lawyer failed to ascertain certain information or advise you on matters beyond what is listed in the agreement.

On the other hand, if you have only a vague written agreement or an oral agreement, any case against the lawyer will probably be bolstered by the fact that it's not clear what was the lawyer's responsibility and what was yours. The lawyer will probably be charged with having more—not less—of a duty to you. ∎

Chapter 2

COMMUNICATIONS PROBLEMS WITH YOUR LAWYER

Each year, I hear thousands of complaints about lawyers. Often, the complaint is that the lawyer has done a terrible job and made horrible mistakes. But more, often the client's unhappiness is the result of poor communication with the lawyer.

Perhaps some poor communication is understandable. It's easy, after all, for lawyers—the ultimate legal insiders—to forget to explain things they take for granted to their sometimes befuddled clients. But it's not forgivable; lawyers, especially those in private practice who make their livings by charging people good money to counsel or represent them, have an affirmative responsibility to keep their clients well-informed—and that includes returning phone calls. It's simply part of the job.

And while lawyers frequently fall down on the job of keeping their clients informed, sometimes the client isn't 100% blameless. In all human relationships—lawyers and clients included—both parties have responsibilities as well as rights. Clients need to understand and stay current with their legal problems. It is never a good idea to simply turn things over to a professional and hope for the best.

While clients are entitled to be kept informed about all important developments in their case, they also should respect the time and other pressures that any busy professional is under. Just because a phone call isn't returned within a few hours, it's unfair to assume your lawyer is arrogant or incompetent. And when the lawyer does call back, don't bombard her with a long litany of personal anxieties and worries. Your lawyer is not your therapist or best friend. While some good Samaritans will concern themselves with your extralegal concerns, this really isn't their job.

Also keep in mind that some lawyers with a poor bedside manner may nevertheless be decent legal craftspeople. I say this not to excuse rude, arrogant or absent communication—as I've said, I don't think that behavior should be tolerated. But I say this to suggest that rather than fire such a lawyer and try to find another who may be no better, you might first try and help the lawyer be a better communicator.

Viewed broadly, this chapter is about efficiently and effectively communicating with your lawyer so your mutual goals can be achieved. Specifically, it covers:

- the type of contact you should expect from your lawyer
- the frequency of contact you should expect from your lawyer
- what to do if you feel ignored or abandoned
- the kinds of questions you need to ask if you think there is a problem, and
- suggestions on how to sensibly try to improve a damaged relationship.

Because communicating with your lawyer is a two-way street, this chapter begins by highlighting client actions that might lead to or exacerbate communications problems. But that section is immediately followed by an extensive discussion on poor lawyer communications and what you can do about it.

Communications Breakdown

If communication has totally broken down and you plan to fire your lawyer, see Chapter 5. If you believe your attorney may be guilty of malpractice and you want to consider suing, see Chapter 9.

A. Are You a Good Customer?

If your relationship with your lawyer is less than ideal, look first at whether you are creating or contributing to the problem. If so, you'll want to take sensible steps to improve how you work with your lawyer. Here are some of the things you can often do to make your interactions with your lawyer run more smoothly.

1. Follow Through on What You Agree to Do

Whether your relationship with your lawyer involves litigation or any other significant legal work, schedules and deadlines will be important. If one seemingly minor thing isn't done on time, it may nevertheless prevent three more important things from happening. So if you tell your attorney you will deliver documents to her office or check records at city hall by Friday, do your best to do it. Your attorney may be waiting for that information before doing anything further.

Of course, real emergencies which prevent things from getting done do happen and are excusable. But, from an attorney's point of view, too often the same clients fail to keep appointments, promptly return phone calls or do other necessary tasks on time. Or, put another way, it's not reasonable to expect your lawyer to do things in a timely manner if you don't do so yourself.

2. Prepare a Written Summary and Chronology

One of the most helpful things you can do—especially early in your relationship with your lawyer—is provide a written summary and chronology of what happened. The attorney can put it in your file and refer to it as needed. You might think it is unnecessary to do this because you expected to (or did) explain what happened at your initial consultation.

But consider this. Few attorneys have perfect memories, and some are better note takers than others. Your summary and chronology may later prove invaluable to your attorney (and indirectly, of course, to you), avoid "miscommunication" problems and maybe even save you money. And even if it does none of these things, it will help you organize your thoughts and is likely to favorably impress your lawyer about how serious a client you are.

3. Tell Your Lawyer Everything

It's human nature to withhold (or forget) embarrassing information. But if something might be important in your case—no matter how small—tell your attorney up front, even if it makes you seem foolish, silly or dishonest. Your attorney is trained to deal with facts, but she can't deal with facts she doesn't know about.

Think of it this way. It is much better for your attorney to know all negative information ahead of time and figure out how to deal with it, rather than to be caught off guard later should the lawyer on the other side unearth the information. Whether you will be filing a lawsuit or obtaining advice on an important business matter, don't withhold information.

4. Understand Your Lawyer's Duty of Confidentiality

Communications with your attorney are private and confidential. They are protected by a legal safeguard called the "attorney-client privilege," which requires your attorney to treat everything you tell her as confidential. This means that you can tell your lawyer things that are embarrassing (that you are having an affair) or things that may be detrimental to your case (that you lied on your employment application), without worrying that your lawyer will tell someone else.

It is possible for *you* to waive the attorney-client privilege—that is, to give your lawyer the go-ahead to talk to others about what you've said. But with few exceptions (discussed below), your lawyer cannot reveal what you have told him (waive the privilege) without you first authorizing it. For example, if you tell your lawyer that you lied on your employment application, your lawyer can't tell your employer unless you say it's okay.

There are a few exceptions to the rule that your lawyer must keep your communications private. The most important is that if you tell your lawyer that you intend to commit a crime or intend to commit fraud, in most states your conversation is *not* privileged. This means that your lawyer can and probably will tell the authorities if you reveal a plan to commit murder, engage in drug smuggling or collect on a fraudulent insurance claim.

A second way to give up your privilege is to tell confidential information to your attorney in a nonconfidential setting. A confidential setting is generally one in which you intend and expect the communication to be confidential. You can't discuss confidential information with your attorney in a loud voice at a crowded party and expect it to be confidential. Even in a quiet business setting you waive the privilege if you discuss your affairs with your lawyer when a third person is present, unless that person works for the lawyer—in which case the attorney-client privilege extends to him.

In addition, conversations you have with any private investigator hired by your attorney are privileged. But that privilege won't extend to investigators you, your friends or your relatives hire on your behalf unless the investigator actually works for (is paid by) your lawyer. In

TECHNOLOGY AND CONFIDENTIAL COMMUNICATIONS

The attorney-client privilege developed when the only means of communications between lawyers and their clients were in person, by letter sent by mail or by letter hand delivered. Today, those are three of the least common methods. And while communications by most methods are still confidential, not all are.

In general, if you have a reasonable expectation of privacy, the communication will be privileged. For example, if your attorney has a fax machine in her office, you can expect that the only people likely to read your fax would be your attorney and members of her staff, and so the communication would be privileged. If, however, your attorney receives faxes through a neighbor's office or commercial establishment, you cannot expect the communication to be private. Similarly, if you e-mail directly to your lawyer's computer or to the computer of someone in her office, you'd have a reasonable expectation of privacy. If your e-mail is sent to a shared computer (with people who don't work for your attorney), you'd have no reasonable expectation of privacy.

Here's a basic guide:

Method of Communication	Privileged	Maybe
In person	✓	
Letter sent by mail or delivery service	✓	
Letter hand delivered by client	✓	
Letter sent by fax		✓
Phone conversation (noncellular phone)	✓	
Phone conversation (cellular phone)	✓	
Voice mail message	✓	
E-mail		✓
Computer floppy disk	✓	
Video tape cassette	✓	
Audio tape cassette	✓	

one case, for example, the court ruled that conversations between a criminal defendant and the investigator hired by his stepmother were not confidential because the investigator did not represent the defendant's lawyer.[1]

As indicated above in the sidebar, communications don't have to be in person or in writing to be privileged. For example, telephone conversations between a client and attorney are usually privileged.[2] Remember, though, the privilege will be waived if you let someone else overhear the conversation. For example, Ms. Harris waived the privilege when she spoke to her attorney over the phone while she was in the presence of a police officer and stated, "Oh, my God, I think I've killed Hy."[3]

Another way to waive the attorney-client privilege is to sue your lawyer for malpractice. The lawyer is likely to reveal your secrets to defend against your claim. For example, if you sue your lawyer for malpractice in handling your employment dispute, expect her to say that she didn't do certain things in your case (what you claim is the malpractice) because she didn't want the other side to find out your secret—that you had lied on your employment application.

If you are concerned about whether what you tell your lawyer will be kept in confidence, ask your lawyer about the rules in your state. Any time you speak to your lawyer in the presence of a third person, ask the lawyer if the communication is covered by the privilege. And once you make a confidential communication to your lawyer, don't tell another person what you said or else you will waive the privilege.

5. Inform Your Lawyer of New Developments

Many relationships between a lawyer and a client can last months or years. Litigation (taking a case to trial), for example, usually takes at least a year—sometimes as many as five—depending upon how crowded your courts are. Even cases that settle often do so just before the trial. Litigation isn't the only area in which you'll almost surely have a relationship with your lawyer over many months or years. Establishing a new business, getting a divorce, filing a patent application or probating an estate are just few of many types of legal actions that commonly take time.

If your legal problem will last for an extended period, you must promptly let your lawyer know about new developments. For example, unless you tell her, she may not find out that a key person has died or become disabled, or that a possible new witness to your accident has come forward. One excellent timesaving way to do this is to send your attorney a note briefly reporting what you've learned and inviting her to contact you for more details if it seems important.

 Tanya's Tip: Ask Your Lawyer How Best for You to Communicate
With so many choices in communications methods, ask your lawyer how he wants to stay abreast of new developments—for example, phone call, letter by mail, letter by fax or e-mail. Most likely, your lawyer will want something in writing that he can easily put in your case folder, such as a letter by mail or fax.

6. Respect Your Lawyer's Time and Schedule

Lawyers understandably become frustrated by clients who interrupt them with daily questions and worries. I stress this because every lawyer I know can reel off a long list of "clients from hell." Typically, these clients call often, repeat the same information over and over and expect their lawyer to play the role of therapist and parent, as well as lawyer.

Of course, some of these lawyers are probably unfairly blaming their own deficiencies on their clients—that is, demonizing the victim. But it's also fair to assume that, human nature being what it is, some clients really are no fun to deal with. Here are a few tips on how to avoid getting on your lawyer's "difficult client" list.

Keep contacts to an appropriate level. Don't pick up the phone and call your attorney every time a thought or question pops into your mind. Unless your concern is really urgent, put it on a list. When your list grows long, call or make an appointment to get your questions answered or your concerns discussed. If you are having trouble reaching your attorney by phone or scheduling an appointment (perhaps the lawyer is in the middle of a trial), send or fax your attorney your list of questions or concerns. Your attorney can call you when the trial is over or fax back answers after business hours.

Don't always insist on talking directly to your lawyer. As with many professional offices, most work in a modern law office is not done by a single lawyer. Just as is true at an efficient medical clinic, it's a team process with several professionals, paraprofessionals and other support personnel working together. Realizing this, it's simply not sensible—and can be insulting—to always insist on talking to "your lawyer." If your lawyer's assistant calls you to ask for information or to set an appointment, treat this as you would if the x-ray department at your HMO called you about a routine test.

Often, you can help your case go more smoothly by asking if a support person such as a paralegal or legal secretary can answer a routine question such as an explanation of legal jargon or the process that leads up to scheduling a hearing. If yours is a workers' compensation, Social Security, bankruptcy, personal injury or other case where a lawyer carries a large case load, it will be routine for you to have your main contact with a paralegal.

Finally, don't refuse to use your lawyer's voice mail if you are referred to it. Instead, thoroughly explain your concerns and questions. This not only avoids telephone tag, but also it allows your lawyer—or an assistant—to understand your concerns and get back to you with the desired information.

Don't leave a message for your attorney to call you at a particular time. In today's overbusy world, it's just not reasonable to assume that your lawyer will be able to return your call at a particular time you set in advance. Even though you are paying good money, you are not the attorney's only client and responding to your phone calls is not the only thing she has to do. Unfortunately, making this type of unreasonable demand is likely to irritate your lawyer who may also be trying to cope with a trial, depositions or just trying to get to her child's Little League game.

Far better is to leave various times when you will be available along with the relevant phone numbers. Or, you can leave a detailed voice mail message clearly asking your question or stating your concern. Unless there is some true urgency to talking to your lawyer pronto (other than your wanting it), be considerate of your attorney's busy schedule.

 Tanya's Tip: Remember How Your Lawyer Is Paid

Understand that your lawyer's willingness to spend time with you answering questions or explaining things may depend upon what kind of case you have and how your lawyer is being paid. If you are being billed by the hour, you are charged for the time you talk with your lawyer and should be able to buy as much as you want.

But if your attorney is being paid a contingency fee (such as with a personal injury claim) or a fee set by your state law (such as a workers' compensation claim), or you have agreed to a set dollar fee for the job, realize that the more time your attorney spends on your case, the less money the attorney will earn per hour. While you are entitled to a reasonable amount of support, having your questions answered and some reassurances, daily or even weekly chats that you are not paying for are out of bounds.

7. Provide Requested Information Promptly

At the start of your relationship, you probably provided your lawyer with considerable information about your legal problem. But typically,

your lawyer will need information as work on your case unfolds. The lawyer may even ask for information you already provided or tried to provide. Realize that no information transfer system and no one's records or memory are perfect. As long as your lawyer is basically handling your problem competently, respond promptly. Your lawyer can't represent you without your help.

Time deadlines are everywhere in the legal system. If your lawyer asks for information within ten days, assume he has a good reason for doing so and meet—or preferably, better—the deadline. If you really can't respond within a requested time, tell your attorney immediately that it will take longer. Never just let the deadline go by without responding. If necessary, your lawyer will try to obtain an extension of the time you have to respond. But realize that because courts are trying to speed up the trial process, it can be difficult, stressful and sometimes even impossible for your lawyer to arrange an extension.

Also understand that a delay in providing information can cost you money if you are paying by the hour. Your lawyer will charge you for obtaining (or trying to obtain) an extension. Similarly, if you have hired an attorney to draft a contract, prepare an estate plan or advise you about a business matter, the longer it takes you to provide information, the more likely it is that your attorney will have to review what you told her in the first place—at her hourly rate. Also, any unnecessary delay on your part sends a message that you are in no hurry. As a result, your project may very well sit in your lawyer's "to do" list for some time.

Tanya's Tip: Take Notes

When you meet with your attorney or talk by phone, note down the details of everything you agree to locate and provide. Especially if this involves doing many things, send a memo to your lawyer confirming exactly what you will be doing. This will give the lawyer a chance to see if you have left anything out and will help both you and your attorney stay organized.

8. Let Your Lawyer Know If You'll Be Unavailable

Working with a lawyer can involve both you and the lawyer doing a number of things on a fairly tight schedule. Litigation, especially, involves time deadlines, many of which can't be predicted. For example, your lawyer might receive a notice from the other side asking to question you under oath (known as taking your deposition) in ten days or two weeks. Not only will you have to be available the day of the deposition, but also you should meet with your lawyer in advance to prepare. Similarly, the other side might send you written pretrial "discovery requests" in which case you will need to answer written questions or provide documents within 20 or 30 days.

It follows that when you are involved in a significant legal action or an ongoing trans-action—be it a divorce, personal injury case, probate or small business formation—you need to be sure your lawyer can readily get ahold of you. If you will be out of town or unavailable for more than a few days, let your attorney's support staff know well in advance and leave a method by which you may be contacted. That way your attorney can obtain needed information before you leave, arrange to change court dates if necessary, and if essential, contact you while you are away. It is very frustrating for an attorney who is trying to do a good job to have the client become unavailable when the lawyer needs her.

9. Help With Research and Legwork That Doesn't Require Legal Training

If you are paying your attorney by the hour, you'll want to do as many things as you can to help your lawyer save time and, in turn, save you money. Even if your lawyer is handling your case for a flat fee or a contingency fee, your constructive efforts to help can result in real benefits, if for no other reason than your lawyer is likely to give a case more attention when a client is actively involved.

Tasks you can do include the following:

- gather documents, such as bank statements
- put documents in chronological order
- index documents, and if you have the skills, put that index into a computer file so your attorney can easily refer to it
- if you are questioned orally at a deposition, summarize the transcript, and if you have the skills, create a computer file cross-referencing key topics
- search public records
- run errands connected with your case, such as picking up or delivering documents, and
- if you are willing to learn a few basic skills, do supplementary legal research that your attorney may not have time for.

Obviously, how much help you can give depends on your time, energy, skills and inclination. But it also depends upon the willingness of your attorney to work with you as a partner. While some traditional lawyers may see efforts to help as time-wasting meddling, increasingly, lawyers welcome client involvement when the client can provide help without using up a great deal of lawyer time in the process.

10. Pay Your Bills

If your lawyer doesn't seem to be doing what you asked her to do, it may be because you haven't paid your bill or sent in your retainer. If you need extra time to make a payment, let your attorney know when she can expect it. From your lawyer's point of view, a demanding client who doesn't pay the bill is asking a lot.

11. Don't Expect Your Lawyer to Be Your Friend

When you hire an attorney, you often tell her things that are very personal and highly confidential. Don't expect this to be a mutual sharing of confidences, and don't encourage it. In fact, be concerned if your lawyer *is* confiding in you. You are sharing your confidences so that your attorney can effectively represent you. You lawyer has no reason to do the same.

Similarly, don't expect your lawyer to become your friend. You are paying your lawyer to solve your problem, not to take you out to dinner or to invite you to her holiday party. A friendship—especially one with romantic overtones—may affect your attorney's objectivity. Far better to keep your relationship on a business level until the legal problem your attorney is handling for you has been resolved.

B. What to Reasonably Expect of Your Attorney

Now let's look at the other side of the attorney-client coin. What types of care, attention and advice should you expect from your lawyer? Although different types of legal work can and often do dictate different types of attorney-client relationships, certain basics generally apply.

Skipping Material

Jump ahead to Section C, below, for information on what to do if your attorney clearly is not meeting your reasonable expectations—for example, your lawyer sends you a bill for five times what was estimated, refuses to return your phone calls for several months or hasn't contacted you in over a year and you have no idea what is happening in your case.

1. Acknowledge That You Are in Charge

The days when an autocratic lawyer could condescend to explain legal issues to grateful clients, if they every really existed, should be gone for good. Today, your lawyer's job is to teach you what is involved in coping with your legal problem, including what is expected of you. Remember that your lawyer works for you. As your highly paid employee, it is your lawyer's job to educate you so you can make intelligent choices and decisions when they arise.

Let me emphasize a key point: You—not your lawyer—should make the crucial decisions. To do this well, you need a sufficient understanding of the legal system, your case and what you can expect to occur. Your lawyer has a responsibility to tell you what will require your input and involvement and to give you the information you need to make those decisions. If your attorney is not adequately doing this, insist. Otherwise, you risk not having sufficient knowledge to make intelligent choices.

Tanya's Tip: Be Educated About Your Case
As I discussed in Section A, above, if you take a lead in educating yourself about your case and do all you can to participate in its preparation, a good lawyer—like any good coach—should look for ways to increase your level of information and participation. If, despite your willingness to learn, your lawyer is unwilling to help, demand better.

For example, say your employer fired you and you are claiming sexual harassment, age discrimination or wrongful termination. If you spend a couple of days in the law library reading up on the subject, including the key court cases in your state, you will have a better understanding of the legal principles which will apply in your case. This could be a big help, for example, if you need to evaluate a settlement offer. Realizing this, your lawyer should be willing to point you to the recent relevant research materials.

2. Tell You What to Expect

Not only should your lawyer explain the laws and procedure affecting your legal problem so you can really stay in charge of your case (Section 1, above), but also he should tell you what his role is and keep you informed at each major step along the way. This means your lawyer should explain what is going on, how long it should take and what kinds of complications may occur, and discuss with you the best ways to cope if problems do arise.

3. Explain When Things Should Happen

Many legal actions—including those involving arbitration or mediation—have a number of deadlines. Although some will be affected by the actions of your opponent and therefore be beyond the control of your attorney, her experience should equip her to give you a good idea of what will happen when. For example, she can tell you when your lawsuit will be filed, when you can expect a response from the other side, and how long the formal evidence-gathering stage (called "discovery") will last and a fairly good estimate of how long it will be until you get to trial.

As time goes by, she should keep you posted of all major developments so you can readjust the calendar you'll inevitably carry around in your head. The wise attorney will also let you know when key crucial deadlines have been met. For example, if you hire an attorney to represent you in your car accident case and you know that October 1 is the deadline for filing your lawsuit, your lawyer should reassure you that it has been filed and send you a copy (stamped with the filing date) for your records. If your lawyer waits until the last few days to file your case, she should not be surprised if you are sitting in the waiting room to be sure it gets done.

 Tanya's Tip: Ask If Your Case Was Filed on Time

One of the most common mistakes made by attorneys is forgetting to file a case before the deadline. In many states, a personal injury lawsuit must be filed within a year or two from when the injury occurred, while a lawsuit based on a breach of contract can often be filed many years later. Don't be shy about asking for the date by which your case must be filed and checking to make sure it has been done.

If you hired an attorney to do a specific task which doesn't depend on outside events, such as drafting a will, preparing an estate plan or drafting a partnership agreement or a contract,

your lawyer should be willing at the outset to tell you how long it will take and stick to that commitment.

 Tanya's Tip: Don't Be Shy About Establishing Your Own Deadline

If you want a project, such as forming a limited liability company or registering a copyright, completed within a specific time, make it clear (in writing) from the outset. If your lawyer can't do the work within that time frame, adjust your expectations to the lawyer's schedule or find an attorney who can get it to you when you need it.

4. Tell You What's Important in Your Case

Depending on your case, your lawyer should discuss with you the following:

- the issues that are in dispute in your case—these may be different than the issues you are concerned about, but remember it's your lawyer's job to identify the *legal* disputes, not every wrong you and the other side can claim against each other
- the important arguments being made by the other side; and
- a strategy for dealing with problems.

It is beyond the scope of this book to discuss every type of case. Nevertheless, what follows are examples of some important matters your lawyer should discuss in common types of cases.

a. What a Lawyer Should Tell You in an Accident or Personal Injury Case

If you were hurt in a car accident or other kind of mishap (such as slipping on a spill in a grocery store), your case is one lawyers refer to as a "personal injury" case.

Issues in dispute. Your lawyer should explain that a frequent issue in dispute in a personal injury case is who caused the accident. While a police report generally isn't considered definitive, it is a good place to start. Your lawyer should also talk to any witnesses. If police reports, witnesses and other routine investigations don't lead to an answer, your lawyer might suggest hiring an expert in reconstructing what happened (called an accident reconstructionist). Other frequently disputed issues in personal injury cases are the extent of the injuries, which will almost always require the testimony of an expert witness.

Arguments being made by the other side. Your lawyer should anticipate common claims from the other side and plan to cope with them. The most common defenses are that you caused (or partially caused) the accident, you knew and accepted the risk of getting hurt (this might be argued if you were injured by a ball, hockey puck or other item during a sporting event) or you're exaggerating your injuries. Exaggerating your injuries is particularly likely to be raised if you've been to many different doctors with no objective injury findings.

Case strategy. Your lawyer should discuss how she plans to preserve witness testimony (for example, obtain witness statements or take depositions), what other evidence she will gather (such as medical bills, medical records, doctors reports, police report, automobile inspections and photographs of the accident scene), whether or not she will retain expert witnesses, and when things should happen. She should tell you the deadline for filing a lawsuit and what generally happens after a lawsuit is filed (for example, the other side will probably take your deposition) and when those things will happen.

If you don't understand what your lawyer tells you, ask for clarification. Although a lot will depend on the nature of your case and the extent of your injuries, here are some examples of the kinds of things your lawyer should be considering and talking to you about:

Your medical condition. Have you completely recovered from your injuries, or are you continuing to have problems? Will you need surgery? How much have you incurred in medical or physical therapy bills? How much more is likely? When will you know?

Police report. Your lawyer will want to get any police report immediately. The police report will let your lawyer form a preliminary opinion about what happened, who was at fault and the names and addresses of possible witnesses.

Witness statements. Your lawyer may have an investigator try to get statements. Obtaining statements from eyewitnesses immediately after an accident can be very effective and inexpensive—the incident is still fresh in the mind. With the permission of the witness, an investigator can record a phone interview. In any case where there is a dispute as to who caused the accident, your lawyer should consider getting witness statements.

Depositions. A witness who won't voluntarily give a statement can be subpoenaed (ordered) to appear at a deposition, where your lawyer can ask what happened. The witness's testimony is given under penalty of perjury and recorded. Usually, your lawyer cannot take the witness's deposition unless the lawsuit has been filed. Your opponent's deposition can also be taken.

Depositions can be expensive (in the range of $1,000 per day). Unless your case is worth more than $25,000, very few depositions—if any—would be economically justified. Your lawyer's strategy may be to delay taking depositions until just before the trial, in the hope that the case will settle and spending the money won't be necessary. This is especially true when your lawyer has favorable statements from eyewitnesses and doesn't really need to develop more evidence.

On the other hand, not taking a deposition even in a low dollar case is a risk. Witnesses move and memories fade over time. If a witness has something significant to say, your lawyer probably should take the deposition as soon as possible.

Reconstructionists. Your lawyer may consider consulting an accident reconstructionist to reconstruct how the accident occurred using time and distance measurements, such as skid marks and the estimated speed of the vehicles, but such a person can be very expensive. If your medical bills are low (say $1,000), and you're not likely to recover more than $25,000, then an accident reconstructionist makes little sense. If, however, your medical costs are already high, and especially if you need surgery, then the amount of your damages will probably justify spending the money on the reconstructionist.

b. What a Lawyer Should Tell You in a Divorce Case

In divorce cases, a common tactic is intimidation:

"You'll get nothing."

"I'll run the business into the ground and there won't be anything left."

"I'll move to Omaha and you'll see the kids once a year."

"I'll quit my job."

"I'll never pay you a penny in alimony."

"I'll take you to the cleaners."

"The kids are mad at you already and by the time this is over, they will despise you."

Divorce lawyers hear these kinds of comments all the time. It is their job to calm you down and provide you with a real picture of how your case will progress.

Specifically, it is your lawyer's job to tell you how the law in your state generally applies to issues, what expectations are reasonable, how a court would likely decide an issue, and what you are likely to receive in your settlement. Your lawyer should also be able to estimate how long your case will take. And your lawyer should talk to you about mediation. Many divorcing spouses are choosing mediation to resolve the issues they are unable to negotiate themselves. Mediation is faster and cheaper than going to court, and really makes sense when the ex-mates will have an ongoing relationship (for example, when they have kids).

In addition, divorce is an area in which you should be able to educate yourself. Many excellent self-help books, including state-specific resources, can be found at your local library or bookstore. For example, to get a handle on the financial issues in your divorce, see *Divorce and Money*, by Woodhouse and Collins, with Blakeman (Nolo Press).

In divorce cases, who wins on a particular issue is often determined by state law unless there is credible evidence that you and your spouse adopted a different plan. For example, assume that in your state, the language in a deed generally controls ownership of a house. Your deed is in tenancy in common (unequal ownership permitted). Your spouse is arguing that you agreed to split the house 50-50, but you know you own 65%. Your lawyer should tell you what you will have to show to prove unequal ownership.

Your lawyer cannot tell you every issue and problem at the beginning of your case. But these are some basic ones to get you started.

Issue in dispute. Whose bank account is it?

Arguments being made by the other side. Your spouse may be arguing that because he had an account before the marriage, under the laws of your state it is his separate property. Just because the two of you made a few deposits of your joint earnings into the account and thereby mixed your joint money with the pre-marital money (called commingling), it doesn't change the fact that it is essentially his account.

Case strategy. Your lawyer should explain to you the law in your state on the issue of mixing marital and separate property. In some states, if you mix marital (joint) money with separate money, it all becomes marital. In other states, you are entitled to one-half of the marital portion and your spouse gets the other half of the marital portion plus the amount in the account from before the marriage. In still other states, whose name is on the bank account raises a presumption of who gets the money. No matter what your state's rules are, your lawyer should explain to you what evidence you will need to prove your position.

Next, figure out how much money is at stake. Is it worth fighting for? If so, how much of a fight should you wage? Your lawyer should help you make this evaluation.

In some situations, you may be entitled to a portion of the money attributable to your wages, one-half of the money that came from your and your spouse's wages or money left over after family necessities were paid for. Figuring out where money came from and went is called tracing and usually requires an accountant.

Tracing has drawbacks. The longer the marriage, the greater number of accounts and activity on those accounts, and the more expensive and time-consuming the tracing will be. Who will pay for the tracing? You? Your spouse? Share equally? Must each spouse hire a different accountant? Can you agree to hire just one accountant to do the work?

Issue in dispute. Can I get back the money I used for the down payment on our house which came from my inheritance?

Arguments being made by the other side. Your spouse may argue that even though you used money you inherited from your grandmother for the down payment on your house, you are not entitled to get that money back because:

- payments were made from a joint account
- you always referred to the house as "ours" and title was taken jointly
- there was never a discussion on reimbursing you
- you bought it ten years ago, and
- real estate values have dropped so that the house is not worth much more than what you paid for it.

Case strategy. Whether you can get back separate money used as the down payment on your house will probably depend both on the law in your state and the details of how you and your spouse hold title to the house, which your lawyer must explain. For example, does it matter:

- whose names are on the deed?
- how much joint funds were used to make mortgage payments?

- how long you've owned the house?
- that you and your spouse never signed a written agreement entitling you to reimbursement—or if you have an agreement, is it enforceable?
- that you claim you and your spouse made a verbal agreement—that money you contributed from your inheritance was yours.

Your lawyer should also explain the laws of your state even if they seem unfair given your situation. Better to get bad news early than to be disappointed later when your expectations are dashed.

For example, say that in your state, you are entitled to be reimbursed for your separate property contributions to a house purchase unless you have a written agreement stating that your contribution was a gift to the marriage. Your mother lived with you and your spouse for several years before she died. When she died, she left you $50,000, which you told your spouse was meant for both of you. You used it to pay the down payment on your house. Now, because of your spouse's behavior, you want to hang on to every cent possible. In this case, the news is good: with no written agreement giving your spouse half of your inheritance, you would be entitled to be reimbursed for the entire amount before the remaining equity is divided.

Although you can win this case, litigating it may nevertheless cost you more than settling it by agreeing to give your spouse a small share. Your attorney must help you evaluate the pros and cons of litigating, mediating or settling.

Issue in dispute. How much is my spouse's business worth?

Argument being made by the other side. Your spouse may be in a vindictive mood and say to you, "The business won't be worth a penny by the time we go to court because I will run it into the ground." Or your spouse may claim that because she owned the business before you got married, all or most of it belongs to her. Or, she may claim that the business is worth little or nothing because a creditor has threatened to force the business into bankruptcy. (It may be a sham threat orchestrated by your spouse just to decrease the value of the business during your divorce proceeding.)

Case strategy. If your spouse is threatening to ruin the business or has orchestrated claims or lawsuits to artificially decrease its value, you and your lawyer need to act quickly to ascertain its real value. You probably need an accountant or an appraiser. You may also need to take the depositions of witnesses. You probably also want to find out if your state generally values assets near the date of separation or near the date of settlement or trial.

If you and your spouse are greatly disputing the value of an asset (business or otherwise)— or how much it has increased since your marriage—one money-saving strategy your lawyer should discuss with you is for you and your spouse to agree to hire one financial expert to determine the value. This could be the business's accountant, although that person probably has a great loyalty to the spouse who runs the business and will keep it after the divorce. An alternative suggestion is a neutral business appraiser, or, at a minimum, an independent accountant to review the calculations done by the business accountant.

If you don't agree on one expert, your lawyer should explain to you how the ultimate value is reached and what factors are considered in the evaluation. With professional practices, for example, state laws vary greatly on whether or not you can count "goodwill" as having a value.

Issue in dispute. How will we divide rental property we own jointly?

Argument being made by the other side. Your spouse argues that you should keep an older apartment building while he takes a newer one with the same market value. He argues that you are better off with the older building because you have no experience in property management, and these properties have an established rental income history, little deferred maintenance, a new roof, lower property taxes and good tenants. This seems reasonable, but nevertheless, you smell a rat.

Case strategy. Your lawyer should warn you that even though the two properties have the same value, your spouse is trying to stick you with the asset for which you originally paid less, and for which you will eventually owe a huge amount on in capital gains taxes. If you will keep the asset that will eventually cost you more in capital gains taxes, you should get other property to compensate. Or, consider selling both properties and sharing the tax bite equally.

Issue in dispute. Will I have to pay alimony— and if so, how much?

Arguments being made by the other side. Your spouse may be arguing that you should pay support based upon your ability to earn (you could go back to work as an emergency room doctor, but you hate it), rather than your actual earnings (from teaching and sculpting).

Case strategy. Your lawyer should explain your state's laws on this issue, which may be fuzzy—courts have made a number of fact-specific rulings as to whether or not professionals must pay alimony based on the income they are capable of earning. For example, in a 30-year marriage in which only one spouse was the wage earner, the nonworking spouse will not get alimony in Texas, but will probably get it for life in California and many other states. In a six-year marriage where a spouse quit her job a few years ago to care for the couple's small child, some states will provide her with large amounts of alimony until the child is in school full time, while other states will give her just enough to get any needed training to reenter the work force.

Specifically, your lawyer should explain whether a court will expect you to work to your full potential (as the payer) or to work at all or go back to school (as the recipient).

If your spouse thinks you arranged a decrease in pay to lower your support obligation, your lawyer should tell you what you will need to prove it, and help you decide whether or not to pursue it.

Issue in dispute. Who pays the attorneys' fees?

Argument being made by the other side. Your spouse may claim that you should pay his attorney's fees because you have more money. You may be thinking that you can't afford to pay your own attorney's fees and his too.

Case strategy. No one likes to pay attorneys' fees; most people shiver at the thought of paying the soon-to-be ex-spouse's fees, too. Nevertheless, the more affluent spouse may have to, and better to know that up front. Your lawyer should explain the general law in your state and specifically what factors a court considers in deciding who pays.

c. What a Lawyer Should Tell You in a Professional Malpractice Case

In a malpractice case against a doctor, lawyer, accountant, dentist, engineer, therapist or other professional, your case will often depend on what others in the field (called "expert witnesses") have to say.

Issues in dispute. The main issue in a malpractice case is whether the professional handled the situation in a way which met the standard of care for the profession. If no reasonable doctor would have treated you in the same manner, the doctor committed malpractice. If a reasonable doctor would have treated you that way, there isn't malpractice.

Other common issues are whether the negligence of the professional caused your damage, and, if so, how you were damaged and how much money will compensate you.

Arguments being made by the other side. The professional will argue that she acted with the standard of care required of similar professionals in the community under the circumstances. She will also argue that she did not cause your damage. For example, in a medical malpractice case against a pathologist who performed a needless mastectomy, the pathologist may argue that her job was only to read the slides and not to advise about the surgery. Her claim is that you should be suing the surgeon, not her.

Case strategy. Your lawyer should explain that to prove your case, you need another professional to testify that the one you are suing rendered services below the standard of care for your community. Of course, you should be told who the expert will be and what it will cost. Your adversary will have an expert who will almost surely say the opposite, which explains why these cases are often referred to as a "battle of the experts." Your lawyer should discuss with you what your expert will say, how the expert has testified before, as well as how your expert will measure up against the one hired by the other side.

Your lawyer's case strategy on what caused the problem may be difficult. For example, if your son was being treated for depression, it will be hard to show that his attempted suicide was caused by improper medical treatment. Your lawyer should talk to you about getting the medical records and having a medical expert review them before a lot of time and money is spent on the case. For example, your expert may find cause if the records show a history of steady improvement, followed by a suicide attempt right after a change to a medication with a documented side effect of suicide attempts.

Your lawyer should also explain that you must prove your damages and should discuss with you whether you will need experts (such as an accountant, actuary or economist) to prove your damage claim.

d. What a Lawyer Should Tell You in a Breach of Contract Case

In a contract dispute, the outcome of the case will often hinge upon the interpretation of a particular clause in the contract.

Issue in dispute. A commonly disputed issue is whether the conduct of one of the parties was a breach of the agreement. For example, in a partnership agreement to run a car repair business, if one partner works on cars on the side and does not put the money in the partnership, the other partner may claim breach of the agreement.

Arguments being made by the other side. The partner doing work on the side may argue that the business partnership operates only during the week and exclusively works on German cars, while the extra work he did was on American cars on the weekend.

Case strategy. Your lawyer should explain how the agreement will be interpreted under your state's law and whether the conduct is likely to be considered a breach of the agreement. Your lawyer should also discuss informal and quick resolutions that are alternatives to suing, as well as mediation, which is often a cheaper, faster and less stressful way to resolve disputes. If a lawsuit seems necessary, your lawyer should discuss the risks and the practical effect of suing. For example, your partnership would probably dissolve. Your lawyer should also discuss fees and costs and whether the loser might have to pay the winner's lawyer's fees.

Issue in dispute. With building contractors, a frequent issue in dispute is who caused delays in construction.

Arguments being made by the other side. Arguments often center around the weather (you couldn't pour concrete in the rain) or the conduct of a third person (the sheet rock guy couldn't work until the electrician was finished).

Case strategy. Your lawyer should discuss whether the excuse would be considered good enough in court. Your lawyer should discuss the evidence you'd need and possible methods of resolutions—informal settlement discussions, propose mediation, request arbitration or file a lawsuit.

Issue in dispute. Many contracts have a provision that the "prevailing party" can recover attorney's fees and costs from the other side. Who the prevailing party is not always clear.

Arguments being made by the other side. Arguments about who is the prevailing party usually center around who breached the contract first.

Case strategy. Your lawyer should explain the significance of the attorney fee provision and the risk of suing. How your state treats such a provision can be critical to your strategy. Once lawyers are involved, especially if a lawsuit is filed, a dispute about a relatively small amount of money can turn into a dispute about who should pay the other's lawyer's fees.

5. Estimate What Things Will Cost

Almost from the outset, you want to have at least a ballpark idea of how much your relationship with your lawyer will cost you. Chapter 3 explains how lawyers charge—the three most common ways are:

- by the hour
- a flat fee for a particular project (such as drafting a will), and
- on a contingency basis—the lawyer doesn't get anything unless you win your case.

In addition to the attorneys' fees themselves, you can (and probably will) be charged for many other things, especially if your legal problem potentially involves going to court. Your fee agreement should specify what costs you have to pay for. Typical fees are listed in Chapter 3, Section H. It is important for you to get a solid estimate of how much these items will be. You will also want to know if:

- you are expected to pay any charges upfront, in the form of a deposit
- you will be billed as these charges are incurred, or
- your lawyer will advance these costs and repay himself when your case settles or you get paid after winning in court.

Most lawyers don't charge for things considered overhead or the cost of doing business. Unless your fee agreement says otherwise, you should not expect to be charged overhead. (Again, these are described in Chapter 3, Section H.)

 Tanya's Tip: Confirm Your Attorney's Cost Estimate

Your lawyer should be able to estimate costs to within about 10% of the eventual amount. Unfortunately, this is often done only orally. To let your lawyer know you take her cost estimate seriously and are budgeting accordingly, send a confirming letter reviewing her cost estimates. And ask your lawyer to speak with you before exceeding the estimate by a material amount (such as 10%) for each expense. This businesslike approach should help your lawyer stick to a plan, and hopefully your budget. Also, as explained in Section A, above, there are often things you can

do—and refrain from doing—that will keep your costs down. (For more information on fee agreements, see Chapter 3.)

6. Help You Analyze the Cost-Effectiveness of Pursuing a Matter

"I'll take you all the way to the Supreme Court!!" is how many people feel when they've been wronged. If your lawyer wholeheartedly agrees with your "damn the torpedoes, full speed ahead" plan, you need a new lawyer.

Law is expensive. And pursuing a losing cause, creating an unenforceable document or suing someone who has no way of paying is foolish and a waste of money. Your lawyer should help you figure out how cost-effective it would be to pursue a particular matter.

There is no set formula to figure out how much money should be spent preparing a case. Nevertheless, ask yourself—and your lawyer—whether the amount of money at stake justifies doing a reasonable, high or extraordinary level of research? If, as is common, the expense of preparing your case is more than you can—or think you should—pay, ask where corners can sensibly be cut.

You may find yourself frustrated with your lawyer for starting to spend more money on your case than you believe it is worth. Raise this concern as soon as it comes up. Ask if he is willing to cut how much work he does so that the total fee is in better proportion to the result you hope to obtain.

Be warned, however, that due in part to the dramatic increase in complaints against attorneys, many lawyers will refuse to take a practical, cost-effective approach for fear of being sued for not having turned over every possible legal stone. In some ways, this urge to practice defensive law is understandable, just as the increase in recent years of lawsuits against doctors who deliver babies has resulted in the increase in cesarean sections.

SAMPLE LETTER LIMITING BUDGET

Dear Ms. Ingram:

Thank you for agreeing to handle my case on a limited budget with a reasonably low cost plan of action. Given that I have been sued for $25,000, it only makes sense for me to fight the battle if I can come out ahead, and have something to show for my effort. As I told you, Patsy will accept a settlement of $18,000. I certainly do not want to pay that, especially since you agree with me that I don't owe it. But, I don't want to be stupid. I will treat this as a business decision, and make an intelligent choice. I certainly don't want to spend more fighting this than it would cost me to get out now.

I appreciate your willingness to handle this for me, keeping this in mind. This is not a case where a "leave no stone unturned" approach makes economic sense. One possibility is to propose mediation and hope Patsy will put her court action on hold while we try to arrive at a compromise settlement we can both live with.

We have discussed a realistic budget for your handling my case assuming we can't divert it to mediation, and I've attached it to the fee agreement you sent to me, which I have signed and enclosed. For purposes of clarity and easy reference, I thought it would be a good idea to put the "litigation budget" that we discussed in writing.

Patsy's deposition	2 hours	$300
Attend my deposition	2-6 hours	$300-$900
Prepare written discovery	1 hour	$150
Respond to plaintiff's discovery request	2 hours	$300
Attend settlement conference	2-3 hours	$300-$450
Misc. (telephone calls, meetings, waiting in court, correspondence)	4-6 hours	$600-$1,200
Legal research/brief writing	4-6 hours	$600-$1,200
Prepare for trial	4-6 hours	$600-$1,200
Trial	10-12 hours	$1,800-$2,400
Total	31-44 hours	$4,650-$6,600

SAMPLE LETTER LIMITING BUDGET

I appreciate your experience and willingness to work within this budget. Otherwise, I'd probably pay the $18,000 to get out. I know you have done your best to give me realistic estimates. If you exceed the estimate in any category, please find a way to shave it out of the budget somewhere else. You have assured me that you will not exceed the total budget by more than 10% which would put an overall "cap" on what I would spend at $7,260. You have told me that you believe you can do an adequate job for me within this budget, and you are willing to handle my case within these parameters. I truly appreciate your efforts to accommodate my need for clarity, a budget and proceeding in a way that makes economic sense.

Again, I thank you for your willingness to do a reasonable job, rather than a perfect one. If you had not been willing to work within a budget that I could live with, I don't think I could have justified the cost of the fight.

I have tremendous confidence in your abilities and hope that we will both benefit from your years of experience.

Cordially,

Clyde Clinkscales

Clyde Clinkscales

7. Explain Delays or Date Changes

Delays are common in the legal system, especially if you are involved in litigation. No matter how experienced your lawyer is and how reasonable the estimates, somewhere along the line getting a court date (even for just a pretrial hearing) or getting the other side to provide you with documents will take longer than expected. And no matter what the reason for the delays, your lawyer should tell you about them.

Here are some common reasons for delays:

- Some courts won't set a date for trial unless certain progress has already been made to assure the court that the case is ready for trial. Even if you have a trial date, the court can postpone ("continue") the trial if the case is not ready.
- If your lawyer asks the other side for documents, and the employee familiar with the documents is on vacation or leave, then the exchange will likely take longer than expected.
- Lawyers may dispute whether one side is entitled to get certain documents from the other—the other may claim they are private and confidential. If the lawyers can't

work out an agreement, they are likely to have a court resolve it.

- Illness (of the attorney, a witness, the judge or anyone else), bad weather, pre-paid vacations, holidays and simple scheduling mistakes all cause delays.
- While working on your case, your lawyer discovers another defendant who should be sued. This could happen if you sue Mr. Taylor, the driver of the car that hit you, and later learned that he was on official business for Xeon, Inc,. at the time of the accident. Your lawyer wants to amend your lawsuit to sue Xeon. If you are close to the trial date, Xeon will request a postponement (which will be granted) to get up to speed.

It is also possible that your lawyer is causing delays. She may not be interested in your case, not know what to do or be too busy to deal with it. Sometimes, lawyers dread talking to a contentious opposing counsel and avoid doing so, causing delays. Sometimes, lawyers get "double set" (two things scheduled for the same time) and must reschedule one of them. If you are paying your lawyer by the hour, count on it costing you money every time she goes to court to reschedule a matter.

If it seems like your case is constantly being rescheduled, perhaps neither your lawyer nor the other side wants to go to trial. It may be worthwhile to explore mediation.

TRIAL DELAYS

Trial delays are often caused by a congested court system. In many counties, clerks schedule for trial on a given day more cases than there will be courtrooms (or judges) available. The assumption is that many cases will settle before the trial date, but of course this doesn't always happen—with the result that some cases get bumped to a later date. In fact, a trial can be continued several times before a courtroom becomes available.

There are other reasons why a case is continued. Your lawyer might ask for a postponement if she isn't ready. In this situation, you may be in serious trouble and should get a second opinion from another lawyer about what needs to be done to prepare the case for trial before the next trial date arrives.

If the delay was due to circumstances beyond your attorney's control—such as a death in the family or medical emergency—and you are paying by the hour, ask your lawyer if she will absorb (not bill you for) the time put in for filing a request with the court to obtain the postponement.

Delays may not be your only frustration. Dates of hearings or meetings may change, too. For example, you may be required (or asked) to attend your deposition, the deposition of the other side or a witness, a settlement conference and the trial. These dates are usually set at least ten days in advance. Your lawyer's office should notify you of these dates and whether your attendance is required. If a date changes, you should be told.

If you show up at court or a meeting only to find that the date has been changed and you weren't told, you have good reason to be angry. This is a sign of disorganization in your lawyer's office and that your lawyer has inadequate client communication. Send a letter to your lawyer immediately.

8. Explain What Your Case Is Worth

If you hire a lawyer to file a lawsuit on your behalf, your lawyer should be able to give you some guidance as to how much your case is worth. Although at the early stage your lawyer probably can't provide more than a very rough estimate, you need some dollar amount on which to base key decisions, such as how much to spend on discovery and how much to settle for.

If your attorney can't or won't estimate how much your case is worth at the outset, ask what needs to happen before she can do so. Do depositions have to be completed? Does legal research have to be done? Does your medical treatment need to end?

SAMPLE LETTER—ATTORNEY FAILS TO NOTIFY CLIENT ABOUT DATE CHANGE

Dear Fred:

I am writing because I was very upset today when I went to have my deposition taken, only to learn that it had been postponed and you had not notified me. I am writing this letter so that you understand what a horrible experience this was for me, and so that hopefully you will figure out a way to be sure it never happens again to me or any of your other clients.

The night before my deposition was supposed to happen, I couldn't sleep. I was nervous and worried. What if I gave a wrong answer? If I couldn't answer the questions, would I lose my case? What if the lawyer talked too fast and I couldn't keep up with her? The list went on in my head all night. I guess you would say I had the nervous jitters.

I finally got up, got dressed, and went to meet you at the coffee shop downstairs from the other lawyer's office. We were supposed to meet at 8:30 a.m., 30 minutes before the deposition was to start at 9:00 a.m. Of course, I got there at 8:10, to be sure I wasn't late. I waited for you until 8:30, and with every minute you were late, my anxiety level got worse. Four cups of coffee into the morning, at 8:40 a.m., you hadn't yet arrived. I went to a pay phone and called your office. I got voice mail and left a message. I was worrying about having to start my deposition at 9:00 without enough time to meet with you first. What if you didn't arrive until just before 9:00? Would you still talk to me first? Would we start late? Or would I have to start unprepared and without talking to you? Would we be rushed? This made me even more nervous. I called your office twice more, at 8:50 and just before 9:00. I left more messages.

At 9:00, I went up to the lawyer's office for my deposition, terrified. I hoped you would be there, and thought maybe I had misunderstood where to meet you. I told the receptionist why I was there and the lawyer who was going to take my deposition came out and told me that it had been rescheduled.

I called your office again from the other lawyer's office. Your secretary told me the deposition had been continued and that a message had been left on my work voice mail late yesterday. This really made no sense since it should have been obvious that I might have already left for the day (which I had because I was so worried about my deposition). Needless to say, I am not looking forward to the new deposition date. This time, I would like to meet with you a day or two in advance with the goal of lowering my anxiety level. If the date is changed again, please call me at home at 312-555-4905 and leave a message if necessary.

This experience did not inspire confidence.

Sincerely,

Maida Wilson

Maida Wilson

HOW LAWYERS ESTIMATE A CASE'S WORTH

To estimate a case's value, lawyers generally rely on their own experience with similar cases and look at published reports of what juries have awarded in cases similar to yours. But drawing meaningful parallels from jury verdicts isn't easy—not only must the cases closely resemble yours, but also, other factors in the case must be considered. And of course, the location of the case or accident, the makeup of the jury and the lawyers will be different. Nevertheless, your lawyer should be able to find very similar cases if you were rear-ended and broke your leg, for example.

The more unusual your case, however, the less likely your lawyer will be able to find verdicts for similar cases and the harder it will be to estimate the worth of your case. Cases with emotional injuries are more difficult to value than cases with physical injuries.

Although looking at jury verdicts is probably the best way to put a value on your case, there is no way to know for sure until a judge or jury renders a verdict in your case. So if your lawyer gives you an estimate of your case's value, ask how she came to the amount. Just her own experience? Reading published verdicts? Talking to other attorneys? And no matter how your lawyer arrived at the value, view it as no more than an educated guess. No matter how much experience your attorney has, or how many verdicts exist for similar cases, you will find that even seasoned lawyers are surprised by jury verdicts (remember the Rodney King case).

To get your own idea of what your case is worth, visit a local law library and look at legal reference materials containing reported jury verdicts. A reference librarian can show you where to find them. Look for cases similar to yours in the last several years. This is a lot like looking at comparable real estate sales. Give the most weight to recent cases, cases in your county and cases with facts similar to yours. If you're in Florida, don't rely on a Minnesota case as being comparable.

To determine the value of a personal injury claim, see *Win Your Personal Injury Claim*, by Joseph Matthews (Nolo Press).

If your case isn't worth all that much, your lawyer should propose your taking your case to mediation in an effort to resolve it quickly and without spending a fortune. Sometimes people go to mediation with their lawyers, and sometimes without. In either case, your lawyer should help you weigh the pros and cons of mediation and help you evaluate your legal position in the event you were to pursue the matter in court.

> EXAMPLE: In a small business dispute or a real estate dispute, you will want a lawyer to help you evaluate:
> - the validity of the contract and the strength of your claim (99% chance of success, 50% or less)
> - the amount of your damages
> - a range of what it would cost you to litigate the dispute
> - whether the winner would have to pay the other side's attorney's fees if you went to court

- who would act as mediator (a lawyer, judge, accountant, mutual friend, someone with mediation training)
- whether lawyers should be present in mediation, and
- how to best present your case in the mediation.

9. Explain the Risks of Going to Trial Versus Settling

If the opposing side offers a settlement, your lawyer should explain the pros and cons of accepting it. As you surely know, trials are risky—you might lose or get less than is fair—and accepting a settlement eliminates risk. But, of course, it only makes sense to settle if the offer is reasonable, given the amount a jury might award and your cost of going to trial.

A settlement offer before your trial is worth more than a jury verdict of the same amount, for a few reasons. First, you get your money now. Second, under many contingency fee contracts, you pay your lawyer a lower percentage of your recovery if you settle before trial than if your case goes to trial. If you are paying your attorney by the hour, you have even more incentive to settle early.

EXAMPLE 1: You are paying your lawyer on a one-third contingency fee which increases to 40% if the case goes to trial:

Settlement:	$35,000	
Contingency fee	– 11,666	
Costs	– 1,000	
Net to you		$22,334

Recovery at trial	$35,000	
Contingency fee	– 14,000	
Costs	– 2,500	
Net to you		$18,500

EXAMPLE 2: You are paying your lawyer $150 per hour:

Settlement	$35,000	
Attorney's fee	– 10,000	
Costs	– 1,000	
Net to you		$24,000

Recovery at trial	$35,000	
Attorney's fee to prepare for trial	– 10,000	
Additional fee of $150 per hour (10 hours per day for a 7 day trial)	– 10,500	
Costs	– 2,500	
Net to you		$12,000

Your attorney should also discuss the following with you to help you decide about accepting a settlement:

- What is a reasonable range of values for your case?
- How long will a trial take?
- When are you likely to get a courtroom?
- How much will it cost for expert witnesses and other expenses in a trial?
- How much more will it cost in attorney's fees?
- How much will you need to get in your trial to end up with the same amount of money in your pocket as you would if you took the settlement offer?
- What does your attorney recommend?

WHO PAYS LITIGATION COSTS AND ATTORNEYS' FEES?

If you lose at a trial, you may have to pay the other side's litigation costs, such as the cost of deposition transcripts, jury fees, filing and motion fees, costs of service of process, costs for the preparation of models, exhibits or blowups for trial and witness fees. While these costs are not as high as attorneys' fees, they can add up. On the other hand, if you win at trial, the other side might be required to pay your costs. Exactly which costs are recoverable will depend upon your state's laws.

Traditionally, plaintiffs and defendants are responsible for paying their own attorneys' fees whether they win or lose a case. In a few types of cases, however, you might be required to pay the other side's attorney's fees if you lose—or the other side might have to pay your lawyer's fees if you win. This is common in contract disputes, such as real estate contracts, construction contracts and business disputes, where a clause in the contract specifically says that attorney's fees will be awarded to the prevailing party in a lawsuit. It is also possible that a law requires the losing party to pay the other's attorney's fee. Be sure to ask your lawyer if there could be an award of attorneys' fees if your case goes to trial or arbitration.

If attorneys' fees and costs can be charged to the losing party in a trial, you will certainly want to consider this in evaluating any settlement offer.

10. Prepare You for Your Deposition

A deposition is a type of pretrial "discovery," the process of evidence-gathering prior to a trial. In a deposition, one party in a lawsuit orally asks questions to the other side or to a witness. The answers must be given under oath, and the entire procedure is recorded by a court reporter or tape recorded if both sides agree.

The purpose behind a deposition is to avoid big surprises at the trial—at the conclusion of a deposition, you should know the other side's evidence.

If the other side schedules your deposition, your lawyer should prepare you for it. For example, your lawyer should probably tell you the following:

- Tell the truth.
- Answer only the question asked—that is, don't give more information than is necessary.
- Listen to your lawyer's objections for clues about what to watch out for.
- If you don't know an answer, say so; don't make up an answer because you think you should know it.
- What is important and what is not.
- It is okay to take a break and ask your lawyer questions.

If your testimony is crucial to the case, and you haven't testified before or you are nervous, ask your attorney to role-play with you so you will have a better idea what to expect. Where a lot of money is at stake, it's also a good idea to take the time to videotape your role play so your lawyer can critique your performance.

Your lawyer should give you an idea of the kinds of questions you'll be asked and the types of questions you don't have to answer (because they might be embarrassing, irrelevant, incriminating or considered a privileged communication). If your lawyer knows the attorney for the other side, your lawyer should tell you a bit about that lawyer's style.

Depending upon the complexity of your case, preparing you for your deposition could take anywhere from 30 minutes to all day. If you need to review a lot of documents, the preparation could take even longer.

When your lawyer will meet with you is a matter of personal style and availability. I find it best to meet with my clients two or three days in advance, so that the important points are fresh on their mind, but that they have enough time to absorb what has been said and sleep on it. This approach also allows for time if either my client or I think of something we should have discussed.

If you have ever testified before on the same or a similar matter—either in a deposition or in a trial—your lawyer should go over that testimony with you before your deposition. It is very important that you give consistent testimony. Otherwise, the lawyer will be able to show at trial that you don't tell the truth and your credibility will die a slow death. If you said "yes" once, and say "no" when asked the same question later, the lawyer for the other side will harp on this inconsistency.

11. Prepare You for Your Trial

If your case doesn't settle as your trial date gets nearer and nearer, your lawyer should spend time with you preparing you for your testimony. As part of doing this, your lawyer should insist that you review your deposition testimony several times to make sure you know what you have said before and don't say anything different at the trial. (The reason consistency is so important is explained just above.)

Your lawyer should also tell you what to expect in the courtroom so you will feel as comfortable as possible given the stressful situation. You should be told how to dress, how to act (don't talk to the jurors) and what to do if you forget an important name, fact or date.

 Tanya's Tip: Take Time to Understand How a Trial Works

Your trial is undoubtedly important to you. So take the time to understand how the process works. The best source of information is Represent Yourself in Court, *by Paul Bergman and Sara Berman-Barrett (Nolo Press). Although it's written from the point of view of a person representing himself, it provides an excellent review of all major aspects of a court case.*

C. Deal With Problems With Your Lawyer Promptly

Don't let problems get worse than they already are before you deal with them. If you are angry or disappointed with your lawyer, mail off a polite letter detailing your concerns. (Keep a copy for yourself.) A written communication is almost always better than a phone call because your lawyer has a chance to think about your concerns and respond thoughtfully. In addition, letters are a good way to document your concerns in the event your relationship deteriorates further.

Hopefully, sending a letter will cause the lawyer to respond to your concerns so that the problem is nipped in the bud.

1. Complaints About Your Bill

You can be sure that your lawyer will read any client letter which raises questions about a bill. The most successful letters not only complain, but also suggest a fair solution.

2. Complaints If Your Lawyer Is Ignoring Your Case

You may be concerned that your lawyer doesn't seem to be working on your case. Sending a polite but firm letter should wake him up. But if your main goal is to get your lawyer's attention, don't threaten to file a malpractice lawsuit or to institute disciplinary action. This type of threat will probably make your lawyer angry and defensive, not attentive.

A sample letter laying out your concerns is below. It is likely to get your lawyer's attention. I know it works. (Years ago, a client sent it to me!)

SAMPLE LETTER—CONCERNS ABOUT A BILL

Dear Ms. Stanley:

I am writing because of the bill you just sent. When I got it, I was surprised as it far exceeded what I had expected. I decided to write because I think I can express my concerns better in writing than over the phone.

When the house I bought in October started sliding off its foundation, I got several opinions from engineers and contractors and figured out that I had a $33,000 problem. That was a lot of money for me, more than I had in savings. I came to you for advice because you were recommended by Dr. Lewis, my physician, and your close friend. I placed my trust and confidence in you and have done everything you suggested.

You suggested that we write a letter asking the seller and his realtor to pay for the problem. If they refused to pay or mediate the dispute, we would file a lawsuit. When I asked if we would win, you said if we could prove that the seller knew about the problem, we should. One of the contractors told me he had looked at the problem before, so the prior owners knew about the problem. After we discussed this, you felt confident that I should proceed. When I asked you what this should cost, you told me that you hoped it wouldn't matter since the other side should pay your fees.

I gave you a retainer of $3,000. You sent the letters, and then filed the lawsuit. The seller and realtor got lawyers, and several depositions were scheduled. You put another lawyer on my case and an assistant. We went to a settlement conference (me, you and your new lawyer). Upon your recommendation, I accepted a settlement of $20,000. Looking back, I don't think your advice at the outset was consistent with your recommendation to settle. Although I know sometimes things don't work out as planned, I am still trying to figure out why my expectations were so different from where I ended up.

After the settlement conference, I got your bill showing I owed you a balance of $17,888. In addition to the $3,000 retainer I paid you, that makes your bill total $21,888. I am worse off by $1,888. I would not have gone through all of this for nothing, had I realized that that would be likely. I don't question that you should be paid fairly for your time, but I think under the circumstances your bill is unfair. I would have known this sooner had you sent me monthly bills, which you agreed to do in your fee agreement.

I have reviewed your bill and see that a lot of time was spent by your assistants preparing for trial. Since we never got close to trial, this could have been postponed, at a minimum, until after the settlement conference.

SAMPLE LETTER—CONCERNS ABOUT A BILL (cont'd)

In addition, you had your associate working on my case. With all due respect, I don't think she ever handled a case like this before—she seems just out of school and as green as could be. I'm sure she'll be a fine lawyer one day and I liked her, but I would not have hired her at the rate you charged for her, with or without your supervision. Quite frankly, I got the impression she was following you around as a learning experience. I was charged for her being at the settlement conference, and she didn't say a word. It seemed to me like she was there to learn.

I don't want to be petty. I want to pay you an additional $8,000 and consider the bill paid in full. That feels fair to me. Please let me know if this is acceptable to you.

Cordially,

Edward Lopez

Edward Lopez

SAMPLE LETTER—IF YOUR LAWYER IS IGNORING YOUR CASE

Dear Tanya:

Even before we spoke last Friday about your bill, I was experiencing a growing concern regarding the work you are doing for me.

Let me just say at the outset that I think very highly of you and I like you very much. You're clear, smart and tough. Even more important, I perceive you as a person of warmth and integrity. I can't think of a better personality to represent me in this case against my former attorney. I came to the decision to go after Lucille Stanley after weighing a substantial amount of professional advice from both accountants and lawyers, one of which sent me to you with highest recommendations. I have little reason to doubt that I am in capable hands. I just don't think I've had your best attention. I have come to wonder if you are truly committed to my case, and I have been losing sleep over this.

Simply stated, I feel like I have been, and continue to be, a very low priority for you. I have been patient and understanding for the past two years as one thing after another superseded my case. I understand the delays that happen in legal cases. But I'm not talking about these. In addition to several extended illnesses, which I know set you back and of course were not your fault, there have been months at a time when you've been virtually incommunicado, because of other matters. I have not complained and have always paid my bills promptly and unquestioningly. About six months ago, however, I began to wonder when—or even if—my case would ever merit your full attention. I called to talk to you about it, but you were unavailable. I had to leave a message with your assistant.

Because of the sporadic nature of your attention, every time you do turn to my case, I have to pay for you to "review and analyze." If your attention was steadier and more concentrated, I would not have had to pay for reviewing time. The pattern has been: momentum gained, paid for, lost, regained and repaid for. I know you are a good lawyer, worth $175 per hour at your best. But I don't always feel I'm getting work that's worth $175 per hour. And sometime I end up paying for it twice.

I would like for us to meet, free of charge to me, to review our relationship and see where we stand. I need to know just how seriously you take my case. I have a lot at stake here. It is not my nature to be indiscriminately litigious. It is also not my nature to throw money at problems. I take the cost of this case very seriously. My first choice is to work this out with you so I can feel better and we can go on to have a successful working relationship. I want to be represented by you wholeheartedly and at your best. Please be frank with me and let me know if this will be possible. I can't tell you how much I hope we can work these things out. This situation has been weighing heavily on my mind.

I look forward to hearing from you soon.

Sincerely,

Edward Lopez

Edward Lopez

If your lawyer does not respond to your letter, or if he does but your subsequent meeting or phone conversation is not fruitful, consider suggesting mediation to work on your communication problems. But it makes sense to do this only if you are interested in continuing to be represented by this lawyer. Remember, some lawyers with poor communication skills are still excellent lawyers, and it can be difficult to find a new lawyer in the middle of a case.

If you feel like you have tried everything but have concluded that you simply can't work with your lawyer anymore, you will probably want to fire your lawyer and find someone new. (See Chapter 5.) You may also want to have a second lawyer evaluate your first lawyer's actions and advise you about challenging any bill you receive (Chapter 7), filing a complaint with your state lawyer disciplinary agency (Chapter 8) or suing the lawyer for malpractice (Chapter 9).

Endnotes

[1] *Parkman v. State,* 742 S.W.2d 927 (Ark. 1988).

[2] *Delano v. Kitch,* 542 F.2d 550 (10th Cir. 1976).

[3] *People v. Harris,* 57 N.Y.2d 335 (N.Y. 1982).

Chapter 3

FEE ARRANGEMENTS—
HOW LAWYERS MAKE MONEY

This chapter looks at how lawyers are paid. If you are in the process of hiring a lawyer, you can use this information to buy legal services at a fair price. If you already have hired an attorney, you can evaluate whether or not you have been overcharged. When you discuss fees with a prospective attorney be sure to ask if there is any possibility that someone else (such as your spouse or the opposing party) will have to pay some or all of them, now or later. (See Section K, below.)

In essence, you want a lawyer who knows the subject matter of your legal problem inside and out, charges fairly, treats you with respect and with whom you can communicate. Allowing for the fact that no lawyer is cheap, you probably can find lawyers that fit this description all over the price spectrum.

Here are some general rules to keep in mind.

There is no such thing as a "standard fee." Fee agreements are negotiable between clients and attorneys unless limited by law (see Sections D.2 and F, below), and are based on several factors, including the lawyer's overhead and reputation, the type of legal problem and what other lawyers in the area charge for similar work. Occasionally, there may be a "going rate" that most lawyers in a particular locality charge for a certain type of job such as doing a trademark search, handling an eviction, filing a bankruptcy or preparing a living trust. But even when most lawyers charge about the same amount for doing a defined legal task, you'll have no problem finding lawyers who charge more and are apt to find one who charges less. This is especially true in the parts of the country with a large surplus of lawyers, where they

are searching for you just as much as you are looking for them.

Cheap isn't necessarily a good thing. While everyone wants to save money, the cheapest lawyer is not necessarily the best, especially if your problem is complicated or specialized. A novice who charges $100 an hour may end up costing more than an expert who charges $225 an hour if the more expensive lawyer has much greater expertise and experience and provides better and more efficient service. If the case calls for a seasoned practitioner, the cheapest fee might lead to an expensive disaster. You might rent a cheap economy car on your vacation in Hawaii, but would you fly there on a plane built by the lowest bidder? Don't let price be your only guide.

Expensive isn't necessarily best, either. I have found little correlation between a premium price and excellent lawyering. More often, the most expensive lawyers are selling you the image that comes with a posh address, a thick carpet and a great view. Again, consider the complexity of your problem. You probably don't need a sophisticated corporate attorney to draft a simple business contract.

A contingency fee can be a bad idea. A lawyer who offers to take your case on a contingency fee (he gets paid only if you win) isn't necessarily proposing a good deal. If it's clear that you or your property were seriously injured and another person who is covered by insurance was at fault, the attorney may be proposing to take a hefty cut (usually 33%–40% of your recovery) of a sure thing. This is especially true if the attorney figures he can settle the case by making a few phone calls. Contingency fees are covered in Section D, below. For now, keep in mind that from your point of view, they can be a good deal when the lawyer is taking a real risk or a big rip-off, when she isn't.

Avoid security interests. Always steer clear of any lawyer who proposes securing his right to collect his fee with a deed of trust or mortgage on your house, or who wants you to pledge other property to pay his fees should you lose the case. These agreements aren't illegal in most states, but if an attorney makes such a request, it's a tip-off that the attorney is more concerned with getting paid than he is with winning your case. Some lawyers have been known to make a good living losing cases and collecting a hefty fee by foreclosing on the houses of

their own naive client. If you cannot otherwise afford to hire a lawyer and must consider this type of offer, at least have your case and the agreement reviewed by a second attorney.

Resolving your dispute without litigation could save you money. The delays, risks, stress and expense of court have led to the increased use of alternative methods of dispute resolution (ADR) to resolve cases. ADR providers are typically retired judges and experienced lawyers available to provide arbitration or mediation services.

ADR is available only if the parties consent to it and are willing to pay for it, unless it is sponsored by a community organization or provided as a free service by a regulatory agency

such as a bar association. ADR has generally proven to be an efficient and economical way to resolve disputes, but the decision to use it must be made in light of the circumstances of each case.

Arbitration is like an informal trial. A neutral party, called the arbitrator, hears the evidence from both sides and makes a decision. Sometimes, cases are arbitrated by three arbitrators. While this has some advantages, it is expensive.

Arbitration is more efficient than the judge and jury system, but it places a great deal of power in the hands of the arbitrator. Arbitrators decide what the facts are, what law is to be applied to those facts, and then make a decision. Depending on the agreement of the parties, the decision can be final, called *binding*, or can be advisory only, called *nonbinding*. If you agree to binding arbitration, you give up your right to a jury trial and to appeal.

In mediation, a third person tries to move the parties toward a voluntary settlement. A private mediator is generally willing to work toward a solution as long as the parties are willing to participate and pay. Mediation is less formal and less legalistic than arbitration, and because it is nonbinding, you can go on to arbitration or trial if you do not resolve the problem.

A. Must Fee Agreements Be in Writing?

The American Bar Association advises (but cannot require) attorneys to state their hourly rate or fixed fee in writing, and further suggests that all contingency fee agreements should be in writing.

AMERICAN BAR ASSOCIATION ADVICE

The American Bar Association is a voluntary membership organization for lawyers. It maintains "Model Rules" to guide attorneys in ethical matters. These rules are not binding on an attorney unless enacted as law in the state where the attorney practices. Disciplinary agencies use the rules as guidance, although the actual rules of your state are likely to be less strict.

Nevertheless, the Model Rules are very helpful in raising ethical and legal issues. For example, your state almost certainly will not require an attorney to provide you with a written accounting of how fees were calculated, but the Model Rules will alert you to the fact that this is an important issue. Knowing the importance, you can incorporate that into your next fee agreement or persuade your attorney to provide an accounting at the end of your case.

A copy of the ABA's Model Rules of Professional Conduct are available in any law library. Ask for the "annotated" version. In addition to the text of the rules themselves, it will provide you with brief summaries of cases and opinions from various states.

The trend is moving toward written agreements, and most states now require that contingency fee agreements be in writing. A chart showing the current state of the law is on the following pages.

REQUIREMENTS FOR WRITTEN FEE AGREEMENTS

State	Contingency Fee Agreements	Other Fee Agreements
Alabama	Yes	Preferred if attorney has not handled matters for client before.
Alaska	Yes	Preferred if attorney has not handled matters for client before.
Arizona	Yes	Preferred if attorney has not handled matters for client before.
Arkansas	Yes	Preferred if attorney has not handled matters for client before.
California	Yes	Cases or matters expected to generate more than $1,000 in fees.
Colorado	Yes	No
Connecticut	Yes	Yes, if attorney has not handled matters for client before.
Delaware	No	Preferred if attorney has not handled matters for client before.
District of Columbia	Yes	Preferred if attorney has not handled matters for client before.
Florida	Yes	Preferred
Georgia	Yes	No
Hawaii	Yes	No
Idaho	Yes	Preferred if attorney has not handled matters for client before.
Illinois	Yes	Preferred if attorney has not handled matters for client before. Yes, when consenting to allow the attorney to share fees with another attorney.
Indiana	Yes	Preferred if attorney has not handled matters for client before.
Iowa	No	No
Kansas	No	No
Kentucky	Yes	Preferred
Louisiana	Yes	Preferred if attorney has not handled matters for client before.
Maine	No	No
Maryland	Yes	Preferred if attorney has not handled matters for client before.

REQUIREMENTS FOR WRITTEN FEE AGREEMENTS

State	Contingency Fee Agreements	Other Fee Agreements
Massachusetts	Yes	No
Michigan	Yes	Preferred if attorney has not handled matters for client before.
Minnesota	Yes	Preferred if attorney has not handled matters for client before.
Mississippi	No	No
Missouri	Yes	Preferred if attorney has not handled matters for client before.
Montana	No	Preferred
Nebraska	No	No
Nevada	Yes	No
New Hampshire	Yes	Preferred if attorney has not handled matters for client before.
New Jersey	Yes	Yes, if attorney has not handled matters for client before.
New Mexico	Yes	No
New York	No	Yes, in family law matters. Section 1400 of the Rules of the Supreme Court Appellate Division provides strict rules for attorneys representing clients in domestic relations cases. Clients must be provided with a detailed statement of rights and responsibilities, fee agreements must be in writing, and nonrefundable retainers are forbidden.
North Carolina	No	No
North Dakota	Yes	No
Ohio	Yes	No
Oklahoma	Yes	Preferred if attorney has not handled matters for client before.
Oregon	Yes It must be written in plain and simple language and must inform the client of the right to rescind the agreement within 24 hours of signing it.	No

REQUIREMENTS FOR WRITTEN FEE AGREEMENTS

State	Contingency Fee Agreements	Other Fee Agreements
Pennsylvania	Yes An "anti-ambulance chasing" prohibition forbids attorneys from obtaining contingency fee agreements from injured clients during the first 15 days of hospitalization for their injuries.	Preferred if attorney has not handled matters for client before.
Rhode Island	The rules say it "should be," not "shall be," which means it's the right thing to do, but is not required.	Preferred if attorney has not handled matters for client before.
South Carolina	Yes	Preferred if attorney has not handled matters for client before.
South Dakota	Yes	Preferred if attorney has not handled matters for client before.
Tennessee	No	No
Texas	Yes	Preferred if attorney has not handled matters for client before.
Utah	Yes	Preferred if attorney has not handled matters for client before.
Vermont	No	No
Virginia	No	No
Washington	Yes	Preferred if attorney has not handled matters for client before.
West Virginia	Yes	Preferred if attorney has not handled matters for client before.
Wisconsin	Yes	Preferred
Wyoming	Yes	Yes

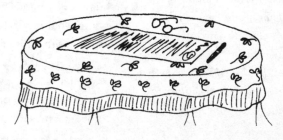

Tanya's Tip: Get It in Writing

The ABA Model Rules propose and a few state laws establish minimum requirements for written fee agreements. You can ask for more. When you hire a lawyer, or if you have one now, ask for a detailed written fee agreement. It should cover the following:

- *the hourly rate, flat fee or contingency percentage*
- *in cases of hourly rates, the minimum time billed (such as six minutes, 12 minutes or 15 minutes) when the lawyer spends less than a full hour on a matter*
- *who will work on the case (lawyers, para-legals, investigators)*
- *the amount of any retainer and what it covers*
- *who may terminate the contract and for what reason*
- *how disputes between you and the attorney will be resolved*
- *who will pay costs and what is included as a cost, and*
- *what is included in the fee—for example does a contingency fee agreement include an appeal, or will the attorney bill for travel time if you pay by the hour?*

The lawyer should be willing to do this regard-less of what your state requires. If the lawyer refuses (or "forgets" to send you one), send or fax the lawyer a letter with your understanding of the fee arrangement and ask for a confirmation. Indicate that you expect to be billed according to those terms unless the lawyer tells you otherwise in writing. The rate is not binding on your lawyer unless he confirms it in writing, but his failure to protest will be strong evidence in your favor if you

have a later fee dispute. A copy of the "Statement of Client's Rights" required in Florida is at the end of this chapter. Although it applies only in Florida, it has some good ideas about what you and your lawyer should agree upon at the begin-ning of your relationship.

If your state requires written fee agreements but your lawyer never put it in writing, do you still owe a fee? Yes, you owe a *reasonable fee,* taking into consideration the following:

- the amount of time the attorney put into the case
- the result
- the general rates charged by other attor-neys in the area for similar types of work
- the amount involved in your case, and
- the degree of risk the attorney undertook in handling the case.

Even though you owe a reasonable fee, you can often negotiate a lower fee than what the attorney demands when something is wrong with the fee agreement.

EXAMPLE: Mercedes' attorney tells her that he expects to be paid a contingency of one-third of whatever Mercedes recovers, but he never gives Mercedes an agreement to sign. In Mercedes' state, all contingency fee agreements must be in writing. Mercedes' case quickly settles for $60,000 and her lawyer demands $20,000. She wants to pay him what is fair, but thinks $20,000 for a few phone calls and a letter is way too much. What does she owe him? A reason-able fee—that is, whatever is fair—which may be $20,000 or it may be less. The fact that she never received a written fee agreement gives her an opening to negotiate a lower fee. (See Chapter 7 for information on fee disputes.)

B. Flat-Fee Arrangements—Knowing Up Front What the Job Will Cost

A flat fee is a set amount of money a lawyer charges to do a certain job, such as $300 to draft a will. Lawyers—particularly those who specialize in one type of work—may charge a flat fee if the time it will take to do a job is easily predictable. Lawyers often charge a flat fee to file a consumer bankruptcy, obtain an uncontested divorce or prepare a drunk driving defense. Also, if you are representing yourself in a lawsuit but consulting a lawyer, he might charge a flat fee to do a particular task, such as prepare a complaint or help you with a deposition.

Flat fees are negotiable. It's always possible that a lawyer will agree to accept less than the originally quoted rate, if you ask. On the other hand, don't be surprised to learn that an advertised flat fee is a minimum and that your problem requires more work—and a higher fee. The flat fee might be for an uncontested divorce, a simple estate plan or a bankruptcy in which none of the creditors challenge the petition.

 Tanya's Tip: Know What You Are Buying

At first glance, a flat-fee arrangement seems like an ideal opportunity for you to do some comparison shopping. But comparisons can be deceptive. Make sure you compare services of equal scope and value.

EXAMPLE: Jenny and Barry have two children. Jenny's mother, Roz, lives nearby and has asked them for some help in finding estate planning advice. Roz has a simple will, but it was written many years ago while Roz lived in another state, before Jenny married and before the birth of her grandchildren. Barry and Jenny realize that they have no estate plan at all, so they embark on a project of finding help for Roz and for themselves. They see an advertisement in the Sunday newspaper which says "Living Trusts: $450" and provides an 800 number for a free consultation. Another ad invites them to a free "estate planning seminar" at a local hotel. As they investigate their options they become confused.

Calling the 800 number gets them a visit from a non-attorney sales representative who will act as a go-between with the lawyer whose office is in another county. The lawyer will review their information and prepare the papers, but they can't actually meet her. The sales rep emphasizes that it is designed to be handled in the convenience of their home. But they are worried about this lack of personal contact. The "seminar" provides some information, but it's mostly a sales pitch. The actual fee for drafting their estate plan seems to depend on several factors which can't be determined until they complete several forms and an in-depth interview.

Their neighbor recommends his brother-in-law, but he specializes in drunk driving cases and other criminal law matters.

They find the right lawyer by reading a do-it-yourself book and then interviewing several lawyers recommended by friends and their tax preparer. They eliminate those who do not specialize in estate planning and who will not give them a free initial consultation. Finally they retain a lawyer who offers them a complete package of services for a flat fee which is higher than the fees in the ads, but which includes several other services which are necessary to make their estate plan fully effective. They also feel like this attorney listened carefully to them, understood their needs, and will be available for the foreseeable future.

C. Hourly Fee Arrangements

The most common way for lawyers to charge for their time is by the hour. Not surprisingly, because lawyers charge big bucks for each hour and keep their own time records, consumers often complain that they have been over-charged.

Common situations in which lawyers charge by the hour include:

- consultations about a legal problem (many attorneys and most prepaid legal plans offer a free initial consultation; also, some attorney referral agencies arrange consultations for a minimal fee, such as $25 for a 30-minute conference)
- advising about business matters or representing a small business
- representing you in a contested divorce

- handling a real estate dispute
- defending you if you get sued, and
- drafting a fairly complicated estate plan.

Hourly bills vary enormously—from about $100 per hour on the very low end up to as much as $500 per hour for a very few high-profile partners in large law firms. Most lawyers are in the middle, charging between $150 and $250 per hour. A lawyer tends to set her hourly rate based on the following factors:

- the lawyer's general experience and reputation
- the lawyer's expertise in the particular practice area
- the complexity of the case or problem
- the area of law involved—if the problem involves law on the cutting edge, such as bioengineering, the hourly fee will probably be considerably higher than average
- where the lawyer is located—an hour of a lawyer's time costs more on America's coasts than in America's center
- the lawyer's overhead expenses—some excellent lawyers work out of reasonably modest offices and charge considerably less than equally competent lawyers who sit on the 40th floor of the most posh tower in town
- how big a hurry you are in
- how much you can afford to pay, and
- how much you are willing to pay.

Start by understanding a critical point: once you agree to a lawyer's hourly rate without a cap or maximum, you will have a difficult time challenging the lawyer's assertion of how much time he spent on a matter, unless it is truly outrageous. For example, if a lawyer claims to have spent four hours reviewing documents, you will have a tough time showing that he spent only two hours. Therefore, it is essential that you take the time to investigate and hire a lawyer whom you trust to be honest, practical and efficient. And it's also wise to negotiate an upper limit on the lawyer's fee; for larger problems, this incentive rewards the lawyer for efficiency.

Your lawyer is likely to be more conservative in spending your money if he knows you will be carefully monitoring the bills and trying to save money. Here are some questions to ask to show that paying only a reasonable amount for good work is a priority:

- What do you think of the idea of proposing mediation to the other side as a way to greatly reduce costs? (If the lawyer has a good reason not to, that's fine, but walk away from any lawyer who simply rejects the idea out of principle.)
- Will you have to conduct any preliminary investigation before filing my case? If so, how many hours will it take and is there any way I can do some of it or help you decide that some of it might not be necessary?
- Does anything else need to be done before you file the complaint? If so, what and how much will it cost?
- What evidence-gathering techniques (called "discovery") do you think will be necessary? How much should they cost? Does this include depositions (orally questioning the other side and witnesses under oath)? Are there any ways to reduce the costs?

- Will we need any expert witnesses (see Chapter 2, Section B.4.c)? If so, approximately how much do they charge? Is there any way I can help you find a qualified expert who might charge less?
- What else do you need to do to prepare my case for settlement, mediation, arbitration or a trial? How much will it cost?

Some costs cannot be anticipated at the outset of a case. Therefore, it is a good idea to periodically review these questions with your attorney.

 Tanya's Tip: Ask to Be Billed Early and Often

The best way to keep from being surprised by a big bill is to insist that your lawyer bill you regularly. In fact, New York attorneys handling family law (domestic) cases must bill at least every 60 days.[1] Most lawyers who bill regularly send monthly statements, but if the lawyer is spending a lot of time on your problem, ask for a shorter billing interval. Not only does getting regular bills let you keep a better eye on what the lawyer is—or is not—doing, but it also prevents the lawyer from padding the bill later on. Also, regular bills give you a great opportunity to ask questions. A lawyer hoping to receive your check should cheerfully answer questions, such as, How is the case progressing? What results can I expect soon? Why is there a $600 charge for research when you are a specialist in this legal area?

1. Questionable Billing Practices

No matter how well you investigate your lawyer's reputation and how clear you are about how you will be charged, you should monitor the lawyer's billing practices closely. On the theory that it pays to know the worst, here are some nasty, but all too common, lawyer billing practices. Ethical lawyers do not stoop to any of these, but many dishonest practitioners do so regularly.

If you spot your lawyer doing any of these things, take action pronto. First, demand an immediate appointment to discuss the matter. If you conclude that it's more than just a misunderstanding, fire the lawyer (see Chapter 5), and consider reporting the lawyer to your state's discipline agency (Chapter 8), suing the lawyer (Chapter 9) or submitting the dispute to mediation or arbitration (Chapter 7).

Billing for work not done. Billing for time not spent is surely the most unethical billing prac-

tice. Many lawyers, especially those who work for large firms, are expected to produce a huge number of billable hours each month—a billable hour is time spent working on an actual case (for which a client can be billed), as opposed to time spent in meetings or doing other nonbillable work.

To meet a firm's monthly billable quota (as much as 175 hours per month), many lawyers are under relentless pressure to exaggerate their hours, and they do it in all sorts of ways. For example, if your lawyer computes his time by rounding up to the nearest 15-minutes (called a 15-minute minimum billing interval) and makes four three-minute phone calls on your case over two days, you will be charged one hour of the attorney's time. Arguably, this would be legally proper (albeit an incredible

deal for your lawyer). But if the lawyer made the four phone calls one right after the other, spending fewer than 15 minutes total but billing you for a full hour, you were cheated.

How would you ever know if the lawyer attempted the four phone calls in a row or at different times? Obviously, if challenged, the lawyer will say she bent over backwards to keep honest time sheets and she billed you properly. This leaves you with little recourse, given that the accuracy of an attorney's time keeping is virtually impossible to prove and difficult to challenge unless totally outrageous.

SOME LAWYERS DIG THEIR OWN GRAVES

Once, I cross-examined an attorney about time he had spent reviewing documents at the opposing counsel's office in the local area. He had billed in excess of five hours. But his own calendar (which I subpoenaed) showed that he had been out of the country on vacation at the same time. Such egregious cheating is rare. To be able to prove it, is even rarer. But when a lawyer bills a lot of hours in a short period of time, it is sometimes possible to show that because he was in court or at a deposition on a different case, the hours on your bill are padded.

Charging two clients for the same hours. Another common, unethical billing practice is to charge two clients for the same time. One place where this often occurs is when a lawyer takes a trip for one client and handles business for another and then bills each as if the other didn't exist. For example, a lawyer travels for client X (bills the client for transit time to the airport, on the plane and to the hotel), and while on the plane works on client Y's case (who is billed for the time on the plane).

Also, charging two clients for the same hours happens when a lawyer makes court appearances for more than one client. Many lawyers charge a minimum fee for a court appearance, such as two or three hours. Given the inevitable delays of traffic and parking, not to mention standing around the courthouse waiting one's turn, this may be reasonable. But it's far from reasonable if the attorney has more than one case in court that morning and bills all the clients the minimum court appearance fee.

This sleazy practice is so common that many lawyers plan to take advantage of it by scheduling three or four court appearances on the same morning. But just because some lawyers believe that this sort of double-billing is acceptable does not mean that is. If you know how long your attorney was in court (because you accompanied her or she told you) and you also know that she handled multiple matters, challenge your bill if you get charged for 100% of her time. (See Chapter 7.)

Charging you more because of a good result. This sometimes happens when a lawyer—often one with experience in a particular field—achieves a good result in a short time and simply decides to up his bill. This practice blatantly violates any hourly fee agreement and is unfair, unless you have agreed in advance to this type of arrangement. You already agreed to pay your lawyer an hourly rate which reflects his experience. And you can bet if things had gone badly and the lawyer took more time to do the job than estimated, you would have been charged for every last minute.

EXAMPLE: In hiring a lawyer to handle her divorce, Sandy carefully selects a family law specialist, even though he charges $50 more per hour than a general practice lawyer who has done good work for her in the past. Then comes a big surprise. When Sandy's lawyer calls her husband's lawyer and presents Sandy's position, he accepts it without any fight. Instead of a long battle, the matter is wrapped up in a couple of hours, when Sandy's lawyer plugs agreed-upon terms into his computerized model property settlement agreement. Despite the lawyer's good work and the favorable result, Sandy should be charged only for the hours her lawyer actually worked. This is true even though an attorney in general practice might have taken two or three times as long to achieve the same result.

Charging you to obtain routine legal knowledge.
A common problem is the lawyer who is unfamiliar with the area of law that affects your legal problem. Instead of admitting this up front, some lawyers who need work will say little, act wise and quote a substantial hourly rate. They then call their buddies who are more expert in the area for advice, and read up on the subject. Ten or 20 hours later, the lawyer is more or less up to speed. This might not be so bad if the lawyer didn't bill you for learning what he should have already known. Unfortunately, you

can't count on this. For example, hundreds of lawyers have bragged to Nolo Press that they have charged clients their hefty hourly fee for information they got from a $25 self-help law book widely available to anyone.

EXAMPLE: Several cousins jointly inherit some commercial property from their grandmother. Many years ago, a gas station occupied the site, and the cousins are worried that it may be contaminated with toxic waste—meaning that the owner could be liable for an expensive clean up—so they consider refusing the inheritance. To learn about their options, they hire an attorney who specializes in real estate. The attorney, who has been in practice for 20 years, charges them at a hefty rate of $250 per hour. He advises them to accept the inheritance and file a lawsuit against the former gas station tenants. Big hourly bills arrive at the first of each month. When the lawsuit seems stalled, the cousins check up and learn that the lawyer normally deals with buying and selling houses, and has no experience in environmental matters. The clients, fed up with paying to educate the lawyer, fire him and hire another—this time a specialist. She charges the same hourly rate, but bills far fewer hours.

This is a situation where there may be little you can do after you receive a lawyer's bill unless it is truly outrageous or his handling of the case was obviously incompetent. It often comes down to this: you hired a bad lawyer and are paying for your mistake. The best way to avoid this is to be sure the lawyer you hire knows what he is doing in the first place. You can reduce the problem by demanding monthly bills and reading them carefully. Don't hesitate to ask whenever you are billed for a substantial number of hours spent on "research."

Doing work prematurely. For legal problems that involve court action, the attorney may spend a lot of time preparing the case for trial. You could wind up with an unnecessary big bill if your lawyer puts in many hours of trial preparation and then settles the case. So if bills arrive with trial preparation items listed, one possible approach is to ask the lawyer to hold off a while and try to settle the case or arrange for mediation.

For example, your attorney should not be working on the preparation of jury instructions or trial exhibits until a trial date has been set. In many instances, I think it's reasonable for an attorney to be deeply into trial preparation 30 days before trial, but usually not more than 90 days before the trial date.

Although the attorney is likely to conduct much of the settlement negotiations by telephone or letter, you should attend all settlement conferences. Courts usually insist that the parties attend these conferences to increase the chance that a settlement will be reached.

2. Billing for Short Intervals

As pointed out in the previous section, it is not enough to know how much your lawyer charges per hour. You also need to know how much he charges for shorter periods, such as a five-minute phone call or a 20-minute research task. One thing you can be sure of—few

lawyers charge for just the actual minutes worked. Most have minimum billing intervals, based on tenths of an hour. The most common minimum billing intervals are one-tenth (six minutes), two-tenths (12 minutes) and three-tenths (18 minutes). If your lawyer works for ten minutes on your case, but has a minimum billing increment of three-tenths, you will be billed for 18 minutes. Obviously, then, your lawyer's minimum billing interval will make an enormous difference in your bill.

> **EXAMPLE:** Audrey charges $200 per hour and bills to the nearest one-tenth (six minutes). Bob also charges $200 per hour, but uses a consumer unfriendly one-half (30 minute) billing interval. If these lawyers return a phone call to someone who is not available, each will spend approximately one minute on the call. Audrey would bill you $20 (one-tenth or $200) while Bob would bill $100 (one-half of $200).

How do lawyers justify exaggerating their time by billing to the nearest billing interval? The usual explanation is that while the lawyer may spend only 30 seconds to make a phone call and leave a message, she will spend at least three or six minutes thinking about it, finding the phone number, making the call, putting a note in the file and putting the file out of her mind so she can move on to something else. This explanation may make sense for a one-tenth or even two-tenth billing increment, but it requires a ridiculous leap of faith to stretch it to justify a longer billing interval. I'd suggest that you avoid any lawyer who bills at 15- or 30-minute minimum intervals.

3. Billing for Others to Work on Your Case

Some cases are sufficiently complicated or document-intensive to require a team effort. This means that in addition to the lawyer you hired, other lawyers, paralegals and investigators may be working on your case. If this is true, you should be told about it up front. If you are, make sure that your lawyer is an efficient administrator or employs someone who is. Otherwise, you'll probably be charged for the same work done by more than one person. In addition, your case may be a disorganized mess, and you'll pay the bill when your lawyer finally puts one person on the case to straighten it all out.

In particular, ask the lawyer—and yourself—the following questions:

- Who is responsible for what tasks? Are too many people doing the same thing? It is probably more efficient for one person to do the document organizing rather than three people.
- How does the firm charge if members of the team change—for example, a person quits the law firm or is taken off the case, and a new person is added to the team? Are you billed for the time the new person spends to get up to the old person's speed? If so, you're being overbilled.
- What hourly rate are you being charged for junior lawyers? Why are so many junior lawyers accompanying the lawyer to court hearings, depositions and conferences? If the junior lawyers appear to just be learning from the experience, you should not be billed for it.

- What hourly rate are you being charged for paralegals? If a paralegal does work, and you are billed at the lawyer's rate, you have a lousy deal.

HOW MUCH DO PARALEGALS COST?

If a lawyer delegates work to a paralegal, you should be billed at a lower rate. Just like lawyers, fees for paralegals can vary considerably, but it's typical to bill paralegal time at $70–$90 per hour or one-third to one-half of the rate billed for an experienced lawyer. Your written fee agreement should tell you if non-lawyer time will be billed, and if so, at what rate.

D. Contingency Fee Arrangements

Historically, attorneys agreed to handle cases on a contingency fee basis when a client couldn't afford to pay a lawyer by the hour. Today, many types of cases, especially those involving accidents (called personal injury cases), are routinely handled this way. Other typical contingency fee cases include products liability cases (in which you are injured by a defective product) and medical malpractice cases. In addition, lawyers often handle some types of cases arising in a business setting on a contingency fee basis, such as cases claiming discrimination, wrongful termination, fraud, interference with economic advantage, unfair competition or breach of contract.

HIGH-VOLUME PERSONAL INJURY LAWYERS

Attorneys who handle a high volume of personal injury cases tend to operate on the law of averages and therefore often take cases that appear to be long shots. That is, they may take ten cases with recovery potential even if none will be easy to prove, with the hope of hitting it big enough on one or two to make an overall profit. They also tend to take cases in which the client has sizable up front costs because they usually have the money to pay for them. And often, they have a lot of trial experience simply because they go to trial a lot. They are also willing to take small cases because their offices are geared toward routine processing of claims.

In a high-volume office, you can expect to see an attorney—although not necessarily the one you met with originally—when you sign the fee agreement, at your deposition, at the settlement conference and, if the case doesn't settle earlier, at your trial. Otherwise, most contact will be with assistants, often called paralegals.

A high-volume law office that specializes in a few types of cases offers the possibility that your case will be handled with great efficiency and expertise. Unfortunately, this is often not the case. For one thing, the quality of your communication with the lawyer is likely to suffer if information always passes through an assistant. One client described this phenomenon by comparing his case to a "two-day-old plate of stale donuts"—his case kept passing from person to person without anyone wanting to keep it. Clients also complain that they must attend crucial events such as settlement conferences, depositions and even the trial, with an attorney whom they had never met and who appeared to know very little about their case.

In a contingency fee case, a lawyer charges a fee that is a percentage of your total recovery. If the attorney charges a one-third contingency fee, and you get a settlement or judgment of $9,000, the attorney gets $3,000. If you get nothing, the lawyer gets nothing. Lawyers like contingency fee cases because they can limit the cases they accept to the strong cases, the easy to prove cases or the ones that will not require a lot of work. And assuming they are adept at choosing the sure winners or easy cases, they have a chance to make far more money than if they did the same work and charged by the hour.

In certain circumstances, a contingency fee case can be a good deal for you. If you have an "iffy" case or one that looks pretty good but will involve a long fight against a tough opponent, the contingency fee shifts most of the risk of losing to your lawyer. And if you cannot afford to pay a lawyer by the hour, it is your only choice. But if your case is a slam dunk—that is, you will obviously win and win a lot without the lawyer doing very much—a contingency fee proposal in definitely not in your best interest.

When Contingency Fee Cases Are Prohibited

In a few types of cases, a lawyer cannot take a contingency fee because of the strong public policy against it. These cases include the following:

• **Criminal cases.** *Contingency fee arrangements are barred because the defendant's liberty, or even life, is at stake. There is too much danger that justice could be corrupted by giving the attorney a financial interest in the outcome of the case.*

• **Lobbying work.** *Contingency fee arrangements for lawyers who do lobbying work are banned because it could lead to bribery.*

• **Family law cases.** *Most states prohibit contingency fees in divorce cases because allowing an attorney's fee to be contingent on the couple getting a divorce might, for example, prevent reconciliation. Public policy also wants ex-spouses and children to receive fair support payments with a minimum of litigation. Contingency fee arrangements would not further that goal.*

While Michigan and New Hampshire prohibit contingency fees in all family law matters, many states (including Arkansas, Connecticut, Idaho, Oklahoma, South Carolina and Wisconsin) allow them in post-divorce child support or alimony collection cases.

If an attorney asks for a contingency fee in a divorce case, be extremely wary and at the very least get a second opinion.

EXAMPLE 1: A shady lawyer asks Della, a non-wage-earner spouse who has been married to a financially successful businessperson for 35 years, for a $25,000 retainer, claiming the issues are complicated. When Della says she doesn't have close to $25,000, the lawyer suggests a contingency fee of one-third of whatever Della recovers in the divorce. But the lawyer has failed to explain that the judge would probably order Della's spouse to pay her attorney's fees, as is common in divorce cases in which one spouse does not earn an income.

EXAMPLE 2: Mitch, married 25 years to a successful doctor, is in the process of divorcing. With little access to cash, Mitch agrees to pay a lawyer one-third of the total value of the property he receives. This turns out to be one-half of the couple's $1,000,000 estate, which means the lawyer gets $166,666. By contrast, if Mitch had paid by hour, the lawyer's fee would have been much less than $166,666.

1. How Big a Contingency Fee Can the Lawyer Get?

Approximately 25% of all states have set some limits on contingency fees. Otherwise, there is no set percentage for a contingency fee. It's a matter of client-lawyer negotiation. Just the same, there are some pretty strong customs which tend to dictate the amount of the contingency fee for different types of cases.

In personal injury cases, for example, lawyers commonly demand a fee of one-third unless the case goes to trial, in which case the lawyer usually wants 40%. In personal injury cases considered "high risk"—for example, the theory of recovery has not yet been tested in the courts —the contingency fees may be 35% (if settled before trial) and 45% (if the case goes to trial). Sometimes, the lawyer agrees to limit the fee to 25% if the case settles before a lawsuit is filed.

In some contingency fee agreements, the percentage the lawyer gets decreases as the amount of the recovery increases. This is normally a matter for negotiation, but occasionally state law will impose it for certain types of cases. (See Section 2, below.) Particularly in cases where

there is a good chance of recovering damages of over $100,000, a decreasing percentage contingency fee on the recovery can make a lot of sense.

EXAMPLE: Ted, who thinks his case should settle for several hundred thousand dollars, agrees to pay his lawyer 40% of the first $100,000 to fairly compensate her if the settlement isn't high. But so she does not get an outrageous windfall from a huge settlement, Ted and the lawyer agree to step down her fee by 5% for each subsequent $100,000 the case settles for, as follows:

$0-$100,000	40%
$100,000-$200,000	35%
$200,000-$300,000	30%
$300,000-$400,000	25%
$400,000-$500,000	20%
$500,000-$600,000	15%

If Ted settles for $600,000, the lawyer's recovery would be $165,000 computed as follows:

40% of the 1st $100,000	=	$40,000
35% of the 2nd $100,000	=	35,000
30% of the 3rd $100,000	=	30,000
25% of the 4th $100,000	=	25,000
20% of the 5th $100,000	=	20,000
15% of the 6th $100,000	=	15,000
		$165,000

If you have a good case, with the likelihood of receiving big damages, you are in a good position to negotiate a reasonable contingency fee—usually an amount less than what the lawyer proposes. At the same time, if you have a case that will be difficult to win or expensive to prepare, the attorney may justifiably propose a higher percentage or even a flat fee up front in addition to a percentage of any recovery. (See Section E, below.)

Here are some tips to successfully negotiate the percentage of a contingency fee arrangement with your lawyer.

Percentage. The percentage the lawyer gets is the obvious place to start negotiating. If your case is strong, you may insist on paying no more than 20% or 25% of the recovery. Some lawyers won't consider it, but at a time when there is a glut of personal injury lawyers, many will. Many others will look carefully to see if your case is strong enough to warrant a lower percentage.

 Tanya's Tip: Paying Costs Up Front Could Reduce the Contingency Percentage

If you agree to pay the costs of preparing the lawsuit, including the court filing fees, deposition fees and expert witness fees (see Section H, below) out of your own pocket, the attorney will be much more likely to reduce her percentage. Otherwise, the attorney will have to lay out this money and then be reimbursed out of your recovery.

Percentage of what? Most attorneys want to be paid their percentage on what they call the *gross* settlement or judgment. That is, if your judgment is $300,000 and the lawyer has a one-third contingency, she gets $100,000 as her fee—plus reimbursement for her expenses. Occasionally, however, an attorney will agree to apply the percentage to the *net* amount, after costs have been reimbursed.

EXAMPLE: Ling's lawyer agrees to a one-third contingency of the net amount of her recovery. Ling's case settles for $400,000 and the out-of-pocket costs which her attorney paid up front are $30,000. Out of the $400,000, Ling's lawyer first reimburses himself for the costs. Then he takes his one-third contingency fee from the remaining $370,000.

Exclude what you've already been offered. If you have a strong case, the other party—or more likely an insurance company for the other party—may make you an offer before you visit a lawyer. It might be worth taking, but remem-

CONGRATULATIONS ARE IN ORDER! I WON.. URR.. I MEAN WE WON! WE WON.. ERR.. I MEAN I WON!

ber this: this insurance adjuster is not on your side. His job is to gather as much information as possible which might help the insurance company defend its claim, and to get your case settled quickly and cheaply if possible. It is generally not advisable to negotiate directly with the adverse party's insurance company.

If you do get an offer before you visit a lawyer, ask that the amount you've already been offered be deducted from the final recovery when calculating your attorney's fees. Why should you pay her a percentage of something you were offered before hiring her? If she refuses, try to negotiate a lower percentage based on the fact that there is already an offer on the table.

> **EXAMPLE:** Mavis was injured in a traffic accident with Walter in which Walter was speeding and had been drinking. Mavis, who has a broken arm and other injuries, is immediately contacted by Walter's insurance company and offered $25,000 to settle the case. Mavis contacts attorney #1 who insists on a minimum of one-third of any recovery. Mavis moves on to attorney #2 who says the case is probably worth closer to $50,000 and offers to represent her for a 25% contingency fee on any recovery before a lawsuit is filed (reduced because Mavis already has an offer), 30% after that, but 40% if it goes to trial.

2. Limits on Contingency Fees

In a few types of cases, states laws establish the maximum contingency fee a lawyer can charge. For example, most states regulate the percent-

age paid to attorneys for recoveries in workers' compensation cases. Connecticut, Michigan, New Jersey and Oklahoma limit contingency fees in all personal injury cases.

More often, the limit is only applicable to medical malpractice cases. In California, for example, the maximum an attorney can charge decreases with the amount of the recovery:

40% of the first $50,000

33⅓% of the next $50,000

25% of the next $500,000, and

15% of any excess over $600,000.

Other states, including Delaware, Illinois, Indiana and New York, also set limitations on contingency fees in medical malpractice cases.

California, Illinois and New York also have methods for limiting the fees an attorney can charge for representing a minor. In California and New York, these fees are subject to court review. In Illinois, fees above 25% must be approved by the court. Also, all contingency fee cases against the U.S. government are limited to a maximum of 25%.

3. Contingency Fees and Multiple Plaintiffs

If several people sue the same defendant(s) and are represented by the same lawyer, it is particularly important to understand *in advance* how the lawyer's fee will be calculated if the lawyer receives a declining percentage as the total recovery goes up. If the fee is calculated separately on the amount each person receives, it will be much higher than if it is calculated on the total recovery. And as the number of plaintiffs increases, the difference will grow.

STATE LIMITS ON CONTINGENCY FEES

Alabama	None
Alaska	None
Arizona	In medical malpractice cases, fees are subject to court review for reasonableness. Rev. Stat. § 12-568.
Arkansas	None
California	In medical malpractice cases, fees may range from 15% to 40% of the net recovery, depending on the size. Bus. & Prof. Code § 6146.
Colorado	None, but Colorado regulations provide suggested forms for the fee agreement and the accounting. Rules of Civ. Pro., Ch. 23.3.
Connecticut	Fees may range from 10% to 33.3%, depending on the size of the recovery. Gen. Stat. § 52-251C.
Delaware	In medical malpractice cases, fees may range from 10% to 35%, depending on the size of the recovery. Code 18 § 6865.
District of Columbia	None
Florida	Fees may range from 15% to 40%, depending on the amount of the recovery and the stage of the proceedings at which it is resolved. Rule of Prof. Con. 4-1.5. Florida rules also provide specific language which must be included in a contingency fee agreement including notice that the client has three business days from the date of signing to cancel it. The client must also be provided with a "Statement of Client's Rights." (See Section K.2, below.)
Georgia	None

Hawaii	None
Idaho	None
Illinois	In medical malpractice cases, fees may range from 10% to 35%, depending on the size of the recovery. Comp. Stat. Ch. 735 § 5/2-1114. Awards of punitive damages are not subject to the contract contingency fee. The fee on punitive damages is decided by the court. Comp. Stat. Ch. 735 § 5/2-1207.
Indiana	In medical malpractice cases, fees are limited to 15%. Stat. 27-12-18-1.
Iowa	In medical malpractice cases, fees are subject to court review for reasonableness. Code § 147.138.
Kansas	In medical malpractice cases, fees are subject to court review for reasonableness. Stat. § 7-121b.
Kentucky	None
Louisiana	None
Maine	In medical malpractice cases, fees may range from 20% to 33.3% of the net recovery, depending on the size. Rev. Stat. 24 § 2961.
Maryland	None
Massachusetts	In medical malpractice cases, fees may range from 25% to 40% of the recovery, depending on the size. Laws 231 §60I. All other contingency fees are subject to court review for reasonableness up to one year after the completion of the case. Massachusetts Rules also contain suggested forms for an agreement and accounting. Sup. Ct. Rule 3:05.

STATE LIMITS ON CONTINGENCY FEES (cont'd)

Michigan	In personal injury and wrongful death cases, fee is limited to one-third of the net recovery after costs have been deducted. Rules of Court 8.121.
Minnesota	None
Mississippi	None
Missouri	None
Montana	None
Nebraska	In medical malpractice cases, contingency fees are subject to court review for reasonableness. Rev. Stat. §44-2834.
Nevada	None
New Hampshire	Contingency fee agreements must be filed with the court. At the end of the case, the attorneys must submit their billing records to the court for review. Attorney fees in cases which result in a settlement or judgment of more that $200,000 are subject to court approval. Rev. Stat. § 508:4-e. In medical malpractice cases, fee is limited to 20% to 50% of the net recovery, depending on the size. Rev. Stat. 507-C:8.
New Jersey	None
New Mexico	None
New York	In medical malpractice cases, fees may range from 10% to 30% of the net recovery, depending on the size. Consolid. Laws Jud. § 474-A.
North Carolina	None
North Dakota	None
Ohio	None
Oklahoma	The fee may not exceed 50% of the net recovery. Stat. § 5-7.
Oregon	None

Pennsylvania	None
Rhode Island	None
South Carolina	None
South Dakota	None
Tennessee	In medical malpractice cases, fees are subject to court review and may not exceed 33.33%. Code. § 29-26-120.
Texas	None
Utah	In medical malpractice cases, fees are limited to 33.33% of the recovery. Jud. Code § 78-14-7.5.
Vermont	None
Virginia	None
Washington	In medical malpractice cases, contingency fees are subject to court review for reasonableness. Rev. Code § 7.70.070. The court will also review an attorney's bill in any other tort action if the client brings a petition within 45 days of receiving the final billing or accounting. Rev. Code § 4.24.005.
West Virginia	None
Wisconsin	In medical malpractice cases, fees may range from 10% to 30% depending on the size of the recovery. Stat. § 655.013.
Wyoming	Wyoming has a special set of "Rules Governing Contingent Fees for Members of the Wyoming State Bar." A copy of the rules must be given to the client, the client has 60 days after the distribution of the money to request a review of the reasonableness of the fee by a committee of the State Bar, and the rules detail the form for the agreement and the final accounting.

EXAMPLE: Martha dies as a result of medical malpractice. She is survived by her husband and two young children. An attorney agrees to represent the survivors on a contingency fee of 40%, which decreases as the recovery increases. The total recovery for the three plaintiffs is $300,000. Compare the difference in the attorney's fee depending upon whether the percentage is applied to the whole $300,000, or whether the percentage is applied separately to the each survivor's recovery.

Fee calculated on a $300,000 total recovery

40% of the first $50,000	$20,000
33⅓% of the next $50,000	16,667
25% of the next $200,000	50,000
Total attorney's fee	**$86,667**

Fee calculated on separate $100,000 recoveries

40% of the first $50,000	$20,000
33⅓% of the next $50,000	16,667
Subtotal	36,667
	X 3
Total attorney's fee	**$110,001**

4. Timing Can Affect the Fee

Many contingency fee agreements contain a provision which increases the percentage as the case gets closer to trial. This can mean substantial savings to you if your case settles soon after the accident. It is possible, however, for this provision to be abused by an attorney who does very little to resolve your case until close to trial when a higher fee is available. The longer your case drags on, the lower your eventual recovery.

Here's what I mean:

Gross Settlement	Fee %	Fees	Net Proceeds (not including costs)
Before filing:			
$250,000	25%	$62,500	$187,500
After filing:			
$250,000	33 1/3%	$83,325	$166,675
Within 30 days of the first trial or arbitration date:			
$250,000	40%	$100,000	$150,000

Or, put another way, to get the same amount in your pocket, you have to get a bigger settlement as you get closer to trial:

Gross Settlement	Fee %	Fees	Net Proceeds (not including costs)
Before filing:			
$250,000	25%	$62,500	$187,500
After filing:			
$281,250	33 1/3%	$93,741	$187,509
Within 30 days of the first trial or arbitration date:			
$312,500	40%	$125,000	$187,500

What can you do to get the maximum recovery in this situation? You can never be 100% certain about when to pursue and when to settle. But you should ask your lawyer the following:

- her strategy for an early settlement
- time estimates about settlements
- her estimated value of your case as it progresses—estimates change from time

to time and you should know if your lawyer's valuation of your case has changed, and

• when considering any settlement offer:
  • what fee percentage applies at that time
  • what the approximate costs are at that time
  • how soon the fee will move up to the next step, and
  • the major costs expected before you move up to the next step.

Tanya's Tip: Insist on Status Reports
I get a lot of complaints from clients who get evaluations from their attorneys only twice: when they are signing the fee agreement (the sky's the limit at that point) and in the courthouse hallway at the time of a settlement conference (the case is terrible and should be settled for whatever you can get). Clients call me thinking they are being cheated. What has usually happened is that the lawyer has failed to communicate with the client about the status of the case and the lawyer has failed to prepare the case for trial—the lawyer generally takes on a huge number of cases and dumps them before trial. It's unethical and it's malpractice, but it is very difficult to prove your damages.

E. Hybrid or Blended Fees

Lawyers who handle cases which are complex, expensive to litigate or where success is very unpredictable often request a fee which combines an hourly rate and a contingency fee. These hybrid or blended fee arrangements are

designed to share the risk of the outcome between the attorney and the client. Because it is hard to know whether there will be a large recovery—or no recovery at all—the lawyer charges a modest hourly rate which lets him cover his overhead, and then shares—at a reduced rate—in any recovery.

EXAMPLE: Patty started her own advertising business 13 years ago. It has grown gradually, and last year grossed $1 million. Her two key employees signed employment contracts when they started working for her agreeing not to leave her employment and compete with her anywhere in the state for five years. But they do leave, form their own similar business and send promotional literature to Patty's clients claiming they can do a better job because Patty is in poor health. Patty's business drops by almost 50% and she wants to sue her former employees.

After consulting with several attorneys, Patty realizes that any lawsuit would face problems. A court might view a five-year noncompetition restriction as too long. Also, the restriction preventing the former employees from competing anywhere in the state might be considered too broad. Nevertheless, Patty may have a good claim against her former employees if she can prove they took her client list and used it to send out promotional literature. In short, there are several unknowns. Patty also faces the problem of limited funds. Although she feels ripped off by her former employees, she is under pressure to put all available money into her business. Patti hopes the lawyer she speaks to will take the case on a contingency fee. After politely pointing out the case's many problems, the lawyer refuses to assume all the risk—but she makes this proposal: Patty would pay out-of-pocket costs such as filing the lawsuit and paying for the deposition, and an hourly fee of $75 up to $15,000 (200 hours). In exchange for charging a lower hourly rate, the lawyer will get a 20% contingency fee of any recovery.

The types of cases for which a hybrid fee arrangement might make sense include:

- a group of homeowners suing a developer and contractor for construction defects
- a home buyer suing the former owner and real estate agent for failing to disclose known defects on the property
- a former employee suing the employer for discrimination or sexual harassment
- an inventor suing for patent infringement, and
- a business person suing for interfering with a business relationship or breach of a distributorship agreement.

 Tanya's Tip: Hybrid Fees Can Help Keep Lawyers Honest

A hybrid fee arrangement may sometimes be better than a contingency fee to keep an attorney honest. Too often with a contingency fee a lawyer has an incentive to settle a case quickly for less than it would be worth at trial. This is because the lawyer typically gets one-third of a settlement, but only 7% more if you win in a trial—and a trial requires much more preparation. So some lawyers push for an easy settlement and pocket a

substantial fee rather than put in the extra work a trial entails. But if the lawyer is getting paid a hybrid fee—which includes some compensation for each hour put into the case—he may be more willing to proceed with a trial if the case looks like a winner.

F. Statutory Fees

Statutory fees are state legislatures' attempts at establishing a maximum fee an attorney can charge for handling certain kinds of cases. Bear in mind that statutory fees set a maximum—nothing prevents you from negotiating a lower fee.

A few states limit statutory fees to a few types of cases, including probate and medical malpractice. In addition, fees are often limited for claims that will go before an administrative agency instead of a court, such as workers' compensation, Social Security appeals and veterans' claims.

EXTRAORDINARY FEES— GETTING AROUND FEE LIMITS

As you might expect, lawyers are extremely creative in getting around fee limitations. One way they do this is to claim that a case involved extra work, and that therefore they should be entitled to exceed the maximum. Often called "extraordinary fees," some lawyers manage to claim them in routine cases, asserting that the work in this particular case was especially time-consuming. These extra fees must be approved by the court for the attorney to be paid. You are always entitled to a copy of any fee request your attorney submits to a court. If you have questions about anything in it, question your lawyer. If you don't get a satisfactory answer, contact the agency or court to which it was submitted. Treat it like a bill. Chapter 7 has tips on challenging an attorney's bill.

1. Workers' Compensation

In workers' compensation cases, most states set a limit on the attorney's fee to somewhere between 10%–12% of the recovery. This is an area of law in which your ability to negotiate a fee is extremely limited. Workers' compensation is a volume business in which lawyers typically handle over 100 cases at any given time. Lawyers are very unwilling to reduce their fee any lower than the state limit.

2. Probate

In a few states, attorney's fees in probate matters are calculated as a percentage of the estate, which decreases as the value of the estate decreases. Probate courts believe they play the role of friend of widows and orphans. (The lobby ceiling of a New York court is decorated with murals in which the court offers protection to the destitute and oppressed.) Of course, attorneys can charge less than the percentage permitted in these states.

In all states, courts must approve the distribution of the assets and the fees paid to the attorneys. Although a few states provide for sliding-scale fees, these are generally only guidelines subject to court approval.

Scrutinize the lawyer's proposal carefully. Don't accept the idea that you will pay the "usual statutory fees" without shopping around. The legal business is more competitive than it used to be, and lawyers will cut their rates to get good business. As with flat fees, be sure you are looking at comparable services and practitioners when you make your choice. You might do best with a straight hourly fee or a hybrid fee.

Formulas for probate fees are treated by the courts like a floor, not a ceiling. The attorney can petition the court for more, called extraordinary fees. When you negotiate your agreement, find out what is included, what is considered extraordinary and how the extraordinary fees will be calculated. One area typically included in extraordinary fees is the preparation of tax returns, yet most probates involve the filing of final tax returns.

Be wary also of attorneys who will charge you for both legal work and their services as executor. Whenever the attorney is named as the executor or trustee, get independent legal advice. It might not have been ethical to get appointed in the first place if the attorney exerted undue influence on the deceased. Beyond that, it still might not be ethical for the attorney to collect double fees as both the executor and the attorney when many of the duties overlap.

During the past several years, many consumers have taken steps so that their heirs avoid probate by setting up living trusts and other probate avoidance devices. This can be a good idea as long as the lawyer charges a much lower fee to avoid probate than it would cost to go through it. It's best to pay a lawyer a flat fee or by the hour for a living trust, which should not cost you more than a few hundred dollars to obtain.

3. Medical Malpractice

Some states cap the amount an attorney can collect in medical malpractice cases. (See Section D.2, above.) In these cases, an attorney is not permitted to charge "extraordinary fees." The amount set by law is the maximum.

G. Retainers and Advances

Lawyers who charge by the hour or by the job often ask for an up-front deposit called a *retainer* or *advance*. They usually do this to avoid the unpleasant task of dunning clients

who are slow to pay or because they are dissatisfied with the lawyer's work.

It is almost always a mistake to pay a large retainer—especially a nonrefundable one—unless you have worked with the lawyer before and trust him completely. Paying a small up-front retainer to cover the lawyer's initial time working on the case is much more reasonable, especially if you haven't worked with the lawyer before. By paying something up front, you can go far toward allaying the lawyer's fear that you may not pay when you are billed.

An attorney normally shouldn't need a reasonable retainer larger than necessary to cover the first 30 to 60 days of work. The attorney can always ask you to replenish the retainer, and can end the representation if you don't pay. An attorney who demands a retainer for work to be done more than 60 days in the future could be using that money for her personal expenses, using that money to pay for other office matters or otherwise mishandling funds. (See Section J.3, below.)

Consider these issues when you are asked to pay a retainer:

- Never pay a fee to simply hire the lawyer.
- Know exactly what the retainer is for. Never pay a retainer to a lawyer unless and until you know exactly what you are buying.
- Is the retainer refundable if you fire the lawyer? Never pay a nonrefundable retainer under any circumstance.
- How will the retainer be credited against work the lawyer does?

Why is it bad to pay a nonrefundable retainer? Because if you fire the lawyer the day,

week or month after you paid the retainer, the attorney could claim that she gets to keep it all. If the retainer is refundable and you fire the lawyer, you are entitled to a refund of the entire retainer, less a reasonable amount to pay the lawyer for work done.

EXAMPLE: Leroy agrees to pay his lawyer a $1,000 retainer toward handling his divorce at an hourly fee of $200. The attorney gives Leroy a written fee agreement which makes it clear that the retainer will be credited against the first five hours the lawyer puts in on the case and is refundable for any reason Leroy decides not to continue to work with the lawyer. In other words, Leroy's attorney must work five hours to use up the retainer. If Leroy reconciles with his wife and fires the lawyer after he's put in one hour of work, Leroy is entitled to an $800 refund.

A retainer is more like a flat fee paid in advance. Its nonrefundability depends on the circumstances, including:

- if the work was completed
- if the work was completed satisfactorily
- if the attorney quit
- if the attorney quit because you made it impossible to do the work, and
- if you fired the lawyer before the work was finished, was it because of incompetence, unethical behavior or unreasonable delay?

Only New York in domestic (family law) matters explicitly bans nonrefundable retainers. But in spite of the lack of specific prohibitions, the basic rule everywhere is that an attorney must refund unearned fees to clients.

H. Costs

In the legal world, a cost is any out-of-pocket expense which a lawyer incurs working on a case, other than attorney's fees. Basically, there are two kinds of costs which lawyers charge to clients: out-of-pocket costs and overhead.

Out-of-pocket costs. Understandably, most lawyers charge their clients for any money they pay on a client's case. Out-of-pocket costs include fees for:

- asset searches (looking to see if the defendant owns property that could be used to pay a court judgment)
- court filing fees (often hundreds of dollars)
- process servers
- computerized legal research charges (a lawyer often spends hundreds of dollars using expensive research tools such as Lexis or Westlaw)
- police reports and medical records
- investigators and researchers
- witnesses subpoenaed to testify at a deposition
- deposition transcripts (paying court reporter for her time and paying for the transcript itself)
- consultant fees (experts who help work up a case but don't testify—often accountants)
- delivery services, special or unusual postage and messengers
- long distance telephone
- mileage, parking and tolls
- travel expenses
- juries

- expert witnesses (doctors, accountants, appraisers, other professionals)
- other witnesses subpoenaed to testify at a trial
- creating exhibits to be used in court (such as blowing up photographs or making large graphs), and
- brief printing and binding (photocopying and binding the large document the lawyer must submit to the court before or after a trial to support her position).

Overhead charges. Years ago, lawyers, like most other businesspeople, paid all their own costs of doing business. Today, however, many try to charge their clients for part of law office overhead. Overhead costs include:

- administrative charges (such as for opening a file)
- charges to send or receive a fax
- document organization expenses
- ordinary postage
- photocopying
- secretarial time
- word processing, and
- other clerical charges (such as for a file clerk).

Not only do many lawyers charge for these types of costs, but some charge for more than the actual cost. The most common example is photocopying. In a large firm with high-speed copiers, the actual cost of making a copy is less than 10¢ per page. But these same lawyers often charge their clients as much as 20¢–30¢ per page. Smaller firms have similar charges, but it's a lot closer to their actual overhead cost for leasing, servicing and operating the copiers. Either way, if your case involves making several thousand copies, this will be a major expense. Many lawyers also inflate the expenses of sending and receiving a fax by charging a hefty per-page fee instead of the actual phone charges.

These types of markups are referred to in lawyer industry slang as "popcorn." In large firms, popcorn—which can even extend to fees for word processing—can be a big money maker. The rationale often given is that the firm charges reduced hourly rates to big clients such as corporations and insurance companies, and need to recover the cost of clerical and secretarial work. That's fine if you are getting a reduced hourly rate, too. But most individuals and small businesses are paying in excess of $200 an hour, which makes adding on popcorn charges just plain insulting.

1. Payment of Costs in Flat- and Hourly Fee Cases

If you are paying your attorney by the hour or the job, you are normally expected to pay all or some of the costs either up front in a retainer or when you are billed for them.

If the attorney asks for a retainer, the money should be deposited into the attorney's trust account (see Section J, below) and withdrawals should be made to pay for costs only as they are incurred.

2. Payment of Costs in Contingency Fee Cases

In contingency fee cases, typically, you don't owe your attorney a fee for his actual work unless you win. But from those winnings, most

lawyers refund themselves all costs such as those listed in the beginning of Section H which are incurred in handling your case. (Sometimes, the court will order the other side to pay your costs if your case goes all the way to trial and you win.)

But what if you lose? Do you still have to pay your lawyer's out-of-pocket costs? Start by reading your fee agreement carefully. If the attorney expects you to pay costs—win or lose—and believes there's a good chance you might not prevail, the lawyer may require you to pay the out-of-pocket costs as they are incurred. But this isn't always the case; sometimes, your lawyer will agree to advance all costs and expect reimbursement whether or not you win.

Tanya's Tip: Paying the Other Side's Costs
To add insult to injury, if you lose in a trial, the court may order you to pay the costs incurred by the other side. These can be substantial, ranging anywhere from $5,000 to $100,000. When costs are very high, cases are sometimes settled after trial by the losing party agreeing to pay the judgment and not appeal in exchange for the winning side agreeing not to collect costs. If you lose and face a big cost bill from the other side, consider using this in negotiation.

I. Referral Fees and Splitting Fees

In some cases, an attorney pays a referral fee to another attorney for sending the first attorney business. Because clients understandably do not like the idea of an attorney getting paid just for referring a client to another attorney, there have been many attempts to stop or restrict the practice. But lawyers, who profit mostly by scratching each other's backs with referral fees, resist. Only Wyoming absolutely prohibits referral fees.

Courts generally allow attorneys to share their fees with other attorneys who did some work in the case. Under guidelines of the American Bar Association, lawyers who don't work for the same office can divide a fee if:

- The division is in proportion to the services performed by each lawyer or, with the client's written permission, the lawyers assume joint responsibility for the representation.
- The client is advised of and does not object to the participation of all the lawyers.
- The total fee is reasonable.

California, Connecticut, Kansas, Michigan and Pennsylvania have rules regarding fee splitting, but do not require that the division be in proportion to the services performed by each lawyer or that the lawyers assume joint responsibility for the representation. New Hampshire follows the ABA Model Rule which requires disclosure to the client, client consent, proportionality and that the total fee be reasonable. Florida adds a requirement that the client consent in writing.

If you hire or consult an attorney who refers your case to a second lawyer and the second lawyer will be paying the first lawyer a referral fee, make sure you are not charged for it—that is, that she does not pay it out of the fee she collects from you. If you can't avoid this, you can fire the first lawyer—who is likely to do little or no work on your case anyway—and hire the second lawyer yourself.

If your attorney tells you that he will be bringing another attorney into the case, ask who will do the work on your case. It is not uncommon for one attorney to hire another to draft motions, do research or even attend depositions. Also, some attorneys hire a trial specialist if the case goes to trial. Also ask how the other attorney will be paid.

J. Trust Accounts

It's common for attorneys to handle money that belongs to their clients. Sometimes the amounts are relatively small, such as when a lawyer collects money in advance from a client to pay court filing fees or a deposition transcript. Other times, large amounts are involved, such as when a lawyer receives a check settling a client's lawsuit.

In every state, attorneys are bound by strict rules and obligations concerning the handling and safeguarding of money and property that belongs to their clients. Usually, this means the attorney must deposit the money into something called a trust account. This is a bank account, separate from the lawyer's own funds, where he keeps money that doesn't belong to him. Because one trust account will contain money belonging to different clients, the lawyer must keep accurate, up-to-date records at all times.

In theory, trust is the fundamental cornerstone of the attorney-client relationship. You should be able to trust that the attorney is your

SAMPLE INVOICE OFFSETTING FEES AGAINST TRUST ACCOUNT

Invoice submitted to:
Susan Marks
4500 West 11th St.
Washington, NY 10001

April 30, 19xx

			Hrs/Rate	Amount
03/14/xx	TS	consulation with G. Smith	0.10 200.00/hr	20.00
	TS	prepare Smith examination; travel to and from SF and attend day I of arbitration; prepare witness exams for next day	10.80 200.00/hr	2,160.00
03/15/xx	TS	prepare examination of R. Jones and R. Schmidt; telephone conferences with R. Schmidt and G. Smith re testimony; travel to, from and attend day II of arbitration	5.40 200.00/hr	1,000.00
03/18/xx	TS	telephone call to client re request for settlement offer from defendants	0.10 200./hr	20.00
	TS	review letter from P. Rideway re settlement; review testimony and prepare closing; instructions to staff re schedules; draft response to P. Rideway re settlement	5.30 200.00/hr	1,060.00
03/19/xx	TS	telephone call from C. Lewis; prepare Lewis examination; prepare closing; instructions re preparation of schedules for closing; prepare, review and revise same	7.20 200.00/hr	1,440.00
		For professional services rendered	28.90 200.00/hr	$5,780.00

			Qty	
		Costs advanced:		
02/22/xx		Bridge toll	1	1.00
02/26/xx		Federal Express to George Smith	1	18.00
02/29/xx		Lexis legal research	1	22.00
03/01/xx		Federal Express to Judge	1	19.76
		Total costs		$60.75
		Total amount of this bill		$5,860.50
		Balance in trust		$10,000.00
		Less this bill		<5,860.50>
		Balance remaining in trust		$4,139.50

advocate and puts your interests above all others, including her own. The willingness to entrust your attorney with your funds is a clear expression of this trust. Unfortunately, it's fairly common for lawyers to violate that trust and mishandle clients' funds. To protect yourself, do not hesitate to insist on knowing what is occurring with any substantial trust account funds on a regular and timely basis. It is your attorney's obligation to let you know, and when a large amount of money is involved, regular inquiry on your part could avert the misuse of your funds.

1. Why Give a Lawyer Money?

Usually, entrusting money to a lawyer is a matter of necessity, not choice. For example, many attorneys require payment of a retainer before they will undertake representation. Also, most lawsuit settlement checks are made out to both the attorney and the client, and mailed to the attorney. Once the attorney and client sign the check, the attorney usually deposits it into the trust account before sending the client his share.

a. Retainer for Fees

No state has rules specifying what an attorney must do before paying himself fees from the trust account—but you should be sure it's stated in your fee agreement. Nevertheless, the attorney should not withdraw money from the trust account for fees until you have been sent a copy of the attorney's accounting for his time. At the same time, attorneys are supposed to withdraw earned money out of the account as

soon as it is earned, rather than let it remain mixed with other client's funds—which means that you should receive regular and prompt statements.

The reason that an attorney's failure to pay himself by withdrawing the fee he's earned from the trust account is an ethical violation is because it amounts to mixing the attorney's personal funds (still in the trust account) with the clients' trust funds. The danger is that if the lawyer doesn't maintain a strict wall between his funds and the clients', the attorney will eventually use his clients' money for his own purposes, either intentionally or by accident.

The attorney should give you a set amount of time to review the bill before withdrawing the money. Suggest that it be spelled out in your agreement. If you don't object after a week or two, the attorney gets to withdraw the money. If you do object, the money is still in the trust account while you work it out.

If the attorney takes out the money before sending you a statement (or simultaneously with sending you a statement) and you object to your bill, you have to convince the lawyer to put the money back into your account—not an easy task.

Many firms will offer to bill you for tasks completed—that is, your flat fee is broken into segments as work is completed. For example, if you hire an attorney to represent you in a dispute over child visitation rights, she may charge you a flat rate for all work done through the first court hearing. In that case, she will have no right to deduct her fee from the trust account until the hearing is over.

b. Retainer for Costs

Lawyers also use a trust account to hold a retainer for future costs, such as court filing fees, deposition transcript fees and other costs of evidence gathering.

Your fee agreement should specify what costs are to be covered by the retainer. The attorney should not withdraw money from the trust account for costs until you have been sent a copy of the attorney's accounting for the actual expenses incurred.

c. Proceeds From a Lawsuit

Trust accounts are commonly used by lawyers to deposit money paid to settle a dispute or lawsuit prior to disbursing it to the client. Here is a typical scenario. You hire an attorney to represent you in an automobile accident case. You agree to pay her one-third of your recovery as a contingency fee and to reimburse her for all costs advanced. You settle the case, and the insurance company for the other driver makes out the check payable to both you and your attorney.

As with most contingency fee agreements, your attorney will probably ask you to endorse the check, and then she will deposit it to her trust account. When the check clears, she will calculate how much you owe for costs and attorney's fees, and will disburse this amount to herself. She will also pay any providers (such as doctors) whose bills are as of yet unpaid. (See Section d, below.) The balance is sent to you as your share of the proceeds.

 Tanya's Tip: Don't Sign the Settlement Check Without Knowing Where the Money Will Go
As suggested in Chapter 7, Section D, before you sign the check, ask your attorney for a detailed record of where every dollar will go. Like any bill, check it over carefully before you endorse the check. A sample accounting, with instructions on how to read it, is in Chapter 7.

Before your lawyer can disburse the money, she must deposit the check and wait for it to clear so that the money really is in her account. Otherwise, she would be paying you with money belonging to other clients. If the check is from an out-of-state bank or in the form of a draft (which requires more processing than a check), it may take one or two weeks to clear. A check drawn on a local bank should clear in less than a week. Once the deposit clears, the attorney should pay you and the providers without delay.

d. Payments to Lienholders

Often, a client who needs medical care after an injury signs a contract, called a lien, giving the medical provider the right to collect from the proceeds of the eventual settlement or lawsuit in exchange for treatment. This lien gives the healthcare provider the right to collect from proceeds before the client gets his share. A medical provider who has a lien against your recovery has a right to be paid whether you win or lose. Practically speaking, however, he is counting on receiving his money when your case is settled or you win at arbitration or trial. To make sure he'll get paid, he will send the lien to your lawyer.

Compromising with the lienholder. Most cases settle—and by reaching a settlement, you and the lienholder (the provider) are sure of recovering something. By contrast, if your case is resolved through arbitration or a trial, there is a risk that you and the lienholder not recover anything. But if the lien is substantial, you may not want to accept a settlement which goes mostly to pay your attorney's fees and your costs (including the large medical lien), and leaves you to pocket very little. Medical providers know this, and will often agree to reduce the amount of a lien to help a case settle before a trial or arbitration.

> EXAMPLE: Mika, who was hurt in a car accident, signs a lien in favor of her chiropractor for the expenses of her treatment. The bills add up to $20,000. Mika gets a

settlement offer of $60,000. If she accepts it, once her attorney subtracts her fees and costs, $35,000 remains. If Mika's attorney pays the chiropractor the full amount of her lien, Mika will pocket only $15,000 of the $60,000 settlement. Mika is unsure about taking the settlement and is considering going to court and hoping for a bigger jury verdict. Her lawyer suggests that she talk to the chiropractor about taking less than the full $20,000. The lawyer points out that this is immediate money, and if Mika rejects the settlement and insists on a trial, there is the risk she will lose and further delay the payments. The chiropractor agrees to cut her fee to $11,000— but only if the lawyer agrees to cut his fee a bit, too.

Disputing a lien. It is possible for you to dispute the amount of a lien, and you especially want to do so if you conclude that once attorney's fees, costs and liens are paid, you'll get very little.

You can also dispute the existence or validity of the lien—for example, if the provider sent you a lien agreement but you never signed it. Whether a particular lien is valid is usually governed by your state law. In most states, the lienholder must follow certain, specific and often picky steps to claim a lien. A provider might file a lien too late or use the wrong language.

If you think a particular lien may not be valid and do not have access to an attorney who knows this area, go to your local law library and consult a lawyers' practice book covering liens to be paid out of lawsuit proceeds. The better books provide quick answers and references to statutes and case law.

If you dispute the amount, existence or validity of a medical or other provider's lien, your lawyer has a legal obligation to hold the money in trust until your dispute is resolved. If ultimately the lien turns out not to be valid (but you do owe money for services provided), the lienholder probably won't be able to hold up the disbursement of your funds, although she could probably sue you to establish her right to collect.

e. Escrow Funds for You and Your Adversary

Often, parties to a transaction or dispute agree that the money involved will be held by a third party (called an escrow holder) until the transaction is complete (for example, the sale of real estate) or until the dispute is resolved (such as how to divide marital property in a divorce). When the matter is concluded, the parties then agree how the money is to be disbursed.

In these situations, attorneys sometimes act as escrow holders. When this happens, it is a good idea to have written escrow instructions. Provide a list of the conditions that must be met before the attorney can release the money. An escrow holder has an obligation not only to his client, but also to the non-client, such as the seller of real estate (if the lawyer represents the buyer) or the other party in the divorce.

What happens if the transaction falls apart or no settlement is reached in the dispute? Typically, the escrow holder must refuse to pay out the money until the parties agree, even if one of the parties is the attorney's client. The reason for this neutrality is that when a lawyer acts as

an escrow agent, her loyalty must be to all parties, not just to her client. If, after an extended period of time, the parties cannot reach an agreement, either the lawyer or one of the parties must turn to a court to have it resolved.

EXAMPLE: Ellie and Fred, a divorcing couple, are entitled to a tax refund but have not decided on how to divide it. Ellie's attorney agrees to act as an escrow holder for the funds until Ellie and Fred decide. Once the attorney has assumed this role, she is obligated to retain the refund until Ellie and Fred agree on the disbursement and provide her with written instructions on how to disburse the refund. If Ellie requests partial disbursement of what she considers her portion, the attorney cannot give her the money without Fred's consent. To act otherwise would be a violation of her obligation to Fred, an obligation the attorney took on when she agreed to hold the funds in escrow.

2. Why Give a Lawyer Personal Property?

It's common for attorneys to hold property as well as money for clients (and sometimes adversaries). The attorney's strict duty of safekeeping money also applies to property. For example, let's say that a divorcing couple owns a valuable piece of art that neither wants the other to have or sell. To keep the peace, one spouse's attorney agrees to hold it in trust for both until the dispute is resolved.

The attorney has an obligation to keep the artwork in a safe place where it is not likely to be damaged or stolen. If she stores it in an unlocked storage room where employees have unlimited access and could easily steal or damage it, she is clearly not meeting this trust obligation.

How many additional precautions the attorney should take depends on the value of the object and how likely it is to be stolen or damaged. If the artwork is really valuable, this might include storing it in a locked, dry and reasonably fireproof place. In some situations, a locked storage room in the attorney's office might suffice, but if the property is extremely valuable and/or perishable, a bank vault or a specialist storage company would be more appropriate.

An attorney may also agree to hold documents which represent the assets of a client or third party, such as stock certificates and bearer bonds. Again, the attorney has an obligation to provide for the safekeeping of these instruments so that they may be returned to the client at the appropriate time. The prudent attorney undertaking this function would rent a safe deposit box to store the instruments.

3. Trust Fund Rules and Obligations

Many rules control how lawyers must carry out their trust fund obligations. This is an area where bar regulatory groups and courts have sincerely attempted to see that a lawyer's clients do not become his victims.

As explained in the beginning of Section J, all states have rules specifying what an attorney must do with funds belonging to clients—such as keep them in an identifiable bank account, maintained in the state in which the attorney

practices law, segregated from the attorney's own funds. The attorney can keep personal funds in the trust account only to pay bank charges and unearned fees and costs. Trust accounts must be maintained in a bank in the state in which the attorney practices so that state lawyer regulators can exercise oversight and prevent the worst types of abuse. Every state, for example, requires banks to report overdrafts on attorney trust accounts to the state bar.

Lawyers must remove their earned fees from trust accounts fairly quickly. Far more egregious conduct, of course, is the attorney who helps himself to clients' trust funds without clients' knowledge and consent. Lawyers call this misappropriation of funds. Everyone else calls it stealing.

Unfortunately, in an era when many lawyers are short of clients and alcohol and drug abuse rates within the profession are on the rise, the temptation can be strong, especially if the attorney kids himself into thinking he can use the funds to make a quick killing and put the money back before the client misses it. But this is *never* okay; stealing is a fundamental violation of the trust inherent in the attorney-client relationship and is a crime.

If you seriously suspect your attorney is mishandling your money, you have several options:

- Immediately file a complaint with your state's attorney discipline agency. Do this both by fax or overnight mail and follow up with a phone call. If your lawyer really is a crook, you have no time to lose in trying to tie up the funds. (See Chapter 8.)

- Call the police.
- Discharge your lawyer and ask your lawyer for the balance in your trust fund account and a full accounting. (See Chapter 5.)
- Go to the lawyer's office, demand your check and cash it immediately.
- If you have lost money and your financial situation allows it, seek anther lawyer to assist you.
- Inquire about whether your state maintains a Client Security Trust Fund from which you can be reimbursed. (See Chapter 8, Section H.)

a. Duty to Keep Good Accounts

An attorney must be able to account for trust funds for each separate client at all times. She must know not only the total amount of funds she holds in trust, but also the amount in the account attributed to each client. If asked, the attorney must promptly account to you for all trust account funds she holds on your behalf. A sample letter making that request is below.

**SAMPLE LETTER
REQUESTING TRUST FUND ACCOUNTING**

Dear Morris:

I'm in the process of updating my financial records. In this connection, please provide me with an accounting of trust fund activity relating to funds held on my behalf since the date of your last statement to me. I would like to know my starting balance, the date, purpose and amount of any expenditures made on my behalf, any deposits received and my current balance.

Thank you for your attention to this matter.

Sincerely,

Cheryl Wong

Cheryl Wong

What type of accounting should you expect to receive? To ensure that the lawyer spends only the funds available to each particular client, she must regularly balance her trust fund account and calculate the amounts available to each client. In doing this, she should keep ledgers showing the following:

- initial deposit made on behalf of the client
- the date, payee and reason for any expenditures made on behalf of the client
- further deposits made on behalf of the client, and
- the ending balance.

As a general rule, the attorney should do this as the activity occurs (or within a few days) and should calculate a monthly balance for every client with trust account activity that month.

The total for all clients should add up to the amount shown on the bank statement so that an audit, whether initiated by a client or a lawyer regulatory agency, can determine if all the money is there. Most states require that a lawyer keep these records at least five years following the termination of the representation.

If you are required to place a significant amount of money in trust with the attorney, ask her what she does to account for the funds. If she does not generally send monthly statements when activity occurs, get her to agree to do so. Remember, you are entitled at any time to an accounting from your attorney of the funds held in trust.

b. Disputes Over Trust Funds

If you and your attorney disagree about how much of the money held in the trust account your attorney is entitled to, he may disburse to himself only the amounts undisputed. The attorney must hold the rest in trust until the dispute is resolved. It's always best to let your attorney know in writing that you disagree with the amount he feels he is entitled to remove from his trust account to cover the fees and costs in your case.

EXAMPLE: Toni agrees to pay her attorney $150 per hour to handle a fairly complicated estate plan complete with a Q-Tip trust (a common marital trust). She gives him a $2,500 retainer to cover attorney's fees, and he deposits it into his trust account. Through December 31 of the year she hired the attorney, Toni received periodic accountings showing she had in-

curred fees for seven hours of work at $150 per hour, using $1,050 of the $2,500. In January, her monthly statement shows that the attorney raised his hourly rate to $175, an amount to which Toni never agreed. The attorney bills Toni for seven hours in January, for a total of $1,225. Toni writes him a letter stating that the bill should be only $1,050, thereby notifying the lawyer that $175 is in dispute. The attorney must keep this amount in the trust account until the dispute is resolved. In this case, because Toni agreed to pay only $150 per hour, the attorney should not charge more. Toni should not be surprised, however, if the attorney attempts to renegotiate the hourly rate as a condition of continued representation.

A client's claim that an attorney simply hasn't done the work billed for is at the bottom of many disputes about who owns money deposited in trust funds. This sort of dispute can arise in a number of ways.

EXAMPLE: Toni notices that on December 27, and 28, her attorney claims to have spent ten hours per day on her case. Because she called his office and got a voice mail message at that time, Toni knows that his office was closed on both those dates and is pretty sure that he had mentioned skiing with his family between Christmas and New Year's. Toni calls the lawyer to inquire about what appears to be a problem, but her call is not returned. She then writes a polite but firm letter to the attorney disputing the bill. The attorney should hold the disputed funds in the trust account until Toni is satisfied that the hours spent are genuine.

Costs are another area where disputes can rise. As discussed in Section H, above, always scrutinize your monthly bill for the costs incurred by the attorney during your representation. Is your divorce counsel billing you for the cost of a meal he ate during a meeting with opposing counsel as well as for his time? Check your fee agreement to see if meals constitute an expense chargeable to you. If the agreement is unclear, the attorney should not ask you to pay for his veal chop.

If you believe there is a question as to fees or expenses you are being charged, and you paid a retainer, promptly contact your lawyer. If you are not able to talk to your attorney and resolve your questions, immediately put your concerns in writing. This makes a record of your dispute and obligates your attorney to hold the disputed funds in trust until it is resolved.

SAMPLE LETTER CONCERNING BILLING ERRORS

Dear Mr. Franco:

This will confirm our conversation where I informed you that your recent billing contains several errors. These errors are as follows:

   [list errors]

Until we resolve this problem, I request that you not charge my balance in your trust account for these funds.

Sincerely,

Walter Owen

Walter Owen

c. Interest on Money Held in a Trust Account

You might like to earn interest on the funds entrusted to an attorney. This is usually not possible, however, because money is held a relatively short time and attributing interest to each client could be an accounting nightmare.

Attorneys in most states have two choices of what to do with the interest earned on trust accounts. Keeping the money is not one of them.

One choice is to participate in a state program called Interest On Attorney Trust Accounts (IOLTA) or something similar. Under IOLTA, interest earned on trust accounts funds legal services for low income people. Under IOLTA rules, the bank pays the interest directly to the legal services foundation.

In most states, the IOLTA program is voluntary. If an attorney does not want to participate, she must notify the state bar association and then figure out how to pay the interest to her clients. Partially because of ease, most attorneys participate. In a few states, including California, Georgia and West Virginia, IOLTA participation is mandatory.

If you will entrust your attorney with a significant sum of money for what may be an extended period, discuss with her the possibility of her opening a separate, interest-bearing account. If IOLTA participation is not mandatory in your state, establishing an interest-bearing account for a significant amount would be in keeping with her general duty to preserve your property. She may, however, require you to pay the bank service charges of a separate account, which seems only fair.

K. Will Someone Else Pay Your Attorney's Fees?

At the initial interview with a lawyer, ask if someone else might pay your lawyer's fee. The right to recover attorney's fees in a lawsuit is a rapidly changing area and would take a book itself to explore. If the attorney you hire is competent, she should know whether or not you have a right to claim legal fees and costs as part of your damages in the lawsuit. Consider it a "trick question" to pop on the lawyer. One who is skilled and experienced in the particular area of law will at least be able to discuss the possibilities with you.

1. Insurance Defense

Your lawyer should immediately explore the possibilities of insurance coverage with you when defending you in any civil lawsuit. If the claim is covered by a policy, the insurance company owes you both a defense and the duty to pay the fair value of the claim. Even if there is some controversy about whether the loss is covered, the insurance company will pay your legal fees, at least until the company makes a determination about coverage. This is done under a "reservation of rights" which means that the insurer will give you the benefit of the doubt while it thinks about the case, but reserves the right to pull out. Attorneys sometimes miss this.

EXAMPLE: The Durhams children build a tree house in their side yard. One day, a child (in the tree house) shoots a slingshot at a passing car. The driver swerves in shock and hits another car causing physical injuries to the occupants of both cars. The injured parties sue the Durhams. They might have a right to be defended by their homeowners insurance carrier if their child shot the slingshot. Their insurance will not cover legal costs if the shot was from a neighbor's child.

2. Recovering Fees From Your Adversary

As a general rule, the winner of a lawsuit is not entitled to get reimbursed (by the loser) for the attorney's fees incurred in bringing the case. There are many exceptions to this rule, however, most of which permit recovery:

- if a contract that has been broken has such a provision
- if a statute authorizes it, or
- if the court awards attorney's fees to the winner as a sanction against the loser for some outrageous behavior (see Chapter 10, Section B.1).

a. Contract Provisions

Provisions for the recovery of attorneys' fees are included in most business and commercial contracts. Common examples of contracts which you would expect to have a provision for the recovery of attorneys' fees would be in:

- promissory notes
- real estate sales contracts
- leases
- listing agreements for the sale of real estate
- mortgages
- deeds of trust
- other security contracts to secure payment of a note
- licensing agreements
- franchise agreements
- building and construction contracts.

Tanya's Tip: Read Your Contract Carefully
In California, if your contact has a provision providing that the other side is entitled to have you pay her attorney's fees if she wins, the clause may be reciprocal. That is, even though it doesn't say so, you may be entitled to have the other side pay your attorney's fees if you win.

b. Statutes

Hundreds of federal and state laws allow for the recovery of attorneys' fees in specific types of cases. Only Alaska has a broad law which simply allows for an award of attorneys' fees in most civil actions.[2]

i. Federal Laws

Federal laws that allow for recovery of attorneys' fees include the following:

- Black Lung Benefits Act
- Civil Rights Act
- Civil Service Reform Act
- Clean Air Act
- Clean Water Act
- Copyright Act
- Employment Retirement Income and Security Act (ERISA)
- Equal Access to Justice Act
- Equal Pay Act
- Fair Credit Reporting Act
- Fair Debt Collection Practices Act
- Fair Labor Standards Act
- Freedom of Information Act
- Handicapped Children's Protection Act
- Individuals with Disabilities Education Act
- Longshore and Harbor Workers' Compensation Act

- Motor vehicle tampering laws, including the former Odometer Act
- Patent cases
- Privacy Act
- Racketeering Influenced and Corrupt Organizations Act (RICO)
- Securities Act
- Securities and Exchange Act
- Sherman Antitrust Act
- Social Security Act
- Surface Mining Control and Reclamation Act
- Trademark Act
- Truth in Lending Act
- Veterans and servicemen's claims.
- Voting Rights Act.

2. State Laws

To find out what laws in your state allow for the recovery of attorneys' fees will require legal research. (Spending some time in a law library should help you find the answer. See *Legal Research: How to Find and Understand the Law*, by Stephen Elias and Susan Levinkind (Nolo Press).)

State laws vary a lot. Many are similar to the federal ones. Others will differ. Although I can't give you specific rules, it is likely that your state has a law permitting the recovery of attorneys' fees in the following kinds of matters:

- divorce, child support, child custody and paternity matters when there is a large gap in the incomes between the spouses or parents
- in matters involving a trust, or the estate of someone who has died or is

incompetent, the court may award fees to a party who sues the fiduciary
- consumer protection and deceptive business cases
- workers' compensation cases
- eminent domain proceedings (public taking of private land for such things as to build a freeway)
- actions to "quiet" title (clearing up title to real property)
- enforcement of mechanics' liens (recorded by a contractor not paid after working on real estate)
- partition lawsuits (forced division or the sale of property owned by more than one person), and
- proceedings for contempt of court.

c. Disputes Over Attorneys' Fees Awards

Even if a contract provision or statute authorizes the award of attorneys' fees, parties often fight over whether the awarding of fees is mandatory or in the judge's discretion. This may depend upon the wording of the contract or statute. A contract or statute that says attorneys' fees "shall" be awarded is mandatory. One that says attorneys' fees "may" be awarded is discretionary. In either case, however, the amount of the fee is usually determined by the court.

Lawyers have generated mounds of case law over what exactly is a prevailing party. Clearly, when the plaintiff wins nothing, the defendant is the prevailing party. But it is not always so clear. Often, a defendant responds with a countersuit against the plaintiff. If they both

FLORIDA STATEMENT OF CLIENT'S RIGHTS

Before you, the prospective client, arrange a contingent fee agreement with a lawyer, you should understand this statement of your rights as a client. This statement is not a part of the actual contract between you and your lawyer, but as a prospective client, you should be aware of these rights:

1. There is no legal requirement that a lawyer charge a client a set fee or a percentage of money recovered in a case. You, the client, have the right to talk with your lawyer about the proposed fee and to bargain about the rate or percentage as any other contract. If you do not reach an agreement with one lawyer you may talk with other lawyers.

2. Any contingent fee contract must be in writing and you have 3 business days to reconsider the contract. You may cancel the contract without any reason if you notify your lawyer in writing within 3 business days of signing the contract. If you withdraw from the contract within the first 3 business days, you do not owe the lawyer a fee although you may be responsible for the lawyer's actual costs during that time. If your lawyer begins to represent you, your lawyer may not withdraw from the case without giving you notice, delivering necessary papers to you, and allowing you time to employ another lawyer. Often, your lawyer must obtain court approval before withdrawing from a case. If you discharge your lawyer without good cause after the 3-day period, you may have to pay a fee for work the lawyer has done.

3. Before hiring a lawyer, you, the client, have the right to know about the lawyer's education, training, and experience. If you ask, the lawyer should tell you specifically about the lawyer's actual experience dealing with cases similar to yours. If you ask, the lawyer should provide information about special training or knowledge and give you this information in writing if you request it.

4. Before signing a contingent fee contract with you, a lawyer must advise you whether the lawyer intends to handle your case alone or whether other lawyers will be helping with the case. If your lawyer intends to refer the case to other lawyers, the lawyer should tell you what kind of fee sharing arrangement will be made with the other lawyers. If lawyers from different law firms will represent you, at least 1 lawyer from each law firm must sign the contingent fee contract.

5. If your lawyer intends to refer your case to another lawyer or counsel with other lawyers, your lawyer should tell you about that at the beginning. If your lawyer takes the case and later decides to refer it to another lawyer or to associate with other lawyers, you should sign a new contract that includes the new lawyers. You, the client, also have the right to consult with each lawyer working on your case and each lawyer is legally responsible to represent your interests and is legally responsible for the acts of the other lawyers involved in the case.

6. You, the client, have the right to know in advance how you will need to pay the expenses and the legal fees at the end of the case. If you pay a deposit in advance for costs, you may ask reasonable questions

FLORIDA STATEMENT OF CLIENT'S RIGHTS (cont'd)

about how the money will be or has been spent and how much of it remains unspent. Your lawyer should give a reasonable estimate about future necessary costs. If your lawyer agrees to lend or advance you money to prepare or research the case, you have the right to know periodically how much money your lawyer has spent on your behalf. You also have the right to decide, after consulting with your lawyer, how much money is to be spent to prepare a case. If you pay the expenses, you have the right to decide how much to spend. Your lawyer should also inform you whether the fee will be based on the gross amount recovered or on the amount recovered minus the costs.

7. You, the client, have the right to be told by your lawyer about possible adverse consequences if you lose the case. Those adverse consequences might include money that you might have to pay to your lawyer for costs and liability you might have for attorney's fees to the other side.

8. You, the client, have the right to receive and approve a closing statement at the end of the case before you pay any money. The statement must list all of the financial details of the entire case, including the amount recovered, all expenses, and a precise statement of your lawyer's fee. Until you approve the closing statement you need not pay any money to anyone, including your lawyer. You also have the right to have every lawyer or law firm working on your case sign this closing statement.

9. You, the client, have the right to ask your lawyer at reasonable intervals how the case is progressing and to have these questions answered to the best of your lawyer's ability.

10. You, the client, have the right to make the final decision regarding settlement of a case. Your lawyer must notify you of all offers of settlement before and after the trial. Offers during the trial must be immediately communicated and you should consult with your lawyer regarding whether to accept a settlement.

11. If at any time you, the client, believe that your lawyer has charged an excessive or illegal fee, you have the right to report the matter to The Florida Bar, the agency that oversees the practice and behavior of all lawyers in Florida. For information on how to reach The Florida Bar, call 904-561-5600, or contact the local bar association. Any disagreement between you and your lawyer about a fee can be taken to court and you may wish to hire another lawyer to help you resolve this disagreement. Usually fee disputes must be handled in a separate lawsuit.

_____   _____
Client Signature   Attorney Signature

_____   _____
Date   Date

win, who is the prevailing party for purposes of attorneys' fees? Generally, it is whoever is the net winner. If the plaintiff recovers $10,000 from the defendant and the defendant recovers $30,000 from the plaintiff on a countersuit, then the defendant has a net judgment of $20,000 and is the prevailing party. Because laws vary so much among states, before proceeding with the expectation of being awarded attorneys' fees based on a statute, read the statute carefully to see if it defines "prevailing party."

Endnotes

[1] New York Superior Court Rules § 1400 et seq.

[2] Alaska Statutes § 09.60.010 and Civil Rule 82.

Chapter 4

CONFLICTS OF INTERESTS— IF YOUR LAWYER ISN'T LOYAL TO YOU

Every state has rules of professional conduct governing how attorneys must act. Although the technical details differ from state to state, the same principles exist in all. The most important is that your lawyer has a fiduciary relationship with you. Stripped of the fancy terminology, this means your attorney must represent you with the highest degree of loyalty, including putting your interests above his own. Central to the concept of fiduciary duty is trust. You can tell your lawyer things in confidence without fear that they will be disclosed.

Here are some of the most common rules of conduct for attorneys:

- An attorney shall represent a client with undivided loyalty.
- An attorney shall keep the client's secrets and maintain the client's confidences.
- An attorney shall not accept representation adverse to a client.
- An attorney shall avoid the "appearance of impropriety."

- An attorney shall not represent multiple parties in the same matter without each client's permission.
- An attorney must exercise independent judgment on behalf of the client.
- An attorney may not represent a client if the interest of the client is directly adverse to that of another client.
- Usually it is okay for an attorney to represent clients whose interests vary in degree or whose interests are divergent, but not in direct conflict.

Failure to adhere to these basic rules means that a lawyer breaches his standard of conduct or fiduciary duty. These lapses are also commonly referred to within the legal profession as conflicts of interest or unethical conduct. Clients generally put it more directly: "Can you believe what my crook of a lawyer actually did?"

This chapter gives you some clues about spotting conflicts of interest. Actually, your own common sense can spot most conflicts—use this chapter to confirm that you're right.

Conflicts questions don't always have simple answers. Legal authorities may come to dif-

ferent conclusions regarding ethical behavior because of subtle differences in facts. This chapter explores the kinds of complaints I hear most frequently from clients and disciplinary agencies hear from consumers. It isn't meant to be exhaustive. If your particular concern isn't discussed here, it doesn't mean that your lawyer is necessarily behaving appropriately. Your lawyer has a duty to serve justice and you. If she's serving herself at the expense of either of those, she's acting unethically.

Despite the many variations, conflicts of interest show up in two basic fact patterns: an attorney has a conflict with his own client's interest, or the lawyer for the other side has a conflict with another party in a matter.

> **EXAMPLE 1:** You are represented by Marsha in your suit against XYZ Corporation for injuries resulting from using a product manufactured by XYZ. Marsha is a major stockholder in XYZ Corporation and thus has a financial interest in the welfare of the defendant.

> **EXAMPLE 2:** You are suing John, a former employee, for stealing trade secrets. John's attorney once represented your company in matters related to those trade secrets, and thus has access to confidential information.

In the two examples, the problems for you are a little different. In Example 1, your attorney might be inclined to put the interests of her investment in XYZ over your right to recover for injuries. In Example, 2 your *former* attorney is in a position to disclose confidential information to your adversary.

If you were in the position of John, your adversary, in Example 2, you would have grounds for a disciplinary complaint and possibly a lawsuit against your lawyer if you were not advised of this possibility and had not waived the potential risk.

HOW TO FIND YOUR STATE'S RULES OF PROFESSIONAL CONDUCT

Most states base their rules of conduct on the American Bar Association (ABA)'s Model Rules of Professional Conduct. The ABA adopted model rules in 1969 and then modified them in 1983. A few states still use the 1969 rules, but most have adopted the stricter 1983 version. But because each state has adopted the rules with changes, you will need to check the rules adopted by your state.

To see a copy of your state's rules or to see how the rules have been interpreted in your state, visit a law library and locate the *Lawyer's Manual on Professional Conduct* (ABA/BNA). Chapter 11, Section A.2, contains a list of the name of each state's ethical rules.

A. Conflicts Involving the Client and the Attorney

Let's look at the rules of professional conduct in the context of real situations. Although I can't detail every possible ethical complaint against lawyers, I do cover the ones I hear most often. Section D, below, covers what to do if you discover that your lawyer has a conflict of interest.

1. My Lawyer Wants to Be Named in My Will (or My Deceased Relative's Lawyer Was Named in the Will)

Among the most callous of ethical violations is the practice of influencing a client to include the attorney in her will, trust or other estate plan. I know it sounds like something out of a soap opera, but many thousands of lawyers do just this—persuade their clients, particularly elderly and ill clients, to leave the lawyers money or valuable property.

Most states have rules allowing heirs to challenge a bequest to a lawyer named as a beneficiary in a will, trust or other estate plan. In one case, a lawyer drafted several wills (each time revoking the previous will) for a client over a period of years. The last will was signed in the hospital, just a few months before the client's death. When the client died, the children found that each successive will had given large gifts to the lawyer, and that the last will gave him most of the estate. The children challenged the validity of the will. The court agreed, ruling that there was a presumption that the lawyer exercised undue influence over the client. The lawyer then had to prove that he did not take unfair advantage of his confidential relationship with the client.[1]

To protect yourself, your inheritance and your own estate plan, challenge any will or trust which makes gifts to the attorney who drafts the document. If you (or an elderly relative) really want to leave property to your lawyer, have a different lawyer draft the will or trust and make a videotape in which you or your relative state that you really want to leave the property to the other attorney.

A similar situation arises when a lawyer who drafts an estate planning document is named the executor of the will or the trustee of the trust. The executor or trustee handles the deceased person's affairs after death. With those responsibilities comes the opportunity to earn a fee and, for a dishonest executor or trustee, to steal from the estate. I don't mean to say that an attorney can never act in this capacity. But you must be alert to the dangers of this kind of arrangement, and the first person who should be alerting you is that very same attorney.

It is unethical for an attorney to name himself as the executor or trustee of a will he is drafting for a client. Every state prohibits it because it amounts to taking unfair advantage of a client. Fortunately, wills and trusts are easily amended. If your attorney has been named as the executor or trustee of your estate, amend the document immediately. If he drafts the new will or trust, refuse to pay any bill for the revision. If you hire a different attorney to draft the new document, send your first attorney the bill for the revision.

2. My Lawyer Is Getting a Referral Fee

In some cases, an attorney pays a referral fee to another attorney for sending the first attorney business. Referral fees among attorneys are covered in Chapter 3, Section I. Courts generally allow attorneys to share their fees with other attorneys who did some work in the case. But that is not necessarily the case if an attorney gets a referral fee from a non-attorney to whom he sends a client. For example, the New Hampshire Bar Association puzzled over that issue in the following situation:

> An attorney settled his client's case for a substantial amount of money, and then referred the client to a financial adviser to assist the client in investing it. The lawyer received a referral fee from the financial adviser, which he disclosed to the client. Although the New Hampshire Bar Association could not come to a final resolution as to whether or not the attorney acted ethically, the disclosure of the fee by the attorney was a key factor in the analysis. The disclosure probably saved the attorney from discipline. In another jurisdiction, in front of another board of examiners, he might have been disciplined anyway.[2]

Disclosure of the conflict (receiving a referral fee) by the attorney and waiver of the conflict by the client will cure most conflicts, but ask yourself if you really want advice from a lawyer who is on someone else's payroll, too. Would you trust an investment adviser whose only quality you really know is the craftiness to pay lawyers to refer their clients?

3. My Lawyer Wants to Change Our Fee Agreement

This is discussed in Chapter 7, Section D, but it bears mention here because it may be an ethical issue. Once you have a fee agreement with your attorney, she has a conflict of interest in advising you about changing the agreement. This is true even if the attorney changes her fee in the normal course of business, unless your agreement permits such a change.

If your attorney ever proposes changing the fee, get an opinion from a different lawyer before agreeing. I have seen many cases where an attorney switches from an hourly fee arrangement to a contingency agreement when it becomes clear that the lawyer can get a windfall in the case—that is, the case is about to settle for a lot of money and very little effort.

There's nothing inherently wrong with changing a fee agreement, as long as you have the opportunity to get another opinion first.

4. My Lawyer Wants to Go Into Business With Me

While there is nothing unethical about an attorney participating in a business deal, ethical problems do arise when the business deal involves the attorney's client. After all, the attorney is supposed to be protecting the client's interests, something that is unlikely if the attorney is party to the transaction and has his own interest to protect.

Here's a common situation. An entrepreneur with a good idea and very little experience approaches an attorney for advice about incorporating, registering a copyright or obtaining a patent. The lawyer recognizes the potential of the idea and offers to do the work in exchange for a portion of the business or shares of stock.

Usually, courts and lawyer discipline agencies find the lawyer's involvement to be unethical unless all of the following are true:

- the arrangement is financially fair
- the attorney discloses the conflict to the client, and
- the client has the chance to get an opinion from a second attorney (referred to as "independent counsel") on whether or not to proceed.

Once you enter into a business deal with your lawyer, your lawyer is working for himself. To protect yourself, get the second opinion before proceeding, use an accountant who is completely independent of your new partner and stay on your toes.

5. My Lawyer Wants to Go to Bed With Me

I made an interesting discovery while doing research for this book. Sexual relations between a client and an attorney has been an index topic to lawyer ethics opinions only since 1990. Clearly, the problem isn't that new. More likely, as with other forms of sexual abuse, the problem is only now being brought to light. As the Supreme Court of Georgia noted in March of 1992, "This proceeding is the first time we have considered whether a lawyer who has a sexual relationship with a client should be disciplined." (See Section A.5.b, below.)

Several states have enacted specific rules which prohibit or restrict lawyers' sexual relationships with clients. Those state rules are discussed in Section A.5.a, below. States without specific rules but which have used other

sources to discipline attorneys for having sex with their clients are discussed in Section A.5.b, below.

It is the opinion of the American Bar Association that a sexual relationship between a lawyer and a client could both be a breach of the lawyer's fiduciary relationship to the client and impair the attorney's ability to represent the client competently.[3] Although the ABA opinion is binding only in those states where it has been adopted, it is an indication of the general opinion lawyer regulators have on the subject.

Most complaints about lawyer-client sexual relations have arisen when a lawyer represents a client in a divorce. Typically, the client claims that the lawyer put his own sexual interest ahead of what was in the best legal interest of the client. Depending somewhat on state law, in a divorce case, if a lawyer is having a sexual relationship with a client it could affect the client's right to alimony, to custody or to having her attorney's fees paid by her spouse. It could also make the lawyer a witness in the divorce case.

Lawyer-client sex is generally governed by state rules of professional conduct or disciplinary rules. Therefore, if your lawyer has sex (or tries or asks to have sex) with you, you should file a complaint with your lawyer discipline agency. (See Chapter 8.)

a. States With Specific Rules Prohibiting a Lawyer From Having Sexual Relations With a Client

These rules have all been adopted since 1990.

PROHIBITIONS AGAINST A LAWYER HAVING SEXUAL RELATIONS WITH A CLIENT

State	Citation	Rule
California	Rules of Professional Conduct, Rule 3-120	A lawyer shall not: • require or demand sexual relations with a client incident to any professional representation or as a condition of any professional representation • coerce, intimidate or use undue influence in entering into sexual relations with a client, or • continue to represent a client with whom the lawyer is having sexual relations if it will cause the lawyer to render incompetent legal services. This rules does not apply if: • the lawyer and the client are married • the sexual relationship predates the lawyer-client relationship, or • the lawyer is a member of a firm representing the client but does not work on the case.
	Business & Professions Code §6106.9	A lawyer is expressly or implicitly barred from conditioning the rendering of professional services on the client's willingness to engage in sexual relations with the attorney. This rules does not apply if: • the lawyer and the client are married or are domestic partners • the sexual relationship predates the lawyer-client relationship • the client consents, or • the lawyer is a member of a firm representing the client but does not work on the case.
Florida	Rule 4-8.4 (i) (Misconduct)	A lawyer may not "engage in sexual conduct with a client that exploits the lawyer-client relationship." This rule does not apply if: • the client is a representative of a corporate client • the sexual relationship predates the lawyer-client relationship, or • the lawyer is a member of a firm representing the client but does not work on the case.
Iowa	DR 5-101(b) and EC 5-25	A client can't waive the conflict or give consent; the belief in Iowa is that it is impossible for a vulnerable client to "consent" to a sexual relationship with the attorney. As a practical matter, a consent or waiver would probably require the advice of second lawyer (independent counsel). Applying this rule, the Iowa bar suspended a lawyer for making unwelcome sexual advances toward a client in the attorney-client meeting room at the county jail. The client was a lesbian; the lawyer insisted on talking to her about sex, rather than the criminal charges against her, and said that he wanted to help her

PROHIBITIONS AGAINST A LAWYER HAVING SEXUAL RELATIONS WITH A CLIENT (cont'd)

State	Citation	Rule
Iowa (cont'd)		change her sexual orientation. He put his hand on her leg, hugged her, put his hands on her face, held her hands and grabbed her buttocks. Law enforcement officers took photographs of his offensive conduct. The lawyer's defense was that he was a "hands-on" counselor due to his 18 years' experience as a clergyman.[4] The court noted that the lawyer had been previously disciplined for having sex with a client in his office and suspended him for 12 months. The court stated that it had "lost its patience with the lawyer's amorous proclivities toward female clients" and warned him that any future similar conduct would surely result in revocation of his license to practice law.
Minnesota	Rule 1.8(k)	A lawyer may not have sexual relations with a current client. This rule does not apply if: • the sexual relationship predates the lawyer-client relationship • the lawyer is a member of a firm representing the client but does not work on the case, or • the client is a representative of a corporate client with whom the lawyer has no contacts.
New York	Court of Appeals Rule 1200.3	A divorce attorney is barred from beginning a sexual relationship with a client during the representation.
Oregon	Code of Professional Responsibility, DR 5-110 [5]	A lawyer shall not have sexual relations with a current client. This rule does not apply if the sexual relationship predates the lawyer-client relationship, or the lawyer is a member of a firm representing the client but does not work on the case, unless the sexual relationship is likely to damage or prejudice the client's representation.
West Virginia	Rule 8.4(g)	It is misconduct for a lawyer to have sexual relations with a client whom the lawyer personally represents during the legal representation unless the relationship predates the lawyer-client relationship.
Wisconsin	Supreme Court Rule 20:1.8(k)	A lawyer shall not have sexual relations with a current client unless the sexual relationship predated the lawyer-client relationship. If the client is an organization, the lawyer shall not have sexual relations with any individual who oversees the representation and gives instruction to the lawyer on behalf of the organization. The client cannot waive the conflict.

b. States Where Sexual Relations May Violate General Rules Governing Lawyer Conduct

Most state's lawyer ethical rules have been interpreted to generally prohibit a lawyer from having sex with a client during the representation.

⚠️ **You Can Consent to Sex With Your Attorney**
In most states, if the attorney advises the client of the potential adverse affects that having sex might have on the legal matter and the client consents, the sex is allowed.

The ethical rules most often used to discipline lawyers for having sex with a client are as follows:

• Rules prohibiting a lawyer from engaging in conduct adversely reflecting on the lawyer's fitness to practice law.
• Rules governing the integrity of the legal profession.
• Rules prohibiting a lawyer from representing a client when the lawyer has a conflict of interest. The theory is that the lawyer's professional judgment should not be affected by the lawyer's personal interests.
• Rules prohibiting a lawyer from engaging in conduct which could make the lawyer a witness in the case.
• Rules imposing a duty on lawyers to maintain client confidences and represent their clients with utmost loyalty.
• Rules prohibiting a lawyer from using information learned during representation to the disadvantage of the client.
• Rules providing that a lawyer shall not engage in conduct which will affect his ability to render competent representation or independent professional judgment.
• Rules providing that a lawyer shall not engage in conduct that is prejudicial to the administration of justice.

The following are some examples of how states have applied these rules to prohibit or restrict lawyers from having sex with their clients.

EXAMPLES OF RULES REGARDING LAWYERS HAVING SEXUAL RELATIONS WITH A CLIENT

State	Decision	Summary
Alaska	Bar Association Ethics Committee, Opinion 92-6 (1992)	A sexual relationship between a client and a lawyer at a firm who is not handling the client's business presents ethical concerns because the lawyer could be called as a witness and this could cause emotional harm to the client. This rule is in contrast to most states, where a sexual relationship is permitted if the lawyer is not working on the client's case.
Colorado	*People v. Good*, No. 94SA402 (Colo. Sup. Ct. 1995)	An ethical opinion determined that, because of the risks inherent in a sexual relationship between a lawyer and client, such a relationship will, at a minimum, almost always violate the rule pertaining to a lawyer's "fitness" to practice law. The opinion held that a sexual relationship between a lawyer and a client during the period of representation can be dangerous and result in injury to the client's legal matter. Noting that the lawyer-client relationship is characterized by the dependence of the client on the lawyer's professional judgment, the court held that a sexual relationship may well result from the lawyer's exploitation of the lawyer's dominant position and presents the strong possibility of a conflict between the lawyer's personal interests and the best interest of the client.
	People v. Crossman, 850 P.2d 708 (Col. 1993)	A lawyer had solicited sexual favors in exchange for legal services from three clients. The court held that the unsolicited sexual advances by the lawyer "perverts the very essence of the lawyer-client relationship." With one divorce client, he offered a reduced fee if she would come to his office wearing "a teddy that you can see through, with nothing under it..." With another divorce client, he insisted on discussing sex, offered to get her a job in which she would have to offer sexual favors to employees, inquired about her sexual habits, requested sexual contact and sexually assaulted her. He was found to have violated two rules: one barring conduct that adversely reflects on the lawyer's fitness to practice law and another barring a lawyer from taking a case in which exercising professional judgment on behalf of the client will or may be affected by the lawyer's personal interests.
	People v. Zelinger, 814 P.2d 808 (Col. 1991)	A lawyer was disciplined for having sexual relationship with a divorce client. The court identified several ethical problems: • it might destroy the chances of a reconciliation • it could cloud the attorney's exercise of independent judgment • the lawyer could be called as a witness against the client, and • if custody is contested, the attorney might become the focus of the dissolution or custody proceedings.

EXAMPLES OF RULES REGARDING LAWYERS HAVING SEXUAL RELATIONS WITH A CLIENT

State	Decision	Summary
Colorado (cont'd)	*People v. Gibbons*, 685 P.2d 168 (Col. 1984)	A lawyer was disciplined for coercing a criminal client into sex as a condition of representation.
Georgia	*Matter of Lewis*, 415 S.E.2d 173 (Ga. 1992)	To engage in sexual relations with a divorce client is considered a violation of ethical rules barring a lawyer from: • representing a client if the lawyer's professional judgment may be affected by his own personal interest, unless the attorney gives a full written disclosure or the client consents • assisting a client in conduct the lawyer knows to be illegal or fraudulent, and • knowingly engaging in illegal conduct or conduct contrary to a disciplinary rule. The court stated that "every lawyer must know that an extramarital relationship can jeopardize every aspect of a client's matrimonial case—extending to forfeiture of alimony, loss of custody and denial of attorneys' fees." The lawyer was suspended from the practice of law for three years.
	Tante v. Herring, 453 S.E.2d 686 (Ga. 1994)	A lawyer handling a client's entitlement to Social Security benefits based upon mental disability engaged in sexual relations with the client, which could have prejudiced her Social Security claim and resulted in emotional injuries. The lawyer's conduct was considered a violation of ethical rules barring a lawyer from misusing confidential information (the client's medical and psychiatric reports) learned from a client solely because of the representation for his own personal advantage. The client was also allowed to sue the lawyer for damages for breach of fiduciary duty.
Indiana	*In re Adams*, 428 N.E.2d 786 (Ind. 1981)	A lawyer was disciplined for grabbing a divorce client, kissing her and raising her blouse. The court said: "conduct of this ilk is particularly repugnant while the client is dependent upon the attorneys for guidance and assistance."
Kansas	Ethics opinion 94-13 (1/13/95)	This opinion recognizes that a sexual relationship between a lawyer and a client has several potential problems, including: • exploitation of the lawyer's fiduciary position • impairment of the lawyer's competent representation, and • a conflict of interest. The opinion further states that a lawyer who pursues a sexual relationship with a client, even a consenting one, leaves most clients in a situation that is not truly consensual. Even so, clients can waive the conflict.

EXAMPLES OF RULES REGARDING LAWYERS HAVING SEXUAL RELATIONS WITH A CLIENT

State	Decision	Summary
Kentucky	*Kentucky Bar Association v. Meredith*, 752 S.W.2d 786 (Ky. 1988)	An attorney had a sexual relationship with a client in a probate matter. After the lawyer was fired, he tried to have the client disqualified as the guardian, using confidential information he learned during the representation. The court ruled that the attorney's sexual relationship violated ethical rules barring a lawyer from: • engaging in conduct that adversely affects his fitness to practice law • accepting employment, except with the consent of his client and after full disclosure, if his professional judgment will be or reasonably may be affected by his own personal interests, and • using confidential information learned during the representation against the client.
Maryland	*Attorneys Grievance Commission v. Goldsborough*, 624 A.2d 502 (Md. 1993)	An attorney who had a propensity for spanking his clients and secretary was held to have violated rules pertaining to the fitness to practice law and to have engaged in conduct that was prejudicial to the administration of justice.
Missouri	*In re Frick*, 694 S.W.2d 473 (Mo. 1985)	A lawyer was disciplined for sexual harassment when he had sexual relations with a divorce client and then engaged in a demeaning letter-writing campaign.
	In re Littleton, 719 S.W.2d 772 (Mo. 1986)	A lawyer was suspended for making sexual advances towards a female client and retaining as a legal fee the money he had accepted to pay her bond.
New Hampshire	*Drucker's Case*, 577 A.2d 1198 (N.H. 1990)	A lawyer was suspended for having sexual relations with a divorce client while handling her divorce. The client was emotionally fragile and seeing a psychiatrist at the time of the divorce. The court ruled that the attorney's conduct: • was a conflict of interest—because his representation was materially limited by his own sexual interest in her and because he used information about her fragile emotional state to her disadvantage by engaging in sexual relations with her, and • impaired his client's ability to make adequately considered decisions in connection with representation because the lawyer did not maintain a normal client-lawyer relationship with her.
	Bourdon's Case, 565 A.2d 1052 (N.H. 1989)	A lawyer was disciplined for engaging in sexual relations with a client. The court emphasized that the lawyer's failure to warn her of the potential effect on her case and obtain her consent was a conflict of interest.
New Jersey	*Matter of Liebowitz*, 516 A.2d 246 (N.J. 1985)	A lawyer was disciplined for sexually assaulting a pro bono client while handling a custody matter. The court noted the lawyer's opportunistic conduct and said that he "brought the pro bono matrimonial counsel program into disrepute." The lawyer's conduct was deemed "prejudicial to the administration of justice."

EXAMPLES OF RULES REGARDING LAWYERS HAVING SEXUAL RELATIONS WITH A CLIENT

State	Decision	Summary
New York	*In re Gilbert*, 606 N.Y.S.2d 478 (N.Y. 1995)	A lawyer was disciplined for making unsolicited sexual advances to a non-divorce client. Such conduct violates rules governing the integrity of the legal profession.
Ohio	*Disciplinary Counsel v. DePietro*, No 92-56, (Ohio Sup. Ct., 12/30/94)	To engage in sexual relations with a client during representation is a violation of two ethical rules: • engaging in conduct adversely reflecting on a lawyer's fitness to practice law, and • a lawyer's professional judgment reasonably affected by personal and financial interests.
Oklahoma	Oklahoma Bar Association Legal Ethics Committee, Opinion 308 (12/9/94)	A lawyer may not engage in a sexual relationship with a client, or the client's representative (in the case of a business, corporation or Opinion 308 (12/9/94) other legal entity), during the time of an ongoing attorney-client relationship unless the lawyer and client are married. To engage in a sexual relationship would violate rules: • requiring a lawyer to provide competent representation • requiring a lawyer to exercise independent professional judgment • requiring a lawyer to avoid conduct that may materially limit the lawyer's representation because of the lawyer's own interests, unless the lawyer reasonably believes that the representation will not be adversely affected and the client consents, and • prohibiting a lawyer from using information relating to the representation to the client's disadvantage unless the client consents.
South Carolina	*Matter of McDow*, 354 S.E.2d 383 (S.C. 1987)	A lawyer was disciplined for having a sexual relationship with a divorce client when the divorce was granted on the grounds of adultery. The court charged the lawyer with: • damaging or prejudicing the client during representation • engaging in conduct which created the appearance of impropriety, and • engaging in conduct prejudicial to the administration of justice.
South Dakota	*Matter of Discipline of Bergren*, 455 N.W.2d 856 (S.D. 1990)	A lawyer was disciplined for engaging in sexual relations with a client who was under the age of 18 in exchange for a reduction in fees. The court held that his conduct violated ethical rules prohibiting behavior that is prejudicial to the administration of justice and conduct and that adversely reflects on the fitness to practice law.

6. My Lawyer Made a Mistake and Wants to Settle With Me

When a client brings a serious problem to the attention of a lawyer, the lawyer should not advise the client to sign away or waive his right to report it to the lawyer discipline agency or to sue for malpractice. Lawyers are ethically barred from entering into an agreement which bars a client from reporting the lawyer to the discipline agency. In addition, it is unethical for a lawyer to advise a client to give up malpractice claims against the lawyer—whether or not the lawyer makes payment to the client—unless he advises the client to get an opinion from a second attorney (independent counsel) first.

EXAMPLE 1: Ken and Ming are in a fee dispute because Ming has not paid several large bills Ken has sent her. Ken does not want to litigate the case because he is afraid Ming will discover malpractice he committed. Ken offers to cut his fee if Ming will agree to sign a release discharging Ken from any civil liability for malpractice. This is unethical.

EXAMPLE 2: Marie hired Juanita to sue the insured driver of a car who was speeding through a red light when he hit Marie as she walked through an intersection. Juanita simply forgets to file the lawsuit on time, and knows that this is a malpractice case Marie could easily win. Juanita admits to Marie that she forgot to file the case and even offers to pay Marie some money. Juanita, who is afraid of being sued for malpractice, is also afraid of depleting her cash reserves if she offers to pay a lot to Marie. So Juanita digs herself into a large unethical hole: she offers $10,000 to Marie (whose medical bills alone are $20,000), saying (incorrectly) that the case had several of problems, and makes the offer contingent on Marie agreeing not to sue Juanita for malpractice.

Even if the attorney-client relationship ended in a dispute, the lawyer has a minimal duty to disclose the fact that there is a conflict and that the client has a right to get a second lawyer's opinion before giving up the right to sue for malpractice.

Less common, although not unknown, are written fee agreements which contain a clause that absolves the attorney in advance of any responsibility should she ever commit malpractice. If you ever see one of these, run. If you already have one, you will probably succeed in challenging it in court if you later sue for malpractice.

7. My Lawyer Is Writing a Screenplay About My Case

Only a very small percentage of legal cases ever make headlines. Nonetheless, if yours is one of them, your lawyer has a conflict if while he represents you, he also negotiates a lucrative media deal. How can he serve your interests faithfully when he hopes someday to earn a percentage of the box office gross or he needs to pump you for details which will draw fantastic ratings on a movie-of-the-week? Not only is he distracted, but he has also created a personal interest in making your story as marketable as possible. In today's world, that means lots of details, particularly about sex and violence.

Every state except California and Virginia has specific rules barring a lawyer from contracting for media rights to a client's story while still representing the client. Even so, California and Virginia disciplinary courts are likely to find a conflict under general conflicts rules.

Not only is negotiating media rights prejudicial to the client, but it also has been used as a basis on an appeal in some spectacular criminal cases. Juan Corona, accused of killing 25 farm workers in California, had a fee agreement which gave his defense attorney all media rights to the story. Needless to say, the lawyer appeared distracted by this gold mine during the time when Corona's case needed his full attention. The attorney even had a writer, with whom he later coauthored a book about the case, sit with him at counsel table during the trial. Whose side was this guy on? That's what Corona asked the California Court of Appeals, which replied:

> [I]t is indisputable that by entering into the literary rights contract trial counsel created a situation which prevented him from devoting the requisite undivided loyalty and service to his client. From that moment on, trial counsel was devoted to two masters with conflicting interests; he was forced to choose between his own pocketbook and the best interests of his client. People v. Juan Corona, *80 Cal. App. 3d 684, 720 (1978).*

After the trial, and presumably after you won, there would be no problem with having a new fee agreement covering representation regarding the rights to the story. At least, not in and of itself. But suppose the lawyer proposes to represent both herself and you in a deal where you will jointly tell your stories, and she shares the royalties with you? That would be a serious conflict of interest. Even so, if the conflict were disclosed and waived, you might agree to it.

8. My Lawyer Wants to Borrow Money

Now and then, a lawyer will ask a client for a loan. This most often happens when a personal injury case is settled for a hefty amount and the lawyer will be holding the money in a client trust account.

Unless you were advised by your lawyer to get an opinion from a second attorney (independent counsel), borrowing money in this context would most likely violate many rules of conduct. The lawyer is taking advantage of his knowledge that you are about to receive the money. And the lawyer is breaching her fiduciary duty to put your interest first because by definition, the lawyer's interest becomes adverse to yours when negotiating the terms (interest rate, security, schedule for repayment) of the loan.

9. My Lawyer Wants to Lend Me Money

What could be wrong with your lawyer lending you money? Plenty. You and your attorney establish a creditor-debtor relationship in addi-

tion to your attorney-client one, which raises many potential conflicts:

- The attorney might use undue influence to obtain your agreement to unfair terms.
- The attorney might later use confidential information obtained during the attorney-client relationship to sue you or to collect the debt.
- The lawyer might make decisions or advise you to make decisions about your case based on his interest in getting repaid (that you settle quickly, for example), rather than your best interest in the case (that you hold out for a bigger settlement, for instance).

This situation typically shows up in contingency fee cases where the lawyer advances the costs and expects to be repaid from the proceeds of the case. (See Chapter 3, Section H.) Traditionally, lawyers were supposed to limit their financial interest in the outcome of a case to their fees. They were not supposed to blur the roles between being an advocate and being an "investor" in a case because an investor-lawyer might become more interested in being repaid than in fighting for the client's cause.

To balance the needs of the client who can't afford to pay costs against the concerns of the lawyer who should not "invest" in a case, most states now allow attorneys to advance costs but require clients to repay them, regardless of the outcome of the case. But some states let lawyers make the repayment of costs contingent on the outcome of the case: no recovery, no repayment. A few states bar lawyers only from paying the client's medical bills or living expenses during a case. Here are some state rules.

STATE RULES REGARDING ADVANCING COSTS

State	Rule
Alabama	The client is legally responsible for repayment whether the case is won or lost. The lawyer can help out in a financial emergency.
Arizona	The client is legally responsible for repayment whether the case is won or lost.
California	A lawyer can lend money to a client if the client makes a written promise to repay. In contingency fee cases, the lawyer may make the client's obligation to repay costs contingent on the outcome.
Colorado	A lawyer can advance particular expenses, such as investigating and obtaining evidence in the case. The client does not have to repay if it would be a financial hardship.
District of Columbia	There is a huge exception to the prohibition: costs may be advanced if they are "reasonably necessary."
Florida	A lawyer cannot advance money for living expenses.
Louisiana	The court allowed a lawyer to advance a client money to pay medical and living expenses. But the court disciplined the attorney for lending another client money where it appeared that the loans were not necessary to continue with the case, but were a marketing device to attract the client.
Maryland	A lawyer can advance costs, but a lawyer cannot pay a client's personal expenses.
Michigan	The client is legally responsible for repayment whether the case is won or lost.
Minnesota	A lawyer can advance particular expenses, such as investigating and obtaining evidence in the case. The client does not have to repay if it would be a financial hardship.
Montana	A lawyer can advance living expenses in cases of financial hardship.
Oklahoma	A lawyer cannot advance costs.
Oregon	The client is legally responsible for repayment whether the case is won or lost. There is an exception if it would be a hardship for the client to pay.
South Dakota	The client is legally responsible for repayment whether the case is won or lost.
Texas	A lawyer can pay the client's expenses, including living and medical expenses. In contingency fee cases, the lawyer may make the client's obligation to repay costs contingent on the outcome.
Virginia	The client is legally responsible for repayment whether the case is won or lost.
Washington	The client is legally responsible for repayment whether the case is won or lost.

WHAT IS INDEPENDENT COUNSEL AND HOW DO I GET IT?

In so many instances where a conflict exists, an attorney is obligated to advise you to get a legal opinion from a second lawyer (called independent counsel). Smart lawyers and ethical lawyers (sometimes they are the same and sometimes not) give that advice in writing. Most states require only the advice, not the writing.

If you have the money to get a second opinion, do it—when your lawyer advises you or you otherwise smell a rat. You can also contact you local bar association. While they won't give you specific legal advice, some will at least steer you toward a case, rule or statute that contains clues about the legality and ethics of what your lawyer is doing or proposing to do.

If you want to learn more about legal ethics and what conduct might constitute a violation, one good place to start is with the published ethics opinions for your state, usually available at a local law library. Also, the opinions of the American Bar Association, although not binding on lawyers, do have great authority and provide an excellent source of information. The ABA's rules and opinions cannot be enforced—no court is required to recognize or follow them. No state bar association can require its members to abide by them. They are, however, persuasive authority. In most states, they form the basis for the applicable rules and laws. Many are adopted word for word; others are slightly altered.

Finally, you can consult the *ABA/BNA Lawyers' Manual on Professional Conduct.* This multi-volume reference work provides a compendium of legal opinions, cases on legal ethics and the text of the ABA's model ethical rules. It is updated twice monthly and provides specific references to local rules. All these materials can be found at a local law library.

10. My Lawyer Wants to Lend Me Money—With Security

Sometimes, a lawyer will ask a client to give back security in exchange for a loan, or as a guarantee that the fees will be paid. Usually, this means giving your lawyer a lien on your house or other real estate. In most circumstances, this is improper. The conflict between the lawyer's financial interests and yours is clear. At a minimum, before engaging in this type of transaction, the lawyer should advise you to get an independent legal opinion. And while you are at it, my advice is that you look for a new lawyer who won't demand a security interest in your home.

B. Triangles and Other Angles: Conflicts Involving Other People

Section A, above, gave examples of conflicts involving a lawyer and client. This section includes possible conflicts between a lawyer and other people or groups.

1. My Lawyer Used to Play Tennis With the Opposing Lawyer

If your lawyer and the opposing lawyer had a fairly close social relationship in the past, your lawyer should tell you. She doesn't have to unless she thinks it would interfere with her duty of loyalty to you, but she should want to just to prevent a potentially embarrassing situation later on. The lawyer is ethically bound to consider if his past relationship will result in a conflict of loyalties or even an appearance of

impropriety. If your lawyer and the other lawyer practice in a town with 150 attorneys who all know each other, that in and of itself isn't a close relationship. If the two lawyers and their spouses had an occasional dinner, that is.

Usually, when a lawyer discloses the social relationship to the client and reassures the client that he will not be swayed in his loyalty to the client's cause, the client will waive the potential conflict in writing. Lawyers get into unnecessary trouble when they don't discuss the relationship with their clients in advance. Clients get very angry when they see their lawyers getting chummy with the attorney for the other side, especially if the case isn't going well. It's not uncommon for a disgruntled client to call my office and offer as "proof" that his lawyer was bought off the fact that the client just learned that his lawyer and the opposing lawyer:

- went to the same law school
- were in the same law school class
- used to work for the same firm
- started working together at the conclusion of the case, or
- socialized together before, during or after the case.

2. My Lawyer Still Plays Tennis With the Opposing Lawyer

The closer and more frequent the contacts are between your lawyer and the opposing lawyer, the more likely there are to be conflicts or appearances of conflicts. Full disclosure and reassurance to you will sometimes cure the problems associated with appearances of

AN APPEARANCE OF CONFLICT

An "appearance of conflict" means the behavior is technically within the rules of professional conduct and the law, but would lead a client or the general public to believe that the lawyer is selling out the client, talking out of both sides of her mouth and putting her interests ahead of her client's. It's the sort of behavior that keeps lawyer jokes in high demand. It also makes clients think they've been cheated. I get calls about these situations frequently, and can't do much more than refer the client to the State Bar. Here are some examples of the complaints I get:

- My ex-husband is an attorney. My lawyer dragged his feet during the divorce and didn't stand up for me. He was more friendly to my ex-husband and his attorney than he was with me. After the divorce he went to work for my ex-husband's firm. I think I was sold out.
- My lawyer told me I had a great personal injury case then, just before trial, he told me to accept a small settlement offer. I think he was working for the other side.
- At the time of my hearing, my lawyer agreed to a last-minute request for a postponement by the other side. He told me it was "professional courtesy," but it's delaying my case and costing me money.

Lawyers are expected to not merely act ethically, they are also expected to avoid appearing unethical. This ideal of professional virtue is included in the ABA's Model Rules.[6] The idea behind it is to maintain public confidence in the law, the courts and the administration of justice.[7] While I agree it is a worthy goal, I suspect it has a lot to do with the fact that it's just plain damaging to the legal business if we don't at least keep up appearances.

The possibilities of what could create an appearance of impropriety are endless. Here's a list of situations, none of which are actual conflicts of interest, but which any client would want disclosed in advance:

- The lawyers have offices in the same building.
- The lawyers live in the same condominium complex.
- The lawyers used to work with each other.
- The lawyers belong to the same golf club.
- The lawyers are on the same softball team.
- The lawyers attend the same church.
- My lawyer used to work for the other lawyer.
- The other lawyer handled a personal case for my lawyer.
- The two lawyers have sued each other.
- The two lawyers have a personal hatred of each other.
- The lawyers used to date each other.
- The lawyers were classmates in law school.
- The other lawyer was my lawyer's professor in law school.
- The lawyers serve on a Bar Association committee together.
- The lawyers are longtime political allies or enemies.

impropriety, and disclosure will at least protect you from surprises. Ultimately, you have to decide whether or not you want to continue with the lawyer. If you find out about a close relationship after the fact, however, you might have grounds to file a complaint against your lawyer with the discipline agency and possibly to sue your lawyer for malpractice if he failed to remain loyal to you because of the relationship.

3. My Lawyer Is Related to (or Having Relations With) Opposing Counsel

There's a great old lawyer movie called *Adam's Rib*. Spencer Tracy and Katherine Hepburn play lawyers, married to each other, who oppose each other in a murder case. My paperback movie guide gives it four stars, but it would get a thumbs down ethics rating from any attorney regulatory group. I know the plot sounds a bit farfetched, but the movie was ahead of its time. With the number of women in the legal profession today, it is not unusual for spouses to encounter each other professionally.

Of course, spouses aren't the only intimates who might act as opposing counsel in a case. In a more recent movie, *Class Action*, Gene Hackman and Mary Elizabeth Mastrantonio play father-and-daughter opposing lawyers in a lawsuit brought by Hackman against a negligent automobile manufacturer, represented by Mastrantonio. Again, thumbs down for ethics.

Whether it's spouses, domestic partners, siblings or a parent and child, it

shouldn't be done. Even if your lawyer discloses the problem in a 24-point boldface writing and you waive the problem in writing, it is still not okay. The problem is not just the conflict of interests, but also the appearance of impropriety. How would you feel if:

- you lost an important case and then found out that the opposing attorney was your lawyer's older, domineering brother
- the expensive bickering in your case seemed motivated by the fact that the attorneys were divorcing each other, or
- you suspect that the two attorneys arranged a "sweetheart deal" to advance their own romantic relationship?

YOUR COURT OR MINE?

4. My Lawyer Is Being Paid by an Insurance Company

Your insurance company must provide you with a defense if you are sued for a claim covered by your liability policy. But there is an old proverb that says that the person who pays the piper calls the tune. If your insurance company pays for the lawyer, won't she be taking orders from the company? Yes. Is this a conflict of interest? Not necessarily, but it can become one.

You are the client. The attorney's duty of loyalty is supposed to be to you. The fact that an insurance company has hired the lawyer is often not a problem because you and your insurer have a common interest in defending the claim. But what happens when the interests conflict?

> **EXAMPLE:** Dale is driving one night and hits the car in front of him. The occupants of the other car claim injuries and sue Dale for damages. Dale's insurance company hires a defense attorney. The attorney's job is to defend Dale in the lawsuit and, if necessary, settle the claim for as little as possible. While talking to the client, the attorney learns that Dale was working part time that night delivering pizza. No one, including the insurance company, knows this or even thinks it's an issue. But the insurance policy excludes payment of claims if the vehicle is used for business. That would probably apply to Dale's pizza delivery and it could mean he has no insurance coverage. Because the attorney works for Dale and, even though he is being paid by the insurance company, his duty of loyalty is to Dale, he should not report the potential problem to the company. (See the ABA Committee on Ethics & Professional Responsibility, Informal Opinion 1476 (1981)).

Even if an insurance company knows from the beginning that there is a potential conflict, it should still hire and pay for the attorney. But the company will take a wait-and-see attitude and will withdraw if it finds a reason to deny coverage. If you are in this situation, immediately get your own attorney appointed to take over the case if the insurance company withdraws.

5. My Insurance Company Is Paying Lawyers on Both Sides of My Case

It is not unusual that your insurance company hires both your lawyer and the lawyer for the other side. This happens more often than you would think—typically when the two people involved in an automobile accident have the same insurance company—and there is nothing wrong with it. The following example can clarify the situation:

> **EXAMPLE:** Mae and Mort are both insured with Big Hands Insurance Company. They get into an accident, are both injured, claim the other side is at fault and hire lawyers to sue each other. Big Hands Insurance Company will hire and pay *separate* lawyers to defend each.

The insurance company has an obligation to provide legal representation to its customers.

Neither it nor the lawyers it hires are doing anything wrong.

6. My Former Lawyer Is Representing My Spouse in Our Divorce

It's fairly common in a divorce that one spouse tries to hire a lawyer who knows the couple and may have even represented the other spouse in the past. In this situation, an ethical conflict arises only if the attorney has access to confidential information which could be used against the other spouse in the divorce.

> **EXAMPLE:** While still unmarried, Jeremy retains Sylvia to advise him on his complex real estate holdings and business interests. Over the years, Sylvia becomes intimately familiar with Jeremy's business practices and assets. Jeremy gets married. Several years later, his wife files for divorce and wants to hire Sylvia to represent her with the idea that she will have access to all the inside information about Jeremy's complex finances. Sylvia should not represent the wife in the divorce. In fact, if Sylvia is familiar with the confidential details of the couple's joint financial affairs, she should not represent either spouse. If Sylvia had represented Jeremy before his marriage in a noise dispute with his neighbor, however, she would probably have no problem representing Jeremy's wife in the divorce, assuming she didn't learn confidential information about Jeremy in that earlier case, which could affect the divorce.

While it might seem that the wife was being clever, she was actually making herself vulnerable to having her lawyer disqualified by a judge. This would be like having your horse shot out from under you in the middle of the race. Not only would it delay the case, but also you would have to pay a second lawyer to go over some of the same ground that your previous lawyer already covered. Of course, if the lawyer failed to advise you of the conflict, you could sue the lawyer for a refund.

> **EXAMPLE:** Juan represented a couple, jointly, in a simple divorce in a state where this is permitted. Later on, a dispute arose between the former spouses over child custody and support. Hoping to save money, the mother hired Juan to represent her interests in the dispute. Juan would be disqualified by the court if the father objected because Juan had access to confidential information from both parents during the divorce proceedings and still has a fiduciary duty to both of them.

Tanya's Tip:
Don't Try to Be Slick With Conflicts

You might think, "That's a great idea. I'll hire an attorney who has inside knowledge about my opponent to gain an advantage." Don't do it. Remember, you can only waive conflicts as to your interests, not those of your adversary. And you might risk more than losing your lawyer in the middle of the case. Depending on the circumstances and local law, you could face sanctions from the court for your tactics, and even an additional lawsuit from your adversary for invasion of privacy and interference with business relations.

7. My Lawyer Used to Work for My Adversary

This is the kind of case where the lines are very finely drawn between what is and isn't unethical. Start by understanding that past representation of the other side is not necessarily a conflict. This makes more sense when you consider that your opponent might be someone other than an individual person, such as a corporation or a government entity. Businesses and government entities have a myriad of legal needs and past representation does not necessarily mean that it bears any relation to the current case.

The basic rule is that after a lawyer has represented a person or business in some case, she should not later represent a different party in the same case or the same sort of case where the new client has interests which conflict with the old client. Contrast these two situations.

EXAMPLE 1: Marta worked for Bus Company several years ago drafting a lease for a parking lot. Now Marta represents you and you are suing that same Bus Company because a runaway bus crashed into your house. It is unlikely that a court would disqualify Marta even if Bus Company complained. The work Marta did for Bus Company did not expose her to any confidential information which would affect the outcome of your case. There is no true conflict of interests here.

EXAMPLE 2: This time, assume Marta had represented the Bus Company in a labor dispute with its drivers. The drivers had complained about safety issues, particularly unreliable brakes, during a strike. Because Marta did do work for your adversary which exposed her to confidential information about its safety practices and records, she would have a conflict of interests and could be disqualified in your case.

As you can see, the key to determining whether an ethical problem exists is whether it is possible that the lawyer has confidential information which can be used against the first client in the service of the new client. In reality, this is not always clear. Courts have developed various tests about how "substantial" the relationship of the new case must be to the previous work and how "material" the effect must be on the old client.

Here are some guidelines:

- If your lawyer is representing you in litigation and the other side disqualifies him because he used to work for them, you may have a lawsuit and an ethics complaint against the attorney for not disclosing the problem to you and the other side, and getting permission from both sides to act as your lawyer.
- If you discover that your lawyer used to represent the other side in a situation where his access to confidential information may cause a conflict of interest, you should explore the possibility that your lawyer does have an actual or potential conflict and ask him to get waivers from the other side, or resign and refund your fees.

8. My Lawyer Represents Me and Others in the Same Lawsuit, But We're on the Same Side

It's not unusual for two or more people injured in the same accident to hire one attorney to represent them both (or all). This seems okay, doesn't it? After all, you are on the same side. But are you sure of that? If it turns out you're not on the same side, whom would the lawyer advise? There are often more than two sides to an argument. Consider these examples:

EXAMPLE 1: Portia and Antonio are injured while riding a bus which skids on ice and turns over. Small, O'Hara and Johnson law firm represents both of them as well as 15 other passengers on the bus. There is no conflict here. Even though there are many plaintiffs, there are only two sides.

EXAMPLE 2: Portia takes Antonio for a ride in her car. Portia's car collides with a bus. Portia and Antonio hire Small, O'Hara and Johnson law firm to represent them in their lawsuit against the bus company and bus driver. This is a potential problem. Facts may be uncovered which indicate that Portia was partially at fault. The attorneys could not continue to represent either party because they have confidential information from both. Portia and Antonio would have to start over with new attorneys.

EXAMPLE 3: The same facts as Example 2, but the attorneys represent Antonio and one of the bus passengers. While this might seem like the lawyers are on both sides of the same case, they aren't. The case is not bus versus car, but passengers versus

drivers. There is a potential problem, explored in Example 4.

EXAMPLE 4: Now, Small, O'Hara and Johnson law firm represents 15 plaintiffs: Antonio and 14 bus passengers. The bus company has a million-dollar insurance policy, but Portia's policy is for no more than $15,000 per person, not to exceed a total of $30,000 per accident. If Portia is at fault, and the injuries are serious, she will not have enough insurance to pay all the claims. Small, O'Hara and Johnson have a conflict as to how the $30,000 insurance policy will be divided among 15 clients claiming the money.

In Example 4, the conflict might be cured by putting the $30,000 into an escrow account and advising the 15 clients to get independent counsel to represent them in the dispute with their fellow victims. But this conflict should have been foreseen by the attorneys and disclosed to the clients.

All states require an attorney to obtain clients' consents before representing them in the same litigation. California, Washington and Wisconsin require that consent to be in writing.

9. My Business Lawyer Is Representing My Business Partner in a Personal Matter

For the sake of simplicity, I generally use examples in which the lawyer is a sole practitioner. But conflicts of interests often involve the handling of multiple matters and representation of multiple clients by large firms. Let's check in with Small, O'Hara and Johnson and their business client, the software development company of Safe Net.

EXAMPLE: Small is a business attorney and has advised the partnership about leases, labor matters, the partnership agreement and taxes for several years. O'Hara is experienced in family law and he has represented two of Safe Net's owners in their divorces. Johnson is involved in civil litigation and is representing a third Safe Net owner is a personal injury case. None of this constitutes a conflicts problem because there are no adverse interests. But what if one owner has a dispute with another? If it's a private dispute, say over the boundary line of adjacent property, the firm could represent one or the other, but probably wouldn't because it would interfere with the business arrangements. If the dispute was between two owners over sharing business profits, there would be a conflict and the firm should not represent either. If the dispute were between one owner and the business over the terms of the agreement, the firm could represent the business to which it has a duty of loyalty regarding business affairs, but not the individual owner. It should not represent the business, however, if it has confidential information from the individual owner which should not be disclosed.

10. My Lawyer's Former Co-Worker Now Works for the Opposing Law Firm

Lawyers, especially those recently out of law school, change jobs a lot. It's not unusual to start at one office in town, move to a second and even possibly a third in a five- or ten- year period. And if the lawyer has developed an area of expertise, the lawyer may move among offices that do similar types of work. So what happens if the associate who used to work for your lawyer now works for the opposing law office? These cases are so intricately related to their facts that they are best discussed by way of example. Let's go back to Small, O'Hara and Johnson.

> **EXAMPLE:** Small has been representing you in your case against Broadway Lights. Broadway Lights is represented by Miles and Miles. One day, you are sitting in the waiting room at your lawyer's office, pick up a legal newspaper and see an announcement:
>
> "Miles and Miles is pleased to announce that L. L. O'Hara, Esq., formerly of Small, O'Hara and Johnson, has joined the firm."
>
> You have every right to feel uncomfortable. Miles and Miles should agree to screen Mr. O'Hara from any involvement with your case, and Mr. O'Hara should agree not to disclose any confidential information he learned while at his former firm. This arrangement is as good as the ethics of the parties involved.

I have actually faced this problem myself. When my partners and I moved our office to another county, one of our secretaries could not make the move with us. She found another job, but with a law firm that mostly handles legal malpractice defense cases and opposed us in several cases on which she had been working. We worked out the confidentiality arrangement so she did no work on any of the cases against our office and no confidential information was disclosed.

11. My Lawyer Negotiated My Office Lease; He Is Also the Business Attorney for the Landlord

Representing both parties in a business transaction violates a number of the rules of conduct, the most important of which is to provide the client with the attorney's undivided loyalty. What is in the best interest of one client is likely to be contrary to the best interest of the other. It is easy to see why this conduct is prohibited. If you trust an attorney to negotiate a lease for you, you want the attorney to exercise his independent judgment on your behalf as required by the rules of conduct. The attorney cannot do that if he is also required to exercise independent judgment on behalf of your adversary.

Even when a proposed deal might objectively be fair to both, an attorney cannot ethically represent both with undivided loyalty, because she surely would be privy to confidential information from both sides. And even in the rare instance when this wouldn't occur, this conduct nevertheless violates of the "appearance of impropriety" rule.

A lawyer also violates the rule that an attorney shall not accept representation adverse to the interests of a client. Dual representation is a serious ethical violation.

12. My Lawyer Used to Represent the Person or Business I Am Suing

Let's assume your attorney used to represent a physician you are suing for malpractice. If the prior representation of the doctor was in a malpractice case, because your lawyer probably learned confidential information—like how the office runs and how certain procedures are conducted—this would almost certainly be a conflict of interest. It would be impossible for the lawyer not to—even unwittingly—use that confidential information against the doctor. The doctor could probably force your attorney off of your case.

If, however, your lawyer's prior representation of the doctor was to review a real estate offer five years ago and you are suing the doctor for malpractice, then there should be no problem. Your attorney should have discussed the prior relationship with you. Failure to disclose this kind of situation is covered by the discussion of the appearances of impropriety in Section B.2, above.

13. My Lawyer Used to Represent the Other Side's Expert Witness

This situation is based on an actual case considered by the ABA Committee on Ethics & Professional Responsibility (Formal Opinion 92-367 (1992)). The attorney in question was representing the plaintiff in a medical malpractice case. The defendant secured an expert witness just before the trial, who happened to be a former client of the plaintiff's attorney. The plaintiff's attorney had defended the expert in a medical malpractice case several years before.

The plaintiff's lawyer was in an ethical bind. His responsibility to his client required him to use all legal and ethical means to discredit the expert. But he also had a duty of loyalty and confidentiality to his former client and could not use information he obtained during the previous case to discredit his former client. And he had no right to force the defendant to find another expert. The lawyer had two choices: get a waiver from the doctor or withdraw from the new case. My advice to the lawyer would have been to immediately inform the client of the situation and ask the expert witness for a waiver. If the witness refused, the lawyer probably should not proceed, even if he has the new client's consent.

14. My Spouse and I Are Using the Same Lawyer for Our Divorce

The public has awakened to the wasteful expenditures involved in divorce. In response, many people do their own, others use lower-cost legal clinics and some employ one attorney to file their divorce papers. By using one lawyer, the spouses get the advantage of legal counsel without dragging out contested litigation. They also pay less than they would pay for having two separate lawyers.

But this arrangement could result in a conflict of interests, particularly where the lawyer was retained first by one spouse. The ethics committees of many states, including

Connecticut, District of Columbia, Kentucky, Maryland, New Hampshire, New Jersey, South Carolina, Virginia and Wisconsin, have been very critical of the practice. Lawyers are likely to be disciplined unless they make the terms of the joint representation clear, obtain the clients' consent and act fairly.

I had a case which was an egregious example of this. The husband and wife together sought legal advice about an impending divorce from an attorney. He assisted them in putting together a settlement which, as was later discovered, cheated the husband out of thousands of dollars. The papers stated that the wife was the attorney's only client and that the husband had an opportunity to consult his own attorney. According to the husband, that provision was explained away as a technicality because court forms require the attorney to fill in the forms as representing only one party. The attorney paid a settlement to the husband and faced disciplinary charges.

California and New York are more liberal. Before agreeing to such an arrangement, read over the fee agreement carefully and have your final papers reviewed by independent counsel before you sign them. Better yet, suggest to your spouse that you choose a neutral mediator to save money and avoid conflicts.

 Tanya's Tip: If You Are Worried About a Possible Conflict of Interest
Before you hire a second lawyer to analyze whether or not a conflict exists and do extensive research, use the resources you have at hand. Tell your lawyer in writing that you are concerned about a conflict of interest and explain why. Ask your lawyer to consider the issue and give you a written opinion about it. I would add, if you are paying by the hour, that you do not expect to be billed for this time.

Your problem might be quickly resolved if the lawyer finds a conflict and offers to refund what you have paid. If you get a response that there is not conflict, however, you probably should get another opinion.

C. Should You Waive a Conflict of Interest?

If you are considering hiring an attorney and she tells you about a potential conflict—or recognizes one when you ask—she should either refuse to represent you or ask you to "waive" the conflict in writing.

If the lawyer believes the conflict isn't serious and suggests that you waive it, what should you do? There is no right answer. You must weigh the degree of the conflict. If you conclude that there is only a small possibility that a conflict exists, then you may wish to sign the waiver. But if you conclude there is a real likelihood that a potential problem is looming, it's obviously best to find a different lawyer. Here are some things to consider in making this decision:

- If the conflict involves your adversary and she raises it later on, you could lose your attorney in the middle of the case through a motion for disqualification. This could result in a large expense and even the loss of the case.

- If you waive the conflict, you may have absolved your attorney from liability for the conflict and from facing disciplinary action.
- Timing is important. Your decision may be different depending on whether the conflict is discovered on the eve of your trial (difficult to get a new lawyer) or early on in the process (almost always better off with another lawyer). Will delay (in finding a new lawyer) work to your advantage or against you?
- Cost is a major factor. Is the cost of getting a new lawyer justified by the risk that the conflict will cause you damages?

 Tanya's Tip: Lawyers, Like Fish, Are Easy to Catch

America has about one million lawyers. If one, or even a few of them, has a conflict by representing you, you are usually best off by tossing the lawyer back. After all, there are a lot more fish in the sea.

D. If Your Lawyer Discovers a Conflict

The rules are simple. If your attorney has a conflict of interest, she can't represent you unless she discloses the conflict to you and you agree in writing that it's not a problem. If a lawyer discloses a conflict before beginning to represent you, the lawyer hasn't violated any rules unless she pressured you into hiring her. This rarely happens, however. Instead, one of the following will probably occur:

- the lawyer will refuse to take the case because of the conflict

- you will refuse to hire the lawyer because of the conflict, or
- you will sign a written waiver stating the conflict isn't a problem.

What happens if you discover the conflict after you have hired the lawyer? Let me repeat: The lawyer must withdraw as your attorney unless you waive the conflict in writing. That's a nice rule, but hiring a new lawyer may be difficult and expensive for you. What if trial is only a month away or you have paid your lawyer a ton of money?

If your lawyer has a conflict of interest and you have to hire a new attorney, who must pay for the time and effort it will take the new lawyer to come up to speed on your case? If the lawyer tells you of the conflict as soon as he becomes aware of it, then, unfortunately, you're probably going to have to pay the bill.

If, however, your lawyer does not disclose the conflict or potential conflict as soon as he realizes it, you should ask that he pay for the time your new attorney spends familiarizing herself with your case.

Similarly, if the opposing side in your case successfully files a motion to have your attorney disqualified from representing you because of a conflict your lawyer knew about but never discussed with you, you probably have a good claim against your attorney for a fee refund and an excellent defense to any claim for fees due.

 Tanya's Tip: Don't Pay If Your Lawyer Didn't Tell You of a Conflict

If your lawyer discloses a (potential) conflict you believe you should have been told about earlier—and the lawyer claims you owe her fees—don't

pay until the issue is resolved. You will have an easier time raising the failure to disclose the potential conflict in a timely manner as a defense to her lawsuit for her fee, rather than using it as a basis for a refund case against her. Why? Because in this kind of lawsuit, whoever brings the case has the burden of proving it.

1. Your Lawyer Has a Conflict Between You and Another Client

There are several steps you can take if you think your lawyer has a conflict in serving your interests and the interests of another client.

Confront the lawyer. If you suspect your lawyer has a conflict of interest, confront her. Ask her to investigate the applicable regulations and to give you a written opinion. You should not be charged for this—after all the lawyer is working to keep her job. If there is a conflict, you might want to waive it by giving the attorney permission to proceed with the case. It all depends on how much you value the work of this particular lawyer and how great the risk is.

If the lawyer tells you there is no conflict, and you are not reassured, get a second opinion. Your first lawyer's written opinion will be a valuable piece of evidence in any lawsuit or disciplinary proceeding you later initiate.

Investigate the rules. Check at your law library and with your state bar for the applicable rules of professional conduct and published opinions. (See Chapter 11, Section A.2.) Also review the model rules and decisions of similar cases in other states so that you have support when you complain to the lawyer or to the discipline agency.

Report the lawyer. Depending on the problem, you might report the lawyer to the disciplinary agency. Learning that your lawyer hired his son-in-law as the expert accountant on your case without disclosing the relationship is a conflict and should be reported. Learning that a new associate in your lawyer's office used to work for the opposing law firm may be a potential conflict, but it probably doesn't call for review by a disciplinary agency.

Sue the lawyer. Not every conflict of interest is grounds for a lawsuit. The deciding issue will probably be damages. If you have lost something of substantial value because of this unethical behavior, you can sue for malpractice on the grounds of breach of fiduciary duty. (See Chapter 9.)

Appeal the decision in your case. If your case was decided against you before you knew of the conflict, and you think the conflict contributed to the outcome, ask for a new hearing or trial, or file an appeal.

Cancel the transaction. File papers with the court asking to have any tainted transaction canceled. For example, just after you signed a lease for office space, you learned that the lawyer who represented you in the negotiations is the business attorney for the owner of the building.

2. Your Adversary's Lawyer (Your Former Lawyer) Has a Conflict Between Your Adversary and You

In this situation, you'll want to take the following steps quickly.

Investigate the rules. On your own, or through your lawyer, research the rules to make sure there is a conflict.

Get a legal opinion. Ask your current lawyer or another one to provide you with an opinion about the situation

Demand a withdrawal. Demand that opposing counsel withdraw from the case. Make a motion to the court for an order if the attorney will not voluntarily comply. In your motion, ask the court for money sanctions—the additional costs and fees you incur by the delay. Act promptly after learning about the conflict; otherwise, you might be considered to have waived it by your inaction.

Report the lawyer. Depending on the problem, you might report the lawyer to the disciplinary authorities. The combined mobility of lawyers switching law firms and corporate mergers creates many inadvertent "conflicts" where no harm is intended or committed. But go to the disciplinary authorities if you have good reason to believe that your former lawyer has misused confidential information.

Sue the lawyer. Again, your decision about whether to sue will probably turn on the amount of damages you incur as a result. In this case your damages are likely to be in the form of additional fees to your own lawyer resulting from forcing the other attorney to withdraw. (See Chapter 9.)

Appeal the decision in your case. See above.

Cancel the transaction. See above.

Endnotes

[1] *Matlock v. Simpson,* 902 S.W.2d 384 (Tenn. 1995).

[2] New Hampshire Bar Association Formal Opinion 1994-95/2.

[3] American Bar Association's formal opinion 92-364 (7/6/92).

[4] *Iowa Supreme Court Board of Professional Ethics and Conduct v. Hill,* Iowa Sup. Ct. No 95-1113 (11/22/95).

[5] Also see Oregon Ethics Opinion 1995-140 (1/95).

[6] Canon 9 of the ABA Model Code of Professional Responsibility reads, "A lawyer should avoid even the appearance of professional impropriety."

[7] *The Law of Lawyering: A Handbook on the Model Rules of Professional Conduct,* 2d ed. (Section 302), Geoffrey C. Hazard, Jr., and W. William Hodes (Aspen Law & Business).

Chapter 5

FIRING YOUR LAWYER

First rule first: you have an absolute right to terminate an attorney's services at any time, for any (or no) reason. It makes no difference what kind of legal problem or court case, or how you agreed to pay your lawyer. You can fire a lawyer simply because you want to. The lawyer does not have to have done anything wrong, improper or unethical.

But before you put down this book and fire a lawyer you are annoyed with, think it through, and then think it through again. Be sure your attorney really is doing a poor job before you give him his walking papers. I caution you against haste for three reasons:

- Changing lawyers can be expensive— you'll normally end up paying twice for at least some attorney time.
- Some attorneys will not take a case if another attorney has been handling it.
- When evaluating whether or not to work with a new client, most lawyers follow this basic assumption: the more often a client has changed lawyers, the more likely the client is a flake, difficult to work with or unreasonable.

 Tanya's Tip: Finding a New Lawyer Isn't Always Difficult

While lawyers often hesitate to take on new clients who change lawyers, this rule generally applies to legal representation involving litigation. On the other hand, you should have little problem finding a new lawyer to draft your estate plan, file your patent, represent your small business or negotiate your house closing.

A. Steps to Take Before Firing Your Lawyer

Okay—you've thought about it. And you're still tempted to change lawyers, but you want to be sure you're making a good decision. Especially if you are having a hard time communicating with your attorney, it may be difficult to tell if she is pursuing your case or legal problem diligently and effectively. As annoying as it is to have a lawyer who is slow to return phone calls, it makes little sense to fire a lawyer solely for that reason. Here are a few suggestions that may help you decide whether you really do want to make a change.

 Tanya's Tip: Don't Fire a Lawyer Because of a Poor Deskside Manner

A lot of hardworking, honest lawyers try and do an efficient job of getting their clients' cases through the legal system. But like any group of people, some lawyers have good communications skills; others don't. It may be that your lawyer is doing a fine job on your case, but a bad job in letting you know it. Before you fire a lawyer who communicates poorly, try to educate him on how he can do a better job of letting you know what's going on and involving you in key decision making. See Chapter 2 for some suggestions.

1. Contact Your Lawyer and Insist on Being Told What Is Happening in Your Case

Send a letter by mail or fax and ask for a written update or status report on your case. Be as direct as possible by asking your lawyer if she thinks you have a good case or a bad case. If she hems and haws, follow up by asking what information she needs to make that evaluation. Assuming you are involved in a contested court case, here are some questions you might want to ask your lawyer:

- What documents have you (the lawyer) reviewed?
- In what way do they have an impact on my case?
- What additional documents do you need to see?
- When will you get them?
- What are you looking for in those documents?
- Whose depositions (oral testimony before the trial) have been taken?
- In what way do they have an impact on the case?
- Are the transcripts available for me to review?
- Will more depositions be necessary?
- In what way might they have an impact on the case?
- Are those depositions scheduled yet?
- If not, when will they be?
- Who will be taking the depositions—you or the lawyer for the other side?
- Is my case set for trial? If so, when?
- If not, when do you expect it will be set for trial?
- Who will testify as witnesses at the trial?
- Will you arrange to have expert witnesses testify at the trial?
- What kinds of experts?
- How much will they cost?

- Have you already arranged for them to testify?
- When will their depositions be taken?
- Is there any way I can help you?
- What else needs to be done in my case?
- When do you plan to do it?

If your lawyer won't talk to you or tells you very little, you'll have to try another approach.

If you've hired the lawyer to handle a legal problem that does not involve contested litigation, you have some different questions to ask, such as the following:

- Have you (the lawyer) started researching the problem?
- Have you gathered the documents you need to work on my problem?
- Have you started drafting the documents I asked for?
- When do you expect to have the documents done?
- Why has there been such a delay?
- Have you drafted these kinds of documents before?
- How many times?
- Do I want a standard agreement or will you have to do custom drafting?
- Will you use a form that is already on the word processor and adapt it, or will you be drafting the document from scratch?
- Do you need anything from me?
- Do you want to do this work for me or are you too busy?
- Is there another way to structure the transaction to avoid the tax consequences?
- Do we need input or advice from an accountant or other professional?
- Is the security adequate?

• Do we need an appraiser or investigator? What would it cost?

2. Visit Your Lawyer's Office and Look at Your File

You have a right to look at your file. (See Chapter 6 if your lawyer won't let you see it voluntarily.) The file should contain correspondence and possibly notes which can tell you the content and demeanor of the exchanges between your lawyer and if yours is a contested case, the lawyer for the other side. If relevant, the file should also contain copies of all court papers filed by your lawyer and the lawyer for the other side. Read them and ask for copies. If your lawyer refuses, write down the case number (it will be on all court papers) and the address of the court (which should be on some of the papers).

3. Visit the Courthouse and Look at the Court File

If yours is a contested case, you always have the right to look at your file at the courthouse. While it will speed things up slightly if you already know the case number (it will be on all papers filed with the court), you can also get it at the courthouse. Ask the clerk to point you to the index of cases filed at the court which lists the names of plaintiffs and defendants.

Once you have the file, you should be able to tell if there are any upcoming hearings, conferences or a trial date. Also look to see if hearings, conferences or the trial itself has been continued (postponed), which can be a sign that your lawyer is not pursuing it diligently. Finally, check to see whether either attorney has been sanctioned (fined) by the court for any reason such as any delay, neglect or raising frivolous arguments.

4. Get a Second Opinion From Another Lawyer

Even if you've had a discussion with your lawyer and looked at your case file, you may still not be sure whether or not your lawyer is doing a decent job. One way to find out is to get a second opinion from a lawyer you are pretty sure is competent to give it. As you might expect, this can be expensive. You are asking an attorney to review your file and give you advice on a course of action. An attorney who agrees to do this will usually write something called an *opinion letter*. Depending on the complexity of the case, such a letter can cost anywhere from a few hundred to many thousand dollars.

Tanya's Tip: Finding a Lawyer to Give a Second Opinion

When getting an opinion from a second attorney, this is not the time to look for a novice who might keep his fee low. If possible, you want a lawyer with years of experience in the area of law your case or legal matter involves. For example, if you're not happy with your divorce lawyer, at a minimum you will want an opinion from someone who specializes in family law—and if your state has such a designation—is a certified family law specialist.

Here are some tips on finding a lawyer to give you a second opinion.

- *Get names from other lawyers of lawyers who specialize in your type of problem. When a name comes up twice, you have a likely candidate for a second opinion.*
- *If you have a litigation matter, you may learn a lot by going to the courthouse and watching lawyers. If one impresses you, get his name and give him a call. If he can't give you a second opinion, ask for referrals.*
- *If you have an injury case or any other case that might go to trial, look in a book that summarizes jury verdicts (these are at a law library) to get the names of local lawyers who have successfully tried cases. If they won't give you a second opinion, ask for referrals.*
- *If your problem is in an area in which lawyers often specialize (tax, bankruptcy, family law or workers' compensation), get the second opinion of a lawyer who specializes in the area. Your state bar association and the Yellow Pages have lists of specialists.*

- *Check continuing education materials for lawyers at a law library to see who has been teaching other lawyers. They are likely candidates for competence, and if they can't give you a second opinion, ask for referrals.*

When you call a lawyer to ask for a second opinion or a referral to another lawyer, tell him how you got his name (another lawyer, jury verdicts, watching him in court). Also, let him know that you expect to pay for his time.

Start by understanding that you can't just call a lawyer's office and ask for simple answers to a few questions. No matter how sympathetic he may be, no competent lawyer will provide answers in this situation. The risk of giving incorrect advice on such a quick and casual basis is just too high. Face it—a second opinion is only worth the trouble it takes to get it if the attorney knows the law in the particular area and has thoroughly reviewed the facts of your case. You can help the attorney by doing the following:

- **Get organized**. Make a brief chronology of your case, complete with key dates and points. If possible, this should fit on one side of a piece of paper. Organize all your documents such as the documents developed by your first lawyer and if relevant, copies of all court papers.
- **Narrow the issues**. What's really bothering you? Have a question or questions in mind that will quickly get to the nub of your problem.
- **Focus on the legal issues.** Go light on discussing any emotional frustration or personality conflicts you have with the

first attorney. Not only are these concerns likely to make any second lawyer wary of getting involved, but also they are a waste of time. If you simply don't like your lawyer or have an emotional problem with your relationship, fire her and don't expect a second lawyer to act as a therapist.

5. Educate Yourself About the Issues in Your Case

The law can be complex, but it isn't inaccessible. There are several ways you can research a question. For example you can visit a library or bookstore and get a copy of any one of Nolo's hundred or so self-help titles, such as *How to Win Your Personal Injury Claim*, by Joseph Matthews or *Sexual Harassment on the Job*, by Barbara Kate Repa and William Petrocelli. You can log onto the Internet or a computer bulletin board. (See Chapter 11, Section D.)

You might also get assistance from a special interest group—either located locally or out there in cyberspace. For example:

- An author worried about whether or not her publisher is treating her fairly could read up on the subject (many books exist on the subject) and could join a regional or national writers group.
- A father who thinks his lawyer is not being aggressive enough in pursuing his child custody or marital property rights might learn a lot through a divorced dads group.
- A disabled person denied rights because of a disability could check with a local independent living center or other disability support group. Some of these groups may

even have libraries of specialized materials on their premises.

So now you have thought about it, have concluded it's more than just poor communication and are thoroughly convinced it's time for a new lawyer. The rest of this chapter tells you what to expect and how to proceed.

B. When Should You Fire Your Lawyer?

During any business association, it can make sense to reassess whether the relationship is working. Sometimes, such a review is triggered by a negative event—such as a judge making an unexpected decision against you or your attorney consistently being late in accomplishing important tasks. Other times, the reasons are more subtle; after doing some of your own research and talking to someone with a lot of experience in the legal area, you conclude that you might receive better legal help elsewhere.

While only you can finally decide if the time has come to fire your lawyer, here are some situations in which you will probably want to find someone new.

You can't communicate. The number one complaint about lawyers is lousy communication. You call to ask what is going on and the lawyer never returns the call. Or if the lawyer does, you can't understand what he is talking about. Obviously, this won't do. You need and want a lawyer who can and will communicate clearly with you. No one should pay as much as most lawyers charge, only to be kept in the dark.

If your lawyer doesn't inform you of the key events of your case and involve you in decision-making, replace her. After all, if your lawyer can't explain things to you in a way you can understand, then she probably can't explain your case to a judge or jury either. But before giving your lawyer the pink slip, review the tips on improving communications in Chapter 2.

Your lawyer doesn't care. If you get the feeling that your lawyer doesn't care about your problem, talk to him. He may be personally unlikeable but professionally competent (see Chapter 2) or he may just feel that your needs for support or reassurance are excessive. But it may also be that he is overworked or over-stressed and really can't cope with your problems. Or, perhaps he has simply lost interest in your case—maybe the lawyer on the other side is so obnoxious that your lawyer can't stomach talking to her. Or maybe he no longer likes you. If for any reason you strongly suspect that your legal concerns are at the bottom of your lawyer's priority list, at the very least it is time for a frank talk.

Even if he says "he'll get right to your legal problem," you may decide that his past lack of diligence is all the reason you need to find someone else. Chances are it will be less expensive to bite the bullet and pay what it takes to educate a new energetic lawyer than to continue with one who has let you down. If you want to give him a second chance, then set a deadline—if significant work (with which you are fully satisfied) isn't done by a certain date, fire him then.

Your lawyer is not making progress, and no end is in sight. Sometimes, a legal problem drags on and on and on. If this begins to happen in your situation, ask why. It is quite possible that you haven't paid your lawyer lately. Especially if you agreed to pay your attorney by the hour, have an outstanding bill, and have not made arrangements about payment, this may explain why your business has become one of her lowest priorities. Lawyers, like everyone else, have a tendency to work much harder on the cases that pay.

If you pay your bills on time, then your case is going nowhere for some other reason. Perhaps your lawyer is in over his head, doesn't know how to handle a problem that has arisen or has lost confidence in your case. But assuming your bill is current (or yours is a contingency or flat fee case), you are likely to have a fight on your hands.

You believe your lawyer is not properly handling your case. Although it's not always easy to spot, my experience is that the level of mediocre lawyering is high. Even a lawyer who performs competently in one matter may not in yours.

If, for any reason, you begin to suspect your lawyer's work is below par, check it out pronto. If you have a question about a particular issue, take it up with your lawyer directly. There could be a misunderstanding. But don't be put off with answers you consider to be nonresponsive or obviously unsatisfactory. It's possible your case is being neglected or mishandled. If you suspect either of these, get a second legal opinion or make your own assessment after taking the time to educate yourself about the underlying legal issues (see the beginning of this chapter). Then, decide if you should fire your lawyer, hire another one, take over yourself or bail out by telling your lawyer to settle the case for whatever is possible.

Your lawyer charges you too much. When you hire a lawyer, you should receive a written estimate of the total cost. (Chapter 3 covers fee arrangements.) But lawyers don't always stick to their agreements and at some point, it may be obvious from the bills you are receiving that you'll have to pay much more. For example:

- Your attorney estimated that a project, for which you are paying by the hour, would take approximately 35 hours. He's already put in 40 hours and says he is not even half done.
- Your attorney quoted a flat fee to draft your document. Now he says that quote was for a relatively simple document and your needs turn out to be far more complex than anticipated.
- Your attorney quoted you a flat fee of $5,000 to handle your divorce, exclusive of court hearings, each of which would cost you $750 more. You've already been through four court hearings with no end in sight.

In cases with a "stepped-up" contingency fee contract, where the percentage of the fee you'll owe increases if the case gets close to trial or arbitration, and then increases again if the case actually goes to trial or arbitration, clients often worry that the attorney will delay serious efforts to settle the case until the increased fee gets triggered. This does happen, but probably more because the lawyer is overworked or lazy, not because the lawyer is deliberately stalling.

EXAMPLE: The defendant is obviously at fault, your injuries are serious, and the defendant has a low or moderate level of insurance coverage and very few other

assets or prospect of getting any. This is the kind of case which should settle quickly, probably without the need to even file a court case. After all, you are probably not going to collect more than the insurance policy and the insurance company is likely to pay out quickly because your claim is worth more than the policy limit. If your attorney does little or no work on the case until close to the trial date, refuse to pay the increased percentage.

Try to prevent this situation by knowing what events trigger fee increases and frequently asking your attorney what she is doing to get the case resolved before the larger percentage goes into effect. Also do some arithmetic.

EXAMPLE: Your agreement states that your attorney's share is 25% if your case settles before she files the lawsuit, 33% generally after that, and 40% once there is a trial date. You're offered $10,000 to settle before the lawsuit is filed. Your lawyer encourages you to file the lawsuit "so they know you mean business," promising you a higher settlement. You reject the $11,000 next offer because your attorney encourages you to take the case to a trial. There, a jury awards you $12,500. All that has gone up is your lawyer's fee:

Settlement or Award Amount	Fee %	Fee Amount	Net (less costs, which increase over time)
$10,000	25%	$2,500	$7,500
$11,000	33%	$3,600	$7,370
$12,500	40%	$5,000	$7,500

LAWYERS WHO CHURN FEES

Anyone who has been around the legal profession for any length of time knows that a small percentage of lawyers consistently and ruthlessly overcharge their clients. Often called "churning fees," this practice commonly involves doing too much research, scheduling too many lengthy depositions or double billing—that is, billing two clients for the same time, perhaps time spent to research one issue relevant to both cases, and just padding bills.

If your attorney is on course to run up a big bill which seems unnecessary or is unexpected, you may have hired a churner. Gather your bills and get a second legal opinion pronto. If this confirms that you are being charged way too much, cut the lawyer off before the situation gets worse. Remember—it's much harder to challenge a lawyer's unfair billing after the fact than it is to get rid of him. Even if you feel you've invested too much in your lawyer to cut loose, I can all but promise you that it will be less expensive in the long run to fire a fee churner and eat your losses.

You are pressured to do things which seem inappropriate or make you uncomfortable. Occasionally, a lawyer will suggest (or even insist) on sexual intimacy. If the attorney won't take a clear "no" for an answer, get rid of him quickly. You know you have a real problem if the lawyer implies that there could be a discount or delay in billing in exchange for dates. Not only is the lawyer behaving in an unprofessional manner, but it is likely that if you do trade intimacy for a discounted fee, you won't get your money's worth.

No one needs the additional pressure that comes with trying to have a personal relationship with one's lawyer in the middle of a lawsuit. An experienced lawyer should know this better than anyone. If he doesn't, he is simply foolish, unprincipled or out of control, all traits you want to avoid.

Tanya's Tip: Leave 'Em Before Loving 'Em
Lawyers are not all unlovable. It's just that your legal business and your romantic life do not make a good mix. Don't let your hormones convince you that your situation is an exception. If you really fall for your lawyer—fire him and tell him why. If both of you are willing, you can continue the personal relationship after you get a new attorney. A lawyer who doesn't understand why you are doing this is not worthy of your trust in law or love.

Your lawyer is nasty or unethical with your opponent. Be wary of dealing with a lawyer who uses sleazy tactics against your adversary. Do you really want to place your trust in someone who suggests destroying or fabricating evidence, makes false accusations, hides assets, tells you to lie or does any number of unethical things? Don't be naive. You can't expect fair dealing from someone who is unfair in her dealings with others.

Your lawyer lies, cheats or steals. Your lawyer gets no second chance here. After verifying that your suspicions are true, get another lawyer—

fast. Even if you weren't the victim, it's silly to put yourself next in line.

C. The Financial Reality of Changing Lawyers

Firing a lawyer has financial consequences. For starters, your attorney may try to get even by aggressively billing you for every minute of time she put in on your matter before you fired her. To keep your last bill to a minimum, take steps to clearly establish the termination date. Do this by sending a letter by fax (and to make sure she gets it, send a copy by regular mail), same-day messenger or overnight mail.

How much, if anything, you owe a lawyer you fire depends to a considerable extent on how your lawyer is being paid. Start by looking at what your written fee agreement says about how your attorney will be paid if you discharge her.

IF YOU WANT TO FIRE YOUR LAWYER BECAUSE YOU'VE RUN OUT OF MONEY

You might be inclined to fire your lawyer (who is being paid by the hour) because you run out of money. A common scenario is for a client to retain an attorney on an hourly basis with only a vague estimate as to the total cost. When the client runs out of money, the client assumes the only option is to fire the lawyer/drop the case.

There may be other possibilities. If your case is one in which you will receive money damages if you win or you can collect attorney's fees from the other side, ask your lawyer if she will continue and agree to be paid out of the proceeds of any recovery. If your attorney is not willing, ask her why. If it's because she doesn't think your chance of winning a substantial recovery is good, it may make sense to drop the case. Or perhaps it's time for your lawyer to make or accept a fairly decent settlement offer.

If you are involved in a divorce or other type case where you are not likely to win a recovery of money, or you lawyer says "no" to a delayed recovery, see the suggestions in Section C.2, below.

1. Attorneys Paid by the Hour

If you are paying your attorney by the hour, he can bill you for his work only as long as he is authorized to act as your attorney. If you send your lawyer a notice that his services are termi-

nated, he generally cannot bill you for work done after that date. If you hire a second lawyer who files a paper with the court to be "substituted in" (this usually happens if you're in the middle of a lawsuit), the lawyer being "substituted out" generally cannot bill you for work done after the substitution paper is signed. The one exception to this rule is that he can charge you any reasonable and necessary fee he incurs extracting himself from your case.

To find out exactly what you might owe, start by looking at your fee agreement. If it doesn't say what you will have to pay, let reason be your guide. If your current lawyer asks your former lawyer for a summary memo or a status letter, expect to pay for it. But, if your former lawyer wants to copy the file, that is his expense (except in Florida).

a. Money You Owe for Work Done

What about the money you owe for work the attorney did *before* you fired him? If your attorney has been working reasonably diligently on your legal problem, but for whatever reason—perhaps you've concluded the lawyer is not smart or knowledgeable enough—you decide to fire her, you must pay all reasonable outstanding bills. You hired the lawyer in the first place and the fact that you now feel you made a mistake is not a legal justification for you to refuse to pay.

But what if you don't think the bill is reasonable (you doubt the lawyer put in as many hours as billed) or you think she was so incompetent that she took 30 hours to complete something most lawyers could have wrapped up in ten? See Chapter 7, Section D, on questioning your bill.

IF YOUR LAWYER HASN'T EARNED HIS RETAINER

If you paid your lawyer a retainer (usually a few thousand dollars to start working on your case) and you fire the lawyer before the retainer is used up, the lawyer may have to refund you the portion yet unearned. See Chapter 3, Sections G and J, for information on retainers and client trust accounts.

---

b. Should You Pay the Lawyer You Fire?

If you have limited funds to complete the case, you will need to budget carefully. Especially if you stand a good chance of receiving a substantial recovery, your remaining funds may be better spent getting a new lawyer to finish your case, rather than in paying the balance owed to the first one. In the meantime, your former attorney may have to wait, like it or not. To assuage that lawyer's anger, consider offering her a lien against your expected recovery. But only do this if you agree that the amount you owe your first lawyer is reasonable—or the lawyer is willing to lower her bill to an amount you agree is fair.

You might also be able to get help from your new lawyer if your first lawyer's bill is outrageous. This would typically be in the form of a written opinion reviewing what has been done and what needs to be done and stating that the first lawyer's bill seems inconsistent with the amount of work that has been done.

IF YOU THINK YOUR FIRST ATTORNEY COMMITTED MALPRACTICE

Malpractice is covered in Chapter 9. If you think your attorney committed malpractice and the attorney claims you owe money, you each have a beef. Sometimes, your relative successes depend not on the merits of your claim, but on timing. For this reason, you will want to resolve your lawyer's claim for unpaid attorney's fees before the period of time (called the statute of limitations) you have to sue your former attorney expires.

The period you have to sue for malpractice is shorter than the period your lawyer has to sue for unpaid fees. Once the statute of limitations on your malpractice claim expires, your allegation of malpractice can be used only to reduce the fees claimed. Your own lawsuit for malpractice claim is gone. Many savvy lawyers who sue clients for unpaid fees wait until the statute of limitations for malpractice expires before suing on the bill. (See Chapter 7, Section A.2.)

---

2. Attorneys Paid on a Contingency Fee Basis

As described in Chapter 3, Section D, under a contingency fee arrangement, your attorney promises to perform services in exchange for a percentage share of any eventual recovery. When you fire a lawyer working on a contingency basis and hire a second, the normal outcome is that the lawyers divide that percentage.

> **EXAMPLE:** Your case settled for $100,000 and you owed a contingency fee of 35%. That is a $35,000 fee which the two lawyers would divide. Although the lawyers can agree to any division they want, you should not have to pay an increased fee because you changed attorneys, unless you made a specific agreement to do so when you hired the second lawyer.

Your fee agreement with the first lawyer probably says that if you terminate his service, he will be paid for the "reasonable" value of his work from *any* eventual recovery. This means that even if you finish up the case with a different lawyer, the first lawyer is still entitled to a fee, assuming he did some work on you case.

a. How Much You Owe the First Attorney

In some fee agreements, an attorney will specify an hourly rate to which she will be entitled to be paid for work done if she is terminated and you win. Assuming the attorney claims a reasonable number of hours, this avoids bickering with the new lawyer over the appropriate hourly rate.

When more than one lawyer has worked on a contingency fee case, the lawyers often settle the fee issue among themselves. Often, the first lawyer is paid according to the number of hours he put into the case, with the other lawyer receiving the balance. For example, if the first lawyer put in only ten hours, and the case later settles so that the total attorneys' fee

is $50,000, the first attorney would typically be paid $150 per hour X 10 hours = $1,500.

If your eventual recovery is insufficient to compensate the first attorney on an hourly basis, then the attorneys would probably divide the fee on a pro rata basis, depending upon how much time each spent on the case. For example, if the first attorney put in 20 hours on the case and the second attorney put in 30 hours on the case and the total attorneys' fee earned was $5,000, then the first attorney would be paid 40% or $2,000 and the second attorney would be paid 60% or $3,000.

MIGHT THE FIRST ATTORNEY EVER WAIVE HIS FEE?

If your first attorney is no longer interested in your case and wants out as much as you do, ask the attorney to agree to waive his fees. If the first lawyer did not put a lot of work into your case and isn't confident it's a winner, he may agree. If your attorney has advanced costs (for example, paid filing fees or for expert witness reports), he may waive his lawyering fee but only if you reimburse him for the costs out of any eventual recovery.

Why would an attorney who has done a decent, but not inspired job on your case agree to waive his fee? Once your fire him, if the case isn't completed (by a new lawyer or you representing yourself), the first lawyer won't recover anything anyway. He also knows that if he waives his fee, it will be easier for you to get another lawyer, which raises the chance that you'll be out of his life forever—remember, he may want out just as much as you do.

b. When to Pay the First Lawyer

Don't pay anything to the first lawyer until the case is over and you have received a recovery. Only then will you owe a fee. The same is usually true for the attorney's costs—contingency fee agreements generally do not require you to repay the costs until the case is ended. But check your fee agreement in the event it requires you to pay costs immediately when you discharge the attorney.

c. Paying the Second Lawyer

It is possible that if the first lawyer has done a fair amount of work on the case, a second lawyer will hesitate to take it without a sweetener, such as a retainer fee or an increased contingency amount.

> EXAMPLE: Lydia agrees to pay 33% to the first lawyer. Before the second lawyer agrees to take over the case, he sees that Lydia's first lawyer has done a good deal of work and that he might only get 15% out of any eventual recovery. Lydia might agree to guarantee the second lawyer 20% of the recovery, if the first lawyer agrees to reduce his share, too, and the second lawyer agrees to handle the negotiations with the first lawyer. Ultimately, even if the first lawyer gets to keep 20% and Lydia agrees to a minimum of 20% to the second lawyer, she may end up paying a 40% contingency fee, rather than the 33% she agreed to initially.

3. Attorneys Paid a Flat Fee

Many attorneys charge a flat fee for handling a specific legal task, such as drafting a document or forming a small business corporation. Let's say you hired a lawyer to draft fairly complicated estate plans for you and your spouse involving several trusts designed to avoid probate and save money on taxes, and agreed to pay him a total of $8,000. After reading up on the subject and talking to a tax attorney, you conclude that your lawyer simply isn't up to drafting the type of plans you want. How do you go about getting rid of him at the lowest possible cost?

First, terminate the lawyer's services in writing. If you paid the fee in advance, ask the lawyer to refund all but a small amount to compensate her for work she has done. If you haven't yet paid her, you may still owe her a small amount. After all, just because you now conclude that you made a mistake, she is still entitled to be paid a reasonable amount for the work she has done. If she refuses to refund any money or reduce her flat fee, you have a fee dispute and your options are described in Chapter 7. The more proof you have that the attorney did not do what he agreed to do, the better chance you will have to win.

4. Costs

Generally, costs are expenses incurred as part of pursuing a trial or arbitration proceeding. In many instances, the client agrees in writing to be ultimately responsible for paying all costs, although the lawyer agrees to "advance" them during the lawsuit. Typical costs are court filing fees, fees to expert witnesses, deposition transcripts, witness fees, jury fees and fees to obtain medical records. (See other examples in Chapter 3, Section H.)

To figure out if you owe costs when you fire your lawyer, read your agreement. In a contingency fee case, your fee agreement should specify whether costs are reimbursed to the attorney only out of any recovery you obtain ("contingent upon the outcome") or whether you have to pay even if you lose the case ("client has ultimate responsibility"). The agreement should state if and when you are responsible to reimburse costs.

Some states, including Arizona, Colorado, Connecticut, Georgia, Iowa, Massachusetts, New Mexico, New York, North Carolina, Ohio, Oregon and Tennessee, prohibit an attorney from actually taking on the legal responsibility to pay costs; in such a situation, legally your attorney is only "advancing" them. That means that the attorney is paying costs on your behalf with the expectation of repayment regardless of the outcome. It is something like a loan, but more like running a bar tab.

In other states, including Alabama, Arkansas, California, Delaware, District of Colombia, Florida, Illinois, Indiana, Kentucky, Maine, Maryland, Minnesota, Missouri, Nevada, New Hampshire, New Jersey, North Dakota, Oklahoma, Pennsylvania, Rhode Island, Utah and Wisconsin, lawyers do not have to insist on being reimbursed.

Even if your agreement requires you to reimburse the attorney for the costs at the end of your case, often the attorney you fired won't pursue you if you lost the case.

In non-contingency fee cases, your fee agreement will probably say that you owe costs "as incurred"—you'll owe your lawyer for the cost or expense when your lawyer sends you the bill.

D. If Your Attorney Wants to Fire You

Although you can fire an attorney for any reason at any time, usually a lawyer cannot just dump you without a good reason, especially if the lawyer is representing you in litigation. To do so might be malpractice. If the lawyer is advising you or drafting a document for you, however, she can usually quit without notice unless it would be prejudicial or harmful to you. A few examples can help you figure out the rules:

EXAMPLE 1: Your lawyer advised you for the past several years about how to keep your car repair business in compliance with various environmental laws and regulations. One day you call her for advice and she tells you she only does criminal defense work now and no longer wants to represent you. She can quit without any notice and it's not malpractice.

EXAMPLE 2: Your lawyer was helping you prepare a bid for a contract to provide child care for a local community college. Just before the deadline to submit the bids, she quits. The paperwork was unfinished, you could not complete it yourself or get another lawyer in the short time remaining and as a result you lost the contract. This is both an ethical violation—client abandonment—and malpractice for causing you to lose the business opportunity.

EXAMPLE 3: You talked to a lawyer about drafting a will or trust for you. He told you that you needed to make several decisions and provide some additional information before the document could be drafted. You procrastinate for several months and, before you get him the information, he sends you a letter firing you. The lawyer

has done nothing wrong, and in fact has probably done you a favor by making it clear that no work was being done on your matter.

EXAMPLE 4: Your mother, who was elderly and ill, consulted a lawyer about making her will. The lawyer said she would take care of it after returning from vacation. Three months later, the lawyer still had not contacted your mother, who died without the will. This may be malpractice.

If your lawyer represents you in a contested lawsuit, he will either need your consent or an order from a court. The order would be granting something called a motion to withdraw. If you ask the attorney why he filed a motion to withdraw, he will probably claim at least one of the following reasons:

- you have not paid his fee as you agreed you would
- you want him to present a claim or argument that is not warranted by the facts and cannot be supported by evidence
- you want him to pursue an illegal course of conduct such as showing you how to fabricate evidence or commit perjury
- your conduct has made it unreasonably difficult for him to work on the case, or
- the attorney-client relationship has broken down—meaning you simply no longer get along or cannot communicate.

Usually, an attorney's motion to withdraw will give only a vague general reason to back up the request. Allegations of "irreconcilable differences of opinion" are not uncommon. While these might seem like weasel words, they serve a necessary purpose. Even when with-drawing, your attorney is bound by confidentiality. He should not make a public record of private information, such as your admission that you were at fault in an accident and lied to the police about it. If he does, it is unethical, and possibly malpractice.

1. How Should You Respond?

If your lawyer files a motion to withdraw from your case, you must be sent notice that there will be a hearing, and you must be given the opportunity to object. In some states, your objection may have to be in writing. If you don't file an objection or come to the hearing and object, the judge will usually allow the lawyer to withdraw and send you a notice after the hearing that the attorney is no longer on your case. In some states, the notice may include a warning that you should talk to another attorney or you may lose valuable legal rights.

Most of the time, you won't want a lawyer who doesn't want you. In such a situation, you have several responses to your lawyer's motion:

- **Ask your lawyer to help you find another.** Perhaps your lawyer is ill, overworked or simply feels he can no longer work with you. Ask him for help in finding a second attorney—whom you obviously will want to check out yourself before agreeing to hire. If your attorney has suddenly become ill, your state bar association may help you find a new lawyer or might even appoint one to take over his cases. Even if you agree to his withdrawing, you will need him to

sign a form called a "Substitution of Attorney" if you are involved in a lawsuit.

- **Ask your lawyer for your file.** Your new attorney will need your file, which contains all court papers, documents and records your first lawyer has accumulated. (See Chapter 6.)

- **Ask your lawyer for a written status report.** No matter why you hired the lawyer—for example, to represent you in a lawsuit or to prepare your company's incorporation documents—your new lawyer will need an overview of the situation, a list of what has been done, what remains to be done and of any scheduled dates for the trial, depositions, settlement conference or appointments with the business owners.
- **Ask your lawyer to reschedule imminent deadlines.** If anything important is about to happen in your case, ask your attorney to try to reschedule them. You will need time to find a new lawyer or to prepare to handle your own case without facing immediate deadlines.

LETTER TO ATTORNEY WHO WANTS OUT OF CASE

(via fax and U.S. mail)

date

Re: *A v. B*, case # 123456

Dear Hank:

You have told me that you want me to get another lawyer to handle my case. I have made several phone calls
to other attorneys, all of whom want information about
the status of my case before they will talk to me. Please
provide me with the following to assist me in my efforts
to find someone who will take over:

1. A copy of my file, including correspondence, pleading, discovery, memos and any legal research you
   have done which might be useful.

2. A brief summary or overview of the case which will
   let the new lawyer know what the case is about,
   what relief and damages we are claiming, the other
   side's positions and what you consider to be the
   most significant areas of disagreement.

3. A list of any depositions which have been taken and
   a list of those which need to be taken. If we have
   any deposition transcripts, please include those.

4. A schedule of any dates which have been set for
   trial, depositions, settlement conferences or any
   other dates which will require an attorney's appearance.

5. Anything else which you think would be important
   for my new lawyer to know.

I will have it all picked up tomorrow at around 2 p.m. If
you need more time to get it together, let me know.

Thank you for your assistance in making this transition
as smooth as possible.

Cordially,

Larry Armando

Larry Armando

It is possible for you to file an objection to
your attorney's motion to withdraw. The court
will usually grant your attorney's request, however, unless it will prejudice your legal position
or that of other litigants.

For example, the court may not grant a
motion to withdraw on the eve of trial when it
would be impossible for you to get another
lawyer, even if you are way behind on your bill.
But if the motion to withdraw is made a few
weeks earlier, the court might agree at the same
time to continue (postpone) the trial for a
reasonable period to give you the chance to get

another lawyer. But while this seems reasonable, it won't always be enough to protect your interests, as would be the case if a key witness were about to die.

You might be tempted to tell the judge that it is unfair to allow a lawyer to withdraw if you have spent a lot of money on legal fees. A court won't force a lawyer to stay on a case for this reason.

Although it can be impossible to keep a lawyer on a case indefinitely, you may be able to get a judge to delay the lawyer's withdrawal until she completes a certain task or gets any upcoming court date postponed. Here are some specific arguments you can make:

- When your lawyer told you he wanted to withdraw, you asked for a recommendation for a new lawyer, your file and a written status report. The lawyer provided none of them, and instead filed the motion to withdraw. Ask the court to delay in granting it until your attorney provides your file and a status report.
- Ask the court to postpone (continue) the motion to withdraw for 30 days to give you and your lawyer time to find someone to take over.

Tanya's Tip: Protect Yourself

If you go to court to oppose the attorney's motion to withdraw—or even just to be present at the hearing—you may face the public disclosure of embarrassing or damaging information. Although a representative from the other side usually does not appear at these hearings, he might be there. Remember that a courtroom is almost always open to the public. So if you think the lawyer might raise issues that are embarrassing (and possibly detrimental to your case), express your concerns to the judge and ask if she can accommodate your need for privacy. The judge might clear the courtroom of spectators or invite you and your lawyer into her chambers for a private discussion.

2. If Your Lawyer Wants Out for Nonpayment

If you are paying your attorney by the hour and you can't afford to pay any more, your lawyer probably will want out. Under many circumstances, this is reasonable. Your lawyer, like everyone else, needs to make a living.

If you hope to recover money in your case, one suggestion would be to ask your lawyer to shift over to being paid on a contingency fee basis—that is, complete your case and agree to be paid the balance of what you owe out of the proceeds of any recovery. If he won't, ask why. If it's because he doesn't think your chance of winning is good, consider whether it's worth continuing the case.

If you are involved in a case where you are not likely to win a recovery of money, or your lawyer says no to a delayed recovery, you could be in a mess. You could try to find a new hungry lawyer who might work for less than your current lawyer wants. If you can save up enough money to get the new lawyer's attention, she may accept it as a retainer and agree to defer the balance until the case is resolved. If she does, make sure your written agreement with the new lawyer says that clearly.

Tanya's Tip:
Ask Your Current Attorney for Help

If your current lawyer drops you for failure to pay but recognizes the possibility that you might win a recovery, ask for his help in trying to find someone else who will work for deferred fees. Attorneys often know the general billing practices of other attorneys—and also may know attorneys hungry for work. Especially if your lawyer feels a little guilty for dropping you, she may help you shop for a new attorney.

E. Hiring a New Lawyer

As I mention at the beginning of this chapter, many lawyers assume that a client who changes lawyers (especially more than once) is a flake, difficult to work with or unreasonable. Many lawyers who already have enough clients will refuse to talk to you, especially if your case is not one likely to bring in a huge recovery. This may be particularly true with a workers' compensation or Social Security disability case where lawyers operate by signing up many clients and process their cases in an assembly line approach.

Probably the best way to get a second or third lawyer to consider taking you on is to offer to pay for the initial interview. Because many clients expect this to be free, the fact that you are willing to pay for the attorney's time will be a big help in getting you and your case taken seriously.

1. When You Are Paying by the Hour or Project

If you find a lawyer willing to take over your case and you are paying by the hour or segment of a project, ask the lawyer to agree in writing to complete your case within a certain budget. Another suggestion is to ask the new lawyer to agree to a fee cap of no more than 10% more than the written estimate. Most attorneys will refuse on the basis that it is too hard to predict how much work a case will involve, but it never hurts to ask. If he does refuse, a fall-back suggestion is to ask if you can pay off any balance which exceeds your budget over a period of time you can afford. No matter what you agree to, get it in writing.

2. When You Are Paying on a Contingency Fee Basis

Often, attorneys are reluctant to take over contingency fee cases—especially if a case doesn't look like it will pull in big bucks. The typical concerns the second attorney will have in deciding whether or not to take over your case are as follows:

- Will your first attorney waive or reduce his fees?
- If not, is the case big enough to justify splitting the fee? The more valuable and certain your potential recovery, the easier it will be for you to get another lawyer. Unfortunately, the reverse is also true.
- How much work did the first lawyer do?

- What work needs to be done and how soon? If deadlines loom, the second lawyer will probably be more reluctant to sign on.
- Has the first attorney damaged the case? The passage of time might make it more difficult or even impossible to win your case. Perhaps a key witness has disappeared without being deposed. Perhaps other witnesses are available, but the time for deposing them has passed. Many cases are lost because an attorney does not meet a deadline for securing a witness. For example, attorneys must tell each other which expert witnesses they will use at a trial. This information must be given far enough before the trial to allow the other side to take the expert's deposition. Failure to do this often results in the court refusing to allow an expert to testify. In some types of cases, you need an expert to prove a plaintiff's case. This is often true in medical malpractice cases.

To summarize, if you have a case with large enough potential damages, your first lawyer didn't work on it much, he hasn't messed it up and a second attorney has time to prepare it, you will probably find another attorney fairly easily. But if your case was marginal to begin with, the trial date is fast approaching and your first lawyer invested considerable time in the case, you will have a difficult time finding someone to take over. ■

Chapter 6

GETTING YOUR FILE

When an attorney represents you, she keeps a file of all materials related to your case or problem. Your file consists of all of your papers (including print-outs of documents on computer disks) and property, such as court pleadings, correspondence, deposition transcripts, exhibits, physical evidence and experts' reports. You may wonder if you have a general right to get a copy of those materials. Legally, no, but if you have a good working relationship with your lawyer, she should be willing to make you copies of everything in your file as long as you pay a modest photocopying fee.

The situation is different if you end your relationship with your lawyer. In most states, once that happens, your file legally belongs to you and you have the right to virtually everything in it. If some materials are on a computer disk, you are entitled to a printout. It makes no difference whether it's you or your lawyer who ends the relationship, what stage your legal work is in or that you owe your lawyer money. If your lawyer wants to keep a copy of your file, he can to do that at his own expense—that is, he cannot charge you for it. The only exception is in Florida, where the file belongs to your lawyer.[1] But it must be made available to you, or copied at your request, if you pay for it.

If you are looking for a new lawyer, but haven't yet fired the person you have been working with, you may want a copy of your file to show around. Unfortunately, you may have a hard time getting it unless your lawyer is as anxious to get rid of you as you are to find a new lawyer. Because your lawyer still represents you, he has no legal duty to give you the file or copies of what's in it, and because you are looking to replace him, he may not do so voluntarily.

Even if he doesn't know why you want the file, if you don't have a good relationship with the lawyer, he probably won't trust you with it. Lawyers don't like to part with their files for a couple of reasons. As long as the lawyer represents you, he needs to refer to the file to work on your case. In addition, the lawyer may not want to give you the file simply to make it difficult for you to hire someone else, to hamper your efforts to have another attorney review his work or if he thinks you may sue him for malpractice. In short, you probably won't get your file until you hire your new lawyer and fire your old one.

 Tanya's Tip: Don't Sign a Substitution of Attorney Form Without Getting Your File

If you are involved in a lawsuit and changing lawyers, you, your first lawyer and your new lawyer must sign a document called a Substitution of Attorney which officially "substitutes" your new lawyer for the old one. Usually, your old lawyer will be anxious for everyone to sign the form so he can get off your case (it's usually

prepared by the new lawyer or by you if you plan to represent yourself); thus, you can use this as leverage to get your file. Refuse to sign the form until your first attorney has your entire file ready for you to pick up.

A. A Lawyer's Notes Are Not Part of the File

As odd as it may seem, while your file includes virtually every document, pleading, deposition transcript and other item relating to your case, it does not include your attorney's notes or other written documents containing his mental impressions and legal strategies of the case.

Documents containing mental impressions and legal strategies are called the attorney's "work product." Some written materials compiled by the lawyer, however, are not considered to be work product. The following, for example, do not constitute work product:

- reminder note of a conversation
- draft of a letter
- phone messages
- transcription of voice mail message
- calendar slips
- notes of conversations if the notes are close to verbatim of what was said—selective note taking that represents the lawyer's interpretation of what was said is probably work product
- indexes of documents which contain the title and date of the document and information taken from the document itself—a chronology of "key events" would be work product because it would indicate what the lawyer thought was "key," and

- a complete chronology of pleadings or documents, unless it includes the lawyer's interpretation of events.

Just because a note is in a lawyer's handwriting does not make it work product. For example, if the note reads "TF OPC 5/20—says no," this would not be work product. Translated, this note means "telephone call from opposing counsel on 5/20—she says no to our offer." But, if the if the note reads "TF OPC 5/20—says no in a stupid and condescending manner," it would be work product because the note reflects the lawyer's mental impressions.

There are many court disputes about what is or is not an attorney's work product. Most of those cases occur in a different context and involve a lawyer wanting written materials from an adversary as part of pretrial preparation, such as witness statements obtained by an investigator, notes of interviews with witnesses or an investigative report prepared for a company to study internal problems which need to be addressed. But the larger point is the same: a lawyer doesn't have to disclose her work product.

When a lawyer withholds items in a file from a former client, the lawyer may apply a broad definition of work product—meaning she'll give you as little as possible. For example, you might not get any handwritten notes, regardless of whether or not they reflect thoughts and impressions of the case.

 Tanya's Tip: A Lawyer Must Turn Over Work Product If You Sue for Malpractice
Although a lawyer need not turn over her work product when she gives you your file, there is an

exception. If you sue her for malpractice, you are entitled to a copy of all papers in your file, even those giving the attorney's thoughts and impressions of your case.

B. How Long Must a Lawyer Keep a File?

Rules vary tremendously from state to state concerning how long a lawyer must keep client files after a case is over, a legal task is completed or the relationship ends for any other reason. The range is no rule at all to seven years—no state requires lawyers to keep files forever. Five to six years is often considered sensible in states with no specific rule unless there is an affirmative reason to keep it longer. States with specific rules are as follows:

Five Years	Six Years	Seven Years
Iowa	Alabama	Illinois
Michigan	Alaska	Mississippi
	Colorado	Nevada
	Florida	New Jersey
	Minnesota	Rhode Island
	New Hampshire	
	North Dakota	
	South Carolina	
	Wisconsin	

In some of the states listed above, attorneys have a duty to use their discretion to hold on to the files longer. For example, guidelines in Alabama suggest a six-year retention period

and state that when a lawyer can destroy a file depends upon what is in it and the circumstances of the case.

Documents that are clearly a client's property and may be of some intrinsic value to the client—such as a will or deed—should be retained indefinitely, recorded, deposited with a court or delivered to the client. Other documents can be destroyed. In a few states such as Alabama, before destroying items of potential value to a client, an attorney must notify the client by either certified mail or newspaper notice stating that the attorney plans to destroy the file after a reasonable period if the client does not claim it, and then keep the file for that period—usually six years. The attorney must also keep an index of destroyed files.[2]

In states without specific time rules, lawyers must usually follow a "common sense" or "type of legal problem" rule. This means that lawyers must keep some files (such as notes to prepare a will) or documents (the will itself) longer than other files (settling an accident case without litigation) or other documents (telephone messages). Factors which should be considered by a lawyer in a commonsense situation include:

- the client's reasonable expectations
- the nature of the documents
- alternatives to destruction of documents—such as lodging them with a court or recording them
- whether or not the items are available elsewhere (as would be the case with public documents)
- the nature of the representation—a file related to creating an estate plan would be

kept longer than a file in a simple automobile accident case

- attempts to locate and return the file to the client
- future value of the files to the client, and
- whether or not destroying the file could possibly prejudice the client's future rights—for example, the possibility that the client might be involved in further litigation and need information in the file.

If you want to find the specific rule in your state (or if there is a rule in your state) concerning how long a lawyer must keep a file or any steps the lawyer must first take before destroying it, try calling your state bar association. If they can't give you an answer, visit a local law library. Ask a reference librarian for help in locating your state's Rules of Professional Conduct or Ethics Opinions from your state's lawyer regulatory agency.

IF A LAWYER GOES OUT OF BUSINESS, IS DISBARRED OR DIES

If a lawyer goes out of business, is disbarred or dies, it may be difficult or in some instances even impossible for you to get your file. The key is to act quickly. As soon as you learn that the lawyer is out of business, write a letter to her last office address (the lawyer may be having mail forwarded or another attorney may have taken over her workload) and ask for your file. Follow up with a phone call. If you don't get anywhere, contact your state lawyer regulatory agency for suggestions.

C. Ask for Your File in Writing

Anytime your relationship with your lawyer has ended (other than at the conclusion of your case when you have a good relationship), ask for your file in writing. This means you should ask for your file if:

- your attorney files a motion with a court to withdraw from your case
- you decide to fire your lawyer—and hire a new one, represent yourself or drop the matter, or
- your case is over but you have a fee dispute, want to file a complaint with your state lawyer regulatory agency or are considering pursuing a malpractice claim against your lawyer.

Give the lawyer a reasonable amount of time to get the file ready—normally three to seven business days, depending upon the volume of material. If the file is unusually large, two weeks might be reasonable. If the file has been closed and sent to an off-site storage facility, add another five days or so. A sample letter follows.

LETTER TO OBTAIN YOUR FILE

[via fax or hand delivery]

October 8, 19xx

Re: Return of my file
    A. v. B., Case # _____

Dear Liane:

Because you are no longer representing me, I would like to have my entire file, including all pleadings, correspondence, notes and memos, deposition transcripts, exhibits, physical evidence, and experts' reports, if any.

This request is for the original file, not a photocopy. If you want to keep a copy for your own records, you may do so at your own expense, provided this does not delay the turning over of my file to me. [Delete this paragraph if you are writing to an attorney in Florida—remember in Florida, your lawyer owns the file and you have to pay the photocopying costs.]

I expect the file to include all papers (including printouts of documents on computer disks) including correspondence, research notes, notes of phone calls, court pleadings, deposition transcripts, exhibits, physical evidence and experts' reports.

[Optional—insert applicable rule from your state, for example: This request is made pursuant to California Rules of Professional Conduct, Rule 3-700 (D).]

I will come to your office after 2:00 p.m. next Thursday, October 14, to pick up my file. [If you are too far away to pick up the file, ask for it to be sent and offer to pay the postage or shipping bill.]

Cordially,

Misha Aranoff

Misha Aranoff

D. Ask for Withheld Items

Lawyers often withhold their notes (work product) when preparing to give a (former) client her file. It is common for a lawyer to have someone in the office "pull my notes" before the file is turned over. But as mentioned, not all notes are work product. Only those that reflect the lawyer's mental impressions and strategies would be. For example, notes of what was said in a telephone conversation with opposing counsel would not be work product. See Section A, above, for a list of items not commonly considered work product.

If you suspect or know that your lawyer has withheld information, ask for an itemized list, including:

- the date of the materials
- the number of pages, and
- a brief description of what each item is about—such as a telephone conversation, legal research, items that needed to be done.

Your lawyer may decide that it is more trouble than it is worth to compile the list, and just give you the items.

LETTER REQUESTING LIST OF ITEMS WITHHELD

[via fax or hand delivery]

October 18, 19xx

Re: Items withheld from my file
   A. v. B., Case # _____

Dear Liane:

Please provide me with a detailed list of what items you have kept from my file and not provided to me, including the following information:

- the date of each item
- the number of pages of each item
- a brief description of what each item is about—such as notes about cross examination strategy, legal research or work that still needs to be done.

I would like to review this detailed list to determine whether or not I am legally entitled to any of the materials you have withheld. Because time is of the essence in finishing up my case, I would appreciate your getting this list to me by next Friday, October 29. If this is not possible, please let me know when I should expect to receive the list.

Thank you.

Cordially,

Misha Aranoff

Misha Aranoff

LETTER REQUESTING ITEMS NOT WORK PRODUCT

[via fax or hand delivery]

October 30, 19xx

Re: Return of items withheld
   A. v. B., Case # _____

Dear Liane:

Thank you for the inventory of the materials you have kept. From the cursory descriptions alone, it is obvious that not everything you have kept qualifies as your work product—the only legal justification for withholding information. For example, if the notes of the telephone conversations with Mr. Osterhouser on February 2, 5, 6, and March 10 are simply notes of phone conversations and do not reflect your mental impressions of the case or your legal strategies, they should be provided to me.

In fact, from the descriptions you sent to me, it appears as though most of the documents, if not all of them, are not your work product.

I expect that this occurred because you delegated the task of segregating my files to someone else. In any event, I would ask that you personally review the materials you have withheld, and provide me with all items not containing your mental impressions or legal strategies.

Again, please clarify what you have continued to withhold.

Cordially,

Misha Aranoff

Misha Aranoff

Assuming you receive a list back from the attorney, review it carefully for items that clearly are not work product. Promptly send another letter requesting the items.

If the attorney still holds on to items you believe you are entitled to, send one more letter. Demand the materials and let the lawyer know that you'll file a complaint with your state discipline agency if she doesn't turn them over to you. You can also suggest that you'll sue her if you have to to get the documents. (See Section G, below.)

LETTER REQUESTING WITHHELD ITEMS ONE LAST TIME

[via fax or hand delivery]

November 7, 19xx

Re: Items continuing to be withheld
  A. v. B., Case # _____

Dear Liane:

I disagree that the documents you continue to hold are your work product. I think I am entitled to them. I do not think that I should have to sue you to get them, and hope that is not my only choice.

[If applicable: As you know, I am out of money and trying to complete this case on a shoestring. I really need the research documents and I can't afford to have the work done again. Your refusal to turn this information over to me "because I haven't paid for it" may seriously jeopardize my ability to obtain a recovery.]

Please reconsider your position and send me the documents and materials you have withheld.

Cordially,

Misha Aranoff

Misha Aranoff

E. Complain to Your State Lawyer Discipline Agency

If the attorney does not respond to your series of requests for your file or for the withheld items, send a letter to your state lawyer discipline agency with a copy to the lawyer. (A sample is below; see Chapter 8 for information on filing a complaint with the state lawyer discipline agency.) Explain that you've asked for your file and your lawyer won't give it to you or that your lawyer won't give you certain items that are clearly not work product. Attach copies of your letters. If you don't have it already, this should get the attorney's attention. Wait about a week, and if you still don't have the file, call the discipline agency and see if you can prod them into action.

LETTER TO REGULATORY AGENCY

State Bar of New York

November 15, 19xx

Re: Attorney Liane Pati
 347 Collins Way
 Binghamton, NY 14000
 (607) 555-6200

To Whom It May Concern:

I have been unable to get my file [certain materials in my file] from my former attorney, Liane Pati.

On October 8, 19xx, I hand delivered a letter to Ms. Pati asking for the return of my file. I received no response. I visited her office at 2:00 p.m. on October, 14, 19xx, to pick up my file. She had not left it for me. [Or: On October 30, 19xx, I received a letter from her in which she stated that she would not turn over several items from my file.] I have enclosed copies of all letters I have sent to and received from Ms. Pati concerning the return of my file.

I need help in getting my file [or the withheld items] returned to me so I can complete my legal matter. Can you help me? Do I need to file a formal complaint with your agency to get help?

Thank you very much.

Cordially,

Misha Aranoff

Misha Aranoff

cc: Liane Pati

Tanya's Tip: Don't Mix Complaints

Limit your complaint to getting your file. Don't include the laundry list of all your complaints against your lawyer for things such as charging you too much, not returning phone calls, doing a bad job or anything else. If you have other complaints against your attorney, file a separate complaint. (See Chapter 8.)

F. Ask Your New Lawyer for Help

Your new lawyer should help you figure out whether or not you really need any of the items that are being withheld. If you do, then a note or a call from your new lawyer may convince your old lawyer to turn over those items. Your new lawyer may be able to explain to the old lawyer why the information is necessary or why it is being withheld unnecessarily, or may be able to arrange for the material to be given to a neutral third person who can decide what is and what is not work product.

G. Sue the Lawyer

If you have tried all of the above suggestions, as a last resort you may want to consider suing the lawyer, demanding that your file (or the withheld items) be returned. It is likely—but not guaranteed—that by filing a lawsuit and having it served on the attorney, you will get her attention and your file returned voluntarily.

One type of lawsuit would be a claim for possession of personal property. (In some states, it's called replevin; in others it's called claim and delivery.) Depending on your state, you may be able to file it in small claims court. If you win, the court would award you a judgment stating that the file (or withheld items) is yours. (This is not a case that can be brought in Florida where the file belongs to the attorney, not you.)

This type of award is called "equitable relief"—as opposed to a case for money damages. Not all states allow equitable relief cases in small claims court. For a list of states that do, see *Everybody's Guide to Small Claims Court*, Ralph Warner (Nolo Press).

If you can't file an equitable relief case in small claims court, you may be able to file a case for money damages and request that a physical item—such as a file—be turned over. (Again, check *Everybody's Guide to Small Claims Court* to find out which states allow this kind of case in small claims court.)

If you can't bring this type of case in your state's small claims court, you will have to file in regular civil court. You should be able to find a lawyer's form book in a law library that can show you how do this on your own. Again, you would request the return of your file (or the withheld items) and money to compensate you for the attorney's refusal to turn it/them over to you.

In small claims court or regular civil court, the money damages you could claim would be the expense of redoing work already done.

If the attorney's refusal to give you your file (or the withheld items) is willful and malicious, you may be entitled to punitive damages (damages meant to punish). Punitive damages,

however, are hard to get. You must prove that the lawyer is withholding your file or the items deliberately. Undoubtedly, the lawyer will say it was an oversight, that he delegated your request to someone in his office and thought that it was handled, or that he sincerely believed that the items withheld were his work product and didn't have to be turned over to you.

If you want to request punitive damages in a lawsuit because the attorney won't turn over anything or is keeping back items that are clearly not work product (such as an expert witness's report), you will have to do some work in advance. Before suing, send a dozen letters over a period of a few weeks by certified mail, fax, hand delivery and overnight mail. Send copies of the letters to all other lawyers in the office. Visit the office to try and get your file. The more you can show your squeaky wheel efforts, the harder time the lawyer will have claiming innocent error.

If the attorney doesn't voluntarily give you the file after you sue, you will have to go to court and get a judgment stating you are entitled to it. If the lawyer still refuses to hand it over, you can give a copy of the judgment to the sheriff (or constable or marshal, depending on your county), and the sheriff, constable or marshal will go get the file for you.

Endnotes

[1] Florida Ethics Opinion 88-11 (Reconsideration), 5/15/93.

[2] Alabama Ethics Opinion RO-93-10, 6/10/93.

Chapter 7

FEE DISPUTES AND FEE ARBITRATION

One of the most common types of complaints about lawyers has to do with their billing practices. Most sound like one of the following:

- My bill is too high.
- My bill is too high and it is not what we agreed to.
- My bill is too high. I'm not sure what we agreed to, but it wasn't this.
- My bill is huge and it's not itemized. I have no idea what my lawyer claims to have done to earn it, and she won't discuss it with me.
- My attorney did a terrible job and I don't want to pay his big bill.
- My attorney won't send me a bill. I am scared that when she does it will be more than I can afford.
- My attorney sued me for unpaid fees—I don't think I should pay because I feel I was overcharged.
- My attorney did a terrible job, sent me a big bill and I want to sue her for malpractice.
- My attorney agreed to a top limit on his fee but his bill is for much more.
- My attorney billed me top dollar for her time when I know her paralegal did most of the work.
- My attorney padded his bill—he billed me 30 minutes for every two minute phone call, even when I called to protest his earlier overbilling.

If you believe you are being overbilled, you have six options:

- You can pay the entire bill and vow not to go near that attorney again.
- You can pay the bill and sue your attorney for a refund. (See Section G, below.)
- You can pay the part of the bill you think is reasonable with a letter explaining why you are refusing to pay the rest.

- You can refuse to pay any of the bill until the lawyer agrees to accept less as full payment.
- In most states and situations, you can request fee arbitration, usually with a panel made up of local lawyers and perhaps one or two nonlawyers.
- Whether or not you pay the bill, you file a complaint with your state attorney disciplinary agency if you think the bill was fraudulent or unethical. (See Chapter 8.)

DOES PAYMENT DEPEND ON HOW THE RELATIONSHIP ENDS?

Normally, if your lawyer is working for an hourly fee, your obligation to pay does not depend on how the relationship ends—whether the work is over, you fire the lawyer or the lawyer quits (assuming she really did the work). The lawyer can claim money for the hours she completed until she is off the case.

If you have a contingency fee contract, the lawyer is not entitled to any fee if she quits before the case is over. This is because her fee was contingent on getting you a settlement or judgment. She will only have the right to get reimbursed for her costs. If you fire her, however, she can claim a reasonable value for her services against your case settlement or winnings. (See Chapter 5, Section C.2.)

Before getting into the details of resolving a fee dispute, start by asking yourself two questions. Is my complaint simply that I've been overcharged? Or do I believe that I've been overcharged in a situation where my attorney's poor handling of my legal problem amounts to malpractice?

A. Fee Disputes, Malpractice Claims and Discipline Matters Are Not the Same

Fee disputes, malpractice claims and discipline matters overlap, sometimes confusingly. Just the same, a claim that your lawyer has charged you too much, a claim that your lawyer has committed serious errors causing you harm (that is, committed malpractice) and a claim that your lawyer violated attorney ethical rules which can trigger action by an attorney discipline agency are not the same. Here's why.

- **Fee dispute.** In a fee dispute, your claim is that your attorney overbilled you. For example, if the lawyer spent (and billed you) for two hours for a task you think should have taken 15 minutes, that's a fee dispute.
- **Malpractice.** In a malpractice claim, your claim is that your attorney committed negligence or fraud which caused you harm. For example, if the lawyer fails to show up at a court hearing and your case is dismissed as a result, that's malpractice. If the lawyer bills you for work he did preparing for the hearing he forgot to attend, you certainly have a fee dispute as well.

• **Disciplinary matter.** In a disciplinary matter, your claim is that your lawyer's conduct violates your state's rules of professional ethics or responsibility. For example, if your lawyer failed to show up at a court hearing and you lost a case you otherwise would probably have won (but you weren't billed for it), that's a disciplinary matter (client abandonment) and it's certainly malpractice—but it isn't a fee dispute.

1. Aggressive Billing Practices Aren't Ethics Violations

Even highly aggressive billing practices—such as charging you two hours for a task that took 15 minutes—are normally not considered ethical violations, at least not by lawyer-regulators. Although you might view the practice as fraud, lawyer-regulators treat it as a breach of contract claim based on the fact that your agreement obligates you to pay only for work actually done. Your options are to sue for a refund (for example, if the lawyer deducted the money from your retainer) or refuse to pay and file a claim for fee arbitration. (See Section F, below.)

Lawyer-regulators generally don't discipline this kind of behavior because they take the position that how long it takes an attorney to actually "work" on a matter is subjective. If a lawyer spends only 15 minutes drafting a document, for example, she will no doubt claim that she spent more than an hour thinking about it, and so that billing you for two hours is more accurate than would be billing you for only 15 minutes. In reality, a lawyer can always claim to

have put in a lot more time on a matter than just the time spent writing, drafting, researching and "doing" other work.

But what if the overbilling is so outrageous that it amounts to just plain cheating? For example, you should not be billed for your lawyer's time if her secretary placed a call or a law student did the research. That's an ethical violation, and if you think you are being cheated, consider complaining to your attorney disciplinary authority. (See Chapter 8.)

2. Whether It's Malpractice or a Fee Dispute Affects How Many Years You Have (or Your Lawyer Has) to Sue

One important difference between a malpractice claim and fee dispute is how long you have to sue your lawyer in court for malpractice or your lawyer has to sue you for breach of contract for not paying your bill. This limit also applies to how long you have to sue your lawyer for a refund. (Filing an ethical complaint with a lawyer disciplinary association will have a separate time limit.) The time limit, called the statute of limitations, is usually shorter for a malpractice case than for a breach of a written contract.

Knowing the time limit is important because a lawyer who is enmeshed with a client over an unpaid bill often thinks like this: "If I sue to recover my fee, the client who thinks I did a rotten job may sue me for malpractice. But I have more years to bring my lawsuit than my client does, so I will wait until the time has passed for the client to sue me for malpractice, and then I'll sue for the unpaid bill."

That a client can no longer sue for malpractice doesn't mean the lawyer will automatically win the fee dispute. Although the client cannot file his own lawsuit for malpractice, he can still defend against the claim for fees, and a valid defense would be that the attorney committed malpractice.

EXAMPLE: Ted's attorney's malpractice in handling his case caused Ted to lose a $5,000 security deposit which he believes should have been refunded by his landlord when he closed down his typesetting shop. The lawyer sends Ted a bill for $1,500. Ted writes back, listing his grievances and refusing to pay the bill. Ted considers filing a malpractice case against the lawyer, but never gets around to it. The lawyer doesn't contact Ted for a year (the length of time Ted has to file his malpractice suit in that state). Ted assumes that after reading his letter protesting the original bill, the lawyer is so embarrassed that she has torn it up. Fourteen months later, the lawyer writes Ted demanding the $1,500. Ted again refuses to pay. A few months later, Ted's lawyer sues him for the $1,500. Ted's defense is that the lawyer committed malpractice. If Ted wins the case, the best result is that he won't have to pay the lawyer's bill. He will not be able to get his own judgment for the $5,000 loss.

CALIFORNIA RELEVANT STATUTES OF LIMITATION

Type of Lawsuit	Time Limit to Sue
Legal malpractice	1 year
Negligence	1 year
Breach of oral contract	2 years
Breach of written contract	4 years

What happens if the lawyer sues for her fees before the statute of limitations period for your malpractice case has run out? If your defense to not paying the bill is the lawyer's malpractice, you have a choice: you can simply raise it as a defense to the fee case and hope that you won't have to pay the bill, or you can file you own paper called a counter-complaint or cross-complaint for malpractice. In either situation, you will have to prove your malpractice case. (See Chapter 9.) If you don't file your counter-complaint or cross-complaint right now, you forever give up your right to do so. This is because the law does not want the same facts litigated twice.

EXAMPLE: Now assume Ted's landlord-tenant deposit case ended five months ago. Even though Ted still has seven months to file a malpractice case, Ted's lawyer has just sued him for the $1,500 fee. Ted must raise the lawyer's malpractice as a defense to the bill to avoid a judgment against him for $1,500. To try to win the $5,000 deposit he lost, he will have to file his own counter-complaint or cross-complaint against the lawyer for malpractice. In most states, he must file this within about 30 days of being served with the attorney's lawsuit.

⚠️ **Statutes of Limitations Vary State to State**
Not only does the statute of limitations depend on the type of legal claim involved, but also they vary from state to state. For example, California has a four-year breach of contract statute of limitations, while Florida's is five years, New Mexico and Arizona's are six years and Illinois's is ten years. Nevertheless, as a general rule a lawyer will usually have longer to file a breach of contract lawsuit for unpaid fees than you will to sue for malpractice. (See Chapter 9, Section B, for information on statutes of limitations.)

The rest of this chapter covers basic fee disputes. If your legal position or case was damaged, consider suing the lawyer for malpractice. (See Chapter 9.) If you were cheated, consider complaining to your state's attorney disciplinary agency. (See Chapter 8.)

B. Fee Clauses in Your Agreement

As mentioned, a fee dispute is essentially viewed as a claim that a contract was broken. But unlike other contract cases, where your and your attorney's rights and responsibilities are determined legally by your agreement, lawyer-client contracts are governed to some extent by laws and the rules of state legal regulatory bodies. In short, while you need to carefully look at any written contract, you also need to look beyond it to the legal rules. (See Section C, below.) Chapter 3 covers various common types of fee arrangements, the important features of each and a few of the ways state law

regulates them. Read that material now if you are not familiar with it.

As you read your contract, ask yourself the following questions. Your answers will provide you with an outline of your dispute and give you direction in resolving it.

- What work did the lawyer agree to do? Has she done it?
- What did I agree to do? Have I done it?
- Are there any conditions which must be met before the lawyer can recover the fee set out in the contract? (For example, did I win my contingency fee case?) Have the conditions occurred?
- Is any provision of the contract unclear?
- Have any letters or conversations changed the contract or clarified any ambiguous provisions?
- Does the contract provide for disputes to be arbitrated? If so, how is the arbitrator chosen and what rules apply? Is the arbitration binding or nonbinding? As you would probably guess, *binding* means that a decision by the arbitrators is final; *nonbinding* means that the parties normally don't have to accept the result. (See Sections F and G, below.)
- Does the contract provide for disputes to be mediated? If so, how is the mediator chosen and what rules apply?

C. Fee Limits Other Than in the Contract

Suppose you don't have a written agreement with your lawyer—or you have a vague one and you get a bill for way more than you expect. Do you have any recourse? Maybe. Lawyers can't always charge "whatever the traffic will bear" and get away with it. Chapter 3 explains that certain types of fees are limited by law or require court approval. But even when that isn't true, lawyers are expected to keep their fees within reasonable limits.

1. Fees Limited by Law

Increasingly, states limit the amount of money lawyers can charge in certain types of cases. Some fee limits are as old as the U.S. republic. Others have been enacted more recently, often in response to public cries for law or "tort" reform. In many instances, the attorney must submit something called a fee petition to a judge before the fees can be paid. Treat any fee petition like a bill. (See Sections D and E, below.)

The following are the most common types of cases for which attorney's fees are usually set by statute or must be approved by a judge:

- personal injury—these fees are capped in some states (see Chapter 3)
- medical malpractice—these fees are capped in some states (see Chapter 3)
- bankruptcy—the bankruptcy judge must approve these fees; most bankruptcy lawyers know the amount judges will approve and charge that amount
- probate—the states that set these fees set them as a percentage of the estate (which may be high), and you may be better off paying by the hour
- workers' compensation—these fees are usually limited to a percentage of the recovery

- Social Security appeals—contingency fees are usually limited to a percentage of the recovery, not more than 25%
- claims of minors or mentally disabled persons—fees must be approved by a judge
- class action cases—fees must be approved by a judge, and
- claims against the federal government—contingency fees are limited to 25%.

2. Excessive Fees

While, generally speaking, a judge, arbitrator or regulatory agency rarely second-guesses an attorney as to the reasonableness of his fees, it occasionally does occur. Fees that are considered "excessive," "overreaching," "extortionate," "fraudulent," "exorbitant" or "unconscionable" may be reduced and sometimes even wiped out.

In one case, for example, a New York court would not allow an attorney to enforce a contract provision giving him a minimum $25,000 fee after the client dropped the case. The judge ruled that it was unconscionable to impose that kind of fee on the client. The attorney was limited to suing for the reasonable value of the services he had actually provided before the client dropped the case.[1] Juries, even more so than judges, may be willing to reduce fees considered excessive or unreasonable. So if your attorney sues you for an unpaid bill and your defense is that the fees charged are outrageous, you may have better luck getting the fees reduced if your case is decided by a jury, not a judge.

In other cases, however, courts allow attorneys to charge huge fees for relatively small amounts of work, if the agreement calling for the fee was fair when the parties made it. In one instance, federal courts agreed that a law firm properly earned a $1 million fee for filing just one document.[2]

The original case involved a lawsuit between two multimillion-dollar corporations, IBM and Telex, in which Telex won a judgment for $259.5 million, and on its counterclaims, IBM won a judgment for $18.5 million. Telex's victory was reversed on appeal, however. Telex wanted to avoid bankruptcy and needed to convince the U.S. Supreme Court to reinstate the trial court's decision.

With very few exceptions, the U.S. Supreme Court picks and chooses what cases it hears. Telex hired the prestigious San Francisco law firm of Brobeck, Phleger & Harrison to file the request, called a Petition for Writ of Certiorari, with the Supreme Court. Telex and the lawyers agreed that Brobeck would receive an initial payment of $25,000, $1 million if they filed the writ on time and additional fees if Telex won at the Supreme Court.

Brobeck filed the writ on time, but Telex got cold feet because the risks of pursuing the case were so great. Without waiting to see if the Supreme Court would take the case, Telex settled with IBM. IBM agreed to drop its $18.5 million judgment and Telex agreed not to try to have the $259.5 million award reinstated. After settling, Telex thanked Brobeck, told them to keep the $25,000 but refused to pay more. Brobeck sued for the $1 million fee for filing the writ and won.

The key factor in the court's decision was that the agreement was reasonable at the time it was made. The fee was high, but Brobeck did not take unfair advantage of Telex. Telex was not ignorant of the terms of the agreement. There were no disguised unfair terms in small print. The court also looked at the results. It pointed out that IBM probably settled because it was threatened by the possibility that the Supreme Court would rule in favor of Telex. Although the fee was high, the court decided that Brobeck's work helped bring about the settlement and Telex was saved from bankruptcy.

Although you probably haven't agreed to pay a lawyer $1 million to file one paper for you, the point here is simple: If you agreed to pay some amount of money—as unreasonable as it may seem now—if your agreement was reasonable when you entered into it, a court would probably uphold your obligation to pay. Keep in mind that judges are lawyers—they almost always approve large fees unless they are way out of line (for example $700 per hour).

D. How to Question Your Bill

Legitimate mistakes and misunderstandings can occur in any context, lawyers' bills included. When you receive a questionable bill, your best approach is to contact your lawyer as soon as possible, especially if you are generally satisfied with his work and wish to continue the relationship. Who knows, it might be a clerical error which can be corrected immediately. Or maybe the lawyer has done more work than you are aware of, and the bill will make sense when he explains it to you.

If, you still believe the lawyer is charging too much, you will want to discuss and hopefully resolve the issue as quickly as possible. After hearing your point of view, your lawyer simply may agree to charge less; especially if you are a long-term client or a likely source of continued business, it is in his interest to resolve your complaint. Even if he refuses, it's likely that you'll clarify your expectations and goals. Or, you may decide to fire your lawyer, but at least the issue won't fester while the bill grows even bigger.

If a lot of money is at stake, you value the relationship and want to try to straighten things out, consider proposing mediation to your lawyer.

E.   When to Question Your Bill

Here are some common warning signs that your lawyer may be overbilling. In any of these situations, speak to your lawyer as soon as possible.

1. No Bill

Under the terms of many contracts—especially if you are paying by the hour—your lawyer should bill you regularly, usually monthly. If you don't get a bill, it typically means there hasn't been enough activity on your case during that period to justify sending a bill. But no news isn't always good news, and despite your lawyer's promise to bill monthly, it's also possible that he is letting several months of billable work accumulate, which means your next bill will be huge.

To avoid this possibility, insist on regular bills, even in months where the balance due is $0. This way you will know what is and isn't being done on your case. If a monthly bill seems too high, it gives you a chance to complain before the situation gets totally out of hand. If the lawyer hasn't done work on your case in six months, it gives you the chance to find out why.

2. New Fee Rate

Your fee agreement with your lawyer is a contract. Any changes in the terms of that contract should be agreed to by both of you. Put more bluntly, your lawyer should not raise fees without your agreement and advising you to consult a second attorney. If suddenly your bills reflect a increased hourly billing rate, a quick discussion is in order—you will want to insist that the rate be reduced to the amount you agreed to.

3. Unexpected Costs

Lawyers' bills are made up of two major components: professional fees and costs. Generally, a cost is any out-of-pocket expense which the lawyer incurred working on your case. Depending on what types of costs the lawyer passes through to you, these can include routine expenses like photocopying and telephone charges, or larger bills such as travel expenses and court reporters' fees. While costs might seem like they would be simple to compute, billing in this area is often abused and needs careful monitoring. Particular items to keep an eye on include:

- **Travel expenses.** Expect to reimburse your attorney for transportation, lodging and meals, but not more than what is necessary to get the job done. Questionable items include first class air fare, luxury hotels and bar tabs. Ask to see receipts and invoices for the expenses. If your lawyer won't give them to you voluntarily, you can probably get copies through the "discovery" process, if you sue. (See Section F.11.a, below.)

- **Charges to be split among several clients.** If your attorney is representing more than one party in your case, make sure you are paying only your share of the costs. Many costs should be split among the clients, while other costs will apply to only one client. For example, the cost of your deposition transcript should be applied to only your case, but the cost of the opposing party's deposition transcript should be split among you and the other clients represented by your lawyer in your case.

- **Clerical expenses.** Your attorney's fee itself should normally cover routine overhead expenses. There are occasions, however, when a case requires an extraordinary amount of secretarial or clerical support— for example, the sorting, identification and filing of hundreds, or even thousands, of documents. This might require the use of outside professional services which could be billed to your case as a reasonable cost.

  Most clients assume clerical services are included in a lawyer's regular fee. That's my practice, but in recent years some lawyers have tried to make an extra dollar by charging for such things as word processing, faxes and even a minimum cost for clerical work. If you are billed for these expenses, whether you should pay

YOU CHARGED ME
FOR A 25 HOUR DAY !!!

YOU SHOULD BE GRATEFUL.
OUR LAWYERS ARE SO SKILLED
THEY CAN TRANSCEND THE
TIME BARRIER.

them depends on what your contract says. If it doesn't specifically obligate you to pay extra for overhead items, protest the bill and refuse to pay this portion of it.

- **Supplies purchased for your case.** (See Tanya's Tip, below.)

Tanya's Tip: If You Paid for It, You Own It
Occasionally, costs include tangible items of evidence, such as photographs of an accident scene. For example, a few years ago my firm was representing a client in a rather odd motorcycle collision case. Because the case was going to be arbitrated in a fairly informal manner, we never went to the expense of having an engineer prepare a model of the accident scene, but we did buy a toy motorcycle and car to demonstrate the accident to the arbitrator. When the client picked up his settlement check, we gave him the toys as well. After all, he paid for them. I mention this because I recently saw a lawyer's bill which included the purchase of an $80 law book which the lawyer added to his office library. We suggested to the clients that they drop by the lawyer's office and pick up the book; after all, they paid for it.

4. Big Bills

Perhaps you want your lawyer to take an aggressive approach to your case and aren't surprised when you receive a fat bill. There is nothing wrong with a large bill—if it is justified. On the other hand, if you receive a bill much bigger than you expect, your lawyer is probably on course to spend big bucks on the case, and you can expect similar bills. Unless this is the approach you want to follow, quickly communicate your expectations to your attorney. If your lawyer explains that future bills will be just as large, or she cannot give you any estimate about the size of future bills, this is a good time to end your relationship.

5. Unfairly Divided Contingency Fee Bill

In most contingency fee cases, the only bill you'll ever receive usually arrives at the end when the case is settled or won. Typically, it works like this. The defendant (or, more likely, his insurance company), sends a check to your attorney's office. The check will be made payable to you and your attorney, meaning that both of you must sign it for it to be cashed. After you and your attorney sign it, your attorney will deposit it into her client trust account (see Chapter 3, Section J), figure out how much she gets and then write you a check for the balance along with a statement of all expenses. (This document is often called an *accounting* or a *settlement of account*.)

Unfortunately, this approach leaves you with no leverage because you have already endorsed the check. Far better to ask your attorney for a detailed record of where every dollar will go before you sign. Check it over carefully and question any unexpected items before you endorse the check.

CONTINGENCY FEE BILL EXAMPLE: John Hannah and Harriet Barbera were injured when a ski lift they were riding on stalled. After being stuck hanging on the lift for six hours, they were both treated for shock and frostbite. The case settled, after arbitration, for $175,000.

STATEMENT AND SETTLEMENT OF ACCOUNT

Total Recovery	$175,000.00
Less Attorney's Fees (40%)	< 70,000.00>
Subtotal	$105,000.00
Less Costs Incurred by Both Clients	
(see separate itemization)	< 2,104.18>
Total Net Settlement Available to Clients	$102,895.80

. . . .

One half to John Hannah	$ 51,477.90
Less Costs Incurred by John Hannah Only	
Med-Rex (medical records copying)	< 49.50>
Lien payment to Dr. Tagano	< 4,291.00>
Lien payment to Health Plan, Inc.	
$ 1,351.00 - $270.20 (20% compromise)	< 1,080.80>
Net total disbursement to **John Hannah**	**$ 46,026.60**

. . . .

One half to Harriet Barbera	$ 51,477.90
Less Costs Incurred by Harriet Barbera Only	
Lien payment to Dr. McCoy	< 2,041.00>
DeLastreet Reporting (Barbera deposition)	< 127.65>
Net total disbursement to	
Harriet Barbera	**$ 49,309.25**

Costs:

10/06/92	Filing fee	$ 182.00
03/02/93	256 copies @ $0.20/copy	51.20
03/11/93	Alco Graphix (copies and bind)	619.19
04/02/93	844 copies @ $0.20/copy	168.80
02/28/93	Rexis (legal research)	20.70
03/01/93	Travel	10.08
04/19/93	Payment for copying from opposing counsel	<251.52>
04/23/93	United Package Service	7.99
05/25/93	25 copies @ $0.20/copy	5.00
08/07/93	Confederated Express	9.00
09/03/93	Filing fee for motions	28.00
12/16/93	Golden Nugget Reporters (Deposition of Chang)	620.50
12/23/93	P. S. Courier	61.00
01/10/94	Reisa M. Hiller (Hearing Transcript)	34.00
05/17/94	Post Jury Fees	150.00
07/01/94	Branch & Sanchez, Inc. (Deposition of Wiener)	78.40
	Parking and tolls	8.00
	Transportation (133 miles @ $0.28/mile)	37.24
	In-house copies (1,323 copies @ $0.20/page)	264.60
	Total Costs	**$2,104.18**

Here are some tips on what to check for on an accounting.

- **Total recovery.** The first thing to check is the total recovery. You agreed to pay your attorney a percentage of your total recovery, but check your agreement to see how that term is defined. It typically includes the money you get from the defendant (or his insurance company) to compensate you for your injuries. Sometimes, but not always, it includes payments to compensate you for property damage. Rarely would it include payments to reimburse your insurance company for your medical expenses.

- **Lawyer's percentage.** Check that your lawyer is taking the agreed-upon percentage of the total recovery. Pay particular attention to the fact that many contingency fee contracts have a "step-up" clause. As discussed in Chapter 3, this means that your lawyer's percentage increases if a certain event occurs in the case. Where this step-up occurs can vary somewhat depending on your agreement, but it is typically when the case is set for arbitration or trial. For example, your contract might provide a 33% fee if settled before the case is assigned a trial date, and a 40% fee if settled after a trial or arbitration hearing is scheduled. If your attorney is taking the stepped-up fee, make sure that the event which triggered it actually occurred.

Clients sometimes accuse lawyers of deliberately delaying a settlement to collect the higher fee. In my experience, most lawyers would rather settle cases earlier so as to get their cut as soon as possible. Nevertheless, if your case settled within a few days or weeks after the event that triggered a higher fee but before the actual trial or arbitration occurred, bring it to your attorney's attention and question whether the higher fee is actually justified.

> **EXAMPLE:** Your attorney and the attorney for the other side have negotiated virtually all of the terms of your settlement. Your attorney agreed to draft the final settlement papers, but due to a busy schedule hasn't gotten around to it. While waiting for the papers to be sent to him, the court schedules the trial date. If your lawyer holds you to the letter of the agreement and demands the full 40% fee, you have good reason to complain.

- **Costs.** As specified in your agreement, your lawyer can legitimately subtract certain costs. These should be carefully itemized so that you can understand them. (See Section E.3, above.)

- **Liens.** A lien (in your lawsuit) is claim for payment by someone who provided you with a service related to your case. Most liens are claimed by medical providers and former attorneys. Usually, a lien comes about when you and your doctor, medical insurer or lawyer (or former lawyer) agree that payment will be deferred until your case is over, at which point the lien will be paid out of your recovery. It goes without saying that before you agree to settle your case, you will want to know who is claiming to be paid out of the proceeds and for how much.

Tanya's Tip: Reducing Liens

As explained in Chapter 3, Section J.1, doctors and other lienholders often agree to reduce the amount of their liens to help a case settle more quickly. They do this because they realize that if liens take all or most of a proposed settlement, you will surely reject it (and a certain recovery) and hope for a bigger recovery at trial (where there is a risk of total loss). If a medical provider agrees to reduce a lien, all savings should be passed on to you, not your lawyer. Unfortunately, I have seen a con game played on clients with lawyers pocketing the amount of the reduction. It's a shameful and fraudulent practice.

> *EXAMPLE: A lawyer convinces a doctor with a $6,000 lien to reduce it to $4,000. The lawyer, however, deducts the full $6,000 from the client's settlement without mentioning the $2,000 savings. She simply pockets the difference.*

If any medical providers or former lawyers have a lien in your case, ask to see copies of the checks sent to the providers or call the providers and find out how much they were paid. Then compare those amounts to what is on the accounting statement you receive.

- **Arithmetic.** Make sure you check the arithmetic. Even in these days of computers and number-crunching programs, mistakes happen.

F. Arbitrating Your Fee Dispute

An unhappy client who gets a large bill may decide not to pay it—after all, in his view the lawyer may not deserve even half of what he is asking. If an unhappy client is dunned repeatedly or is served with a lawsuit to collect the bill, she is likely to fight back by filing a malpractice lawsuit or a misconduct complaint against the lawyer.

Not surprisingly, lawyers have been motivated to set up processes to settle fee disputes before they escalate into a lawsuit. Occasionally, that may mean a mediation—a process in which a neutral third party, without any actual decision-making authority, tries to get the parties to reach an agreement acceptable to both.

More often, however, the alternative is arbitration. Arbitration is a process in which a neutral party hears evidence and makes a decision regarding a dispute. While arbitration is generally designed to be faster and less formal than a court trial, all arbitration procedures have some rules governing how each side can present evidence and question the other side. These rules govern what happens in any particular arbitration.

1. What Will the Arbitration Include?

For many clients, the shortcoming of fee arbitration is that it is too limited in scope to let you raise issues like incompetence, negligence or other misconduct. This is especially true of local bar association fee dispute programs, in which the arbitrator does not have the authority to hear other complaints. The only issue at the hearing will be whether your attorney performed the services for which you are billed.

In such a situation, the arbitrator might not be willing to consider the quality of the work, the results of the work or other issues related to how your case was handled, such as your claim of a conflict of interest, unprofessional conduct or negligence. Or even if the arbitrators do consider some or all of these issues, they will do so in the context of whether or not your lawyer's fee is appropriate. A claim that the lawyer's poor work or ethical violation caused you to lose your case normally won't be considered.

So before you agree to any fee arbitration process, make sure you understand exactly what issues can and cannot be raised in the process. If yours is a simple fee dispute, with no malpractice issues, you may decide to go ahead—particularly with nonbinding arbitration. (See Section F.4, below.) Otherwise, I advise against it. I have been contacted by many people who were shocked when they were not allowed to present evidence about their attorney's negligence or other misconduct at a fee arbitration hearing.

2. Is Fee Arbitration Required?

You might have already agreed to arbitrate your fee dispute. If you have a written contract with your lawyer, look to see if it has an arbitration clause. If so, study the language carefully. It may specify that fee disputes must be arbitrated. Or it may simply state that you and your attorney agree to arbitrate any dispute.

a. States in Which Fee Arbitration Is Mandatory for Lawyers

Alaska, California, the District of Columbia, Maine, New Jersey, North Carolina, South Carolina and Wyoming generally mandate that

attorneys submit their fee disputes to arbitration. In New Jersey, attorneys must submit fee disputes to arbitration, although clients still can take their complaints directly to court. Despite the claim of lawyers that this was discriminatory, the New Jersey law was upheld in federal court in 1990.[3]

The District of Columbia Bar Association requires all lawyers to submit a fee dispute to binding arbitration if the client requests it. In New York, a lawyer must arbitrate all fee disputes in matrimonial (family law) cases. In any state, fee arbitration may be required of an attorney if the client originally located the attorney through a lawyer referral agency. This is because the referral agency may have required the attorney to agree to arbitrate any dispute arising in a case referred by the agency.

In Alaska, California and New Jersey, an attorney must notify a client of her right to have a fee dispute arbitrated before the lawyer files a lawsuit. If the lawyer sues without first giving the client notice of that right, the client can have the lawsuit stayed—that is, suspended —and choose arbitration instead. North Carolina has a similar law, although it applies in only some counties.

b. States in Which Fee Arbitration Is Not Mandatory

In some states (other than the ones listed above), mandatory fee arbitration clauses are not legal. This is because your attorney, in her capacity as your fiduciary (trusted professional adviser), is ethically prohibited from presenting you with an agreement in which you waive your right to sue the attorney in court.

The background for this position is simple— federal and state constitutions give you the right to a jury trial in civil cases like contract disputes. When you agree to arbitration, you give up that right. Because you might be better off going to court, a lawyer acting as your fiduciary shouldn't stick an agreement under your nose containing an arbitration clause in which you agree to substitute compulsory arbitration for your day in court. (See Chapter 4, *Conflicts of Interests*.)

Despite the fact that mandatory arbitration clauses in lawyer-client agreements are often ethically questionable, lawyers increasingly insert them in their agreements. They argue with some plausibility that because arbitration is usually cheaper, faster and easier than a civil court trial, it's in everyone's best interest.

If you were not advised by your lawyer that you were giving up your right to a jury trial and that you should get an opinion from a different lawyer on the issue, you may be able to challenge the agreement. You can go to court to get an order (called an injunction) against allowing the arbitration to proceed. Another option is to ask the arbitrator to rule that the agreement is invalid.

3. Is Arbitration Possible If It's Not in Your Agreement?

Even if your agreement does not include an arbitration clause, you and your attorney can agree to arbitrate your dispute. Most states have voluntary fee arbitration programs, which allow either a lawyer or a client to suggest arbitration. And as mentioned above, a few states

STATE FEE ARBITRATION PROGRAMS

State	Type of Program	Participation	Arbitrators
Alabama	Local bar	Varies	Varies
Alaska	Statewide	Mandatory	Lawyers and lay people
Arizona	Statewide	Voluntary	Lawyers
Arkansas	No program	Not applicable	Not applicable
California	Statewide and local	Mandatory	Lawyers and lay people
Colorado	Statewide and local	Voluntary	Lawyers
Connecticut	Statewide	Voluntary	Lawyers and lay people
Delaware	Statewide	Voluntary	Lawyers and lay people
District of Columbia	Districtwide	Mandatory	Lawyers and lay people
Florida	Statewide and local	Voluntary	Lawyers and lay people
Georgia	Statewide	Voluntary	Lawyers and lay people
Hawaii	Statewide	Voluntary	Lawyers
Idaho	Statewide	Voluntary	Lawyers and lay people
Illinois	Statewide and local	Voluntary	Lawyers and lay people
Indiana	Local bar	Varies	Varies
Iowa	Local bar	Varies	Varies
Kansas	Local bar	Varies	Varies
Kentucky	Statewide	Voluntary	Lawyers and lay people
Louisiana	Statewide	Voluntary	Lawyers and lay people
Maine	Statewide	Mandatory	Lawyers and lay people
Maryland	Statewide and local	Voluntary	Lawyers
Massachusetts	Statewide and local	Voluntary	Lawyers and lay people
Michigan	Statewide	Voluntary	Lawyers
Minnesota	Local bar	Pilot program in St. Paul only	Varies
Mississippi	Statewide	Voluntary	Lawyers

STATE FEE ARBITRATION PROGRAMS

State	Type of Program	Participation	Arbitrators
Missouri	Statewide	Voluntary	Lawyers and lay people
Montana	Statewide	Voluntary	Lawyers and lay people
Nebraska	Statewide	Voluntary	Varies
Nevada	Statewide	Voluntary	Lawyers and lay people
New Hampshire	Statewide	Voluntary	Lawyers
New Jersey	Statewide and local	Mandatory	Lawyers and lay people
New Mexico	Statewide	Voluntary	Lawyers and lay people
New York	Local bar	Varies	Varies
North Carolina	Local bar	Mandatory	Varies
North Dakota	Statewide	Voluntary	Lawyers and lay people
Ohio	Local bar	Varies	Varies
Oklahoma	Local bar	Varies	Varies
Oregon	Statewide	Voluntary	Lawyers
Pennsylvania	Local bar	Varies	Varies
Rhode Island	Statewide	Voluntary	Lawyers
South Carolina	Statewide	Mandatory	Lawyers
South Dakota	No program	Not applicable	Not applicable
Tennessee	Local bar	Varies	Varies
Texas	Local bar	Varies	Varies
Utah	Statewide	Voluntary	Lawyers, judges and lay people
Vermont	Statewide	Voluntary	Lawyers
Virginia	Local bar	Varies	Varies
Washington	Statewide	Voluntary	Lawyers and lay people
West Virginia	No program	Not applicable	Not applicable
Wisconsin	Statewide and local	Voluntary	Lawyers
Wyoming	Statewide	Mandatory	Lawyers

require an attorney to take a fee dispute to
arbitration before filing a lawsuit, while still
making participation by the client voluntary.
Other states simply require the attorney to
notify you that you have the right to choose
arbitration.

In Washington, D.C., a legal malpractice
claim can be arbitrated along with the fee
dispute if both parties agree.[4] Attorneys have
consented to arbitration in about one-third of
the malpractice cases filed with the program.
But this has been pretty terrible for clients.
During one recent year, all of the cases that
reached the hearing and award stage (some
cases in which the parties agreed to arbitration
settled before the hearing) were decided in favor of the attorney.

4. Is Arbitration Binding?

Arbitration can be binding or nonbinding.
Binding arbitration means you and you lawyer
are bound by the arbitration decision—neither
of you can appeal. An arbitration clause in an
attorney-client fee agreement usually calls for
binding arbitration. In it, you give up the right
to sue in civil court and the right to have your
case decided by a jury. In exchange you will get
a quick, informal and final result. But as discussed just above, such a clause may not be
legal, and you may be able to reject any arbitration unless it is nonbinding.

Nonbinding arbitration means that either
side can reject the arbitrator's decision and file
(or continue with) a lawsuit. Arbitration by a
local or state bar's fee arbitration panel is usually nonbinding. But nonbinding arbitration

still has rules—one of the most important being
how and when you can reject an award you find
unsatisfactory. Often, if you fail to take certain
steps within ten-30 days, the decision becomes
binding and final. For example, to reject a nonbinding arbitration decision in some states, you
have to file a lawsuit within 30 days.

In some states, by contrast, you need to take
affirmative steps to make a nonbinding award
binding. For example, you may be required to
file a copy of the arbitration decision with a
local court along with a formal written motion
to have the decision made into a court judgment.

 Tanya's Tip: If Arbitration Is Nonbinding, Why Bother?

*An arbitration proceeding which produces a non-
binding award could be a waste of time—but not
necessarily. For starters, it will give you an opportunity to organize your case and have a practice
run before deciding whether or not to sue. And
there is always a chance that you and the lawyer
will either settle the matter during the process or
accept the arbitrator's award.*

5. Who Serves as Arbitrators?

In most situations in which you arbitrate your
dispute voluntarily, state or local bar associations have set up fee dispute arbitration panels.
Most states have statewide programs, although
in about a dozen states, the program is admin-
istered by the local bar association.

In 20 states and Washington, D.C., non-
attorneys may volunteer to be arbitrators.
Otherwise, all arbitration panels are drawn

from pools of volunteer lawyers. If state law allows, steer clear of all-lawyer panels. Having lawyers as arbitrators is not uniformly bad because many lawyers who volunteer to arbitrate fee disputes have a sense of public responsibility and a genuine interest in weeding out unfair practices. Nevertheless, the risk of insider favoritism—of having the reasonableness of a lawyer's fee judged by other lawyers—is unacceptable for two reasons.

First, the arbitrator may be friends with the attorney. Second, even if they aren't friends, the arbitrator, who makes her living as an attorney collecting fees, is likely to be predisposed to the lawyer's point of view.

If you complain to your lawyer or a state lawyer regulatory group about your lawyer's fee, and you are told that a state or local bar association arbitration panel is your only choice, know that it isn't necessarily. Unless your attorney refuses to agree, you and your attorney can agree to have any mutually agreed-upon person serve as the arbitrator. Insist that someone other than a local attorney play this role and suggest any of the following as a way to find an arbitrator:

- **American Arbitration Association.** AAA has over 30 branch offices in the U.S. Check with directory assistance in the largest nearby city or send a letter requesting the phone number of the closest office to AAA, 140 W. 51st Street, New York, NY 10020.
- **Telephone directory.** Look under Arbitration, Mediation or Dispute Resolution.
- **Bar associations.** Ask for private referrals to lawyers who do arbitration.

- **Court administrators.** Many county courts now have dispute resolution referral panels. Don't forget to call the closest federal court if your local county court has no referral.
- **Retired judges.** You can probably get a referral to a private judge—or to a group that employs private judges as mediators and arbitrators—from the bar association or a court administrator.

6. What Does Arbitration Cost?

If you are in a fee dispute with your lawyer, you've already learned that justice usually has a price. Fees for private dispute resolution can be high. Agencies usually use one or two methods to establish fees: by the hour or a percentage of the amount in dispute. Be a smart shopper. If the amount in dispute is a lot, but the situation is straightforward, go for an hourly rate. On the other hand, if the amount in dispute is small but the situation is complex, choose a provider which charges a low fee, such as 10% of the amount in dispute. Otherwise, you are going to be very angry if you sit in an office for six hours paying an hourly rate for an arbitrator while your former attorney meticulously examines every witness.

Generally, arbitration provided by bar associations is at no cost to the client other than a small administrative filing fee. Even that often can be waived if your income is low.

If your agreement calls for private arbitration or you voluntarily choose private arbitration, you will have to pay for it. Private arbitration organizations usually charge based on the

HOW DO I FIND A NEUTRAL ARBITRATOR I CAN TRUST?

In selecting an arbitrator, you will be faced with the fact that most are lawyers or former lawyers. You usually can't avoid this. So how can you be sure that the arbitrator won't have a personal or professional bias? The truth is that you can't, but you can take some preventative steps.

- Ask the prospective arbitrator (in writing) to disclose any previous personal or professional connections with the other party. (Send a copy of your letter to the other side.)
- Obtain and review the arbitrator's qualifications (usually a resume or curriculum vitae is available). Look for experience and professional training in arbitration.
- Ask for references—the names and phone numbers of legal consumers who brought their disputes to this arbitrator. The arbitrator can contact former claimants and ask for their permission to disclose identities to you.

- Look for an arbitrator located outside your immediate geographical area. This does not guarantee that the attorneys don't know each other, but it reduces the chances that your outcome will be affected by past, or potential future, business connections.
- Select an arbitrator who practices (or practiced) a different kind of law than the type your former attorney practices. This will reduce the chances of professional connections between the arbitrator and your former lawyer, but it means that your arbitrator will be less knowledgeable about how cases like yours are handled.

If you cannot bring yourself to trust a lawyer as an arbitrator, and your former lawyer won't agree to a non-lawyer arbitrator, consider using a three-person arbitration panel. You and your former lawyer each choose one arbitrator and they select the third. The only other way to put the decision-making power into the hands of non-lawyers is to sue the lawyer and take the case to a jury.

amount being disputed or by the hour. Either way, you may well conclude it is too expensive unless the amount in dispute is large. But if your alternative is going to court to fight over an unpaid bill, private arbitration will usually cost less.

To get an idea of how much a particular arbitration is likely to cost, carefully review the arbitration rules of the organization. Typically, the party requesting arbitration will pay the fee to begin the arbitration. After that, unless you have an agreement or a local rule which determines who pays for the arbitration, you and the lawyer will probably split the fee equally.

7. Who Pays the Arbitration Bill?

Arbitrators sometimes have the power to decide who ultimately pays the cost of the arbitration. In your written materials and oral presentation, be sure to ask the arbitrators to "award you the costs of the arbitration"— meaning that the lawyer would pay it all. If the rules permit it, arbitrators usually require the losing party to pay the fee if they find that the loser acted unreasonably in the dispute. To avoid the risk of losing the arbitration and having to pay the entire arbitrator's fee, don't volunteer to participate unless the bill will be split or it won't cost you anything.

8. Challenging the Form of Arbitration

If your fee agreement provides for private arbitration and you were not advised by your attorney that you were giving up the right to a cheaper arbitration procedure provided by state

law (such as a bar association program), you can very likely challenge the enforcement of that provision. You have two choices in challenging the arbitration. You can file a lawsuit in court challenging the arbitration provision in your agreement or you can simply raise it with the arbitrator.

More than likely, you'll want to raise it with the arbitrator. Going to court to challenge an arbitration provision is frequently complex and expensive and very difficult for a nonlawyer to handle himself or herself.

When challenging the provision with the arbitrator, be sure to raise it at the beginning and at every opportunity thereafter. Include your protest in the first paper you file, all subsequent papers and with the arbitrators when you meet with them. Emphasize that the arbitration provision in the agreement should not be enforced because your attorney had a conflict of interest (see Chapter 4) when he asked you to sign the agreement without advising you that you were giving up your rights to a jury trial and to appeal. Ask the arbitrators to rule on this issue before hearing the merits of your case, but be prepared for the arbitrators to rule against you or to have you proceed with the case while they consider the issue.

If your attorney rejects your challenge and insists on taking you to expensive private arbitration, file your fee dispute with the bar arbitration panel anyway and report your lawyer to the state lawyer regulatory agency for violating conflict of interest restrictions. (See Chapter 8.)

Challenging an award after binding arbitration is likely to be a losing battle unless you can show that the arbitrator committed fraud or had a conflict of interest, or that the arbitration agreement was invalid. The trend is to uphold arbitration agreements and enforce arbitrators' awards. Nevertheless, if you think you were tricked into signing an arbitration agreement in the first place, or that the arbitrator was prejudiced or grossly unfair to you, you can file a petition in court asking a judge to issue an order overturning the arbitrator's award. You should simultaneously file a lawsuit against your lawyer based on the fee dispute. Be aware of the risks. Depending on the terms of your arbitration agreement and your local law, if you lose in court you will probably have to pay your lawyer interest, additional attorney fees and her legal costs.

9. Can I Maintain Privacy in Arbitration?

Arbitration is private. It often happens in a lawyer's office or conference room of the arbitration company. By contrast, only in exceptional circumstances (not involving lawyer fee disputes) are court trials and files closed to the public. By suing, you make your dispute public, which means most details of your case will be available to anyone interested, including the media. Unless there is a specific agreement that the arbitration remain private and confidential nothing prevents one side or the other from talking about it. Because arbitration hearings don't take place in public, however, they rarely generate mediate attention or are watched by gawkers.

Before you worry too much about losing your privacy, consider that your lawyer is probably far more concerned about privacy than you are. In a small city or county, a lawyer might be embarrassed to appear as a defendant in a court action involving fees, especially if you also claim malpractice. This is true—no matter what the population of your city or county—if the lawyer is newsworthy or has political ambitions. For example, in a recent election for city attorney in a major U.S. city, one candidate included his opponent's record of malpractice claims and fee disputes in his campaign literature.

10. How Do I Get Started With Arbitration?

The arbitration process starts by one party filing a petition or claim, and if required, paying a filing fee. This is similar to starting a lawsuit. You must describe your claim and the basis for it, and give notice to the other side. The procedures are in the arbitration rules published by the bar association or private arbitration group you use. Usually, you can notify the other side by mail; personal service by a process server is rarely required.

The person filing the petition or claim is called the petitioner or claimant, which is similar to being a plaintiff. The other side is generally referred to as the respondent.

11. How Do I Prepare for Arbitration?

Make sure you have a copy of the arbitration rules and understand the deadlines for filing papers and conducting any discovery in the form of written questions, requests to produce documents or oral questions to learn about your opponent's case. If the award will be nonbinding, you'll also need to know how to either reject or accept it.

a. Gather Your Evidence

The arbitrator needs evidence to make a decision. In a fair hearing, the winner is the party who produces the best evidence designed to prove her case. Some evidence will be in the form of your testimony and the testimony of the lawyer. But because this may amount to little more than your word against hers, you will want to produce as much additional evidence as possible to convince the arbitrator that you are right. Other evidence will likely include the following:

- your written fee agreement with the lawyer
- letters or memos discussing the attorney's fee or legal costs
- canceled checks indicating that you have paid bills
- bills from the lawyer—particularly if these are not itemized
- any statement of account (see sample and explanation in Section E.5, above)
- client ledger card—if the bookkeeping is done manually, your attorney should have a ledger showing fees, costs and payments made providing a history of billing and payments, and
- printout of any computerized information related to your fees—your bill was probably computer-generated using a billing or spreadsheet program; get a printout of all costs, hours, bills, payments and credits.

If you don't have any of these, you are probably entitled to get copies from your lawyer. Consult the arbitration rules regarding "discovery." Discovery procedures provide for the exchange of evidence and information prior to the arbitration.

b. Organize Your Evidence

Arbitrators are more likely to read documents which are easy to find. A good way to organize them is to attach a numbered tab (just start with 1) to each piece of your evidence. Then make a cover sheet listing each item, with its tab number, and attach the cover to the evidence.

JANE SHUMOTO'S LIST OF EVIDENCE

Contract dated July 1, 19xx—indicates the fee agreement.

Letter from Martin Delgado (attorney) dated July 28, 19xx—confirms term of fee agreement.

Bill from attorney dated October 1, 19xx—shows bill is more than agreed amount.

Check to attorney (#2234) dated October 15, 19xx—shows payment consistent with fee agreement.

Etc.

c. Submit Any Required Documents

Check the rules of arbitration about evidence. Sometimes, you must give copies of all documents to the arbitrator and the other side several days or even weeks before the hearing. Failing to do this could mean that the arbitrator will not consider your evidence.

Have at least two extra copies of every document you intend to use. Give one to the arbitrator and one to the other side.

d. Arrange for Your Witnesses

Testimony from witnesses is not easy to organize. Even witnesses testifying for you have to be reminded to show up at the hearing. Check the arbitration rules to see if the arbitrator has the power to issue an order (called a subpoena) ordering your witnesses to appear at the hearing. If you are asking "unfriendly" witnesses to testify on your behalf (such as the attorney's law clerk with whom you had a discussion about the fee), you'll definitely want to have the arbitrator issue a subpoena ordering that person to show up. Even friendly witnesses may need a subpoena to get the time off from work.

e. Don't Contact the Arbitrator

A basic rule of arbitration is that neither party should communicate with the arbitrator before the hearing. An administrative staff person or secretary in the arbitrator's office should be able to answer your questions. If that person cannot, you should not attempt to talk to the actual arbitrator unless the other side participates or is present.

12. How Is the Hearing Conducted?

Although not as formal as a trial, arbitration should be taken just as seriously and the arbitrator should be given the same respect as a judge. Let the arbitrator set the level of formality or informality. If in doubt, refer to the arbitrator as "your honor."

Unlike a trial, there is usually no court reporter or tape recording system to record what goes on. Some arbitrators let the hearing be taped if you bring your own equipment, but you will probably have to agree to provide the other side with a copy.

Generally, the arbitrator will discuss the rules with you and your former lawyer before letting you present evidence. If you aren't clear about what is happening, now is the time to ask. The arbitrator can provide some guidance, but cannot step out of the neutral role and give you legal advice.

Some arbitrators require that you submit a written statement (called a brief) before, at or after the hearing. Check the arbitration rules. If they are silent, ask the arbitrator's staff ahead of time to find out. A brief should cover the same points you will present at your hearing, except on paper. Explain what the disagreement is and what your position is. Describe the evidence which supports your case and attach copies of all documents. Finally, tell the arbitrators what decision you would like them to reach.

Normally, an arbitration hearing follows the same format as a trial. (See Sidebar.) Some arbitrators, however, don't follow a court-like scenario, and instead ask questions in an effort to isolate the main issues in dispute.

Try to make your case presentation unfold like a story. If you wrote a brief (summary of your case) for the arbitrator, use it to guide you. Otherwise, make a simple outline of what you want to present and check off each item as you present it.

PRESENTING YOUR CASE IN ARBITRATION

Normally, your case will proceed as follows—tell, show and tell again:

1. **Opening statement:** The best strategy is to assume the arbitrators know nothing about the case. Your job is to educate them. Try to make your opening statement simple, direct and specific. Tell the arbitrators what you are going to prove and how you are going to prove it. Make it chronological—for example, "My agreement with my attorney was that he would charge $175 per hour and not exceed 15 hours of work without my authorization. A letter dated January 22, 19xx, will prove that. On March 9, 19xx, I received a bill for 28 hours of work. I will present that bill as evidence."

2. **Presentation:** Now you must show the actual proof of your case. When you present your case, try to follow the same chronology you used in your opening statement and your evidence list. Present your evidence and call your witnesses one at a time.

3. **Closing statement:** Finally, tell the arbitrator what you have shown and how you have shown it. Go over the evidence again and point out the significant points each piece of evidence proves. "The fee agreement, Exhibit 1, shows what our agreement was. Mrs. Garibaldi testified that my attorney was out of the country on the date he billed me for a court appearance in Exhibit 2." Then sum it all up and tell the arbitrator how you want her to decide the case.

For more help on representing yourself at an arbitration hearing, take a look at *Represent Yourself in Court*, by Paul Bergman and Sara Berman-Barrett (Nolo Press). The book is written for people representing themselves in a court trial; however, it applies equally to arbitration hearings.

Fact	Witness	Evidence	Check when done
Attorney promised to handle may case for $500 flat fee	Me	$500 canceled check (#8901)	
Attorney sent me a bill for $1,000		Bill of February 21, 19xx	
Attorney explained at March 11, 19xx, meeting that case was more complicated than expected so he charged more than he said he would	Spouse		
Attorney overcharged me for costs	Process Server	Ledger card and bill showing charge of $50 for service of papers	
		Process server's actual bill of $35	
Attorney sent a new fee agreement for services to be billed at $250 per hour		New fee agreement dated March 29, 19xx	
I fired the attorney and hired a second one, who finished the case for $2,500		Letter firing first attorney dated April 13, 19xx	
		Bills from second attorney dated May 1, 19xx, June 1, 19xx, July 1, 19xx	

As mentioned, you will need to be prepared to make an opening and closing statement. Your opening statement should explain why you filed (or agreed to) the arbitration and what you intend to prove. Your documents and witnesses, as well as your own testimony should then attempt to prove every point you made in your opening statement. Your closing statement should remind the arbitrator what you set out to prove, how you proved it with evidence and what decision you want the arbitrator to make.

13. When Will I Get the Decision?

Arbitrators rarely give their decisions at the hearing. Instead, you will be notified by mail—normally anytime from a few days to a few months after your hearing. Even before you receive the decision, be prepared for your next step by knowing what you must do to reject or accept the decision.

14. Summary: Should I Arbitrate or Sue?

Is arbitration quicker, cheaper, better? Generally it is quicker and usually less expensive. Whether it is better depends upon your case. There is no certain way to determine exactly which process fits your situation, but reviewing the following chart may help you make a choice.

CHOOSING A METHOD TO RESOLVE YOUR FEE DISPUTE

My Situation	Mediation	Binding Arbitration	Nonbinding Arbitration	Small Claims Court
I can't afford to hire another lawyer.		✓	✓	✓
I want privacy.	✓	✓	✓	
My former lawyer doesn't want publicity, but I want the proceeding out in the open.				✓
I want to get this over with.		✓	✓	
I want to keep all other options open to me.	✓		✓	
The amount the lawyer claims I owe is small.		✓	✓	✓
I can't afford arbitration.				✓
I am intimidated by formal, public proceedings.	✓	✓	✓	
I need to educate myself more about this process.	✓		✓	
I don't mind paying an arbitrator just to get this over with.		✓	✓	
I want to work out this problem and continue to work with this lawyer.	✓			
I don't trust another lawyer or a judge to see my side of the dispute.	✓			
This dispute is more about personal issues (trust, respect, communication, courtesy) than about fees.	✓			

MEDIATION: A BETTER WAY?

Most lawyers and clients would agree that the common forms of dispute resolution used today, lawsuits and arbitration, represent enormous progress over previous methods such as challenging your opponent to a duel or having a gunfight down at the corral. Even so, our contemporary models are still competitive and even combative. In that atmosphere, the party that can command the most resources has an edge.

Mediation offers a different perspective. A mediator has no power to impose a decision. The parties retain the power to resolve the dispute cooperatively. A mediator offers expertise in reaching the essence of the dispute. The role of the mediator is to listen to the parties and to reflect back the positions so they can see both positions more clearly. A mediator also acts as a "translator" when the parties speak different "languages." The classic example of this language barrier arises between a person who is rigidly logical and someone who is emotionally volatile. The goal is to reach an agreement which both sides find acceptable. See the chart which precedes this sidebar for some examples of when mediation can be the best choice.

G. Suing

If you decide that arbitration or mediation aren't right for you (and you're not forced into arbitration), your only option if you want to be proactive in resolving your fee dispute is to sue. (Your other option is to wait to see if your lawyer sues you.) In every state, you can sue in the regular formal court, or if the amount at stake is small enough, in your state's small claims court. (Most state's small claims court limits are between $2,000 and $7,500.)

Going to small claims court is often a very viable option as compared to having your dispute considered by a local fee arbitration panel. Because small claims is a court like any other, you can raise issues other than that your attorney charged too much, such as your attorney's negligence or fraud. In fact, if you choose small claims court, it's wise to include all possible legal claims in your complaint. Otherwise, you might be giving up the right to raise them later.

Small claims is not appropriate for a dispute with your lawyer about an *unpaid* fee. These courts generally can only make money awards and do not have the power to make a ruling that you do not have to pay a bill. That type of case is called a declaratory relief action and most small claims courts do not have the power to rule on those kinds of cases. Instead, you normally have to pay the bill and sue for a refund, or hope that your former attorney sues you for an unpaid bill.

Generally, you will find small claims to be less formal and less expensive than arbitration. In theory, it may be more public than arbitration (because court filings are public records), but very few people ever pay attention to small claims court filings. Your budget, your stage-fright and your desire for privacy may dictate your choice.

If you don't qualify for small claims court—perhaps the amount at stake is way over your court's limit or you don't want to pay the bill and sue for a refund—you must sue in regular civil court. The rules applicable to a fee dispute won't be substantially different from any other lawsuit. But one thing might surprise you—even if you file a lawsuit, your court might order your case to be arbitrated. This type of arbitration is not much different from the arbitration described in Section F, although it

might be more formal. In this arbitration, however, you present all issues raised in your lawsuit—the fee dispute and the malpractice claim.

Court-ordered arbitration usually results in a nonbinding decision, but that decision will become a binding court judgment unless one party files a request with the court to continue with the lawsuit. Again, read the rules of the arbitration.

H. A Fee Dispute Strategy Guide

Let me summarize. Assuming you disagree with your lawyer's bill and the two of you can't resolve it informally, what specifically should you do? This will depend on who starts the proceedings.

⚠️ **Malpractice Claims and Fee Disputes**
If you have both a malpractice claim and a fee dispute, review Chapter 9 and incorporate your malpractice claim into your fee dispute.

1. Your Former Attorney Demands You Pay the Fees

Is fee arbitration mandatory—that is, does your state require that your attorney submit to fee arbitration or inform you of the option to do so before suing?

Yes: If you prefer arbitration, ask for it when you are notified of your right to do so.

No: If you prefer arbitration, and neither the law nor the contract require it, propose voluntary arbitration.

If you have a choice, this is the time to opt for binding or nonbinding arbitration, or even to attempt mediation. See the chart, above, in Section F.14, Should I Arbitrate or Sue? for some guidelines.

2. Your Former Attorney Sues You for Fees

Is there an arbitration clause in the contract?

Yes: Assuming it binds your lawyer (see Section F.4, above) and you want to arbitrate, ask the court to "stay" the lawsuit and send the dispute to arbitration. If you don't want to arbitrate the dispute, respond to the lawsuit by filing an answer or other response.

No: If you prefer arbitration, ask the court to "stay" the lawsuit and send the dispute to arbitration. The court should not let your lawyer sue you if your state or your contract requires arbitration. If you would just as well fight the case in court, do nothing.

⚠ Is it Too Late for Arbitration?

If you have already filed a lawsuit against the attorney, you may have given up the right to submit to or be notified of arbitration.

3. You Challenge Your Former Attorney Over Fees

Is there an arbitration clause in the contract?
Yes:
- If you prefer arbitration, start arbitration proceedings.
- If you don't want to arbitrate, look to see if the arbitration clause is binding. (See Section F.4, above.) If it isn't, sue.

No:
- Check with the local and state bar associations to see if the attorney is required to arbitrate.
- Propose an agreement to arbitrate anyway.

Endnotes

[1] *Gross v. Russo*, 351 N.Y.S.2d 355 (N.Y. 1974).

[2] *Brobeck, Phleger & Harrison v. Telex Corp.*, 602 F.2d 866 (9th Cir. 1979).

[3] *Guralnick v. Supreme Court of New Jersey*, 747 F. Supp. 1109 (D.N.J. 1990).

[4] See *Resolving Disputes Over Attorneys' Fees: The Role of ADR*, by Alan Scott Rau, 46 Southern Methodist University Law Review 2049, n. 157 (Summer 1993).

■

Chapter 8

FILING A COMPLAINT WITH YOUR LAWYER DISCIPLINE AGENCY

Each state has a system of attorney oversight, including a discipline system, which, at least in theory, is designed to keep attorneys in line. If you hire an attorney and conclude at the end of your case that your attorney did not serve your interests properly, this may motivate you to file a complaint with your state attorney disciplinary agency. Alternatively, if you are currently involved in a malpractice or fee dispute with your attorney, you may be able to gain leverage by reporting him to your state attorney disciplinary agency.

The effectiveness of the disciplinary systems varies from state to state. All have been justifiably criticized as being run by and for attorneys, not the consuming public. Increasing public awareness and outcry at the large numbers of complaints that go ignored, however, has led a number of states to make at least some improvements to their attorney disciplinary system. Today, if your complaint has merit, it will be taken somewhat seriously in many states, and the very fact that you have put it on record is likely to prompt some lawyers to attempt to resolve the problem to your satisfaction.

A. What Conduct Does an Attorney Discipline Agency Regulate?

When making a complaint to a state disciplinary agency, it is important to frame it in a way that will grab the attention of the employee who initially investigates your complaint. To best do this, you need to understand the types of attorney conduct about which regulators are most concerned. State disciplinary agencies generally focus on intentional attorney misconduct such as stealing client funds, or on incompetence induced by drug or alcohol abuse. They very rarely prosecute or discipline lawyers for garden variety incompetence, instead forcing you to file a malpractice lawsuit in such a situation.

When to Complain:

• The attorney is stealing your money.
• The attorney has just been convicted of a crime.
• The attorney hasn't returned your calls for an extended period.
• The attorney did not show up for trial or other court matter and had no valid excuse.
• The attorney talked you into an unfair business deal or one in her self-interest (such as buying her property or signing over your bonus to her).
• The attorney is abusing alcohol or drugs.
• The attorney took your money but did no work.

When Not to Bother to Complain:

• The attorney is not working fast enough.
• The attorney is slow to return calls.
• The attorney communicates with you only through a paralegal or secretary.
• The attorney was criticized by a judge or another lawyer for poor preparation.
• The attorney was negligent in handling your case with the result that you lost money or important rights.
• The attorney's hourly rate is too expensive.
• The attorney lost your case.

Again, it is crucial to understand that attorney disciplinary agencies have traditionally been interested in only truly bad behavior on the part of lawyers, such as stealing or completely abandoning a client. They generally don't care about stupid, careless or mistake-prone lawyers. Or put even more bluntly, if an incompetent lawyer screws up repeatedly to the serious detriment of clients, the agency won't intervene unless someone can show that the lawyer is abusing drugs or alcohol or is obviously mentally impaired. Of course, this is ridiculous.

It is fair to ask: What's the point of licensing and regulating lawyers if you don't even try to protect consumers by weeding out incompetent practitioners? Even those who cause their client devastating and highly unfair losses? Sadly, there is no decent answer. The lawyer discipline system historically has been designed to protect the profession, not the public. Lawyers claim that consumers are protected by their right to file a malpractice lawsuit, a claim that most objective observers consider ludicrous given the difficulty and expense of pursuing a malpractice case. (Chapter 9 covers suing your former attorney.)

There is one situation in which incompetent attorneys who are not also thieves, drunk, drugged or mentally impaired possibly may be disciplined. At least some state discipline agencies may act if they find that an attorney took on legal work that he clearly did not have the skills to handle. This is because state rules of professional responsibility generally require an attorney to have the skills necessary to handle the legal matters he agrees to work on. If

he doesn't (for example an attorney who handles criminal cases accepts a personal injury matter), he must get some relevant training or associate himself with a lawyer experienced in the field.

As potentially useful as this rule sounds, a discipline agency rarely takes action when an unqualified lawyer screws up. Because attorneys are not required to take specialist examinations and are authorized to handle cases in many different areas of law, regulators feel that as long as a lawyer has passed the state bar examination, she is qualified to take on any type of case. Logically, this is nonsense, given that law is becoming highly specialized and increasingly more difficult for someone to work in as a generalist. Nevertheless, only if you can show that the lawyer botched a case way outside of his normal area of expertise might a discipline agency step in.

WHO REGULATES LAWYERS?

Most lawyer disciplinary bodies are run by a state agency. In some states, such as New York and Colorado, that agency is the state courts. In other states, including California and Pennsylvania, the attorneys' professional (bar) association disciplines its own. Still other states, like Michigan and Minnesota, have established a specific state agency to invoke discipline. In a handful of states, such as New Jersey, local ethics committees administer lawyer discipline. But no matter who regulates lawyers in your state, one thing is sure: the overwhelming majority of the people doing the regulating will be lawyers, a fact that goes a long way in explaining why all state agencies tend to see attorney discipline cases from the point of view of the lawyer, not the consumer.

In recent years, lawyer regulators have been under pressure to clean up the profession. While some positive steps have been taken in some states, on the whole discipline is still lax. For this reason, if you plan to complain to your state's (or a local) attorney discipline agency, it's a good idea to first browse through your state's rules of professional responsibility (see Chapter 4) and phrase your complaint in language that will be most likely to get the agency's attention.

For example, lawyer regulators get angry when they hear that an attorney has abandoned a client, but are far less concerned if a busy lawyer hasn't returned a client's phone calls for a few weeks. So if your attorney has not communicated with your for an extended period and you have tried to deal with the problem following the suggestions in Chapter 2, your complaint should say something like this: "My attorney has consistently failed to communicate with me over a long period of time, and as a result I feel abandoned."

Similarly, if you expected your attorney to accompany you in court for a hearing, but she never showed up and didn't have a good excuse, your complaint would be more likely to grab the attention of the disciplinary investigator if you state "My attorney's failure to show up at my preliminary hearing on July 12, 19xx, and his failure to return my subsequent phone calls has led me to the conclusion that my lawyer has abandoned me."

COMPLEX CASES AND BIG FIRM LAWYERS

Most lawyer discipline agencies will not take on complicated matters or cases involving lawyers at large law firms. Rather, investigations tend to focus on lawyers who work on their own or in small offices and are accused of minor transgressions or something easy to prove—such as keeping inadequate trust fund records. (Chapter 3 has information on trust funds.) And if that wasn't enough protection for lawyers, discipline systems contain all sorts of procedural rules which put the rights of attorneys to protect their reputations and practices ahead of your right to fast and meaningful action.

B. Has Your Attorney Been Previously Disciplined?

If you're considering filing a complaint against a lawyer, you may be interested in finding out whether anyone else has done so. If others have complained for the same or similar conduct, you may be able to convince a lawyer disciplinary agency that the attorney is engaging in a pattern or practice of conduct that warrants its intervention. Unfortunately, you probably won't be able to find out who else has filed a complaint because in virtually all states, complaint records are kept secret. In fact, in many states, you won't even be able to find out whether your lawyer has ever been disciplined.

Typically, state agencies will tell you only if a lawyer has been seriously disciplined—such as being disbarred or suspended—but not if lesser (and more common) discipline has been taken, such as a private reprimand. Also, most states won't say whether a complaint has been filed if the matter is still pending. So, for example, in New Jersey, where it typically takes five years to disbar a lawyer and where pending complaints are kept secret, getting the discipline record against your attorney won't usually be of much help unless discipline was imposed more than five years back.

There are a few exceptions to this rule. In Oregon—perhaps the most consumer friendly state when it comes to regulating lawyers—you can get the following information over the phone about an attorney:

- the number of complaints that have been made against a lawyer
- when they were made, and

- the disposition of the complaints—be it a dismissal, reprimand, suspension or disbarment.

If you want additional information in Oregon, such as the nature of the complaints, you can set up an appointment with the Oregon State Bar to look at the attorney's file, or you can have the attorney's file copied and sent to you at your expense.

Both Florida and West Virginia allow access to information if the disciplinary agency decides to prosecute the attorney for violating ethical rules, but not if the agency drops the matter. Most states allow access to information only if and after discipline has been imposed. In a handful of states, including Iowa and New York, there is no access to attorney discipline records except in limited situations, such as when an attorney requests records about himself or herself. This hostility to consumer access is best exemplified by the situation in California a few years ago. The state attorney regulatory agency obtained a toll-free phone number for complaints, but then kept the number unlisted. When asked why, bar officials responded that they feared getting too many calls if they listed the number.

What this amounts to is that while it's good to try and check on a lawyer's previous discipline record, chances are you'll have to write up your complaint without having the lawyer's complete discipline history. If you do find a record of discipline—especially for conduct similar to what you're complaining about—definitely mention the prior discipline in your complaint. If your lawyer has seriously breached an ethical obligation more than once, the more likely it is the discipline agency will do something. Of course, if your investigation reveals extensive prior discipline against your attorney, you'll also probably want to end your relationship immediately. (See Chapter 5.)

If the discipline agency sees a pattern of extensive complaints against an attorney, it may be more willing to act. This is true even if those complaints claim that the attorney is incompetent (something normally left to malpractice lawsuits)—if the regulators conclude that the lawyer is so bad that she is a danger to the public. Another reason the agency may take action is that numerous complaints about a single attorney are often a sign of drug or alcohol abuse or some sort of mental illness, all of which regulators do take seriously.

This may offer cold comfort to most people who have been harmed by an attorney who wasn't obviously drunk or stoned, or who does not have a complaint record the length of a gourmand's grocery list. Even in the unlikely event that the discipline agency does investigate and finds the attorney to be incompetent, nothing is likely to be done.

 Tanya's Tip: Don't Go Public Unless You Are Sure You Have a Good Claim

The attorney regulators' refusal to weed out incompetent lawyers has made some frustrated clients so angry that they've placed ads in local newspapers asking other clients of a particular attorney to contact them so they can approach the discipline agency as a group.

Before you undertake this sort of action, be sure you can back up your claim of incompetence. An angry and embarrassed lawyer may sue you for

libel, claiming that you are publishing falsehoods and damaging his reputation. Although truth is a defense to a libel lawsuit, you'd still have to defend yourself in court.

C. Why File a Complaint?

If you are unhappy with the result of a matter your attorney handled but no specific ethical violation jumps out, it is probably not worth your time and effort to complain. It is an especially bad idea to file a complaint if you need your attorney to continue representing you because you are at a critical phase of your case. Filing a complaint would probably mean the end of the relationship.

 Tanya's Tip: Don't Threaten to Complain for Frivolous Matters

Make sure that your proposed complaint has merit. Making idle threats to report your attorney for conduct she knows won't be disciplined may undermine your credibility and unnecessarily anger your lawyer. For example, because a disagreement over a case strategy will not result in a disciplinable matter, it's silly to think your lawyer will be more responsive if you threaten to file such a complaint. In this situation, you'd probably be better off firing the lawyer.

But there are a few good reasons to complain to an attorney disciplinary agency.

1. To Get the Lawyer Disciplined

If a lawyer is a thief or a drunk or otherwise obviously unfit, you'll want him disbarred or suspended before others are hurt. Lawyer regulators will usually take action in these types of situations.

If your attorney has abandoned you and your rights have been compromised or your attorney has stolen your money, it is very likely the discipline agency would impose some form of discipline. By complaining, you have done all you possibly can to keep your lawyer from abandoning another client or stealing another client's money.

If your lawyer works for a law firm, it may even be possible to have the entire firm disciplined and the objectionable practice stopped. In May of 1996, the New York Supreme Court amended the state's lawyer disciplinary rules to specify that an entire law firm can be disciplined—not just the offending lawyer—for failing to adequately supervise its lawyers and monitor their compliance with the state's lawyer ethics rules.

2. To Get the Lawyer to Take Action

While the vast majority of states keep disciplinary investigations confidential, the attorney usually is aware of both the complaint and the investigation. In most states, if the agency finds something worthy of investigating, the attorney will be told your name and the nature of your complaint, and will be invited to prepare a response.

In some circumstances, a complaint to a discipline agency may get a lawyer who has not been communicating with you or paying attention to your legal problem to mend his ways. Even though the agency isn't likely to discipline

a lawyer guilty of garden-variety laziness or unresponsiveness, your attorney might pay you more attention if for no other reason than to get you off his back.

 Tanya's Tip: Contact the Lawyer Directly Before Filing a Complaint

From a lawyer's perspective, reporting an attorney to a discipline agency is a serious measure, so drastic that it will probably irreversibly damage any rapport you have with the attorney. A lawyer is likely to file a motion to withdraw from your case (in a lawsuit) or drop you as a client. If your basic problem is the unresponsiveness of your attorney—not that your attorney is a thief or incompetent—first try to improve communication. See Chapter 2 for suggestions on effective communications with a lawyer.

3. To Get Money or Property

If your lawyer has stolen your money or property, filing a complaint with a discipline agency won't directly result in your getting it back. But it can sometimes have this effect.

A disciplinary proceeding against a lawyer, like any legal matter, can be settled. Sometimes, a discipline agency negotiates a deal with the attorney that includes repaying ("making restitution" with) the client. In other situations, a disciplinary board may suspend the lawyer's right to practice law and require him to make restitution before working again. Obviously this only works with lawyers who can be rehabilitated. Unfortunately, by the time an agency acts, many lawyers are too far gone.

Finally, the majority of states maintain something called a client security fund for the benefit of clients who have had money stolen by their attorney. This fund can provide some limited restitution for clients who have been victimized by a dishonest attorney. Although these funds aren't directly related to attorney discipline, some states require a client to file a disciplinary complaint against an attorney to be eligible to recover from the fund. (See Section H, below.)

D. Document Your Attorney's Conduct

If you're pretty sure your lawyer is stealing from you or is otherwise guilty of serious misconduct, file a complaint with the attorney discipline agency P.D.Q. But if as is more likely, your case is less black-and-white, the more you can document the behavior the better. Otherwise, it is likely to come down to your story against the lawyer's.

One good way to get documentation is to write letters to your attorney pointing out the problem—be it the failure to communicate, pay you settlement money or attend court hearings with you. This will put the lawyer (and if you later complain, the agency) on notice that you have identified a problem and asked that something be done to rectify it.

This may also be your best strategy if you suspect (but aren't sure) there are problems with your attorney and you are still hoping to salvage your relationship. Chapter 2 has information on sending your attorney a letter which will hopefully produce positive results without inflaming the situation.

Another way to generate documentation is to make notes of phone conversations you have with your attorney, and, if something significant is said, follow up with a confirming letter. Put your notes—which should contain the dates of your contact with your attorney—and copies of all correspondence in your case file. If your attorney tries to defend herself by accusing you of missing appointments or failing to turn over information, your records should be able to show your efforts to cooperate.

SAMPLE LOG

July 18: Attorney calls and says I must be at deposition on August 30; asks me to bring financial documents related to starting my business.
July 25: I call attorney and leave message asking when we will meet to go over deposition.
August 15: I leave second message, having received no response to first.
August 20: I leave third message.
August 25: Secretary calls back and says attorney has been busy. Not to worry about a "routine" deposition. There is no need for a conference.
August 30: I show up for deposition. Attorney never makes it. Other attorney appears surprised and agrees to my suggestion that we reschedule.

Tanya's Tip: Tell the Discipline Agency About Your Records

If you file a complaint, let the discipline agency know that you have kept a careful record of contacts with the lawyer and why you believe they show misconduct. Attorneys at the agency who prosecute discipline cases are just as interested in winning as are attorneys in private practice. If the agency lawyer assigned to your case thinks your records will carry the day, she may be more likely to follow through on the charges against your lawyer.

E. When Should You File a Complaint?

As a practical matter, the most important factor in deciding when to file a complaint is whether you still need your attorney to do work for you. If you need the lawyer to stay, you may decide not to file a complaint at all unless the lawyer has been guilty of truly outrageous conduct such as stealing. After all, why poison your relationship with your attorney if you see no alternative but to have that person finish your case.

EXAMPLE: Nelson's attorney is handling his personal injury case for a contingency fee. Nelson suspects she is dragging her feet because his case may not result in as big a settlement or jury verdict as some of her other cases. The attorney has even suggested that Nelson find another attorney if he is not satisfied. But when Nelson interviewed several other lawyers, all declined on the basis that his case is too far along. Despite the fact that the lawyer is treating Nelson badly, this is probably not the time for him complain to the discipline agency for two reasons—first, the discipline agency is unlikely to take action and second, the complaint could be just the excuse the attorney needs to get out and leave Nelson on his own. A court is not likely to make the attorney continue when the attorney can show that the level of conflict with the client is so great that there is no longer trust and confidence between them.

Of course, if your lawyer is really awful, dump him, file a complaint and move on. Even if yours isn't a highly desirable case, you are better off putting your energy into trying to find someone competent to help you than continuing to work with a jerk.

You'll always want to file a complaint promptly if any of the following is true:

- Your case is over and you will not deal with the lawyer again.
- Your attorney has stolen your money or you suspect he may have done so. In fact, the faster you act, the better your chance of getting some of it back, either from the attorney or from a client security fund.
- Your attorney has been convicted of a serious criminal offense.
- Your attorney has threatened you in any way, such as suggesting that your case won't be pursued unless you engage in sexual relations, lend him money or invest in his pet project.
- Your attorney committed obvious malpractice, such as missing a filing deadline and then lying to you about it.

- Your attorney has abandoned your case and your rights have been compromised—for example, you lost a hearing because your lawyer didn't show up.
- Your attorney disclosed confidential information you gave her when it was not necessary to protect your rights—for example, when you disputed her bill, she retaliated by informing the IRS that you had unreported income.

There is another consideration in deciding when to file a complaint. Most states have rules as to when a complaint must be filed. Usually, as long as you file a complaint at the time the bad conduct occurs (or you discover it) or soon after you fire your lawyer, there will be no problem. If you wait until later, however, the discipline agency will consider your complaint only if it's filed within about one to two years after you discharge the attorney. Specific deadline information is available from your state's discipline agency.

F. Should You Tell the Lawyer You Plan to File a Complaint?

As mentioned in Sections C.2 and C.3, if you want your lawyer to do something positive, such as pay attention to your case or pay you money she owes, it makes sense to tell her you plan to file a complaint if she doesn't otherwise respond the way you want. For example, if your case is over, and your attorney is delaying preparing a financial accounting necessary before you receive your settlement money, your threat to file a complaint may shake it loose.

Some sample letters are below.

SAMPLE LETTERS THREATENING TO REPORT TO DISCIPLINE AGENCY

Dear Sharon:

Since I signed the release and the settlement check over one month ago, I have had no indication from you as to when I can expect my share of the settlement. In addition, my several phone calls to your office have not been returned. If I do not hear from you by this Friday, my only option will be to file a complaint with the Attorney Discipline Board to see if they can get any information concerning my settlement proceeds. Please send my money immediately or contact me to discuss this matter.

Dear Andrew:

After I inspected my file at the courthouse, I learned that my case was dropped from the trial calendar and that there is no new trial date. You did not inform me of this. My case is almost five years old and as you know, I am extremely anxious to get it resolved. Please contact me no later than Friday, January 26, to let me know why the case was dropped and what you are doing to obtain a new date. If I do not hear from you, I feel I have no option but to report this instance of client abandonment to the State Bar. I look forward to hearing from you promptly.

Dear Lisa:

My husband called to ask why we have not responded to his latest settlement offer regarding the property and support issues in our divorce. This is the second time you did not tell me about a settlement offer. I know you are busy, but I also think it is important for an attorney to communicate with her clients. This case is costing both me and Phil money we could better spend on our children as well as a huge amount of stress. You know I cannot afford to hire a new attorney—and pay for the time it would take to educate him about my case. If we continue to have this communication problem and I am forced to spend funds I don't have, I feel I would have no choice but to report you to the Lawyer Discipline agency based on your serious and repeated failure to communicate with me. Please give me a call so that we can try to get my case back on the right track.

G. How Attorney Discipline Systems Work

As mentioned, attorney discipline systems have been justly criticized because the attorneys who control them do not effectively police their own. Although it is fair to say that most states have made progress in dealing with some of the worst lawyers—those who engage in criminal conduct or obviously abandon or abuse their clients—discipline agencies have a long way to go before they can be called legitimate consumer watchdogs. Even in states that have improved their discipline systems, complaints are still handled very slowly, investigations and hearings are for the most part secret and, worst of all, there remains little or no effort to deal with the fact that thousands of attorneys are incompetent.

 Fee Disputes Are Not Usually Handled by Discipline Agencies

Many complaints filed with discipline agencies involve fees—usually accusations of overcharging. Unless you also charge client abandonment or fraudulent billing—such as billing for hours not spent on your case—these complaints will be referred to a separate fee dispute procedure. We cover resolving fee disputes procedures in Chapter 7.

1. File Your Complaint

Most complaints to a state discipline agency start with your written complaint, either on a preprinted form or in a letter. Below is a list of state lawyer discipline agency addresses and phone numbers. Call or write to obtain the proper form for making a complaint. (It is possible that you will be contacted by the discipline agency in response to a complaint filed by another client or if the attorney is being investigated by the district attorney.)

EXAMPLE 1: My complaint is about attorney Nancy Jones, 128 Scenic Drive, Watertown. She accepted a retainer from me of $5,000 to represent me in my divorce, telling me "don't worry; I will take care of everything." When I hired her, I gave her a copy of the Petition for Divorce which had just been served on me. I have just been notified that a default judgment was taken against me because I did not file a response. The judgment is not fair—my wife has been awarded most of our property and sole custody of our son. I have placed numerous calls to Ms. Jones's office, only to get an answering machine. Each time I left a phone number and when I could be reached. I have no idea why Ms. Jones abandoned me and won't communicate with me. I also have no idea what happened to my money and I do not have funds to pay another attorney to straighten out this mess. I realize that if I don't act promptly I might lose important rights forever.

This letter highlights that the attorney violated rules against failing to communicate and client abandonment. Depending on what Nancy Jones did with the money, it may also involve stealing client funds. Such a letter should get the attention of the disciplinary agency.

EXAMPLE 2: I am writing to complain about attorney Mark Rowan whose office is located at 1818 First Street, Bank Tower Building, Suite 300, Smithville. We were in court on my child custody case and I smelled alcohol on his breath and his eyes were bloodshot. The judge said that Mr. Rowan had not filed some papers on time and as a result, the hearing to decide whether or not I will get to spend time with my kids was postponed for two months. After court, Mr. Rowan told me that he needed another $2,000 to prepare for the next hearing. When I asked him what hap-

pened to the money I already gave him, he told me he spent it preparing for the hearing we just had, even though nothing happened except the judge chewed out Mr. Rowan and gave us a new hearing date. I believe that Mr. Rowan's drinking negatively affects his ability to perform as an attorney and directly contributed to the debacle in my case.

An attorney's failure to file papers on time would not ordinarily concern a disciplinary agency. Combined with signs of alcohol abuse, however, it may pique the agency investigator's interest. Of course, don't make such an accusation if it isn't true. But if your attorney's lack of performance is possibly due to drug or alcohol abuse, bring it to the attention of the disciplinary agency.

EXAMPLE 3: This complaint is about attorney Sara Green, 77 Mayfair Way, Greenville, who I hired to represent me in a lawsuit concerning the death of my late husband. I do not believe that Sara was qualified to handle this case; furthermore, she misrepresented the fee arrangement and never put it in writing, which I have since learned is required in our state.

When I met Sara, she told me she could get me a big settlement from the driver of the car that killed my husband. Nothing happen on the case for years, and then one day she told me the trial was a few weeks away and that she needed $10,000 to prepare. This was a shock to me. Sara had told me that she would charge me nothing unless I won. I looked for another attorney, but no one would take my case so close to the trial. I gave Sara the $10,000 and then another $5,000 two days before the trial. At the trial, she did not seem to know what she was doing. The other side objected to everything she did, and then she would just drop the subject. Needless to say, we lost the trial. After the trial, I found out that she had never handled a case like mine and that her entire practice had been writing wills. It doesn't seem right that she could take my money when she had no experience in the type of case I had. If I had known that, I would have found another attorney.

This letter may or may not get a discipline agency to take action. Most discipline agencies do not pursue accusations of attorney negligence; however, an attorney is required to have a certain level of competence. If an attorney takes on a matter in which she has no experience, she must either gain the skill and learning required or bring in another lawyer who can guide her in the process. In the above example, the disciplinary agency may move to punish Sara if she really had no experience in the field and neither sought to gain any nor brought in a competent lawyer to advise her.

STATE LAWYER DISCIPLINE AGENCIES

State	Disciplinary Board Address/Phone
Alabama	Alabama State Bar Center for Professional Responsibility Disciplinary Commission P.O. Box 671 Montgomery, AL 36101 334-269-1515
Alaska	Bar Counsel Alaska Bar Association P.O. Box 100279 Anchorage, AK 99510 907-272-7469
Arizona	State Bar of Arizona Disciplinary Dept. 111 West Monroe, Suite 1800 Phoenix, AZ 85003-1742 602-252-4804, Ext. 225
Arkansas	Committee on Professional Conduct Arkansas Supreme Court Justice Building, Room 205 625 Marshall Street Little Rock, AR 72201 501-376-0313
California	Office of Intake/Legal Advice State Bar of California 1149 South Hill Street Los Angeles, CA 90015-2299 213-765-1140
Colorado	Disciplinary Counsel Supreme Court of Colorado Dominion Plaza Bldg. 600 17th St., Suite 510 South Denver, CO 80202 303-893-8121
Connecticut	The Statewide Bar Counsel 387 Main St., 2nd Floor East Hartford, CT 06118-1885 203-568-5157

State	Disciplinary Board Address/Phone
Delaware	Office of Disciplinary Counsel Delaware Supreme Court 200 West 9th St., Suite 300A P.O. Box 472 Wilmington, DE 19899 302-571-8703
District of Columbia	Office of Bar Counsel Board on Professional Responsibility District of Columbia Court of Appeals 515 Fifth St. NW, Bldg. A Washington, DC 20001 202-638-1501
Florida	Programs Division Florida Bar 650 Apalachee Parkway Tallahassee, FL 32399 904-561-5839
Georgia	Office of General Counsel 50 Hurt Plaza, Suite 800 Atlanta, GA 30303 404-527-8720
Hawaii	Office of Disciplinary Counsel 1164 Bishop Street, Suite 600 Honolulu, HI 98613 808-521-4591
Idaho	Idaho State Bar P.O. Box 895 Boise, ID 83701 208-334-4500
Illinois	Attorney Registration & Disciplinary Commission of the Supreme Court of Illinois 130 East Randolph, Suite 1500 Chicago, IL 60501 312-565-2600

STATE LAWYER DISCIPLINE AGENCIES (cont'd)

State	Disciplinary Board Address/Phone	State	Disciplinary Board Address/Phone
Indiana	Disciplinary Commission of The Supreme Court 115 W. Washington St. Suite 1060 South Tower Indianapolis, IN 46204-3417 317-232-1807	Massachusetts	Board of Bar Overseers 75 Federal Street, 7th Floor Boston, MA 02110 617-357-1860
Iowa	Ethics Administrator 521 E. Locust Des Moines, IA 50309 515-243-3179	Michigan	Attorney Grievance Commission Suite 256 Marquette Building 243 W. Congress Detroit, MI 48226 313-961-6585
Kansas	Disciplinary Administrator 3706 So. Topeka Ave., Suite 100 Topeka, KS 66609 913-296-2486	Minnesota	Lawyers Professional Responsibility Board 25 Constitution Avenue, Suite 105 St. Paul, MN 55155 612-296-3952
Kentucky	Bar Counsel 514 W. Main St. Frankfort, KY 40601-1883 502-564-3795	Mississippi	General Counsel Mississippi State Bar P.O. Box 2168 Jackson, MS 39225 601-948-4471
Louisiana	Louisiana State Bar Association 601 St. Charles Avenue New Orleans, LA 70130 504-566-1600	Missouri	Fee Dispute Resolution Missouri Bar P.O. Box 119 Jefferson City, MO 65102 573-635-4128
Maine	Board of Overseers of the Bar 97 Winthrop St. P.O. Box 1820 Augusta, ME 04332-1820 207-623-1121	Montana	Commission on Practice of the Supreme Court State of Montana Room 315, Justice Bldg. 215 North Sanders Helena, MT 59620-3002 406-444-2608
Maryland	Attorney Grievance Commission 100 Community Place, Suite 3301 Crownsville, MD 21032-2027 800-492-1660 (instate) 410-514-7051	Nebraska	Ethics Office 635 So. 14th Street Lincoln, NE 68508 402-444-2608

STATE LAWYER DISCIPLINE AGENCIES (cont'd)

State	Disciplinary Board Address/Phone
Nevada	Attorney Discipline State Bar of Nevada 201 Las Vegas Blvd. South, Suite 200 702-382-2200
New Hampshire	New Hampshire Supreme Court Commission on Professional Conduct 4 Park St., Suite 304 Concord, NH 03301 603-224-5828
New Jersey	Office of Attorney Ethics Director and Counsel Supreme Court of New Jersey Richard J. Hughes Justice Complex, CN-963 Trenton, NJ 08625 609-292-8750
New Mexico	The Disciplinary Board 400 Gold Ave. SW, Suite 1100 Albuquerque, NM 87102 505-842-5781
New York	If lawyer's office is in Bronx or Manhattan: Departmental Disciplinary Committee 41 Madison Ave., 39th Floor New York, NY 10010 212-685-1000

	If lawyer's office is in Brooklyn, Queens
	  or Staten Island:
	Grievance Committee for the 2nd and
	  11th Judicial Districts
	Municipal Bldg., 12th Floor
	210 Joralemon St.
	Brooklyn, NY 11201
	718-624-7851

	If lawyer's office is outside of NY City: Call for nearest office: 212-417-5872

State	Disciplinary Board Address/Phone
North Carolina	Grievance Committee North Carolina State Bar 208 Fayetteville Street Mall P.O. Box 25908 Raleigh, NC 27611 919-828-4620
North Dakota	State Bar Association of North Dakota P.O. Box 2136 Bismarck, ND 27611 919-828-4620
Ohio	Office of Disciplinary Counsel Supreme Court of Ohio 175 South 3rd St., Suite 280 Columbus, OH 43215-5196 614-461-0256
Oklahoma	General Counsel Oklahoma Bar Association 1901 N. Lincoln Blvd. P.O. Box 53036 Oklahoma City, OK 73152 405-524-2365
Oregon	Disciplinary Counsel's Office Oregon State Bar P.O. Box 1689 Lake Oswego, OR 97035-0889 503-620-0222 800-452-8260
Pennsylvania	Disciplinary Board of the Supreme Court of Pennsylvania 2100 No. American Bldg. 121 So. Broad St. Philadelphia, PA 19107 215-560-6296

STATE LAWYER DISCIPLINE AGENCIES (cont'd)

State	Disciplinary Board Address/Phone	State	Disciplinary Board Address/Phone
Rhode Island	Executive Director Rhode Island Bar Association 115 Cedar Street Providence, RI 02903 401-421-5740	Virginia	Grievance Department Virginia State Bar Eighth and Main Building 707 E. Main Street South, #1500 Richmond, VA 23219-2803 804-775-0570
South Carolina	Board of Commission of Grievances & Discipline South Carolina Supreme Court P.O. Box 11330 Columbia, SC 29211 803-734-2038	Washington	General Counsel Washington State Bar Association 500 Westin Building 2001 6th Avenue Seattle, WA 98121-2599 206-727-8207
South Dakota	Disciplinary Board State Bar of South Dakota 222 E. Capitol Pierre, SD 57501 605-224-7554	West Virginia	Lawyer Disciplinary Board Office of Lawyer Disciplinary Counsel 210 Dickinson St. Charleston, WV 92201 304-558-7999
Tennessee	Tennessee Lawyers Fund for Client Protection 511 Union St., Suite 1430 Nashville, TN 37219 615-741-3096	Wisconsin	Supreme Court of Wisconsin Board of Attorney's Professional Responsibility 110 E. Main St., Suite 400 Madison, WI 53703-3383 608-267-7274
Texas	Call for nearest office 800-932-1900	Wyoming	Bar Counsel Wyoming State Bar P.O. Box 109 Cheyenne, WY 82003-0109 307-632-9061
Utah	Office of Attorney Discipline Utah State Bar 645 S. 200 East Salt Lake City, UT 84111-3834 801-531-9110		
Vermont	Bar Counsel Professional Conduct Board 59 Elm Street Montpelier, VT 05602 802-223-2020		

2. If the Agency Doesn't Follow Up or Contact You

Because most states discipline attorneys in secret, you probably won't know what, if anything, is happening after you file a complaint. Too often, you wouldn't be happy if you did know, given that in many states underfunded discipline agencies take years to get around to most complaints. If you are contacted by investigators and given a chance to make a statement, it is some indication that the agency may be taking your complaint seriously.

If you don't hear anything significant from your state discipline agency, call and inquire about the status of your complaint. Or, if you can't get past the inevitable mechanized phone answering system, send a fax requesting that someone call you. If you still receive no response, consider sending copies of your complaint to:

- the Chief Justice of your state's highest court (called the Supreme Court in most states, but called the Court of Appeals in New York)
- your elected state representatives—that is, the people who represent you in your state capitol, or
- the legal affairs correspondent at the nearest metropolitan newspaper.

3. How Might Your Lawyer Respond?

What your complaint may persuade your attorney to do depends greatly on the person and situation—in the best case, it may spur an overbusy, but decent lawyer to focus on your legal problem. Or it could put the fear of God

in a lawyer who has been disciplined before and wants badly to avoid further trouble. But if the lawyer has a clean record and believes that you are being highly unreasonable and that she has done nothing wrong, she may file a motion with the court asking for permission to withdraw as your attorney. If she has already been disbarred—or knows she is about to be—she is likely to ignore your complaint.

 Tanya's Tip: Your Attorney Must Know You Filed a Complaint

For your complaint to wake your attorney up and start noticing you, he must know that you filed it in the first place. In the states where attorneys are routinely contacted within a short period of time, this won't be a problem. But many states lack the resources to move quickly enough to make any difference in your case. If it appears that your attorney doesn't know about your complaint (he doesn't say anything or change his ways), send him a copy of your complaint.

4. How an Agency Handles Complaints

In most states, your written complaint will land on the desk of an intake officer. This person typically decides whether the complaint should be acted on pronto or put on the back burner. If he decides that your allegations aren't disciplinable—for example, you file a complaint challenging a strategy your lawyer pursued in a case—he can also terminate the process right then. You will probably get a letter or other notice stating that your complaint is not being acted upon.

If you have alleged something that is disciplinable, the intake officer will assign your case to an investigating officer. You will probably receive a notice stating that your complaint is being investigated. Unless your allegations are extremely serious (you suspect your lawyer has stolen your money and plans to flee to Brazil), getting even this far can take months in many states, which have large and growing case backlogs. Eventually, however, the agency will notify the attorney of your complaint and request a response. If your lawyer does not offer a satisfactory explanation, or if the investigating officer does not believe the explanation, your complaint will proceed to the prosecutorial arm of the discipline agency.

5. If Your Attorney Is Prosecuted

If the discipline agency prosecutes your attorney, it will issue formal written charges against him. He will be given a chance to defend against the charges at a hearing. At this stage, especially when the lawyer has been charged with less serious offenses (such as keeping inadequate trust fund records but not alleging theft of money), your attorney may be able to plea bargain his case. This means that he agrees to accept (not contest) discipline at a less serious level than he is charged with. If this occurs, you have a real opportunity because often the discipline agency will accept this only if the attorney takes care of your problem. This might include your attorney agreeing to finish your case or refund your money.

In states with many lawyers, actual prosecution—assuming you can get this far—is likely to consist of a trial-like hearing. The agency will be represented by an attorney who will present the case for discipline like a District Attorney presents a criminal case. Your former attorney may or may not have his own lawyer, although, if the matter has gone this far, it is likely that he will.

The lawyers for the discipline agency and for your former attorney will ask questions of the witnesses. Witnesses would testify about the facts and, if applicable, about the character of the attorney. You can expect to be called as a witness to testify about her conduct—of course, you will be interviewed and prepared ahead of time. In most states, there is a privilege as to anything you testify about in a discipline hearing. This means that the attorney cannot later sue you for slander. The reason for this rule is to encourage people to testify honestly without fear of repercussion.

In states with relatively few lawyers, prosecution will probably be more informal. Typically, the attorney accused of violating the state rules and an attorney for the discipline agency would meet to discuss the conduct and circumstances that led to the complaint. In advance of the meeting, the people who will make the decision about discipline will probably talk to any witnesses. You can expect to be contacted.

At the end of the hearing (in states with many lawyers) or meeting (in states with fewer lawyers), the decision-maker either:

- decides whether or not discipline should be imposed and if so, what discipline, or
- makes a recommendation to the discipline agency about whether or not discipline should be imposed and if so, what discipline; the agency then decides whether to accept or reject the recommendation.

If the officer or agency finds that your attorney should be punished, discipline will be imposed. Depending on the state, there are several types of possible discipline.

Private reprimand. Private reprimand means that the attorney receives a private scolding from the discipline agency. It is the lightest discipline, and in most states does not become part of the attorney's public record. If comprehensive discipline records are available in your state for public review, the fact of a private reprimand might be disclosed, but not information concerning the circumstances. If the attorney is subject to discipline for another incident, however, the fact that the attorney was in trouble at an earlier time would be known to the discipline agency and could mean a more severe punishment.

Public reprimand. This is a public scolding of the attorney. If disciplinary records are available for review in your state, anyone could see that the attorney was scolded and why.

Probation. Probation means that the attorney can still practice law, but his work will be monitored either by the state agency or another attorney appointed to do the job. Usually, the attorney on probation must meet regularly with his monitoring attorney and submit reports concerning the area in which he was disciplined. For example, if the attorney was disciplined for improperly keeping trust fund accounts, he would have to submit reports concerning how he is keeping his trust funds. Sometimes, a condition of probation is that the attorney complete the legal work he was doing for the complaining client.

Suspension. Suspension means the attorney can't practice law. The suspension can be for any amount of time. Typically, suspensions are imposed for at least 30 days, and in extreme circumstances, as long as three years. Suspension is often coupled with a period of probation once the suspended attorney begins to practice law again. Often, suspended attorneys must pass a lawyer ethics exam as a condition of being permitted to resume the practice of law.

Disbarment. If the conduct is particularly egregious, the attorney can be prevented from practicing law. Depending on the state, disbarment has a number of meanings. Sometimes it amounts to a permanent or at least long-term bar to future law practice. But it can also be for a shorter term. For example, in California and Texas, no matter how awful the conduct, a disbarred attorney can petition for reinstatement after five years. Disbarment differs from suspension in that a suspended attorney's right to resume the practice of law is automatic; a disbarred attorney must apply to become a member of the bar and must prove that she has been rehabilitated and is fit to practice law again.

No matter what the decision, the attorney will have the right to appeal, as the ultimate disciplinary authority lies with your state's highest court. Usually, the court accepts the decision of the regulatory agency, but occasionally it changes the decision—often to go easier on the offending lawyer.

6. If the Agency Won't Prosecute

If the agency decides not to prosecute, you may have a right to appeal. Contact the discipline agency to find out if such a procedure exists. If there is no formal process, write a letter of protest and direct it to the supervisor of the person who signed the letter stating that no action would be taken. Appealing is not necessarily a waste of time. In California, for example, an estimated one-third of all appeals are referred back to the discipline agency for further investigation. This does not guarantee that action will be taken, but it does require the agency to take a second look.

If your state does not have a formal appeal procedure, you may still be able to pursue the matter by appealing directly to the courts. In South Dakota and Wyoming, for example, if the discipline agency decides not to prosecute, you can simply file your complaint directly with the state Supreme Court. If you are persistent enough, your complaint may get a second chance.

H. Obtaining Money From a Client Security Fund

Many states maintain a client security fund. Financed by a small portion of attorneys' annual dues, the fund is designed to compensate clients up to a specified amount when the discipline agency finds that the attorney has stolen their money. You probably won't be able to recover your entire loss, however. Most states have limits on the amount recoverable, which can be as low as $10,000 per claim and $50,000 per attorney. If your attorney has stolen more than that, your only hope is to find him and your money. Even worse, client security funds don't compensate clients for losses due to an attorney's negligence or incompetence, or abandonment of the client.

EXAMPLE: Emily hires an attorney who settles her case. The lawyer does not pay Emily her share of the settlement, but instead gambles the money away. Emily is entitled to compensation from the state Client Security Fund. If Emily had received no settlement because the attorney incompetently failed to file the lawsuit on time, Emily would not be entitled to compensation from the Fund. Instead, she would have to file a malpractice lawsuit against the lawyer.

The distinction between compensating a client whose money is stolen but not when a lawyer is grossly incompetent is not entirely logical. Nevertheless, it's part and parcel of all attorney regulatory agencies' operation. Given that most states require a very low level of continuing legal education, no state requires periodic skills testing, and only Oregon requires attorneys to buy malpractice insurance to protect clients, it is just plain disgusting that clients who are victims of attorney negligence are not protected by a client security fund.

To collect from a client security fund, you will have to make a written claim and provide some documentation of your loss. Before making your claim, get a copy of the security fund recovery rules and make sure you state your claim in a way that qualifies you for reimbursement. If you haven't kept copies of your settlement papers, documentation may be a problem if your attorney has stolen your settlement proceeds and skipped town. Contact the attorney for the other side, explain the problem and ask her to send you a letter

describing the settlement to submit with your claim. Your claim will be evaluated by a decision-maker, who will determine the validity of your claim and the amount you can recover.

If your claim is rejected, you can usually appeal—at least informally. Make it clear that there were identifiable funds (not just a potential recovery from a lawsuit) and that your loss was due to your attorney's dishonesty, not negligence. If you are unsure and you have a large claim, it may pay to consult with an attorney familiar with your state's lawyer ethical rules for help in wording the claim in such a way that it falls within the criteria for reimbursement.

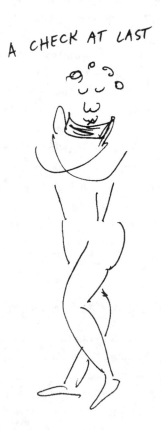

A CHECK AT LAST

CLIENT SECURITY TRUST FUNDS

State	Address/Phone	State	Address/Phone
Alabama	**Client Security Trust Fund** Executive Director, Alabama State Bar Center for Professional Responsibility Disciplinary Commission P.O. Box 671 Montgomery, AL 36101 205-269-1515	Connecticut	**Client Security Trust Fund** Assistant Executive Director Connecticut Bar Association 101 Corporate Place Rocky Hill, CT 06067 203-721-0025
Alaska	**Client Security Trust Fund** Bar Counsel Alaska Bar Association P.O. Box 100279 Anchorage, AK 99510 907-272-7469	Delaware	**Fund for Client Protection** Court Administrator Delaware Supreme Court 200 West 9th Street, Suite 300B P.O. Box 472 Wilmington, DE 19899 302-652-2117 302-577-3706
Arizona	**Attorney Grievance State Office** Chief Bar Counsel State of Arizona 111 West Monroe, Suite 1800 Phoenix, AZ 85003-1742 602-252-4804, ext. 225	District of Columbia	**Client Security Trust Fund** Assistant Executive Director 1250 8th Street, NW Washington, DC 20005 202-737-4700, ext. 237
Arkansas	**Client Security Trust Fund** Clerk, Arkansas Supreme Court Justice Building, Room 205 625 Marshall Street Little Rock, AR 72201 501-682-6849	Florida	**Client Security Trust Fund** Programs Division Florida Bar 650 Apalachee Parkway Tallahassee, FL 32399 904-561-5812
California	**Client Security Trust Fund** State Bar of California 1149 South Hill Street Los Angeles, CA 90015-2299 213-765-1140	Georgia	**Client Security Fund** Assistant General Counsel 50 Hurt Plaza, Suite 800 Atlanta, GA 30303 404-527-8720
Colorado	**Client Security Trust Fund** Executive Director Colorado Bar Association 1900 Grant Street, Suite 950 Denver, CO 80203-4309 303-860-1112	Hawaii	**Fund for Client Protection** 1164 Bishop Street, Suite 600 Honolulu, HI 98613 808-599-2483

CLIENT SECURITY TRUST FUNDS (cont'd)

State	Address/Phone
Idaho	**Client Security Fund** Idaho State Bar P.O. Box 895 Boise, ID 83701 208-334-4500

Illinois	**Client Security Trust Fund**
	Attorney Registration & Disciplinary
	    Commission of the Supreme Court
	    of Illinois
	130 East Randolph, Suite 1500
	Chicago, IL 60601
	312-565-2600

Indiana	**Client Security Trust Fund** Executive Director State Bar of Indiana 230 East Ohio Street, 4th Floor Indianapolis, IN 46204 317-639-5465
Iowa	**Client Security Trust Fund and Attorney Disciplinary Committee** Administrator Supreme Court Commission State Capitol Des Moines, IA 50319 515-246-8076
Kansas	**Client Protection Fund Commission** Kansas Judicial Center, Room 374 301 SW 10th Avenue Topeka, KS 66612-1507 913-296-3229
Kentucky	**Client Security Trust Fund** Bar Counsel Kentucky Bar Association W. Main at Kentucky River Frankfort, KY 40601 502-564-3795

State	Address/Phone
Louisiana	**Client Security Trust Fund** Louisiana State Bar Association 601 St. Charles Avenue New Orleans, LA 70130 504-566-1600
Maine	**None**
Maryland	**Client Security Trust Fund** 208 Calvert Street Salsbury, MD 21801-2804 410-543-8410
Massachusetts	**Client Security Trust Fund** Bar Counsel Massachusetts Board of Bar Overseers 75 Federal Street, 7th Floor Boston, MA 02110 617-357-1860
Michigan	**Client Security Trust Fund** State Bar of Michigan 306 Townsend Street Lansing, MI 48933-2083 517-372-9033, ext. 3026
Minnesota	**Client Security Trust Fund** 25 Constitution Avenue, Suite 105 St. Paul, MN 55155 612-296-3952
Mississippi	**Client Security Trust Fund** General Counsel Mississippi State Bar P.O. Box 2168 Jackson, MS 39225 601-948-4471
Missouri	**Client Security Trust Fund** Director of Programs, Missouri Bar P.O Box 119 Jefferson City, MO 65102 314-635-4128

CLIENT SECURITY TRUST FUNDS (cont'd)

State	Address/Phone
Montana	**Client Security Trust Fund** Executive Director State Bar of Montana P.O. Box 577 Helena, MT 59624 406-442-7660
Nebraska	**Client Security Fund Committee** 10050 Regency Circle, #200 Omaha, NE 68114-3721 402-397-5500
Nevada	**Client Security Trust Fund** Staff Administrator State Bar of Nevada 201 Las Vegas Blvd. South, Suite 200 Las Vegas NV 89101 702-382-2200
New Hampshire	**Client Indemnity Fund Committee** Bar Association of New Hampshire 112 Pleasant Street Concord, NH 03301 603-224-6942
New Jersey	**Office of Attorney Ethics** Director and Counsel Supreme Court of New Jersey Richard J. Hughes Justice Complex, CN-961 Trenton NJ 08625 609-984-7179
New Mexico	**None**
New York	**Client Security Trust Fund** Executive Director 55 Elk Street Albany, NY 12210 518-474-8438

State	Address/Phone
North Carolina	**Client Security Trust Fund** North Carolina State Bar 208 Fayetteville Street Mall P.O. Box 25908 Raleigh, NC 27611 919-828-4620
North Dakota	**Client Security Trust Fund** State Bar Association of North Dakota P.O. Box 2136 Bismarck, ND 58502 701-255-1404
Ohio	**Client Security Fund** 175 South 3rd Street, #205 Columbus, OH 43215 614-221-0562
Oklahoma	**Client Security Trust Fund** General Counsel Oklahoma Bar Center 1901 N. Lincoln Blvd. P.O. Box 53036 Oklahoma City, OK 73152 405-524-2365
Oregon	**Client Security Trust Fund** Staff Liaison Oregon State Bar P.O. Box 1689 Lake Oswego, OR 97035-0889 503-620-0222 800-452-8260
Pennsylvania	**Lawyers Fund for Client Security** Supreme Court of Pennsylvania Executive Director 1515 Market Street, Suite 1425 Philadelphia, PA 19102 215-560-6335 800-962-4618

CLIENT SECURITY TRUST FUNDS (cont'd)

State	Address/Phone
Rhode Island	**Client Security Trust Fund** Executive Director Rhode Island Bar Association 115 Cedar Street Providence, RI 02903 401-421-5740
South Carolina	**Client Security Trust Fund** South Carolina Bar P.O. Box 608 Columbia, SC 29202-0608 803-769-6653
South Dakota	**Client Security Trust Fund** Executive Director State Bar of South Dakota 222 E. Capitol Pierre, SD 57501 605-224-7554
Tennessee	**None**
Texas	**Client Security Trust Fund** General Counsel State Bar of Texas P.O. Box 12487 Capitol Station Austin, TX 78711 512-463-1463
Utah	**Client Security Trust Fund** Bar Counsel Utah State Bar 645 S. 200 East Salt Lake City, UT 84111-3834 801-531-9077

State	Address/Phone
Vermont	**Client Security Trust Fund** Staff Administrator Vermont Bar Association P.O. Box 100 Montpelier, VT 05602 802-223-2020
Virginia	**Client Security Trust Fund** Virginia State Bar Eighth and Main Building 707 E. Main Street South, #1500 Richmond, VA 23219-2803 804-775-0502
Washington	**Client Security Trust Fund** General Counsel Washington State Bar Association 500 Westin Building 2001 6th Avenue Seattle, WA 98121-2599 206-727-8200
West Virginia	**Client Protection Fund** West Virginia State Bar 3006 Canawha Blvd. East Charleston, WV 25311 304-558-2456
Wisconsin	**Client Security Trust Fund** Legal Services Assistant State Bar of Wisconsin P.O. Box 7158 Madison, WI 53707 608-257-3838
Wyoming	**Client Security Trust Fund** Bar Counsel Wyoming State Bar P.O. Box 109 Cheyenne, WY 82003-0109 307-632-9061

[insert name, address and phone number from chart in Section G.1.]

COMPLAINT FORM

Your Name _____

             First   Initial   Last

Address _____

_____

Phone   (   ) _____   (   ) _____

          Home   Business

Attorney Complained of _____

             First   Initial   Last

Address _____

_____

Phone   (   ) _____   (   ) _____

        Business   Fax

Details of complaint against attorney (attach additional sheets if necessary):

Have you filed a civil or criminal action against this attorney? If so, give the case name and number and the court in which it is filed.

Please list by name, address, and phone number all witnesses to your complaint.

Attach all relevant documents.

Note: This is a sample form only. If possible, use any form provided by your state's discipline agency to insure that you provide the information needed.

Chapter 9

SUING YOUR FORMER LAWYER

f you're furious at your lawyer for messing up your case, you may be thinking—or at least fantasizing—about filing a lawsuit. It's a natural thought. Just as medical negligence can result in permanent injury or even death, lawyer negligence can have serious, even life-threatening, ramifications. Although not every bad result (from either a lawyer or a doctor) indicates negligence, it is true that there is plenty of negligence around—probably more than you would think. Here are a few examples of negligent things lawyers do on a daily basis:

- failing to file a lawsuit on time or missing other important deadlines
- failing to comply with mandatory administrative agency regulations before filing a lawsuit
- suing the wrong person
- failing to sue all of the right people
- suing on the wrong grounds (called "causes of action")
- failing to investigate the facts before filing a case
- failing to conduct discovery (evidence-gathering before trial)
- failing to prepare for trial, including failing to secure expert witnesses
- failing to show up for trial or a court hearing
- not having the experience needed to handle a case
- failing to tell you that if you lose, you'd have to pay your opponent's attorney's fees
- failing to tell the other side about expert witnesses (it is required to let the other

side take the expert's deposition before the trial and arrange for his own expert)
- failing to get a debt discharged in bankruptcy, and
- failing to advise you about tax consequences of a transaction.

⚠️ **Proving That the Lawyer Did Wrong and Proving That You Are Entitled to Monetary Compensation Are Not the Same**

As I explain throughout this chapter, establishing that a lawyer was guilty of malpractice is only part of the battle when it comes to recovering money from the lawyer for malpractice. You must also prove that you would have won your case had the lawyer not been incompetent, and that you would have been able to collect the judgment.

A. Grounds for Suing

There are three different types of lawsuits you can file against a lawyer who messes up:

- malpractice
- breach of fiduciary duty, and
- fraud or other intentional conduct.

Let's look at each one in detail.

1. Malpractice

"Malpractice" simply means that a lawyer failed to use the ordinary skill and care that other lawyers would be expected to use in handling a similar legal problem or case under similar circumstances.

EXAMPLE 1: You hire a lawyer to handle your personal injury case and hear nothing for many months. You call the lawyer's office and leave messages asking about your case, and are told that your lawyer is very busy and will get back to you. You finally reach the end of your rope, and go see another lawyer who finds out that your lawyer never filed the lawsuit and because a one-year statute of limitations applied to your case, it is too late to do so now. In short, your case has been lost because your lawyer didn't prepare the necessary paperwork and get it to the court clerk's office on time. There is no question that your lawyer committed malpractice in not filing your lawsuit before the deadline expired.

EXAMPLE 2: Your father died; his will names you executor of his estate. You hire an attorney to handle the legal matters for the estate. The lawyer never tells you that you must file a tax return for the estate. Eventually, the estate is assessed interest and penalties by the IRS. The lawyer committed malpractice in not advising you to either file a tax return or hire a tax preparer to do it for you.

EXAMPLE 3: You hire a lawyer to help you sell your business. You agree to finance the sale, and the buyers agree to make monthly payments to you, secured by the assets of the business. The lawyer prepares the paperwork, but fails to record the "security document," meaning that your security interest doesn't exist. The buyers default on the payments, and you try to foreclose on the business assets. You discover that they have already been pledged as security to another creditor who properly recorded its security interest. The lawyer committed malpractice in not recording your security interest.

Also keep in mind that your lawyer is responsible for mistakes made by her employees or others who work for her on your case. If your lawyer missed a deadline because her secretary made a calendaring mistake, your lawyer is responsible and it is considered the lawyer's malpractice. Similarly, if the lawyer you hired to advise you had a law clerk do legal research, and the law clerk missed an important case which caused your lawyer to give you incorrect advice, the mistake is your lawyer's.

2. Breach of Fiduciary Duty

As explained in Chapter 4, *Conflicts of Interests*, your lawyer has what is called a "fiduciary relationship" with you. This means she must represent you with undivided loyalty, even if it means putting your interests above her own. You are entitled to tell your lawyer things in confidence without fear that they will be disclosed or used to the attorney's personal advantage.

Legal claims for breach of fiduciary duty usually involve a lawyer having a personal interest which conflicts with the client's interest. But they can also occur when a lawyer agrees to represent two people with conflicting interest, with the result that one client is harmed. Thus, the two major types of claims for breach of fiduciary duty arise from:

- a lawyer's duty to maintain your confidences, and
- a lawyer's duty to handle your matter with undivided loyalty.

The following are examples of breach of fiduciary duty:

EXAMPLE 1: An attorney who is a partner in a real estate partnership which owns a shopping center agrees to represent you (as a prospective tenant) in negotiations to lease space in the shopping center.

EXAMPLE 2: The lawyer handling your adoption sends a copy of the adoption petition to the birth parents. In doing so, your identity and whereabouts are revealed, which were supposed to remain confidential.[1]

EXAMPLE 3: You consult with a real estate attorney about buying a ranch you learn is about to go into foreclosure. You think you can pick it up at a bargain price. Before you decide about making an offer, your lawyer mentions the "business opportunity" to someone else who contacts the seller and buys the property.

EXAMPLE 4: The lawyer advising you to accept a settlement in a case has a job offer from the law firm representing the other side.[2]

EXAMPLE 5: The lawyer handling your divorce pressures you to accept a settlement. Immediately after your case closes, you find out that your lawyer is merging her law practice with that of your ex-spouse's lawyer.[3]

3. Fraud or Other Intentional Conduct

To qualify as fraud or other intentional misconduct, a lawyer's action must be intentional, knowing that it will harm a client or someone else. Unfortunately, because many lawyers are ethical dunderheads, lawsuits against lawyers for intentionally harming a client (or other person) occur with regularity. Here are a few examples of the common types of these claims:

- stealing a client's money
- destroying evidence or lying to the other side about what evidence exists
- "creating" evidence, such as forging an adversary's signature
- accepting a favor or bribe to handle a client's case poorly, or
- lying to a client about key aspects of a case.

What is unusual about a lawsuit for fraud or other intentional misconduct—as compared to malpractice or breach of fiduciary duty—is that it may not only be brought by a client, but it can also be initiated by any person injured by the lawyer's actions, including an adversary (someone on the other side of a case). Unlike a malpractice or breach of fiduciary duty case, there is no need to show that the attorney you are suing had agreed to represent you. (See Chapter 10 on suing the lawyer for the other side.)

B. How Much Time Do You Have to Sue?

Every state has laws, called statutes of limitations, which specify how much time you have to sue in different types of cases. Statutes of limitations exist because it is best to resolve disputes soon after they arise. As time passes, it becomes more difficult to litigate a case because witnesses move, die or forget and documents often become difficult to find.

Depending on your state and the type of lawsuit you want to file (malpractice or breach of fiduciary duty, for example), you may have as little as one year to sue or as many as 20 years after the incident occurred or you discovered the lawyer's mess-up.

To complicate matters, you might have grounds to sue your attorney under more than one category, each with a different statute of limitations. For instance, in Ohio you have only one year to file a lawsuit against a lawyer for negligence, but six years to sue for breach of an oral contract or 15 years to sue for breach of a written contract. (Section 1, below, has information on each state's statutes of limitations.)

Given how difficult it can be to figure out the statute of limitations, coupled with the increasing difficulty in winning a case that's old, the best advice is always *file your lawsuit promptly.*

ARGUING ABOUT WHETHER YOU FILED ON TIME

If a year or more has passed since the date you claim your lawyer screwed up or you discovered the screw-up, the lawyer will probably claim that you have not filed your case on time. (See Section H.1, below.) Who wins this issue will depend on how the law of your state applies to an often complicated fact situation. In short, once you file your lawsuit, you may spend months—or sometimes years—getting this issue settled before actually moving on to resolve your malpractice or other claim.

1. Statute of Limitations for Malpractice

Skip Ahead if the Malpractice Just Occurred
If it's been only a few weeks or even months since your lawyer committed malpractice, skip ahead to Section C—and be sure to file your case promptly.

In a malpractice case, the date from when the statute of limitations starts is called the "trigger" date. In legal lingo, once a statute has been triggered (starts), it begins to run. This means that if a state has a one-year statute of limitations for attorney malpractice and the trigger date is April 1, the statute of limitations period runs from April 2 to the following April 1.

Your State May Count Differently
In a few states—Georgia, Kansas, Kentucky and Wisconsin—the statute of limitations starts to run on the day the malpractice occurred, and therefore would run from April 1 to the following March 31.

If you don't file within that period, your claim against your lawyer is said to be "barred" by the statute of limitations, because the limitations period has run out. What triggers the start date in a malpractice case differs from state to state—and in many states, two or more events can trigger the start date. The most common trigger dates are:

- the date you sustained damage as a result of the malpractice (damages rule)
- the date the malpractice occurred (occurrence rule)
- the date you discovered or should have discovered the attorney's mistake (discovery rule), or
- the date the attorney last represented you (last representation rule).

These are explained in more detail in Section B.1.b, below.

a. Which Statute of Limitations Will Apply?

Very few state statutes of limitations specifically include cases for legal malpractice. In most states, you use the statute of limitations for another kind of case, such as breach of contract or tort (general civil wrong, such as negligence). Which kind isn't always clear, meaning that lawyers frequently argue over it.

STATUTES OF LIMITATIONS APPLICABLE TO LEGAL MALPRACTICE CASES

Legal Malpractice	Professional Malpractice[4]	Tort	Breach of Contract	General Civil Cases
Alabama	Florida	Alaska	Arkansas	Delaware
California	Idaho	Arizona	Hawaii	District of Columbia
Illinois	Kentucky	Colorado	New Jersey	Indiana
Louisiana	Massachusetts	Connecticut	New Mexico	Iowa
Montana	Michigan	Mississippi	New York	Maine
Nevada	Nebraska	Oklahoma	Utah	Maryland
Rhode Island	New York	Oregon	Virginia	Minnesota
South Dakota	North Carolina	Texas	Washington	New Hampshire
	North Dakota	Wisconsin		Pennsylvania
	Ohio			South Carolina
	Tennessee			Vermont
	Wyoming			

Note: In New York a legal malpractice claim may be either a professional malpractice or a breach of contract claim.

Below are two charts:
- Chart 1—Number of Years to Sue for Malpractice, and
- Chart 2—Actions that Extend the Statute of Limitations.

 Use Charts Only as a Place to Start Your Research

Defense lawyers, in an effort to defeat malpractice claims, often claim that the statute of limitations has expired. Indeed, because it is such a reliable winner, lawyers raise and litigate this defense in virtually every malpractice case. The result is that every state has a wealth of hypertechnical and sometimes contradictory case law relating to statutes of limitations. So use the charts in this chapter only as a place to start your research.

In researching the question of statute of limitations, you will want to begin with your state statute (Chart 1). Unless it is absolutely clear that your case is well within the statutory time, you will want to read some cases interpreting the statute. (See Chapter 11 for information on doing legal research.)

i. States With Specific Legal or Professional Malpractice Statutes

States which have a specific legal or professional malpractice statute tend to describe in detail how many years you have to file your lawsuit and from what date the statute starts to run. For example, Florida's law states that you must file within two years from the date the cause of action was discovered, or through the exercise of

CHART 1—NUMBER OF YEARS TO SUE FOR MALPRACTICE

State	Statute	Number of Years
Alabama	6-5-574(a)	Within two years after act or omission or failure giving rise to claim; if cause of action is not discovered and could not reasonably have been discovered within such period, then action may be commenced within six months from date of such discovery or date of discovery of facts which would reasonably lead to such discovery, whichever is earlier; in no event may action be commenced more than four years after such act or omission or failure, except, an act or omission or failure giving rise to a claim which occurred before August 1, 1987, shall not in any event be barred until expiration of one year from such date.
Alaska	09.10.070	Two years.
Arizona	12-542	Two years.
Arkansas	16-56-105	Three years.

California	CCP 340.6	• Within one year after plaintiff discovers, or through the use of reasonable diligence should have discovered, facts constituting wrongful act or omission, whichever first occurs. In no event shall time for commencement of legal action exceed four years except that period shall be tolled during time that any of following exists:
		  ▪ plaintiff has not sustained actual injury
		  ▪ attorney continues to represent plaintiff regarding specific subject matter in which alleged wrongful act or omission occurred
		  ▪ attorney willfully conceals facts constituting wrongful act or omission when such facts are known to attorney; this shall toll only four-year limitation, and
		  ▪ plaintiff is under legal or physical disability which restricts plaintiff's ability to commence legal action.
		• In action based upon instrument in writing, effective date of which depends upon some act or event of future, period of limitations provided for by this section shall commence to run upon occurrence of such act or event.

Colorado	13-80-102(1)(a)	Two years.
Connecticut	52-577	Three years.
Delaware	10-8106	Three years.
District of Columbia	12-301 (8)	Three years.
Florida	95.11(4)(a)	Within two years from discovery of cause of action or from when it should have been discovered with exercise of due diligence. [Not applicable to people who did not hire attorney, such as intended beneficiary of will.]

CHART 1—NUMBER OF YEARS TO SUE FOR MALPRACTICE

State	Statute	Number of Years
Georgia	9-3-25	Four years—general breach of contract statute usually applies.
	9-3-33	Two years—general tort statute may apply in some cases; exceptions to two-year rule: injuries to reputation (one year); injuries involving loss of consortium (four years).
Hawaii	657-1 (1)	Six years.
Idaho	5-219(4)	Within two years of wrongful act or omission.
Illinois	735 ¶ 5/13-214.3	Within two years from time the person bringing the action knew or reasonably should have known of injury but no later than six years after occurrence of act or omission.
		If client dies and injury does not occur until death, action may be commenced within two years after date of person's death unless letters of office are issued or person's will is admitted to probate within that two-year period, in which case, action must be commenced within time for filing claims against estate or petition contesting validity of will of deceased person, whichever is later.
		For minors and others under other legal disabilities when cause of action accrues, statute does not begin to run until minor reaches age of majority or other legal disability is removed.
Indiana	34-1-2-2	Two years [specific statute of limitations for physicians and other professionals does not apply].
Iowa	614.1(4)	Five years.
Kansas	60-512	Three years—general oral or implied contract statute.
	60-513(a) & (b)	Two years—general injury to rights of another statute usually applies; does not begin to run until substantial injury, but there is ten-year cap from date of negligent act or omission.
Kentucky	413.245	Within one year from date of the occurrence or from date when cause of action was, or reasonably should have been, discovered.
Louisiana	9:5605	Within one year from date the alleged act, omission or neglect is discovered or should have been discovered but not later than three years from date of alleged act, omission or neglect.
		Possible ten-year breach of contract statute could apply if attorney expressly warrants specific result and fails to obtain it or if attorney agrees to perform certain work and does nothing whatsoever.[5]

CHART 1—NUMBER OF YEARS TO SUE FOR MALPRACTICE

State	Statute	Number of Years
Maine	14-752	Six years.
Maryland	5-101	Three years.
Massachusetts	260-4	Three years.
Michigan	600.5805	Two years from occurrence or six months of discovery, whichever is later.
Minnesota	541-05, Subd. 1(5)	Six years.
Mississippi	15-1-49	Three years.
Missouri	516.120	Five years.
Montana	27-2-206	Within three years after plaintiff discovers, or through use of reasonable diligence should have discovered act, error or omission, whichever occurs last, but no later than ten years from the date of the act, error or omission.
Nebraska	25-222	Within two years after act or omission, but if not discovered and could not have been reasonably discovered within such two-year period, then within one year from date of such discovery or from date of discovery of facts which would reasonably lead to such discovery, whichever occurs earlier, but no later than ten years from date of act or omission.
Nevada	11.207	Within four years after damage is sustained and facts constituting cause of action are discovered or reasonably should have been discovered; statute is tolled if attorney conceals fact-constituting negligence which are known or reasonably should be known.
New Hampshire	508:4	Within three years of act or omission, except that when injury and its causal relationship to act or omission were not discovered and could not reasonably have been discovered at time of act or omission, within three years of time plaintiff discovers, or in exercise of reasonable diligence should have discovered, injury and its causal relationship to act or omission complained of.
New Jersey	2A:14-1	Six years.
New Mexico	37-1-4	Four years.
New York	213 (2)	Six years—breach of contract claims.
	214(6)	Three years—malpractice (negligence) claims.

CHART 1—NUMBER OF YEARS TO SUE FOR MALPRACTICE

State	Statute	Number of Years
North Carolina	1-15	Four years from the last act giving rise to claim; if the injury is not readily apparent at time of its origin ("hidden injury"), and is discovered or reasonably should be discovered two or more years after the occurrence of the last act giving rise to the claim, the lawsuit must be filed within one year from the date the discovery is made. In no event could this be less than three years or more than four years from the last act giving rise to the claim.
North Dakota	28-01-18(3)	Two years.
Ohio	2305.11	One year.
Oklahoma	12 95 (3)	Two years.
Oregon	12.115(1)	Ten years from occurrence.
Pennsylvania	42-5525	Four years.
Rhode Island	9-1-14.3	Within three years of occurrence of incident giving rise to claim, unless injuries were not reasonably discoverable, then within three years from discovery or when discovery reasonably should have occurred.
South Carolina	15-3-530(1)	Three years.
South Dakota	15-2-14.2	Within three years after malpractice occurred.
Tennessee	28-3-104	One year.
Texas	16.003(a)	Two years.
Utah	78-12-25 (1)	Four years.
Vermont	12-511	Six years.
Virginia	8.01-246 (2)	Five years—breach of written contract statute rarely applies.
	8.01-246 (4)	Three years—breach of oral contract statute usually applies.
Washington	4.16.080 (3)	Three years.
West Virginia	55-2-12	Two years—torts statute usually applies.
	55-2-6	Five years—breach of oral contract statute sometimes applies. Ten years—breach of written contract statute rarely applies.
Wisconsin	893.53	Six years.
Wyoming	1-3-107	Within two years of act, error or omission or within two years from when it was discovered or should reasonably have been discovered.

reasonable diligence, should have been discovered. In Illinois, you must file within two years from the time you know or reasonably should have known of the injury, but not later than six years from when the negligent act occurred.

ii. States Using General Civil Statutes of Limitations

In states that apply a more general limitation statute to malpractice claims, such as Maine, which requires that all civil actions be filed within six years, the statute begins to run the day after the negligent act, omission or event took place—that is, the date your lawyer did something wrong or made a mistake.

If you lawyer's negligence was in failing to do something—such as failing to file an appeal notice on time—the date of the negligence is the actual date your lawyer should have done something and didn't. If your lawyer made a series of mistakes or omissions over a period of time, the date is likely to be the date of the last act or the last date when your lawyer was supposed to do something but didn't. Here are some examples of the dates of a negligent act, omission or event:

- Your lawyer put the wrong amount of support "on the record" when reciting the terms of the agreement in court and the time limit for filing a correction expired.
- Your lawyer failed to show up in court.
- Your lawyer didn't file a complaint on time.
- Your lawyer was supposed to draft a will and didn't. The negligence would be when the lawyer should have done it and didn't. Although lawyers might disagree about

when that date is, it is likely that a court would rule that the negligence occurred on the last possible reasonable date the lawyer could have drafted the will.

b. Extending the Statute of Limitations

Often, you don't know about your lawyer's negligence until well after it occurred—perhaps because you aren't damaged until sometime later. For this reason, states have rules that extend (toll) the statute of limitations. A few states put their tolling rules into the statute of limitations law and are covered in Chart 1. But most of the rules that extend the statute of limitations to file a malpractice case have evolved over time through case law (decisions by courts followed by other courts). The four most common are:

- the statute of limitations may be tolled (doesn't start running) until you are damaged as a result of the malpractice
- the statute of limitations may be tolled until you discover or should have reasonably discovered the attorney's mistake
- the statute of limitations may be tolled while important facts about your case are concealed from you, or
- the statute of limitations may be tolled until the attorney stops representing you.

EXAMPLE 1: Your lawyer failed to disclose to the other side the names of your expert witnesses, who were therefore barred from testifying on your behalf at your trial. Although you were actually damaged when you lost your case on June 5, 1996, you don't learn of your attorney's mistake until you consult with a second lawyer on November 22, 1996, who explains why the absences of expert witnesses caused you to lose your case. In the many states which use both the damage and discovery rules, the statute of limitations does not begin until November 23, 1996. This means that if your state has a one-year statute of limitations for malpractice claims, you would have to file your lawsuit by November 22,1997.

EXAMPLE 2: You lose your case at trial, which is the date you were damaged. Your lawyer files an appeal and represents you through the end of the appeal process. You lose on appeal as well. The statute of limitations does not start to run until the appeal is over and the lawyer stops representing you. This is true even if you discovered or should have discovered the damages earlier.

In some circumstances, you may find that although one type of statute of limitations prevents your case from being heard, another one allows it to go forward.

EXAMPLE: You hired an attorney to represent you in a divorce filed by your spouse and paid the attorney a $3,000 retainer fee. Your attorney never filed your response and as a result, a "default" divorce was obtained against you with unfavorable terms. When you demanded the return of your $3,000, the lawyer said she no longer had it. You want to sue for malpractice (a one-year statute of limitations) and breach of fiduciary duty and embezzlement (a

two-year statute of limitations). It's been one and one-half years since your divorce. Although your malpractice claim is no longer good, you can claim breach of fiduciary duty and embezzlement. (In addition, you should also file a claim of abandonment with the lawyer discipline agency in your state. See Chapter 8.)

If it appears that all of the statutes (or the only statute) of limitations have passed, but there is room to argue the other way, then you will need to do a cost-benefit analysis of whether it is worth the fight. If you may be able to win large damages, it may be worth it. If the inevitable court fight over which statute of limitations date applies is likely to cost you more than the damages involved, then you will want to forget proceeding with the case.

Chart 2 summarizes each state's tolling rules. A blank means that no statute or case law exists on that issue in your state. Although this might seem unusual, understand that malpractice cases against lawyers started "booming" in the 1970s and legal precedents are very recent. *Legal Malpractice*, the first major treatise on legal malpractice (for lawyers) was written by my former boss, friend and frequent adversary, Ronald E. Mallen. Originally published in 1977 as a single volume, in 1996 the fourth edition came out as a four-volume set, indicating how much law has been made in the last 20 years.

⚠ Use This Information as a Place to Begin
As with Chart 1, do not use the material as a comprehensive analysis of how the tolling rules work in your state. The chart is a starting place only.

CHART 2—ACTIONS THAT EXTEND THE STATUTE OF LIMITATIONS

State	Statute tolled until you are damaged	Statute tolled until you discover or reasonably should have discovered mistake	Statute tolled while facts constituting claim are concealed from you	Statute tolled until attorney stops representing you
Alabama	yes	yes	yes	
Alaska	yes	yes	yes	probably
Arizona	yes	yes	yes	yes
Arkansas	yes	no	yes	
California	yes; actual injury required	yes; but four-year cap	yes	yes
Colorado	probably; on tort claim, when injury is known, cause of action accrues	yes	yes	probably
Connecticut		maybe	yes	maybe
Delaware	yes	yes	yes	
District of Columbia	yes	yes	yes	
Florida	yes	yes	yes	yes
Georgia	yes		yes	
Hawaii			yes	
Idaho	yes	no	yes	no
Illinois	yes	yes; but six-year cap	yes	no
Indiana	yes	maybe	yes	
Iowa	yes	yes	yes	probably
Kansas	yes; substantial injury required	yes	yes	yes
Kentucky	yes	yes	yes	yes
Louisiana	probably	yes; but three-year cap	probably	probably not
Maine	probably	maybe	yes	
Maryland	yes	yes	yes	
Massachusetts	yes	yes	yes	yes; unless consulted with second lawyer while first lawyer continues to represent you
Michigan	yes	yes	yes	yes
Minnesota	yes	yes	yes	probably

CHART 2—ACTIONS THAT EXTEND THE STATUTE OF LIMITATIONS

State	Statute tolled until you are damaged	Statute tolled until you discover or reasonably should have discovered mistake	Statute tolled while facts constituting claim are concealed from you	Statute tolled until attorney stops representing you
Mississippi	yes	yes	yes	yes
Missouri	yes	maybe	yes	no
Montana	yes	yes; but ten-year cap	yes	no
Nebraska	maybe	yes	yes	yes; unless negligence discovered during representation
Nevada	yes	yes	yes	
New Hampshire	probably	yes	yes	
New Jersey	yes	yes	yes	
New Mexico	yes	yes	yes	no
New York	probably not	no	yes	yes
North Carolina	yes; damages required for discovery of hidden injury	yes; but four-year cap	yes	maybe
North Dakota	yes	yes	yes	yes
Ohio	yes	yes	yes	yes
Oklahoma	yes	yes	yes	maybe
Oregon	yes; but ten-year cap cap	yes; but ten-year cap	yes	maybe; but ten-year
Pennsylvania	yes	yes	yes	yes
Rhode Island		yes	yes	
South Carolina		yes	yes	
South Dakota	probably not	no	yes	yes
Tennessee	yes	yes	yes	
Texas	yes	yes	yes	maybe
Utah	no	yes		no
Vermont	probably	yes		
Virginia	yes		yes	yes
Washington	yes	yes	yes	
West Virginia	yes	yes		maybe
Wisconsin	yes	yes	yes	no
Wyoming		yes		

i. You Weren't Yet Damaged

The most common reason for tolling the statute of limitations is that you haven't yet been damaged. In fact, most states require that you be damaged by your lawyer's malpractice before the statute of limitations begins to run. What is necessary to constitute damages varies, depending upon the facts in your case and your state's rules of interpretation.

Here are some examples of damages.

You incur attorney's fees. Paying another lawyer to try and sort out your first lawyer's mistake is probably the most common type of damage in a legal malpractice case. In most states, the statute of limitations starts to run as soon as you pay a second lawyer to represent you.

> **EXAMPLE:** Your lawyer made a mistake in drafting a contract and you were sued as a result. You paid a second attorney a $1,000 retainer to defend you in the lawsuit.[6] Over the next several months, the second lawyer negotiates a settlement and you pay $50,000 to settle the dispute. You were damaged when you paid the $1,000 retainer and the statute of limitations begins to run from that date.

In general, as soon as you pay any attorney's fees, you have been damaged and the statute begins to run. In a few states, your damages occur on the date you knew you had to hire a second attorney to handle a matter that arose as a result of your first lawyer's malpractice. (This might be the date you were sued.) In other states, your damages occur when you incur the debt or you receive the bill from the second attorney, whether you pay it immediately or later.

An adverse judgment is entered against you. If you lose a lawsuit because of your attorney's malpractice, you are damaged when the judgment is entered against you. For example, your lawyer tries your medical malpractice case but does not call any expert witnesses. As a result, you lose your case and a judgment is entered against you. The date the judgment is actually entered in the court records is the date you are damaged.

You learn that a security agreement prepared by your attorney is not effective. When a person lends money or sells property, she often receives a promissory note backed up by a security agreement in exchange for agreeing to receive all or part of the payment in installments. The security agreement allows you to foreclose on the property pledged as security (often a house or other real estate) if you aren't paid. But if the security agreement is invalid or not properly recorded, foreclosure won't be available to you if you aren't paid. In most states, you are damaged when the debtor fails to make an installment payment and you learn that you have no recourse against the security. In Alabama, however, a court ruled that because unsecured property (the promissory note) is worth less than secured property, the damage occurred when the promissory note was received.[7]

You receive notice of tax deficiency. If, as a result of a lawyer's mistake, you receive a notice of tax deficiency from the IRS or other taxing authority, you are damaged when you receive the notice, not when you challenge it or pay the tax.[8]

Your attorney errs in drafting your marital settlement agreement. The date an erroneous marital settlement agreement becomes final is the date you are damaged. Usually this is the date the agreement is signed by you and your ex-spouse, but in some states, it may be the date the agreement is incorporated into a court judgment.

ii. You Didn't Yet Discover the Facts

In most states, the statute of limitations is delayed (tolled) until you know or have reason to know the facts which would give rise to the claim against your lawyer. This "discovery rule" makes sense because law is a highly technical field and it's common that you won't learn about a mistake your lawyer has made until sometime after the fact.

As soon as you know that you possibly have a claim against your lawyer, you probably have "discovered" the facts necessary to start the statute of limitations running. You don't have to know exactly what your lawyer did. You just have to know that there is a problem.

> EXAMPLE: You call your lawyer to find out the status of your case, but are given no information. You then visit the courthouse and check the file which tells you that your case was dismissed. The statute of limitations starts to run from this date—the date you discovered the problem—even if you don't know what, if any, damages you have incurred.

In Illinois, Missouri, North Carolina and Rhode Island, the statute of limitations is tolled until you discover or should have discovered your damages, rather than until you discover or should have discovered the facts giving rise to your claim.

> EXAMPLE: Your lawyer handled the paperwork when you purchased property in the country. Although the title company showed an easement on the title report, the lawyer misread it or failed to tell you about it. Before you build your home, an adjacent owner has who has an access easement across the part of the property you plan to build on cuts a road across your land. Three months later, you drive to the country to visit your land and discover the road. The statute of limitations against your lawyer starts to run when you discover your damages—the road.

Remember that the statute of limitations is tolled until you discover or *should have discovered* the facts giving rise to the problem. Obviously it's not always easy to determine when something "should" have been discovered. But if you call your lawyer's office for several months in an effort to find out what's happening in your court case but never get an answer, the law probably will require that you do something more to quickly ferret out what seems to be a problem—sit in your lawyer's office until you get some answers or go to the courthouse and look at the file. Certainly, if you learn or strongly suspect that your case was dismissed, you now have discovered a problem.

In many situations, whether a particular fact situation will trigger the statute of limitations to start to run will depend on:

• your level of sophistication

- the facts of your case
- what you hired the original lawyer to do, and
- your lawyer's excuses.

If you are a business person who regularly handles your company's legal matters, you will be expected to be more familiar with legal systems and have a greater ability to see through your lawyer's excuses than if you have never had any experience with lawyers or the legal system. In short, the statute of limitations probably will be tolled for a shorter time for a business person than it would be for a less sophisticated client.

YOUR NEW LAWYER'S ACTIONS ARE ATTRIBUTABLE TO YOU

The date your new lawyer reasonably should have learned of a mistake will be attributed to you for purposes of determining when the statute of limitations runs. This date will depend on several things, including:

- the status of the case when your new lawyer took over
- the complexity of the case
- the other matters your lawyer had scheduled, and
- whether your first lawyer delayed in handing over the files.

Discovering facts or damages can happen years after the lawyer's negligent act or omission. So that lawyers can't be sued indefinitely for their mistakes, a few states—California, Illinois, Louisiana, Montana, North Carolina and Oregon—impose a maximum number of years for filing a lawsuit, even if you don't discover the facts giving rise to your claim until many years after the malpractice occurs.

For example, Illinois allows a lawsuit to be filed within two years of discovery, but in no case more than six years from the date of the negligent act. If your Illinois lawyer made a mistake in 1993, and you discovered it in 1995, you must file by 1997. But if you don't discover it until 1998, you must file by 1999 because of the six-year cap.

EXAMPLE—HOW THE DISCOVERY RULE WORKS: You hire Adam (first lawyer) to help you sell your business. Adam drafts a promissory note and security agreement which the buyers sign. They agree to pay you $1,000 per month for five years. The note is secured by the assets of the business, which means that if the buyers don't pay, you can repossess the assets. After ten months, the payments stop. You hire Bill (second lawyer) and pay him a retainer to repossess the assets. Bill learns that Adam never recorded your security agreement. Bill further finds that the buyers had pledged the business assets to a bank to secure a loan and defaulted on that loan, and that the bank has already taken the assets and sold them at an auction. You have just discovered your damage and the statute of limitations starts to run against Adam.

iii. Your Lawyer Concealed Information From You

Every state (with the possible exceptions of Louisiana and Oregon) tolls the statute of limitations if your lawyer conceals important information from you about your case. (Concealment is also fraud—see Section B.2, below.) In this situation, the statute of limitations will not start until you learn—or reasonably should have learned—what your lawyer was hiding.

Concealment can take two forms. In every state, telling an overt lie is considered concealment. In addition, in most states, failing to tell you something is considered concealment.

Here are some common examples of concealment.

• **Your lawyer agrees to file a personal injury case, but doesn't.** After you and the lawyer sign a contingency fee agreement, you call your lawyer to find out the status of your case. She refuses to take your calls. Eventually you get distressed and call the other party's insurance company. They know nothing about your case. You visit the courthouse and can't find any record of a case filing with your name on it. Your lawyer's conduct in avoiding your calls and not telling you that the complaint was not filed is concealment. You discover the problem when you learn that the insurance company knows nothing about your case. You confirm your discovery when you go the courthouse and find no record that your case was filed.

• **Your lawyer settles your case but doesn't pay you anything.** After not being able to contact the lawyer you retained to work on your personal injury case for several months, you call the insurance company and learn that they paid a settlement in your case a number of months before. You have never seen the money. Your lawyer has probably concealed the fact that she stole your money. You discover the facts that give rise to your claim against your lawyer when the insurance agent handling your claim tells you that the claim has been paid.

• **Your lawyer insists that you accept a settlement that seems low and is far less that what he told you to expect.** In urging you to take the small settlement, your lawyer explains several reasons why the case is not as good as he originally thought. He fails to tell you, however, that the real reason why your case has gone south is that he missed the deadline to secure expert witnesses. You discover facts giving rise to a claim against your lawyer when you learn from your adversary that your lawyer missed the deadline to disclose expert witnesses.

• **You take financial papers to your divorce lawyer and ask what they are.** She says to leave them with her and she'll look into it. Your forget about the papers, your lawyer never mentions them again, and your divorce eventually settles. Later, you remember the papers and call your lawyer to find out what happened to them. She has no idea of what you are talking about. You ask your ex and learn that they were bearer bonds and could be used by anyone just like cash! Not only do you have concealment, but you may also have stealing. You

discover the facts giving rise to your claim against your lawyer when you learn from your tax accountant that what you gave your lawyer was the equivalent of cash.

iv. You Were a Minor, Imprisoned, Disabled or Unavailable

In Louisiana, Skip This Section
None of the grounds for extending the statute of limitations discussed below apply in Louisiana.

If you are trying to find extra time to file a lawsuit, do some legal research (see Chapter 11) or have a lawyer check to see if any of the following (called "legal disabilities") are grounds for tolling a statute of limitations in your state:

- you were in prison or jail
- you were a minor
- you were hospitalized
- you were mentally or physically disabled, or
- you or the lawyer you want to sue were out of the country.

EXAMPLE: Montana tolls the statute of limitations if you are imprisoned for up to five years. If you serve 20 years, it will be too late to sue when you get out because Montana has a ten-year statute of limitations for malpractice cases and you can delay the time at which it begins for only five years. If you serve only three years, however, the statute of limitations does not start to run until you get out.

v. Your Lawyer Still Represented You

In most states, if your lawyer continues to represent you, the statute of limitations against that attorney is tolled for as long as the lawyer represents you on the same matter in which your lawyer was negligent. If your lawyer is handling two different matters for you, once the case on which the lawyer committed the malpractice ends, the statute of limitations no longer is tolled, even if the lawyer is doing other legal work for you.

EXAMPLE: Your lawyer is handling your personal injury case and your divorce. The personal injury case settles, and your lawyer continues to handle your divorce. The continuing representation in the divorce would not give you extra time to sue your lawyer for a mistake in the personal injury case.

Sometimes, you and your lawyer both know that your lawyer made a mistake, but you agree to let your lawyer try and correct it. In most states, this situation results in the statute of limitations being tolled for the length of time your lawyer takes trying to fix the problem. In

Nebraska, however, once you discover your lawyer's negligence, the continuing representation rule does not toll the statute of limitations.

Here are common examples of when the representation is over and the statute of limitations starts to run:

- the lawyer finishes what he was hired to do
- you send a letter firing your lawyer
- you and your lawyer sign a document in which you agree that the lawyer no longer represents you
- a court grants a motion letting the attorney withdraw from your case
- your lawyer dies
- you file a complaint with your state's disciplinary agency concerning your lawyer's conduct
- your lawyer sends you a notice of fee arbitration, or
- your lawyer sues you to collect her fees.

vi. You Appealed or Tried to Fix the Error

A few states, including Arizona, Iowa and Kentucky, toll the statute of limitations while your case is on appeal or while you take other remedial action, such as file a motion to set aside a judgment or a motion to reconsider the outcome—even if you handle it yourself or hire a second lawyer to take the case.

Most states, however, including Alabama, California, Colorado, District of Columbia, Idaho, Michigan, Nebraska, New Jersey, New Mexico, Ohio, Oklahoma and Oregon, will not extend the statute of limitations while your case is on appeal or while a motion to set aside a judgment or to reconsider the case is pending

unless the lawyer who made the error in the first place continues to represent you.

WILL THE LAWYER AGREE TO EXTEND THE STATUTE OF LIMITATIONS?

You may decide to try to fix your lawyer's mistake yourself or with a new lawyer and defer your decision about whether or not to sue for malpractice. But this may put you in a bind if the law in your state does not toll the statute of limitations while you appeal or file a motion. To protect yourself, you can ask the attorney who made the mistake to sign an agreement extending the statute of limitations. Most lawyers will cooperate in your effort not to sue them—if they think about it. Some lawyers (or their insurance companies) will even pay for your efforts to try to fix their mistakes. If the lawyer agrees to give you extra time, put the exact date in the agreement, such as July 1, 1997, rather than just saying "an additional one-year period of time to sue for malpractice."

vii. Other Ways to Toll the Statute of Limitations

Here are a few other grounds used to toll or extend the statute of limitations in legal malpractice cases.

The lawyer files for bankruptcy. A court may toll the statute for the length of time your former attorney is in Chapter 11 bankruptcy.[9] This is because, in general, you are barred from suing or pursuing a lawsuit against the lawyer once she files for bankruptcy.

Corporation suspended because of lawyer's malpractice. A court may toll the statute for the length of time a corporation was suspended from doing business for failing to comply with state law.[10]

Corporation controlled by fraudulently behaving officers or directors. If you are suing a lawyer for a bank or a corporation along with some of the officers or directors, a court may extend the statute for suing the lawyer for the time that the officers or directors controlled the bank or the company.[11]

2. Statute of Limitations for Breach of Fiduciary Duty or Fraud

If you have a claim against a lawyer for intentionally breaching her fiduciary duty (duty of loyalty) or for defrauding you, the statute of limitations which applies in most states in most circumstances will be that for fraud. How long this is varies from state to state, but is generally two to ten years from when the fraud is discovered or reasonably should have been discovered.

It is important to understand that for the fraud statute of limitations to apply to a breach of fiduciary duty claim, your lawyer must have intentionally breached the fiduciary duty to you. If the breach was accidental, such as a clerical error, the statute of limitations for malpractice (discussed in Section B.1, above), applies.

EXAMPLE: Your lawyer's secretary accidentally sends a copy of your child's adoption papers to the birth mother, thus revealing your identity and the whereabouts of the child. This information was supposed to remain confidential. The malpractice statute of limitations will probably apply because the secretary made an honest error. If your attorney deliberately revealed your identity to the birth mother, however, the fraud statute of limitations would apply.

Usually, the statute of limitations does not begin to run until you discover you have been defrauded. This is because the wrong is usually hidden from you, at least for a while. This gives you extra time to file your lawsuit.

EXAMPLE 1: Your lawyer settled your case without telling you, forged your name and took your money in 1994. You figure it out in 1996. You live in California which has a three-year statute of limitations for fraud. You have until 1999 to sue.

EXAMPLE 2: Your adoption lawyer revealed your identity to the birth mother of your child. She comes to visit and tells you how she learned of your identity and location. You just discovered your claim against your lawyer and the statute of limitations starts to run.

Chart 1 in Section B.1.a, above, does not include fraud. Each state has a separate statute of limitations which applies to fraud claims. Your state's statutes are in a law library or large public library. Look in the index to your state's statutes under "statutes of limitations" or "limitations of actions" to find the statute of limitations for fraud. For a shortcut, look at

Chart 1, which gives your state's statute for the statute of limitations for malpractice. The statute of limitations for fraud may be in the same statute or close by.

C. Who Should You Sue?

Below is a list of all the possible people (called "defendants") you should consider suing. Anyone responsible for your loss can be sued. If the lawyer and law firm who were primarily responsible for your loss have adequate insurance (see Section D, below), it probably won't be necessary to name every possible defendant. If, however, the insurance is inadequate, naming all possible defendants can make the difference between collecting and not.

The lawyer you hired. In all cases, sue the lawyer you hired to handle your matter.

The lawyer who was primarily in charge of handling your matter. This is usually the lawyer you hired. But if you hired a lawyer who works for a law firm and the lawyer gives your case to another lawyer in the firm (perhaps because the other lawyer has the time or expertise), sue that lawyer as well.

Any lawyer who worked on your matter. A lawyer may hire another lawyer with whom he does not work to do particular tasks in a case. If you hired a solo practitioner or someone without insurance, be sure to sue both the lawyer you hired and any other lawyers who worked on your case.

In law firms, junior attorneys often do legal research, brief writing and simple discovery, while a senior attorney supervises the junior attorneys and does the important or complex work, such as a deposition or trial. If you are suing a law firm, the firm's insurance will cover the acts of its employees or outside lawyers hired to work on your case. If there is adequate insurance, it isn't necessary to name every lawyer who worked on your case.

Each partner in the law firm. Partners in a law firm are responsible for law work done by each other. If three partners are in the firm and only one worked on your case, all three are responsible for any mistakes. If the firm has adequate insurance, you can sue just the firm and the lawyer who handled your case. If the insurance is inadequate, however, sue each partner.

Law firms often do business under fictitious names, such as Keeting and Howe, Attorneys at Law. The name of the firm can give you a good idea about who some of the partners are. Lewella Keeting and Bernard Howe are probably partners in the firm. If other lawyers work there, some of them may be partners, even if their names are not part of the firm's name. Be aware that in long-established firms, some or all named partners may have died; traditionally, their names remain part of the firm's name. To find out the names of all current partners, you'll have to do discovery.

Some firms now do business as limited liability partnerships (LLPs) or limited liability companies (LLCs). Under these creations, partners are not responsible for the negligent acts of each other. If the firm you want to sue is an LLP or LLC, you probably can't sue the partners who did no work on your case.

The law firms where a lawyer worked while doing work on your case. The law firm where your lawyer worked may have merged with another law firm or added a partner and changed its name. Or, the lawyer working on your case may have changed law firms and taken your case with her. In either situation, be sure to sue the original firm and the new firm.

The lawyer who referred you to the lawyer who committed the malpractice. If one attorney sent you to another attorney who was not qualified to handle your matter, you would have a claim against the first attorney for negligent referral. Although these cases are rare (in 19 years, I have brought this claim only once), it should not be overlooked.

The lawyer referral service or legal insurance plan that referred you to the lawyer who committed the malpractice. Lawyer referral services and some legal insurance plans make referrals. Some referral services and insurance plans have their own insurance to cover a lawyer for matters which they refer. The most common claims against referral services and legal insurance plans are for inadequate screening of the lawyers to whom they refer or inadequate training and supervision.

The lawyer's estate (if the lawyer has died). If your lawyer has died, you can sue your lawyer's estate, but you will be treated like any other creditor and must file your claim within the time period allowed by your state. This time is generally much shorter than the time allowed to sue for malpractice.

D. Can You Collect If You Win?

Lawsuits are time consuming, emotionally draining and expensive. The only thing you can win is money. Early on, you need to figure out if it is worth it to proceed—that is, can you collect if you win?

If the amount of your claim is modest and an attorney responsible for your loss is still working, you probably won't have a problem collecting. Most judgments can be collected as many 20 years after they are awarded and in some states judgments can be extended.

If the amount of your claim is six figures or more, you might have a more difficult time collecting. First and foremost, you want to find out whether any attorney responsible for your loss has malpractice insurance. Not all attorneys do. Only Oregon requires lawyers to have malpractice insurance.

1. Finding Out If the Lawyer Has Insurance

You often cannot find out if a lawyer has malpractice insurance until you file a lawsuit. To find out sooner, you can ask—preferably an employee or former employee. If you ask the lawyer herself and get a "yes," it is probably a truthful answer. But don't rely on a "no" unless the lawyer is willing to confirm it in writing, under oath.

Another way to check out malpractice insurance before you sue is to visit your local courthouse and look at the court filings to see if your lawyer or his law firm has been sued before for malpractice. If you find other cases, call the lawyers who represented the plaintiffs in those other cases; their phone numbers will be on the court papers. Ask about insurance—how much coverage, the name of the insurance company and any other claims they know about. Because a lawyer had insurance once does not mean he still does, but it is a sign that he is (or at least was) willing to pay for it.

If you don't find out before you sue whether or not the lawyer has insurance, you certainly will afterward. If the lawyer has insurance, she will be represented by a lawyer hired by the insurance company, and insurance companies usually hire lawyers from "insurance defense firms."

Of course, you won't know whether or not the lawyer is with an insurance defense firm just by looking at the response papers. Your own attorney (or lawyer friends) might know. Or, you can check a lawyer directory for your state or the nation to see how the firm describes itself. A local law library will have such directories. You might also get a clue by calling the lawyer's office and asking the receptionist.

Once your lawyer files a response to your lawsuit, you can use the discovery process (usually written questions called interrogatories) to find out about insurance. Ask whether there is insurance, the name of the insurance company and how much insurance coverage is available (called the policy limit).

2. If the Lawyer Doesn't Have Insurance

If you're suing a large law firm (50 or more lawyers) and it doesn't have insurance, don't despair. Many large firms self insure—meaning they pay for their own malpractice errors, rather than pay insurance premiums. Unless you have a multimillion-dollar claim, it is unlikely that collection will be a problem if you successfully sue a large law firm.

If you sue a solo practitioner or small firm with no insurance, you will only be able to collect your judgment from the assets of the individual lawyer or lawyers. You can't ask questions about the lawyers' assets until you get a judgment. This will be after your malpractice lawsuit is over.

So before suing, you will want to informally investigate. First, you can visit your county land records office, do a search and find out if the lawyer owns real estate. Second, you can hire an investigator to do an asset search. Although there is no assurance that the lawyer will still own the assets once your case is over, this will give you a good idea about what kinds of assets the lawyer has available.

CASE STRATEGY WHEN YOUR LAWYER DOES NOT HAVE INSURANCE

- Sue all possible defendants.
- Check the assets of each.
- Be reasonable and realistic about a settlement figure.
- Expect and ask for a modest recovery, one which won't bankrupt the lawyer—if the lawyer files for bankruptcy, you get nothing unless you prove the lawyer committed fraud or you recover punitive damages, neither of which can be eliminated in bankruptcy.

3. If the Lawyer Does Have Insurance

There are several things you should know about legal malpractice insurance policies:

Fixing the problem. If the problem you have with your lawyer might be correctable, the insurance company may hire a different lawyer to try and fix it. Insurance companies call these "claims repair programs." For example, if a judgment against you might be set aside or reversed on appeal, the insurance company may hire a new lawyer to try to get the judgment reversed. Don't agree to this unless you get a written promise from the insurance company that you can proceed with your lawsuit if the problem is not corrected.

Lawyer's consent to settle. Legal malpractice insurance policies usually require the lawyer's consent for any settlement. A second clause, however, gives the lawyer incentive to settle. It typically states that if the lawyer does not consent to a settlement the insurance company recommends as reasonable, and the person suing later wins an amount which exceeds the recommended settlement, the lawyer must personally pay all amounts above the suggested settlement. Lawyers call these "hammer clauses" or "blackmail clauses."

Policy amount. If your damages are the approximate amount of the policy (even if they slightly exceed it), demand a settlement for the policy amount. The lawyer will want the demand paid so that his personal assets are not at risk in the event you later win a judgment for an amount in excess of the policy limit. If the insurance company refuses your demand and you later win a judgment for more, the insurance company may be required to pay it all because it rejected a reasonable settlement offer and put the lawyer's personal assets at risk.

Costs of litigation deducted from policy amount. In many malpractice insurance policies, the costs of defense (attorneys fees and litigation costs) are deducted from the policy limits. This means that the amount of insurance available to pay your damages is reduced. If you have damages of $125,000 and the insurance policy limit is only $100,000, you'll want to quickly accept a settlement for the policy amount before litigation costs reduce it.

Some policies will pay full policy limits as long as defense costs don't exceed a certain amount. For example, on a $100,000 policy, the insurance company may be willing to pay up to the full $100,000 as long as defense costs don't go over $50,000. If the insurance company spends $35,000 defending the claim, the full

$100,000 policy limits will be available to pay out. If the insurance company spends $60,000, however, then only $90,000 would be available to pay out.

Claims not covered. Several claims are not covered by legal malpractice insurance.

• Claims for intentional conduct, willful, deliberate or malicious acts, criminal conduct or punitive damages. If you want insurance coverage to be available, call the conduct both negligent and intentional when you file your lawsuit and let the insurance company and the lawyer fight it out.

• Claims for work done in the area of securities. Coverage for lawyers who do securities work is very expensive and usually is included only if the policy contains a special securities endorsement for which the lawyer has paid an extra premium.

• Negligence which took place before the lawyer had the policy.

• Negligence which took place after the policy expired, unless the lawyer purchased a special endorsement or extension on the policy called "tail coverage."

• Conduct arising out of business ventures of the attorney, other than law business.

Who is covered. The lawyers who work for the firm, the law firm itself (which may be a partnership, corporation, limited liability company or limited liability partnership), employees of the firm and usually any independent contractors the firm hires to work on your case will be covered by the policy. The policy limit does not apply separately to each, however. A $100,000

policy is for $100,000 total, not $100,000 per defendant.

E. Proving a Malpractice Case

To prove (win) a case against an attorney for malpractice, in every state you must prove four basic things. Lawyers call them the "elements of your cause of action or case."

Let me emphasize the necessity of all four elements being present by comparing a malpractice lawsuit to baking a cake. To make a successful cake, you need eggs, flour, sugar and baking soda. If any one of these is missing, you end up with no cake. The four ingredients (elements) of your legal malpractice recipe (cause of action) are:

• **Duty**—that the attorney owed you a duty to act properly

• **Breach**—that the attorney breached the duty, was negligent, made a mistake or did not do what he agreed to do

• **Causation**—that this conduct caused you damages, and

• **Damages**—that you suffered financial losses as a result.

And just as it is true that you will have no cake if you leave out one of the essential ingredients, if one of elements of your cause of action is missing your malpractice case will fail.

1. Duty

Duty usually means that you had an attorney-client relationship or that the attorney was acting as *your* attorney. In other words, you need to show that the attorney was representing you. (See Chapter 1, Section C, for examples of situations in which there is *not* an attorney-client relationship.)

You can usually prove that the attorney was "your" attorney with canceled check(s) showing you paid a fee to the attorney, with a copy of a signed fee agreement or with correspondence between you and the attorney indicating that the attorney was advising or representing you.

But it is not necessary for you to have paid a lawyer a fee for the lawyer to have owed you a duty. If the lawyer offers you a free consultation through a bar association or other referral panel, that is sufficient to establish a duty, although it would be extremely limited if the attorney didn't agree to represent you further.

In some cases, an attorney may owe you a duty even though you did not hire or consult with her. This commonly occurs with the attorney who drafts a will or does an estate plan. In most states, courts have ruled that the beneficiaries named in the will or other estate documents are "intended beneficiaries" and therefore, the lawyer owes them a duty because they will benefit when the client dies. In other words, the attorney owes the intended beneficiaries a duty to insure that they inherit what was intended for them.

> **EXAMPLE:** Your father lived in the same house in Seattle, Washington, for 40 years. Your mother died many years ago, and your father remarried late in life. When he remarried, he asked a lawyer to fix it so that when he died, the house would go to his new wife. The lawyer prepared a joint tenancy deed, so that at your father's death, title to the house would automatically go to his wife. After a few years, your father decided that he wanted to leave his interest in the house to you, not his wife. He went back to the lawyer and the lawyer prepared a will, which your father signed, leaving his interest in the house to you. When your father died, because the joint tenancy designation takes precedent over the will, the entire house passed to his wife and you got nothing. You have a complaint against the attorney for malpractice. In addition to preparing the will, the lawyer should have recorded a tenancy-in-common deed, which would have destroyed the joint tenancy deed with the result that your father could have left half of his interest in the house to you.

2. Breach

If, as you just learned, your attorney owes you a duty, the next logical question is "to do what?" The answer is to act competently. If he fails to do this, he has "breached" his duty to you and the second element of your malpractice claim is in place. The level of competence required of the attorney is to use the skill, care and knowledge "ordinarily" used by other attorneys in the same or similar circumstances. This does not mean the attorney has a duty to do a good job. He need only meet this "ordinary" standard of care, even if the ordinary standard in a particular community or on a certain type of case isn't very high.

ESTABLISHING LOCAL, STATEWIDE AND NATIONAL STANDARDS OF CARE

Depending upon the law of your state and the particular area of the lawyer's practice, you will need to measure "ordinary" skill and care by other attorneys in the community, statewide or nationally. This can sometimes be tricky.

Establishing that a divorce lawyer breached the ordinary standard of care would be best done by getting another divorce attorney (an expert witness) from the same general geographical area—certainly from the same state—to testify to your lawyer's breach (failure to use ordinary care). This is because divorce law and practice is intensely local with many laws and procedures which vary from state to state and sometimes from county to county.

Compare this to a claim against an attorney for negligence in handling a corporate merger or bankruptcy reorganization. These matters are generally governed by federal law. For the most part, a fairly small group of legal specialists headquartered in major metropolitan areas do this work all over the country. Therefore, it would be fine to have an expert from New York testify on your behalf in a suit claiming that a Dallas attorney breached his duty of care to you. And chances are the Dallas attorney would have little luck claiming that in Texas, attorneys don't bother to do many things considered to be good practice in the rest of America.

To prove that the attorney breached her duty of care, you must show that the attorney did something or failed to do something which no reasonable attorney would have done or failed to do. To prove this in court, it is essential to find another attorney who is willing to say the lawyer you are suing screwed up (failed to meet the standard of care). This is called expert testimony and it is almost always the very heart of any legal malpractice case. Although it may be

possible under certain very limited circumstances to establish that a lawyer breached her duty of care without an expert, I do not recommend trying it.

EXAMPLE: You have a biopsy done on a lump on one of your breasts. The pathologist tells your surgeon that the initial indications from the frozen sections appear malignant. Your surgeon recommends and performs a double radical mastectomy immediately, without waiting for the permanent slides from the lab. Several days after your surgery, the permanent slides come back benign. Your radical double mastectomy was unnecessary. You hire a lawyer to handle your case. Your lawyer sues the surgeon for malpractice, but fails to produce expert testimony—the opinion of another surgeon—that it was below the standard of care to do the surgery before the permanent slides were read. You lose your medical malpractice case against the surgeon. You sue your lawyer for malpractice. To win the case against the lawyer, you will need a second attorney who handles medical malpractice cases to testify that trying a medical malpractice case of your kind without a doctor to testify as an expert was below the standard of care. The lawyer will need to explain that no reasonable attorney would have tried the case without such expert testimony, and that such testimony would have been available.

WHEN A LEGAL SPECIALIST BREACHES THE STANDARD OF CARE

Legal specialists are attorneys who advertise—hold themselves out—as possessing superior knowledge about a particular legal area and usually charge higher fees than general practice attorneys. Many states and some private organizations offer lawyers the opportunity to take a test to become certified as a specialist in areas of law such as tax, family law, workers' compensation, criminal law, bankruptcy, probate and trial practice. In addition, many lawyers can and do loudly claim to be specialists even if they haven't taken or passed one of these exams.

If an attorney claims to be a specialist by putting the fact that he has qualified under a state or private certification program on stationery or in a Web-site or phone book ad, the attorney will be held to a higher standard of care than nonspecialists. This makes sense. After all, if you claim to be a great cook or car mechanic, people have a right to expect that you won't burn the eggs or forget to tighten the spark plugs.

In other words, rather than being held to the standard of "ordinary" care, a specialist will be held to an "expert" standard. The higher the standard of care, the easier it will be to establish breach if your case goes wrong. You will have to make sure that the expert witnesses who testify that your specialist lawyer screwed up are specialists too.

3. Causation

The third element needed to establish a successful malpractice case is to be able to prove that the attorney's mistake caused your loss. It is not enough to show that the attorney made a mistake; you must also show that the lawyer's screw-up caused your loss.

For example, a car runs a red light and hits you. You are hospitalized with a broken leg and can't work for two months. The police report says it was the other driver's fault. An attorney agrees to take your case and you sign a fee agreement. When you call to check on your case, the attorney tells you that she is sorry, but you are out of luck because she forgot to file your case and the statute of limitations has run out.

Can you win a malpractice case against your lawyer? You can establish duty, because there is no question that the attorney agreed to represent you. You can also establish breach; that the lawyer did not file the case before the statute of limitations in your personal injury claim expired clearly fails to meet her duty of care to you. But can you prove that the attorney's mistake caused your loss? To do this, there are two items you will have to prove—that you would have won the underlying case and that you would have collected what you won in the case.

a. Winning the Underlying Case

As just noted, to prove that your lawyer's breach of her duty of care caused your loss, you will have to prove that you would have likely won the underlying case. This is often referred to as the need to prove the "case within a case,"

and essentially means that to win your malpractice case, you have to prove two cases. If you can't show that you would have probably won the underlying case that the lawyer messed up, then your lawyer's malpractice was not the cause of your loss. And winning the case within the case is very difficult because of many reasons, not the least of all the passage of time—witnesses move or die, memories fade and evidence gets misplaced.

If you file your case, the attorney will certainly raise the defense of "So what? You wouldn't have won the case anyway, so the fact that I screwed up and didn't file the case in time didn't cost you anything." (Lawyers who love sports analogies often call this the "no harm, no foul" defense.)

b. Collecting on the Underlying Case

You will also have to show that if you would have won the underlying case, you would have been able to collect from the defendant. In the example above, this means you'd have to show that the driver had money or insurance. If the driver was uninsured and unemployed, for instance, this might be impossible, unless you can show that the driver had other assets which could have been used to pay the judgment. The reasoning here is similar to that discussed above—if you couldn't have collected your judgment, the lawyer's mistake did not cause your loss.

This puts the burden on you to show how you could have collected had you won. But you don't have to prove that you would have been able to collect the judgment immediately. Because in most states court judgments last as many as ten years and can often be renewed, you probably will prove causation if you show that you would have been able to collect at some point in the future. If you can show that the defendant had a strong earning history or potential (even if unemployed at the time of your case), you could probably show that you would have been able to collect eventually. If the defendant was sporadically unemployed, never insured and overwhelmed by debts, however, you probably won't convince anyone that you would have ever been able to collect.

It's worth noting that Florida has created an exception to when the burden is on you to prove collectibility. In Florida, a court ruled that if "the negligence of the attorney makes it impossible to prove the collectibility of the claim, the burden should be shifted to the attorney to prove that the judgment…was uncollectible."[12] In the particular case, the attorney failed to petition the state legislature for special permission to claim extra damages. Because the plaintiff could not prove that the legislature would have granted the petition, the court shifted the burden to the lawyer to prove that the legislature would not have granted it.

4. Damages

The fourth element of your malpractice claim is damages. If you cannot prove that you were damaged by your lawyer's malpractice, then your case will fail. For example, even though your lawyer may have failed to show up in court, if the no-show did not adversely affect your case, you weren't damaged.

It is your burden to prove that you were damaged. If you only suspect that your lawyer's lack of attention to your case adversely affected the outcome, you have no claim. Without proof of damages, you will surely be faced with the "So What?" defense to your malpractice case.

> EXAMPLE: In your personal injury case, your lawyer hired an accident reconstructionist to demonstrate how the accident happened and to show that the accident was caused by the other person. Your lawyer failed to follow the court rules requiring him to disclose the fact that you planned to present the testimony of an expert witness (the accident reconstructionist) and as a result he was prohibited from testifying. Your lawyer tried the case anyhow and the jury decided that the other guy was at fault—but awarded you very little money because they also decided that you contributed to your injuries by not wearing your seatbelt. You were not damaged by your lawyer's failure to disclose the expert because the jury decided in your favor on the issue to which the expert would have testified. Instead, your damages were low because of your own actions. So what that your lawyer made a mistake? You weren't damaged and you have no claim for malpractice.

Section G, below, discusses the different types of damages you may be able to claim.

5. Duty, Breach and Causation Examples

Because duty, breach and causation are such important aspects of proving malpractice, here are a few typical examples of attorney malpractice situations to help you understand what is required to bring a successful case. In each situation, I focus on explaining how and why duty, breach and causation must be present.

EXAMPLE 1: After talking to several lawyers, you conclude that your divorce attorney settled your case for far less than what you should have received under the laws of your state. You want to sue him for malpractice. To succeed, you will have to prove:

- Duty—that the attorney was representing you (this probably won't be difficult).
- Breach—that in recommending the settlement, the attorney acted in a way below the standard of care, or that no reasonable attorney would have recommended the settlement. You will need expert testimony.
- Causation—Did your lawyer's screwup cause your loss? You will have to prove what would have happened if your attorney had handled it properly. This means proving that if your divorce had gone to trial, you would have received a significantly larger amount than you did in the settlement. You will have to prove the whole divorce case, not just the part that you think was messed up.

EXAMPLE 2: You and your former husband owned two pieces of real property. As part of a divorce settlement, you each received one. You accepted this because you agreed to split the property 50-50 and you believed that the two parcels were worth about the same amount. Later, you learn that the property your ex got was worth $200,000 more than the one you received. You are upset that you were shorted your half, or $100,000, and want to sue your attorney. If you do, your case won't be as simple as showing that your lawyer gave you substandard advice regarding the value of the two pieces of property and that the property your husband got was obviously worth more. Why? Because your former attorney will argue that you have to look at the big picture. Even though this particular division of real property might have worked to your ex's advantage, you may have received an offsetting bonus in the division of other property.

It's most likely that you will have to prove the values of all of the assets and show that you didn't get half of the total. This will mean getting appraisals for all real estate, business interests, artwork and

anything else with no easy-to-establish sales value. And if alimony is a part of the divorce, you'll have to show both spouses' income and expenses to determine the proper level of support. This is because you might have gotten more support to compensate for less property.

Even if you establish that the divorce was unfair, you still have work to do. You must prove that you did not get what you were entitled to in the divorce because of your lawyer's negligence. This isn't easy. If your ex would have gambled the money away and you took what you could get before it was all gone, then your lawyer's negligence probably didn't cause your loss. If you were so afraid of your ex-husband's violence that you insisted on a fast settlement even though your lawyer would have been willing to push for more, then your lawyer's negligence didn't cause your loss.

EXAMPLE 3: You hire an attorney to handle your personal injury claim and your lawyer fails to file your case before the statute of limitations expires. If the lawyer agreed to handle your case, you have established duty. By not filing your case on time, you have established breach. If you suffered physical injuries in the accident and were unable to recover damages because your case was not prosecuted, you have been damaged. The critical element likely to create an obstacle to your recovery from your lawyer is causation. You must show that your lawyer's failure to file your claim prevented your recovery of money damages. If the person responsible for your in-juries had no job, no insurance and no assets, you probably wouldn't have been able to collect. Unless you can show a specific source of funds from which you could have recovered money, your claim against your lawyer will fail because you would not be able to prove causation.

EXAMPLE 4: You hire an attorney to handle your bankruptcy. The lawyer fails to list a debt and as a result, it was not eliminated (discharged) in bankruptcy. You will have little problem establishing duty if the lawyer filed the papers for you. And the failure to list the debt certainly caused you damage because now you have to pay it. The likely difficulty here will be in showing breach—was it your lawyer's fault? Your lawyer may argue that she listed all of the debts you told her about. Most bankruptcy lawyers have their clients prepare a list of the debts for just this reason. If your lawyer gave you paper to prepare a list and you forgot this debt, then the omission of the debt was probably not your lawyer's fault. If you told the lawyer about the debt, however, and the lawyer forgot to put it on the list, then the lawyer breached her duty to you. What actually happened was probably in the middle. Your lawyer may have given you the list, you left off the debt, but then called later remembering it and the lawyer forgot to write it down. A note to your lawyer or letter would prove your case. Without evidence indicating that you told your lawyer about the debt, you will probably not be able to show that your lawyer breached her duty to you.

F. Proving a Breach of Fiduciary Duty, Fraud or Other Intentional Conduct Case

Each state has rules that govern the conduct of lawyers, such as representing their clients with undivided loyalty, maintaining their client's confidences and putting the interests of their clients above their own interests. Breach of fiduciary duty cases involve a lawyer's failure to abide by these rules of conduct. Fraud and other cases involving intentional conduct (such as theft or battery) usually involve conduct for which the lawyer could be prosecuted criminally.

1. Breach of Fiduciary Duty

To win a case against an attorney for breach of fiduciary duty, you must prove the same four elements you must prove in a malpractice case: duty, breach, causation and damages.

a. Duty

In a breach of fiduciary duty case, you will need to prove that you had an attorney-client relationship (your attorney owed you a duty to act properly). To prove this duty, see Section E.1, above.

In a breach of fiduciary duty case, you will also need to prove that your attorney had a specific duty to maintain your confidence and represent you with undivided loyalty. The exact nature of this duty will be set out in rules adopted by your state lawyer discipline agency. Most states have adopted rules similar to ones promulgated by the American Bar Association (ABA) such as the following:

A lawyer shall not reveal information relating to representation of a client unless the client consents after consultation. [Model Rules of Professional Conduct Rule 1.6(a) (Discussion Draft 1983).]

A lawyer has an obligation to preserve the confidences and secrets of a client. [Model Code of Professional Responsibility Canon 4 (1980).]

A lawyer should exercise independent judgment on behalf of a client. [Model Code of Professional Responsibility Canon 5 (1980).]

Except with the consent of his client after full disclosure, a lawyer shall not accept employment if the exercise of his professional judgment on behalf of his client will be or reasonably may be affected by his own financial, business, property, or personal interests. [Model Code of Professional Responsibility DR 5-101(A) (1980).]

A lawyer shall not enter into a business transaction with a client if they have differing interests therein and if the client expects the lawyer to exercise his professional judgment therein for the protection of the client unless the client consented after full disclosure. [Model Code of Professional Responsibility 5-104(A) (1980).]

A lawyer shall decline proffered employment if the exercise of his independent professional judgment on behalf of a client will be or is likely to be adversely affected by the acceptance of the proffered employment, or if it would be likely to involve him in representing differing interests. [Model Code of Professional Responsibility 5-105(A) (1980).]

A lawyer who has formerly represented a client in a matter shall not thereafter represent another person in the same or a substantially related matter in which that person's interests are materially adverse to the interests of the former client unless the former client consents after consultation. [Model Rules of Professional Conduct Rule 1.9 (Discussion Draft 1983).]

Review the rules of professional conduct in your state which tell you how lawyers are supposed to conduct themselves. Any violation of a rule can be the basis of a claim for breach of fiduciary duty.

b. Breach

The failure of an attorney to maintain a client's confidence or represent a client with undivided loyalty as required by a particular state rule often gives rise to a claim for breach of fiduciary duty. Because these rules are usually spelled out in some detail, proving the breach may not be very difficult and may not require the testimony of an expert witness.

If your lawyer's conduct is not a clear violation of a rule or may be subject to a more benign or innocent interpretation, however, you will want an expert witness to testify. This is especially true in a jury trial, where having an expert explain how your lawyer's conduct violated a state ethical rule can be a big help, given that your expert will have a chance to explain the purpose of the rule as well as why your lawyer's conduct violated it. To accomplish this, many trial lawyers often hire former prosecutors with the state discipline agency, law school professors or retired judges to testify.

In a breach of fiduciary duty case, you do not have to prove that the breach was intentional. Accidental disclosures of your confidences would be a breach of your lawyer's fiduciary duty. Nor do you have to prove that your lawyer intended to harm you—only that you were harmed. (If you can prove that your lawyer intentionally breached your confidence or intended to harm you, you probably have a claim for fraud. See Sections F.2 and G.6, below.)

c. Causation

You must be able to show that your lawyer's breach of the fiduciary duty caused your loss. Causation in a breach of fiduciary duty case is no different than causation in a malpractice case. (See Section E.3, above.)

d. Damages

Finally, you must prove that you were damaged. If your lawyer stole your settlement, your damages are the amount you didn't receive. If your lawyer's conduct was not so blatant, such as representing you when he had a conflict of interest, you may have trouble showing that the lawyer's conduct resulted in damages. A few states, including California, Ohio and Texas, allow damages for emotional distress with claims for breach of fiduciary duty. (See Section G.3.b, below.)

2. Fraud

The most important characteristic of fraud is that someone intended to do you wrong. Unlike claims of legal malpractice and breach of fiduciary duty, a claim of fraud is not unique to lawyers. You prove a case for fraud against a lawyer like a case for fraud against anyone else.

You must prove five elements in a claim for fraud:

- a lie (misrepresentation) or a cover-up (concealment) of something important
- the lawyer knows the lie or cover-up is false or is aware that she doesn't know whether or not it is true
- the lawyer intends for you to rely on the lie or cover-up
- you rely on the lie or cover-up and your reliance is reasonable, and
- you were damaged as a result.

a. Lie or Concealment

The lie or concealment must be about something important. For example, in your automobile accident case, your lawyer takes the deposition of a witness who had told your lawyer before the deposition that he had an unobstructed view of the accident and that it was clearly the other party's fault. To the surprise of your lawyer, at his deposition he testifies to the opposite—that the accident was your fault. The value of your case has sunk by miles.

You're not present at the deposition, your lawyer doesn't tell you about the testimony (which is clearly relevant to your case) and your lawyer tells you it would be a waste of your time to read the deposition transcript. You still think your case is worth a lot and reject all settlement offers because they are very low. You instruct your lawyer to prepare for

trial, hire accident reconstructionist experts, medical experts and generally incur other expenses, assuming you'll get a big award. You lose at trial, based on the testimony of the witness. Your lawyer is guilty of concealment (not telling you about the deposition testimony) and lying (telling you it would be a waste your time to read the deposition transcript).

b. Knowledge

To be guilty of fraud, your lawyer must know she is lying. If she accidentally gives you false information it might be malpractice if her negligence was below the standard of care, but it isn't fraud. For example, if you ask questions about the status of your case, and your lawyer makes something up to get you off her back, she is committing fraud. If you ask for legal information the lawyer isn't familiar with and she concocts a false answers, she is committing fraud. But if your lawyer gave you the same incorrect information accidentally, there is no fraud (she didn't know the information was wrong).

Innocent mistakes do happen and fraud is hard to prove. One way to prove fraud is if an employee (preferably a former employee with no ax to grind) will testify. For example, if a former employee will say that he was told to pay all of the settlement proceeds to the lawyer and none to you, that would indicate that the disbursement of all of the money to the lawyer was no accident.

Others who may have information to help establish fraud would be the lawyer or insurance representative for your adversary who could testify that your lawyer gave instructions to write the settlement check payable to the lawyer alone. If you can get ahold of your case file, you may find correspondence to that effect. Finally, you may have notes of your conversations with your lawyer of things she said she'd do but did not which would help you to establish fraud.

c. Reliance

The third element you must prove in a fraud case is reliance on the false information provided by your lawyer or on the concealment. Your reliance will usually be implied from the attorney-client relationship. Or put another way, because your lawyer is a professional working for you, she knows—or should know—that you are relying on the advice or information she provides.

d. Reasonableness of the Reliance

The fourth element you must prove in a fraud case is that your reliance on the false information provided by your lawyer or on the concealment was reasonable. As with the reliance itself, the reasonableness of your reliance will usually be implied by the attorney-client relationship. It is justifiable for you to believe what your lawyer tells you or to expect that your lawyer will tell you what is important.

e. Damages

The final element you must prove in a fraud case is damages. As with any other case, you must prove you were damaged. (See Section E.4, above.) In addition, you may be able to recover punitive damages which are designed to punish your lawyer for outrageous conduct (see Section G.6, below) or triple damages if your state provides for special damages for particular kinds of conduct (see Section G.5, below). Punitive damages are not recoverable in Nebraska.[13]

3. Other Intentional Misconduct

A lawyer is not immune from claims for a long list of antisocial or criminal acts, such as assault (threatening to touch you), battery (unlawful touching), intentional infliction of emotional distress (intending to cause you grief), false imprisonment (holding you against your will) or embezzlement (stealing your money or property). There is nothing special about an attorney or the attorney-client relationship which makes this kind of claim against a lawyer different from this kind of claim against your neighbor, the mail carrier or your business associate.

As with fraud, the most important element of an intentional tort case is that the attorney intended to cause you harm. The most common of these kinds of claims by clients against their former lawyers are for sexual assault or battery. (See Chapter 4, *Conflicts of Interests*.) If you are suing the lawyer for the other side, see Chapter 10. And in addition to suing the lawyer, when the act is criminal (such as taking your money), you can always report the lawyer to the district attorney for possible prosecution.

G. Damages: How Much You Can Win If You Prove Malpractice, Breach of Fiduciary Duty, Fraud or Other Intentional Conduct

If a malpractice case goes to court and you prove both that you probably would have won your underlying case for which you would have been monetarily compensated and that your lawyer's negligence caused your loss, you will receive a judgment for money damages. How much, exactly, will vary from case to case. This section explains how much you can expect to be compensated for your attorney's mistakes or intentional acts.

1. Actual Damages

Actual damages (also called compensatory damages) are designed to compensate you for what you actually lost as a result of your attorney's errors. These damages are usually for out-of-pocket losses or direct economic losses which result from the attorney's mistake. In most states, you must be able to establish (prove) actual damages or direct out-of-pocket losses to sue your attorney in the first place.

Here are some examples of how actual damages would be calculated:

- If you lost your personal injury case because your attorney failed to file it before the statute of limitations expired, your actual damages would be the amount a jury would have likely awarded you if the case went to trial.

- If your case was settled for too little as a result of your attorney's bad advice, your actual damages would be the amount you should have received in a reasonable settlement minus how much you actually did receive.

- If your attorney's mistake was incompetently structuring a business transaction, your actual damages would be the extra money you had to pay because of your lawyer's misunderstanding of the law.

  EXAMPLE: You agree to sell your business equipment for $200,000 and the buyer is willing to write you a check. But your attorney suggests that you take the payment as an installment sale so you don't have to pay all of the taxes at once. Over the years, you have depreciated the equipment, with the result that your tax basis is $50,000, meaning you will have to pay federal capital gains taxes on a gain of $150,000. Your lawyer prepares the agreement so that you are paid $50,000 per year for four years, telling you that your $150,000 gain on the sale of the equipment will be allocated over a four-year period. You expect your tax bill to be about $12,000 per year for the next four years. When it is too late to change the deal, your accountant explains that you must report the entire gain of $150,000 in the "year of sale." In short, your current year's tax bill will be about $50,000, rather than $12,000. You don't have the extra $38,000 and need time to pay it off. The IRS agrees, but charges interest and penalties. Your damages are the interest and penalties, as well as the money you paid the lawyer to negotiate this worthless installment transaction.

- If you spent money pursuing or defending a case which was lost due to your attorney's error, what you spent in pursuing or defending the case would be actual damages. (If you lost a case you brought, your damages might also be the amount you should have won had your lawyer been competent.) If you were sued and your lawyer failed to argue that the lawsuit was barred by the statute of limitations, then whatever you spend in attorney's fees to defend the case on other grounds would be damages.

• If you settled your divorce case on the advice of your lawyer for way below what you were entitled to, your actual damages are the difference between what you were entitled to receive and what you actually received in the property settlement. You must reduce this amount by the additional costs and attorney's fees you would have incurred if your case went to trial.

• If your lawyer's malpractice resulted in your losing a case in which you would have recovered punitive damages (damages designed to punish bad conduct), such as a fraud case against a dishonest securities broker, the amount of the punitive damages you didn't receive are part of your actual damages against your lawyer.

You are also entitled to collect interest on your actual damages from when you should have received it. The rate of interest is governed by state law, and usually ranges from 5% to 15%.

2. Nominal Damages

Nominal damages are "token" or "negligible" damages awarded when the plaintiff suffered no real monetary damage. It is based on the law of some states (such as Georgia), which presumes that if an attorney made a mistake, the client must be entitled to recover some amount (such as $1).

Nominal damages aren't available in most states. Instead, you must be able to show that you suffered actual damages in order to sue an attorney for malpractice or fraud. In addition,

to collect punitive damages in most states, you must have suffered actual damages—nominal damages alone are usually not enough to collect punitive damages. Georgia, North Dakota and Texas, however, will allow you to claim punitive damages if you win only nominal damages.

3. Consequential Damages

Consequential damages follow from (are caused by) the attorney's negligent representation, but are not immediately apparent. The most common type of consequential damage is for fees paid to a second lawyer to try and correct the mistakes made by the first one.

a. Fees Paid a Second Attorney

As just stated, these are the most common types of consequential damages. For example, if you accepted a terrible settlement in your divorce because your lawyer told you to, and later a second attorney tried to get it nullified (called "setting it aside"), you could claim as consequential damages the fees you paid to the second attorney and the costs you incurred. And these fees and costs would be recoverable whether or not the second attorney's efforts to set the settlement aside were successful, as long as the fees were reasonable.

b. Emotional Distress Claims

Clients often complain that their attorney's mistakes caused them to suffer emotional distress or mental anguish. In general, you cannot recover money for the emotional anguish or mental pain and suffering which result from an attorney's malpractice. These damages are usually recoverable only in a claim for intentional wrongdoing, such as fraud or breach of fiduciary duty.

In recent years in a few states, however, courts have allowed emotional distress or mental anguish damages when a client's liberty or emotional well-being, not merely her wallet, has been affected by the attorney's errors. For example, in a California case, a court ruled that a client could sue for emotional distress in a malpractice case against a lawyer who had bungled a criminal case with the result that the client went to jail.[14] Similarly, an Oregon court allowed a claim for emotional distress against an attorney who negligently handled a child custody proceeding with the result being that the client lost custody of the child.[15] And in New Jersey, a client was able to claim emotional distress damages against a lawyer who inadvertently disclosed her name to the birth parents in an adoption.[16]

Although courts are reluctant to award monetary damages for emotional distress claims in malpractice cases, they are more willing to allow these damages in cases involving the breach of a fiduciary duty or fraud. For example, a California court held that a client might be able to recover emotional distress damages against her attorney who pressured her to accept a settlement so that the attorney could merge her practice with that of opposing counsel.[17] A Texas court allowed emotional distress damages for weight loss, ulcers and an eventual divorce when a lawyer consented to the assessment of a tax penalty without the client's authorization, resulting damaged credit for the client.[18] An Ohio court allowed emotional distress damages against an attorney who consulted with a wife about her divorce and then represented her husband.[19]

4. Speculative Damages

Damages which are not directly related to the claimed malpractice or intentional act, or which are extremely remote, are not recoverable. This makes sense. Your ex-lawyer isn't going to be held liable for damages unless they really exist. This does not mean, however, that you must be able to calculate the amount of actual or consequential damages precisely. Sometimes damages can be estimated with enough precision to allow a court judgment.

> **EXAMPLE:** You are able to prove that a lawyer delayed in getting you a recovery for 18 months. The fact that you suffered harm (damages) is certain, as you lost use of the money for the 18 months. Your damages would be calculated based on allowing you a reasonable rate of return on the money, such as your state's legal interest rate. You could not claim that you would have invested the money in a real estate venture which would have generated a 300% profit. This would be considered speculative and not allowed.

a. Future Adverse Tax Consequences

It's fairly common to claim that an attorney's malpractice has resulted in your having to pay additional future taxes. Because in many situations the amount of future taxes is highly speculative, these claims are often not allowed. But if the adverse tax consequences are immediate and can be calculated, such as the IRS sends you a notice of deficiency or you reach a settlement with the IRS to pay additional taxes and accountant fees to resolve the deficiency, you can make them a part of your claim for damages.

EXAMPLE: In your divorce, there were two pieces of real estate with equal market values and equal equity values (market value minus mortgage and other debts). Based on the advice of your lawyer that it constituted an equal division, you and your ex each take one piece of property. But one property was bought 15 years earlier and has a very low tax basis. When it sells, the owner will have a huge taxable gain. The other property is only one year old. If it were sold now, the owner would have no taxable gain. Can the spouse who took the property purchased 15 years earlier sue the attorney for malpractice based on the fact that she overlooked the difference in the tax status of the two parcels? No. Because there is no immediate or specific tax which can be computed. It is expected that, at sale, taxes will be due. But many things could happen before the property is sold, which would affect how much tax is due. The real estate market could crash with the result that there is no taxable gain. The owner could die and leave it to an heir who would not have to pay taxes because the property qualified to have its tax basis increased ("stepped-up") to its fair market

value. Or, if the owner is over age 55, the owner might be able to deduct up to $125,000 from the taxable gain.

b. Lost Profits

Another type of speculative damages is lost profits. For example, if you claimed that your lawyer's delay in negotiations caused you to lose profits, your claim for damages would probably be considered speculative and not allowed because it requires you to anticipate what the other side would have done if your lawyer had approached the negotiations differently. For example, it would be almost impossible to show that if your lawyer had promptly responded to an offer to negotiate a settlement more quickly you would have been making profits sooner. It is just as likely that the other side would have thought your lawyer too anxious and you wouldn't have been able to close the deal at the price you ended up paying.

5. Statutory Damages

Some states have laws which specifically provide for the following types of damages:

- Triple (called "treble") damages in cases of intentional conduct, such as theft, fraud, deceit or dishonest acts. Because most claims are for attorney malpractice, treble damages usually won't apply. But if your claim is for fraud, breach of fiduciary duty or other intentional misconduct, you might be entitled to extra damages.
- Extra penalties or interest may be allowed if your lawyer delays in turning over your

settlement funds or if your lawyer misappropriates money which was supposed to be held in the lawyer's trust account for your benefit.

6. Punitive Damages

Punitive damages are designed to punish or make an example out of a bad actor. These damages are not designed to compensate you for losses sustained. Punitive damages are only recoverable if you prove intentional conduct, such as fraud, deceit or intentional misrepresentation, or you prove malicious conduct or gross disregard for the rights of others. A claim for malpractice generally will not allow for a claim for punitive damages.

H. Common Defenses Raised by Lawyers Who Are Sued

Sections E and F explain what you have to prove to win a case against your former attorney. Of course, it is important to remember that you won't be bringing your case in a vacuum. When you file your lawsuit, your former lawyer will not roll over and play dead. He will fight back, probably viciously. He may lie, make things up, destroy documents, distort things you told him and otherwise make your life (through the litigation) miserable. Certainly, he will raise every possible legal defense, the most common of which are described below. If your former attorney succeeds with these arguments, he can prevent you from winning your malpractice case or he can dramatically reduce the amount of money you recover.

ARE COMMUNICATIONS WITH YOUR FORMER LAWYER STILL PRIVILEGED?

If you sue your lawyer for malpractice, fraud or breach of fiduciary duty, the attorney-client privilege (described in Chapter 2, Section A.3) is gone, at least to the extent the lawyer needs to divulge your otherwise privileged communications to defend himself. He cannot, for example, call your business competitor and reveal your confidences just out of spite.

1. You Waited Too Long to Sue

As explained in Section B above, you must sue within the appropriate period as defined by the statute of limitations which affects your claim. The claim that the statute of limitations has expired is one of the most common lawyer defenses. If the lawyer is right, then your case will be dismissed and you won't be able to proceed, even though the lawyer's conduct many have been as horrible as it was damaging.

2. The Mistake Didn't Cause Your Harm

Attorneys will often defend their conduct by saying that it was not their mistake which caused your loss. (This is sometimes called the "so what" defense.) For example, your lawyer failed to file your automobile accident case on time. You sue him for malpractice and he defends by pointing out that the person you intended to sue had no insurance or other assets to pay any judgment—that is, that the other person's poverty was the real reason you wouldn't have been made whole. (See Sections E.3 and F.1.c, above, for more on this.)

3. You Failed to Mitigate Damages

If you know your attorney made a mistake and it cost you money, you nevertheless have a legal duty to try to minimize your losses. In legal lingo, this is called the "duty to mitigate damages" and your failure to do so is a defense lawyers sued for malpractice often raise. Put simply, if you do not take reasonable steps to reduce your damages, your damages will be reduced by the amount you could have saved with reasonable efforts.

How can you try to mitigate damages resulting from a malpractice case? Especially if your ex-lawyer's mistake was recent, consult another attorney to see what, if anything, can be done within reason to reduce your damages. You might be able to bring a motion to set aside or modify a judgment if it was obtained based on a mistake. For example, if your divorce settlement agreement did not divide your spouse's pension (maybe you didn't even know your spouse had a pension), then you may be able to reopen your divorce case to include the asset, rather than sue the lawyer for omitting it. The fact that you sought and followed advice on keeping your losses to a minimum is evidence that you took reasonable steps to mitigate your damages.

 Tanya's Tip: You'll Need to Consult Two Attorneys

It's a good idea to get advice about keeping your losses to a minimum from an attorney other than the one you will hire to sue your first attorney. This is because the attorney with whom you consult will probably be a witness concerning the question of whether you took reasonable steps to mitigate your damages.

Here are examples of other actions which might mitigate your damages:

- Appeal an adverse decision.
- File a writ asking an appeals court to reverse an incorrect ruling made by the lower court.
- File a motion asking the judge to reconsider her ruling, because you have newly discovered evidence.
- File a motion asking the court to set aside a default entered against you because of your lawyer's negligence.
- Ask the lawyer who made the mistake to fix it at his expense.
- Ask the lawyer's insurance company to hire another lawyer to fix the problem.

You are only required to take reasonable steps to mitigate your damages. You need not take expensive action with little likelihood of success.

4. The Attorney Is Not Liable for Errors in Judgment

The defense that an attorney is not liable for errors in judgment is peculiar to legal malpractice cases. It recognizes that lawyers must advise clients about likely outcomes, and that predicting likely outcomes can be difficult. For example, a case might involve issues of law so new or unsettled that no one can reasonably predict how a particular judge will rule. Or, in an accident case, there might be contradictory eyewitness accounts making it difficult to predict who will be believed.

In these and similar situations, courts routinely rule that if a lawyer cannot be certain about how a court will rule or what an outcome will be, then the attorney need only exercise his best judgment in advising the client. The advice need not be correct.

But while an attorney cannot be held responsible for malpractice for a genuine error in judgment concerning an uncertain area of the law or where believable witnesses have contradictory stories, this defense goes only so far. If the attorney failed to consider a legal issue at all, the attorney will be liable. For example, if the lawyer failed to call an expert witness in a medical malpractice case, the lawyer probably will not be able to use this defense—it is generally recognized that expert testimony must be used in most malpractice cases.

5. You Failed to Establish Duty

Generally speaking, you can only sue an attorney if there was an attorney-client relationship (if the attorney represented you) or if you were an intended beneficiary of the attorney's work, such as the beneficiary of a will. When and how a duty comes into existence is discussed in more detail in Sections E.1 and F.1.a, above, and in Chapter 1, Section C.

6. You Waived the Conflict of Interest

As explained in Section F.1, above, your lawyer has a duty to represent you with undivided loyalty, even if it means putting your interests above her own. The lawyer must tell you about any conflicts of interest and generally refuse to represent you if a conflict exists, unless you waive it—that is, say that the conflict doesn't bother you.

If you sue for breach of fiduciary duty, the attorney might raise as a defense that you knew about the conflict, and knowingly waived it. If the lawyer can show that the nature of the conflict was explained to you, and you nonetheless agreed to hire the lawyer, then you "waived" the conflict and the lawyer may have a successful defense.

Usually, an attorney will not raise this defense unless you signed a written waiver. Even then, you might still be able to sue if you did not receive an adequate explanation of the conflict so as to understand what you were waiving.

I. Settling Your Claim Without Going to Court

Resolving lawyer-client disputes without going to court is not new. For years, in many states fee disputes have been resolved through arbitration. (See Chapter 7.)

But using dispute methods other than litigation to resolve malpractice claims is new. As of June 1996, a handful of states have adopted mediation programs to resolve complaints against lawyers. Mediation is a private, informal way to resolve a dispute. A neutral third person (mediator) helps the disputing parties reach a mutually agreeable solution. A mediator cannot impose a decision.

The first state to adopt a program was New York. Since 1989, the Disciplinary Committee of the New York Supreme Court, the Bar Association of the City of New York, the New York County Lawyers' Association and the Bronx County Bar Association have been participating in a program that includes mediation to resolve "low level" complaints, such as failing to return papers or records, ambiguous withdrawing from a case and refusing to provide an accounting.

In New York, when the disciplinary committee receives a complaint, those complaints appropriate for mediation are referred to a volunteer attorney who is trained as a mediator. The mediator arranges a conference between the lawyer and complaining client. There is no cost for the service to either the lawyer or client and the entire process is kept confidential.

At the conference, the mediator listens to both sides of the dispute and then may talk privately with the lawyer and client to encourage or suggest resolutions. The parties will meet again with the mediator to try to come to a solution.

New York is not the only state to adopt mediation. California's local fee arbitration panels are authorized to set up mediation programs. As of June 1996, only six (out of 42) have, and they are slow to get going, but mediation should become more widespread in the Golden State.

The California Bar Association estimates that about 60% of the 110,000 telephone complaints it receives would be good for mediation. Unfortunately, the Bar only suggests mediation when a complaint is received on paper, so again, mediation is under-used.

Other states that have adopted some mediation programs include Arizona, Colorado, Minnesota and Missouri. In these states, mediation is primarily used to handle complaints that:

- would be rejected by the disciplinary process
- involve only a small number of issues
- do not allege dishonesty, and
- usually involve poor communication.

Although only a few states offer mediation, many more are considering it. It can provide a quick resolution of a dispute, give a client redress for minor—albeit important—complaints and help reduce court caseloads.

Endnotes

[1] See *Kohn v. Schiappa*, 281 N.J. Super. 235, 656 A.2d 1322 (N.J. 1995).

[2] See *McCafferty v. Musat*, 817 P.2d 1039 (Colo. 1990).

[3] See *Stanley v. Richmond*, 35 Cal. App. 4th 1070, 41 Cal. Rptr. 2d 768 (1995).

[4] Indiana has a statute of limitations for actions against physicians and "other professionals," but it does not apply to legal malpractice cases. *Shideler v. Dwyer*, 417 N.E.2d 281 (Ind. 1981).

[5] See *Lynn v. Brown, Williams & Tucker*, 655 So. 2d 675 (La. 1995).

[6] See *Gulf Coast Investment Corp. v. Brown*, 813 S.W.2d 218 (Tex. App. 1991).

[7] See *Ladner v. Inge*, 603 So. 2d. 1012 (Ala. 1992).

[8] See *Key Trust Co. of Maine v. Doherty, Wallace, Pillsbury and Murphy, P.C.*, 811 F. Supp. 733 (D. Mass. 1993).

[9] See, for example, *California Aviation, Inc. v. Leeds*, 233 Cal. App. 3d 724, 284 Cal. Rptr. 687 (Cal. 1991).

[10] *Watson & Assoc., Inc. v. Green, MacDonald & Kirscher*, 253 Mont. 291, 833 P.2d 199 (Mont. 1992).

[11] See *In re American Continental Corp./Lincoln S&L Securities Litigation*, 794 F. Supp. 1424 (D. Ariz., 1992); *Resolution Trust Corp. v. O'Bear, Overholser, Smith & Huffer*, 886 F. Supp. 658 (D. Ind. 1995); *FDIC v. Nathan*, 804 F. Supp. 888 (Tex. 1992); *FDIC v. Cocke*, 7 F.3d 396 (4th Cir. 1993).

[12] *Fernandes v. Barrs*, 641 So. 2d 1371 (Fla. 1994).

[13] Constitution of Nebraska, Article VII § 5; *Abel v. Conover*, 104 N.W.2d 684 (Neb. 1960).

[14] *Holliday v. Jones*, 215 Cal. App. 3d 102, 264 Cal. Rptr. 448 (Cal. 1989).

[15] *McEvoy v. Helikson*, 277 Or. 781, 562 P.2d 540 (Or. 1977).

[16] *Kohn v. Schiappa*, 281 N.J. Super. 235, 656 A.2d 1322 (N.J. 1995).

[17] *Stanley v. Richmond*, 35 Cal. App. 4th 1070, 41 Cal. Rptr. 2d 768 (Cal. 1995).

[18] *Rhodes v. Batilla*, 848 S.W.2d 768 (Tex. 1993).

[19] *David v. Schwarzwald, Robiner, Wolf & Rock Co., L.P.A.*, 607 N.E.2d 1173 (Ohio App. 1992).

■

Chapter 10

TAKING ACTION AGAINST THE LAWYER FOR THE OTHER SIDE

There is an old Mexican curse that goes like this: "May you have a lawsuit in which you know you are right." The wisdom in this is that the process of bringing any lawsuit is so awful, you'll end up miserable even if you win. Against this background, this chapter looks at the most common types of complaints against lawyers for the other side and explains what, if anything, you can do about them.

ACTIONS AGAINST THE LAWYER FOR THE OTHER SIDE

In the 17 examples of complaints against the lawyer for the other side, I refer to several potential remedies available to you, including:

- ask the court to impose sanctions against the lawyer
- sue the lawyer for malicious prosecution
- sue the lawyer for abuse of process
- sue the lawyer for false arrest or false imprisonment, and
- sue the lawyer for defamation, invasion of privacy or trespass.

These concepts are explained in Section B, below.

A. Common Complaints Against a Lawyer for the Other Side

Is the lawyer for your adversary unfairly getting in the way of settling your divorce case? Is the conduct of your wife's divorce lawyer so bad that she has violated court rules? Have you been sued in a situation where the other party (and his lawyer) had absolutely no good reason to file the lawsuit except to harass you? These and other serious complaints are often leveled against lawyers. Sometimes they are unfair—after all, your adversary was entitled to the same energetic effective representation you expected to receive. But sometimes lawyers do run amok, and when they do, you may be able to do something about it.

1. Frivolous Lawsuits

If you have successfully defended against a lawsuit and you can show that the attorney who sued you had no reasonable basis to believe the lawsuit had merit, you may be able to sue him for what is called "malicious prosecution." If the case is not over yet, and you can convince the judge that the lawsuit has absolutely no merit, the judge might impose sanctions, such as a monetary fine, against the lawyer to be paid to you.

Showing that a lawyer had "no reasonable basis" to sue you or that a lawsuit has absolutely no merit is not an easy task. Probably everyone who wins a lawsuit feels they shouldn't have been sued in the first place. But most of the time if you win a lawsuit, you can't sue the lawyer who sued you. Lawyers have a lot of leeway in what constitutes a legitimate legal case, and in most states, lawyers are entitled to rely on what their clients tell them when deciding whether or not to sue. In some circumstances, however, if you can show that the lawyer who sued you knew that the case was totally without merit—a difficult thing to show—you may be able to sue the lawyer for having filed a frivolous case.

2. Costing You Money by Suing in the Wrong Court

If an attorney files a lawsuit against you in the wrong state, county or federal district, and you spend money getting the lawsuit moved, you have two possible courses of action:

- sue the attorney for what is called an "abuse of process," or
- request that the court award you sanctions against the lawyer.

3. Refusing to Engage in Settlement Discussions

You cannot force the other side to pay you money to settle your case or to accept your settlement offer. In most courts, however, parties and their attorneys must at least participate in good faith in a settlement conference conducted at the courthouse. Some courts also require attorneys to discuss settlement possibilities before the conference, and to submit to the court a written statement describing their client's settlement position. If the opposing

attorney complied with all court rules and court orders regarding settlement discussions, documents and court appearances—but simply refuses to settle the case—you cannot force a settlement and you have no basis to pursue a claim against the attorney.

On the other hand, if the attorney violates a court rule or order requiring her to attend a settlement conference, submit a written statement or make a settlement offer (even if the offer is zero), you can ask the court to award you sanctions. The court will be more likely to award sanctions if the lawyer shows a deliberate disregard for court rules. If the lawyer cannot offer a plausible excuse to the court for noncompliance, the court will likely award you sanctions. If the lawyer has engaged in a pattern of non-compliance, sanctions are more likely to be imposed and with greater severity.

4. Unreasonably Escalating the Litigation

Litigation often takes a long time to resolve. In the course of nearly every lawsuit, attorneys schedule hearings, conduct evidence gathering (discovery)—and generally engage in pre-trial posturing for weeks or months at a time. A process that seems intensely frustrating to you may be par for the course for others.

Some lawyers, however, make matters worse by filing multitudinous motions such as repeated motions to continue a trial, routinely attempting to postpone hearings and depositions, requesting extra time to respond to every court paper you file, filing unreasonable discovery requests on Christmas Eve and refusing to cooperate with your lawyer's reasonable discovery request until a judge orders it. If this type of scorched-earth lawyering describes the modus operandi of the opposing attorney in your case, and you can convince a judge that this behavior is in bad faith, she may award you monetary sanctions—especially if the opposing attorneys' tactics have caused you to incur unnecessary lawyer's fees. The more outrageous the conduct, the more likely a court will be to award you a hefty sum.

> **EXAMPLE:** Your lawyer noticed the deposition of the other side and prepared for the deposition, and you took off work to attend. You and your lawyer waited with the court reporter and the other side pulled a no-show. It is not likely that a court would impose sanctions if the lawyer's office had made an innocent calendaring mistake. When it happens a second time, however—with the same innocent calendaring mistake excuse—a court would likely award you sanctions at least to pay for the court reporter's fee (maybe $100) and something for your lawyer's wasted time (maybe $250). When it happens a third time—a court would likely award you significant sanctions, such as $750 to $1,000, intended to punish the other lawyer.

5. Failing to Participate in Discovery

An attorney may fail to show up at a deposition or fail to get his client to attend. Or, a lawyer may refuse to turn over documents you request or answer written questions you ask of his client. Courts generally do not look favorably

on an attorney who impedes this evidence-gathering part of a lawsuit without a very good reason. Depending upon the why the attorney had failed to cooperate and whether it occurs more than once, a court may award you a sum of money in the form of sanctions.

6. Violating Court Order or Court Rule

In the course of any case, courts make decisions. If those decisions require either party or their lawyer to take certain action, that ruling is called a court order. Similarly, courts have certain procedures that all litigants must follow, usually relating to deadlines and content of papers filed. These are called court rules.

If an attorney violates a court order or a court rule, you can ask the court to award you sanctions to compensate you for any financial losses or to make an order to discourage additional violations. The court's decision will depend upon the reason for and the frequency of the violations.

> **EXAMPLE:** The lawyer for the other side files a motion opposing your using a certain witness at trial. Your lawyer calls the opposing lawyer to try to convince him that your witness is qualified to testify, but the opposing lawyer won't budge. Your lawyer then spends 20 hours (and thousands of your dollars) filing an opposition to the motion. When your lawyer goes to the court for the hearing, he discovers that the lawyer for the other side withdrew his motion right before your lawyer filed your opposition, but never bothered to tell your lawyer. As sanctions, the court may very

well order the lawyer for the opposing side to pay your attorney's fees for preparing your opposition.

7. Giving False Testimony

Anyone who lies under oath commits the crime of perjury. It's no different for an attorney. It's not all that unusual for a lawyer to testify in a trial. For example, a lawyer might testify as to how documents were preserved before the trial and what documents were given to the other side. If the lawyer attempts to introduce a critical document at the trial which she did not exchange before the trial, the judge may become very angry, especially if it appears that the lawyer lied about the document. If the judge is angry enough, he may refer the perjured testimony to the local prosecutor.

The likelihood that the prosecutor will do anything is remote, unless the lie is big, bold and clearly false. Even then, it is not likely that the prosecutor will bring charges unless the case or the lawyer has some notoriety or has received some degree of publicity.

Engaging in criminal activity such as perjury also violates the ethical rules governing attorneys in your state. In a situation which outrages the judge (such as the above example of the withheld document), the judge is likely to refer the matter to the state lawyer discipline agency. In such a situation, the agency is likely to seriously investigate the lawyer. By contrast, if you or your lawyer complained to the agency, the complaint would not get immediate attention, unless there was a strong paper trail proving a lie.

Finally, if the lawyer is convicted of perjury or disciplined by the discipline agency, the attorney may be ordered to pay you restitution if you have monetary damages. Or, you may have to file a separate lawsuit against the lawyer to recover your damages.

8. Presenting False Evidence in Court

If a lawyer presents false evidence in court (something either the lawyer knows a client faked or the lawyer faked), you cannot sue the attorney for damages. You can file a complaint with your state attorney discipline agency, however. (See Chapter 8.)

The attorney discipline agency will not take you seriously unless you have good documentation. For example, this could be a note or letter from or to the lawyer about a "double" set of books that had been kept—a real one and a fabricated one shown to the court's accounting expert who was conducting a business valuation. In the rare instances when a paper trail exists to prove such conduct, it usually comes to light through an employee or former employee who is offended by the fraud and "whistle blows" either to a government agency or to the party likely to be harmed.

9. Making False Statements About You or the Case

No matter what the lawyer for the other side says about you, she is immune from liability if the statements relate to your case—even if they are outrageous. In most states, this includes statements made in anticipation of litigation, as well as statements made after a lawsuit is pending. The purpose of the immunity is to not limit the lawyer in her representation of the client, and it is designed to prevent you from later suing the lawyer. For this reason, the immunity has been liberally construed in favor of attorneys—questions about whether a statement is related to litigation will almost always be resolved in favor of the lawyer.

Although it would be practically impossible to sue the lawyer for the other side for something she said about you, you could ask the court to issue sanctions or ask your state lawyer disciplinary agency to impose discipline for malicious lies the lawyer says about you.

Similarly, if the lawyer intentionally lies in court (unless she is testifying under oath—see Section A.7, above) and the lie is related to the case, she is immune from liability.

10. Entering Your Property or Taking Pictures Without Your Permission

If the lawyer for the other side hires an investigator (including a junior lawyer from his office) who enters your property without your permission or takes pictures of you or your property without your permission, you may be able to sue. For entering your property without your permission, you can sue for trespass; for taking photos without your permission, you can sue for invasion of privacy. The economic damages from such a trespass or invasion or privacy would probably be negligible, unless you were in the business of providing privacy and you lost business as a result of the photograph.

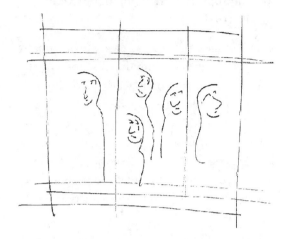

11. Orchestrating Your Arrest So You Spend Time in Jail

Let's say you are behind on your child support. The attorney for the other side hauls you into court on a Friday afternoon (any other day of the week was possible) just to have the court hold you in contempt and throw you in jail. You may have grounds to sue the attorney for abuse of process—generally considered a misuse of the legal system.

12. Threatening to Have You Jailed to Collect a Debt

A lawyer cannot threaten criminal prosecution to collect a debt—such as back rent, your credit card bill or a defaulted student loan. If a lawyer makes such a threat, you may have grounds to sue the attorney for abuse of process (misuse of the legal system) and to file a complaint with your state attorney discipline agency.

13. Improperly Releasing Money Held in Trust

Often, money owed to you or to the other party in a case is deposited into the trust account of your lawyer or your opponent's lawyer until it is ready to be disbursed. As discussed in Chapter 4, in such a situation, the attorney has a fiduciary duty to both parties—so if your lawyer deposits the money, she has a fiduciary duty to your opponent and if your opponent's lawyer deposits the money, he has a fiduciary duty to you.

If your opponent's lawyer releases the money without your consent, or uses it to cover his client's bill for attorney fees, that would be a breach of his duty. You would have grounds to sue the lawyer for the unauthorized release of the funds.

In a similar situation, you may not be a party to the lawsuit, but you are owed money out of the recovery—for example, you are a doctor who hasn't been paid yet by the injured party. If you file papers giving yourself a lien on the recovery, but the lawyer holding the funds distributes the money without paying your lien, you have grounds to sue the lawyer for interference with economic advantage.

14. Improperly Releasing Your Tax Returns

In many cases—especially divorce cases—a party must give copies of his or her tax returns to the opposing side. If the lawyer for the other side discusses or releases those tax returns to anyone (such as your business competitor), you have grounds to sue the lawyer.

EXAMPLE: You have one of the only two businesses of its kind in town. Your ex-spouse's lawyer gave your tax returns to your competitor who used them to "pitch" his business as the one in town on superior financial footing. You might have a claim for damages if you could show that you lost customers as a result.

15. Breaching an Ethical Rule

Lawyers must abide by an extensive list of ethical rules. (See Chapter 4.) For example, the lawyer for the insurance company can't contact you directly, behind your lawyer's back, and encourage you to accept a settlement contrary to your lawyer's advice. This would be a violation of the ethical rules for lawyers. You couldn't sue the lawyer for damages; however you could file a complaint with your state attorney disciplinary agency. (See Chapter 8.)

16. Behaving Rudely

Sorry, but there is nothing you can do to make a lawyer be polite. Nevertheless, repeated and serious rude conduct could subject the attorney to disciplinary action; more likely, a judge might impose sanctions for particularly offensive behavior.

17. Committing Malpractice

If the attorney for the other side commits malpractice, you have no basis to sue. This is because the lawyer owes a duty only to her client, not you. (See Chapter 9 for a discussion of malpractice.)

B. Claims Against the Lawyer for the Other Side

Other than reporting the lawyer to your state discipline agency or to a government prosecutor, such as the district attorney or attorney general if the lawyer engaged in criminal conduct, you can normally take one of two kinds of actions against the attorney for the other side:

Request that the judge award you sanctions. Sanctions are money damages or a court order going against your adversary.

File a separate lawsuit for damages. Usually these lawsuits amount to a claim that your adversary's attorney engaged in intentional conduct unrelated to the litigation that caused you harm. Unfortunately, because the rules governing these lawsuits are stacked against you, your chances of success are poor. In theory, most of these claims may be brought against both your former adversary and her lawyer. Because your former adversary is likely to defend by stating that she relied upon the advice of her attorney, this chapter only discusses claims against lawyers.

1. Request for Sanctions

Sanctions, which are normally awarded during a lawsuit, not after it has concluded, take the form of either a money fine levied on the offending lawyer or a court ruling that goes against the party represented by the errant attorney. A monetary fine can be awarded against a party, the party's attorney or both. The court may order that the fine be paid to you, your attorney or the court to be put toward administrative expenses. A court ruling is usually designed to penalize conduct or deter harassing behavior.

Here are some examples of situations in which sanctions may be awarded:

- An attorney schedules a deposition of one of your witnesses and then reschedules it without notifying your lawyer. Your lawyer and your witness appear at the date and place noticed, but no one else does. A court may order the opposing attorney to pay your lawyer's fee for the time spent traveling, waiting and figuring out what happened.
- The opposing attorney schedules your main witness's deposition. The witness, your lawyer and the court reporter appear at the date and place noticed, but the lawyer does not. A court may order the opposing attorney to pay your lawyer's fee for the time spent traveling, figuring out what happened and rescheduling the deposition.
- The opposing attorney schedules your deposition and doesn't show up. You, your lawyer and the court reporter do. A court may order the opposing attorney to pay your lawyer's fee for the time spent traveling, figuring out what happened and rescheduling the deposition and may impose sanctions against the lawyer to compensate you for the time you took off work.
- An attorney schedules a deposition, reschedules it without notifying your lawyer and proceeds without your lawyer being

there. The sanction the court may impose is to prohibit the deposition testimony from being used at the trial.

- Your lawyer schedules a deposition of the opposing party, who doesn't show up because her lawyer never told her about it. A court may order some or all of the following as sanctions:
  - that the lawyer for the other side be precluded from taking any depositions until the deposition you scheduled takes place
  - that the lawyer (and/or party) for the other side pay your lawyer's fee for the time spent waiting, figuring out what happened and rescheduling the deposition, and/or
  - that if the lawyer and party for the other side do not appear for deposition when it's rescheduled, that they pay monetary sanctions of a specified amount.
- An attorney continually violates a court order, such as an order to comply with a request to answer written questions asked by your lawyer, called interrogatories. The court may order that the case be dismissed, and/or that the attorney be referred to the state attorney discipline agency.

Other situations in which a court might award sanctions include when an attorney:

- uses harassing litigation tactics, such as sending multiple sets of interrogatories (written questions for you to answer under oath) which are repetitive or absurd given the issues

- files an obviously groundless lawsuit
- pursues a frivolous claim or defense, such as claiming that an accident was caused by an unknown third party when no facts or witnesses support the claim that a third person was involved
- files a frivolous appeal, such as one done for the sole purpose of delaying the entry of a judgment to allow the defendant sufficient time to hide his assets
- repeatedly interferes with a deposition by interrupting or coaching the person whose testimony is being taken or ordering a person not to answer proper questions
- fails to answer interrogatories (written questions about the lawsuit) or produce requested documents
- fails to file reports required by the court, or
- fails to show up for a hearing.

Sometimes, a judge will impose sanctions on her own motion, without any request by an opposing party or the party's attorney. More often, however, the opposing party (or his lawyer) will bring a problem to the judge's attention and ask for sanctions to be awarded.

A court decides whether and what sanctions are appropriate depending upon the circumstances. Whether sanctions will be ordered in a particular situation will vary considerably from one judge to the next. But with the growing dissatisfaction with the legal system and the out-of-control behavior of too many lawyers, courts and judges are intervening and awarding sanctions more than they used to in a deliberate attempt to control unreasonable lawyer conduct.

As a general rule, federal judges are more apt to play the role of careful watchdogs over how lawyers conduct litigation and are more willing to award sanctions than are state court judges. One reason for this is that federal court rules require an attorney to do some investigating as to the validity and merit of a case before filing it. Unlike some state courts, in our federal system an attorney cannot simply rely on what a client says as a basis of filing a suit.

2. Lawsuit for Malicious Prosecution

Malicious prosecution (sometimes called "abusive litigation") is the lawsuit most people would dearly love to bring against the lawyer for the other side. In it, you claim that:

- a former lawsuit brought against you (or criminal charges instigated against you) was filed knowingly and maliciously
- the lawyer knew the case was without merit or had no probable cause to think that it could succeed
- the case did indeed fail, and
- you were damaged (the most common damages that are claimed are the attorney fees and costs you spent defending your position).

Unfortunately, although many former litigants consider, threaten and some even file a malicious prosecution lawsuit, this type of case rarely succeeds. If the lawyer for the other side had any reasonable and honest belief that there was even an arguable (tenable) claim, the claim for malicious prosecution will fail.

Even if you can overcome this hurdle and can show that the lawyer for the other side filed a completely meritless case, you still face other obstacles. First, you must show that the underlying lawsuit has been completely resolved in your favor. Lawyers call this the "favorable termination" requirement. This means that if in order to avoid years of litigation you settled a frivolous case for a nominal sum instead of fighting it through to ultimate victory, you can't sue for malicious prosecution.

Furthermore, some states impose the nearly impossible requirement of showing a "special" injury. Special injury is discussed in Section B.2.c, below.

➡ Immunity for Government Prosecutors
Skip this section if you want to sue a government prosecutor, such as a district attorney or state's attorney, for malicious prosecution. They are absolutely immune from liability for such claims.

a. Examples of Malicious Prosecution

Here are several examples of malicious prosecution cases:

- A false report given to the police results in your arrest. After considerable time, expense and trouble, the charges are dropped. If your accuser hired an attorney to pass the information on to the police (perhaps an attorney who represent the person in civil matters), for you to win a claim of malicious prosecution against the attorney, you must show that the attorney gave a false report to the police or communicated information which he knew to be false.

- A business competitor hires a lawyer to report your business to a state regulatory agency, which leads to your being investigated and cleared. You can sue the attorney who made the report if you can show either that the attorney knew he was reporting false information or that he reported the information as true without knowledge of whether or not it was.
- A voters' association circulates written materials opposing a real estate development. The developer hires a lawyer to sue the association for libel, claiming the written materials contained false statements. The case is eventually dismissed because the developer doesn't pursue it. To sue the attorney for the developer, the association must show that the lawyer filed the case knowing the developer had no intention of prosecuting it, but did so for other reasons—such as the resulting publicity or to intimidate the other side.

  (In such a situation, you will want to look into whether your state has a SLAPP (Strategic Lawsuits Against Public Participation) law. California, Colorado, Massachusetts, New York, Washington and other states have laws designed to prevent meritless lawsuits from being filed against citizen groups for the purpose of silencing them. The laws are most often used by citizen groups, public interest groups or political groups who oppose real estate developments or actions proposed by landlords.)
- An immigrant wife marries a U.S.-citizen husband and petitions for a green card.

The husband, as the wife's immigration sponsor, signs an Immigration and Naturalization Service (INS) form promising to support her for three years. They divorce immediately and the divorce court denies the wife's request for alimony. Her attorney then sues the husband in federal court for support, claiming that he agreed to support her for three years. The federal court dismisses the case based upon clearly established law holding that the form filed with INS is a promise made to the U.S. government only—not to the wife. To win a malicious prosecution case, the husband must show that the wife's attorney had no reasonable belief that the lawsuit would prevail—or failed to investigate the validity and merit of a case before filing it—a federal court requirement.

b. Elements of a Malicious Prosecution Case

This section provides detail concerning the four elements of a malicious prosecution case. In most states, you must prove all four to win.

A civil or criminal proceeding was instituted or prosecuted against you. Satisfying the first element is easy, since it requires only that a lawsuit was brought against you or that criminal charges were filed against you. Neither has to have been prosecuted to conclusion. It is enough if you were sued and then the case was dismissed or that criminal charges were filed against you and then dropped.

Lack of probable cause to believe lawsuit had merit. This is an extraordinarily difficult standard for a person bringing a malicious prosecution case to meet. For starters, an attorney needs only to have a reasonable basis that a claim might be valid to defeat your malicious prosecution case. The claim doesn't have to be good or strong. It's well known that speculative and innovative claims which may seem weak at the outset are often the ones that break new legal ground. Also, it's a lawyer's job to be creative—even aggressive—in advocating for a client.

EXAMPLE: A lawyer represents grandparents in a custody action against the parents of two young children. Based on the legal presumption that parents—not grandparents—have the primary right to parent their children, the parents win the case and then sue the grandparents' lawyer for malicious prosecution. The lawyer could defeat the malicious prosecution case as long as she can show that her clients had convinced her that there was a reasonable belief that the children were being neglected, had

been abandoned, or that continuing to live with their parents was harmful in some other way.

The rules vary from state to state as to what is necessary to show probable cause. In many states, an attorney has the right to rely on the facts as presented by his client, unless he knows the client is lying. This means that an attorney does not have to undertake an independent investigation into the alleged facts on which he intends to base his legal claims.

In some states and in federal courts, however, an attorney must conduct a reasonable investigation of the facts presented by the client as well as researching the law he believes supports his legal claim before filing a case. How much investigation and research is required depends on the particular case and court, but generally the research standard is fairly low. For example, an attorney does not have to show that he conducted an extensive investigation of the facts or spent many hours researching the legal theories in a case. As long as he can show that he did some investigating and researching, he'll almost surely defeat any malicious prosecution case.

⚠ More Research Is Often Required for Medical Malpractice Cases

States requiring independent investigation into the facts often require it specifically in medical malpractice cases. There, before a doctor can be sued, the attorney for the plaintiff must check with another doctor about the reasonableness of the first doctor's actions—that is, whether there is a legitimate claim for malpractice. An attorney who fails to do this checking will have a hard time showing probable cause to sue.

BEWARE OF THE SUMMARY JUDGMENT MOTION

A motion for summary judgment is used when an attorney for the other side asks the court to throw out your case before trial based on the fact that there is no issue to be tried (legally, you have no case). Virtually all lawyers sued for malicious prosecution file such a motion, claiming that there was probable cause to file the first case and that therefore there is no way a malicious prosecution claim can win. Judges—lawyers themselves—are usually at least somewhat sympathetic to lawyers sued for malicious prosecution and tend to grant summary judgment motions when it appears that anything which would support the lawyer's claim for filing the suit in the first place was present, even minimally.

A motion for summary judgment can be expensive to oppose. You must follow technical rules and provide the court with documentary evidence supporting your position. If a lawyer does the opposition paperwork for you, it will cost you several thousand dollars. If you do it yourself, you will have to meticulously comply with the rules or your response won't be considered by the judge. If your adversary's lawyer's motion is granted, you have lost your malicious prosecution case. Now the only way to proceed is to appeal.

If your claim for malicious prosecution gets as far as a trial, you have a choice of requesting a judge or jury trial. In a judge trial, the judge decides all questions—factual and legal. If the judge believes that no reasonable attorney would have concluded that the first case had merit, the judge will rule for you by finding that it lacked probable cause.

In a jury trial, the jury decides factual questions and the judge decides legal questions. The ultimate question of whether the attorney had probable cause to file the first case is a legal question. What steps the lawyer took to decide whether he had probable cause to file the first case—such as what investigating and researching the lawyer did—however, are questions of fact. The judge will decide whether or not there was probable cause based on what the jury finds.

Malice. The third element you will have to prove in a malicious prosecution case is malice. Malice is hatred, spite or ill will directed toward someone else. It is improper to pursue a lawsuit because of hatred or spite for the purpose of harassing the defendant. Either an attorney personally acting with improper motive or an attorney acting on behalf of a client whom she knows has improper motive is malice. So if a lawyer knows her client hates the other side and is motivated solely by that hatred to prosecute a case, the client's malice may be attributed to the attorney.

Malice is often hard to prove, and so judges often allow a person suing for malicious prosecution to imply malice. For example, if the lawsuit filed against you obviously had no merit (a judge finds your opponent's case lacked probable cause), you can probably imply malice. Why? Because otherwise there would be no reason for the lawyer to prosecute a groundless case.

Winning the first lawsuit. The final element you must prove in most states to win a malicious prosecution case is that the first case is over and you won. This is called the "favorable termination" test. Only Georgia, Tennessee and Washington do not require it. In those states, when you are sued in the case you claim to be frivolous, you must (Georgia) or may (Tennessee and Washington) countersue claiming the case has no merit.

In all other states, favorable termination means the case is absolutely over—it has not been appealed and the time for filing an appeal

has expired. It also means that you won the case on its merits. This does not necessarily mean the case had to proceed through a trial. Generally, it means that the manner of termination of the case supports your claim of innocence. A few states require that a judge determine the issues in the case.

Here are some examples of what does and does not constitute favorable termination:

Favorable Termination

- Winning at trial.
- Winning at arbitration which is final, binding and can't be appealed (or time to appeal expired).
- Summary judgment granted in your favor.

Possibly Favorable Termination

(check state law)

- Voluntary dismissal by the plaintiff (person suing you).
- Dismissal for failure to prosecute—that is, after case filed, plaintiff did nothing else and the court dropped the case.
- Case dismissed as a sanction against your adversary or her lawyer.

Not Favorable Termination

- Settlement.
- Case dismissed because of statute of limitations (unless attorney filed case knowing that time to file had expired).
- Dismissed on technical grounds for procedural reasons—for example, failing to return a form showing proof of the service of the summons to the court within the required time limit.
- Dismissed for lack of jurisdiction—that is, court did not have authority to hear case.

c. Damages

If you prove the elements of a malicious prosecution case, you are entitled to damages. The kinds of damages usually claimed include:

- attorney fees and costs incurred in defeating the frivolous claim
- injury to your reputation—this is a particular favorite of lawyers who are sued for malpractice and win and then sue their former clients for malicious prosecution—the lawyer claims that the case besmirched his otherwise spotless reputation
- damage to your credit—for example, you were wrongfully sued for not making payments on a note that you didn't owe and it was reported to a credit bureau; you would be damaged if you were later denied credit and suffered from embarrassment and humiliation
- increased insurance premiums—for example, the lawyer for the other side refuses to remove a wrongfully recorded lien which causes your homeowner's insurance premiums to increase
- emotional distress, and
- punitive damages—damages simply meant to punish.

In some states, you must show "special injury" damages—and quite frankly, it will be nearly impossible to successfully win a case for malicious prosecution in those states unless you were imprisoned. Attorney's fees and costs to defend the first case are not special injury damages. Nor are damages for emotional distress. Unfortunately, it is difficult to articulate exactly what damages might meet the special injury test, other than incarceration. Probably for this reason, many states have eliminated or limited the special injury requirement.

If your state requires a showing of special injury, the following types of injuries will probably not meet the test:

- humiliation
- embarrassment
- emotional distress
- injury to reputation
- injury to business credit
- injury to business goodwill
- lost time, and
- expenses paid for defense of the action or increased insurance premiums. New Jersey does permit the loss of insurance and the inability to practice a profession to be a special injury.[1]

As of late 1995, Delaware, the District of Columbia, Georgia, Hawaii, Iowa, Louisiana, Maryland, Michigan, New Jersey, New York, Ohio, Oregon, Pennsylvania, Rhode Island, Texas and Virginia required a showing of special injury in all cases. Illinois requires it in all but medical malpractice cases. Kentucky allows you to claim damages for injury to reputation as a special injury. If your state is listed above, you'll probably need to do some legal research to see if any of your damages would be considered "special" or to see if your state has eliminated or redefined the requirement. (See Chapter 11 for information on doing legal research.)

3. Lawsuit for Abuse of Process

Abuse of process is a claim that an attorney misused the legal system for a purpose for which it is not intended. You must prove that the lawyer intended to misuse the legal system. Accidental mistakes will not support a claim for abuse of process.

Abuse of process differs from malicious prosecution in one major way: there is no requirement that the first lawsuit must result in a termination favorable to you. This means that you can raise a claim for abuse of process as a countersuit in the first case or your opponent's suit against you or in an independent lawsuit later. You could also raise it if you settle the case to avoid litigation costs.

a. Examples of Abuse of Process

Most claims against lawyers for abuse of process arise in the context of wrongful debt collection practices. The increased use of sanctions has done away with much of the need for these cases. (See Section B.1, above.) Nevertheless, here are some examples of possible abuse of process claims against lawyers:

- The lawyer representing a collection agency files a lawsuit in the wrong state or county:
  - to make it inconvenient and expensive for you to respond
  - to coerce you into agreeing to an unfair settlement, or
  - to increase the possibility that you will default and the collection agency will automatically win the case.
- The lawyer for a creditor owed a negligible sum of money records a lien against your real estate and forces a sale of your property—which is worth many times more

than what you owe.[2] If the creditor asked for payment and you refused to pay, this probably would not support a claim for abuse of process. The lawyer would have to have some illegitimate purpose. For example, if you and the creditor had other litigation pending, you could show abuse of process if the lawyer was trying to force you to unfairly compromise the second claim.

- A lawyer representing a creditor with a judgment against you makes false statements in an affidavit to obtain a court order called a "writ of execution" which allows the lawyer to seize your property or take a portion of your wages out of your paycheck to satisfy the debt.
- A lawyer representing a creditor with a judgment against you attempts to seize property which cannot be taken to pay a debt under the laws of your state. You incur expenses stopping the proposed seizure.
- You have sued your former employer for wrongful termination. The lawyer representing your former employer has documents served on you demanding that you provide your former employer with copies of records already in the employer's possession. The only reason the lawyer served you with the papers is to harass and intimidate you, hoping you will dismiss your case.
- A lawyer representing your business competitor illegally obtains a document called a "writ of possession" which allows a sheriff to seize your business records.

- A lawyer representing a creditor knowingly obtains a judgment against you for money you clearly do not owe—such as a debt that was expressly eliminated in bankruptcy.
- A lawyer representing a creditor to whom you do owe money threatens you with criminal prosecution for nonpayment or files unfounded criminal charges to force you to pay.
- A lawyer representing your ex-wife orchestrates your arrest for nonpayment of child support late on a Friday afternoon of a holiday weekend so you have to sit in jail for three days.
- A lawyer issues subpoenas on 100 employees of the same company, requiring them to appear in court at the same time, and refuses to cooperate with their employer to stagger the schedule.
- Attorney files lawsuit alleging fraud, sends announcements to newspaper, sends the news clippings to the opposition and then dismisses the case. The opposition may have claim for abuse of process if she can show that the case was filed for the purpose of gaining favorable publicity and in the hopes of coercing a settlement in another matter.

b. Elements of an Abuse of Process Case

To win an abuse of process claim, you must prove the following:

Improper use of the legal system, a legal procedure or a legal tool. Examples include a subpoena, lien, garnishment, attachment or arrest. For example, if a lawyer used legal means to collect an already paid judgment, that would be an improper use of the legal tool called a writ of execution. Other examples are just above.

Purpose other than that for which the process was intended. The focus here is more on what was said, threatened or intended than what was actually done. This requirement is a lot like extortion: "Pay me money or I will file a lien against your house." This requirement is like the requirement of malice for malicious prosecution, except that it does not require spite or hatred.

c. Damages

If you prove both elements of an abuse of process case, you are entitled to damages. The kinds of damages usually claimed include:

- attorney fees and costs incurred in fighting the lawyer's abusive action (the most common damages claimed)
- injury to your reputation
- damage to your credit
- lost profits
- loss of use of property wrongfully seized
- emotional distress, and
- punitive damages—damages simply meant to punish.

As with malicious prosecution cases, a few states require a showing of "special injury" for abuse of process claims. As of late 1995, only Georgia, Kentucky, New York, Pennsylvania (maybe) and Texas had such a requirement. The discussion in Section B.2.c, above, on special injury in malicious prosecution cases applies here as well.

Tanya's Tip: Help Prove Your Abuse of Process Claim—Send a Letter

In pursuing a claim for abuse of process against a lawyer, it will help you to show that the lawyer was put on notice of your claim that he was misusing the system. Send a letter telling the lawyer how the process is being misused. "You have sued the wrong person. I don't live at the place where the incident happened." Include documentation to prove that you live elsewhere. (If you have a lawyer, she should send the letter for you.) If the lawyer continues with the claim against you, file a countersuit for abuse of process—and ask for sanctions as well. Use the letter and documentation to show that the lawyer proceeded after being put on notice that she was misusing the court's process.

4. Lawsuit for False Arrest or False Imprisonment

To win a case for false arrest or false imprisonment, you must have been physically restrained or detained against your will. For example, if a lawyer (or anyone else) either makes a citizen's arrest or furnishes false information to the police, which causes the police to make a wrongful arrest, the lawyer may be liable for damages if the lawyer knew that the information used as the basis for the arrest was false.

Here are some examples of false arrest or false imprisonment.

- An attorney represents a client in a dispute with you over the ownership of property. The attorney reports the property (which is in your possession) to police as stolen. If you are detained or arrested by the police,

the attorney may be liable for false arrest or false imprisonment.

- An attorney represents a husband in a divorce case and the couple has not yet divided their marital property. The wife takes and uses the family car and the lawyer—knowing she has it—reports it to the police as stolen. If the wife or any passenger with her is detained or arrested by the police, the husband's attorney may be liable for damages.

a. Elements of a Claim for False Arrest or False Imprisonment

You must prove two elements to win a false arrest or false imprisonment claim.

Unlawful detention. This involves a restraint on a person's individual freedom to come and go. It does not require incarceration in a jail. It could simply involve the police pinning you to the wall, searching you and not letting you go for a short period of time.

The confinement must be in a limited area, such as a house, car, street (especially if it is roped off) or a small island. If someone takes your plane ticket and prevents your departure, that may be considered confinement to the city from which you intend to depart.

Confinement must also include no reasonable means of escape. If the only way to get out is to crawl through a sewage pipe or jump off of a second story balcony, that is not reasonable. Similarly, if you do not have the wherewithal to purchase another plane ticket or the flight is booked, you are being confined.

Intent. There must be an intent to confine you. If you are locked in a basement on purpose, there is intent. But, if someone locks your basement door with no idea that you were asleep inside, there is no intent.

b. Damages

If you prove both elements of a false arrest or false imprisonment case, you are entitled to damages. The kinds of damages usually claimed include:

- attorneys' fees and costs incurred in getting out of jail and defending the charges
- inconvenience measured by attributing an hourly wage to the amount of time you were inconvenienced, lost time or lost wages
- physical discomfort
- emotional distress, humiliation, mental suffering, shame or embarrassment
- nominal damages (such as $1), and
- punitive damages—damages meant to punish.

5. Lawsuit for Defamation

Defamation is a false statement that damages someone's reputation. Truth is an absolute defense. This means that if a statement is true, you cannot claim defamation no matter how much you were damaged by the statement.

Successfully suing a lawyer who represented your opponent for defamation would be rare and most unusual. This is because attorneys have absolute immunity for statements they make during a legal proceeding. Only if a statement made has no reasonable relationship to the legal proceeding could you win. Although the issue of what is reasonably related to a judicial proceeding varies from state to state, attorneys are given broad leeway and the benefit of the doubt.

Here is the kind of situation which might give rise to a claim of defamation. You are sued by your former business partner who alleges that you manipulated the books, stole money and generally caused the business's failure. A jury rules in your favor on all counts, but the lawyer for your former business partner won't give up. As you leave the courthouse, the lawyer runs after you, shouting, "There goes a liar and a thief." In many states, this would support a claim of defamation. So would speaking to a reporter or giving a press conference and saying the same thing.

6. Lawsuit for Invasion of Privacy or Trespass on Your Property

Invasion of privacy or trespass means that someone has unlawfully sought or disclosed information about you or entered your property. For example, in certain types of lawsuits—particularly in family law proceedings involving support—you are required to exchange tax returns with the other side. But at the same time, tax returns are considered to be confidential. If the attorney for the other side discloses your tax returns, for example, to your business competitor, he could be liable for invasion of privacy. Just because you had to give the other side your tax return for a limited purpose does not mean that you agreed to waive your right to have it remain confidential.

Not all acts of invasion of privacy or trespass are done by lawyers—but the acts still may be attributed to them. For example, if a lawyer hires a person to investigate the facts you assert related to a lawsuit, the lawyer is liable for all unlawful acts done by the investigator. And because the law places limitations on how such an investigation may be conducted, an attorney would be liable (for a claim of invasion of privacy and/or trespass) if an investigator:

- obtained entry to a premise unlawfully or under false pretenses
- obtained information unlawfully or under false pretenses
- placed an illegal wiretap, or
- photographed your premises without permission.

7. Lawsuit for Unauthorized Release of Funds

Often, money owed to you or to the other party (or for which ownership is in dispute) is deposited into one of the lawyer's trust accounts until it is ready to be disbursed. In such a situation, the attorney has a fiduciary duty to both parties—so if your lawyer deposits the money, she has a fiduciary duty to your opponent and if your opponent's lawyer deposits the money, he has a fiduciary duty to you.

If a lawyer releases the money without your consent, or uses it to cover his client's bill for attorney fees, that would be a breach of his duty. You would have grounds to sue the lawyer for breach of fiduciary duty—that is, the unauthorized release of the funds.

Here are some examples of this breach.

- You and your spouse are divorcing and your spouse's lawyer agrees to hold some money until you and your spouse agree how to divide it or a court orders it to be divided. Your spouse tells the lawyer that you are behind on support and the lawyer releases the money to your spouse to cover what you owe. You can sue your spouse's lawyer for any damages you suffer as a result. For instance, if you were planning to use the money to pay your taxes and you now can't, you can sue for the interest and penalties you will owe the IRS for paying your tax bill late and you sue for the money itself to be replaced into the trust account.
- You and your tenant are disputing how much rent she owes you. The tenant agrees in writing to pay the entire amount you claim is owed to her attorney to be held in trust, until you resolve the dispute. The attorney agrees to collect the rent and act like an escrow agent. Later, before the matter is resolved, the tenant asks her attorney to return what she has paid, and the lawyer does it. You can sue the tenant's lawyer for any damages you suffer as a result, such as whatever lost rents you cannot collect.

8. Lawsuit for Interference With Economic Advantage

If an attorney knows of a business relationship you enjoy and maliciously interferes with it, the attorney may be liable for damages for something known as "interference with economic advantage." State laws vary about what is required to win these claims, but generally all of the following elements must exist:

- a business relationship, either existing or expected
- knowledge of it by the attorney
- intentional interference with it (intent means malice; see Section B.2.b, above), and
- damages.

Here are some examples of interference with economic advantage:

- You quit your job to start a competitive business and encourage customers of your former employee to patronize you. Your former employer threatens to sue you for taking her business. Her lawyer calls the customers and tells lies (such as claiming that you are selling substandard merchandise or are under criminal investigation for selling stolen merchandise) with the hope of getting the customers to return to her client. You may have an action against your former employer's lawyer if you lose your new customers as a result of the lawyer's lies.
- You are a real estate agent and show a property to a client who is looking to buy. The seller's lawyer contacts your client directly to buy the property and cut you out of your commission. You may have a claim against the attorney for the lost commission.
- In certain types of lawsuits—particularly divorce cases involving support—spouses must exchange tax returns. As mentioned above (in Section B.6), if the attorney for the other side discloses your tax returns, for example, to your business competitor, he could be liable for invasion of privacy.

He might also be liable to you for interference with economic advantage if you lose business because of the disclosure.

- You are a contractor who has just finished a remodeling job. The property owner refuses to pay you, causing you to place a mechanic's lien on his property. You (and several others who supplied goods and labor) later sued the property owner and reached a settlement. The attorney for the property owner disburses the money to the other contractors, but does not pay off your lien as required by the settlement. You have a claim for interference with economic advantage.

Here is an action that is *not* considered interference with economic advantage, but is a common complaint against opposing lawyers. Let's say the attorney for your adversary advises her client not to do business with you. This seems like an interference with your economic advantage; however, the attorney has an absolute privilege and is considered to be just doing her job.

9. Lawsuit for Violating the Federal Securities Act

The federal Securities Acts require that when you buy an investment, you sign a document called a subscription agreement.[3] In it, you must agree that you:

- have read about the investment, and
- meet the qualifications to purchase it.

The subscription agreement usually requires that you answer questions about your net worth, whether you have an investment advisor and whether you have made similar investments before. In addition to the subscription agreement, the seller must give you a big, fat booklet called a prospectus. It is supposed to explain the investment and its risks. A lawyer will have participated in preparing it and the lawyer must be sure that nothing important is omitted.

If you bought an investment subject to these rules which goes bad, you may have a claim under the Securities Act against the attorney who signed the offering memorandum, offering circular or registration statement. Lawyers are required to do a reasonable investigation of the facts contained in the offering documents and cannot simply rely on information provided by a client as being accurate. If the facts represented in the offering document were incorrect, and the lawyer did no independent and reasonable investigation, you may have a claim against the lawyer.

EXAMPLE: You bought an interest in a recreational real estate venture on a remote location, only to learn the property had been misrepresented (or perhaps doesn't even exist). If a lawyer signed the offering materials, you would have a claim against the lawyer as well as the others involved in the sale.

 You Will Need Advice From an Attorney Familiar With Securities Litigation

This is not the kind of claim you can handle on your own. Securities are governed by very complex laws and regulations.

10. Lawsuit for Violating the Racketeer Influenced and Corrupt Organizations Act (RICO)

The Racketeer Influenced and Corrupt Organizations Act (RICO) allows private citizens to file lawsuits for damages arising out of organized crime, commonly known as racketeering.[4] Although RICO was intended to deal exclusively with organized criminal activities, it has been interpreted to apply to almost any bad business behavior involving at least two people if there is an allegation of conspiracy, as long as there is a pattern or history of bad action.

RICO claims against attorneys most often arise in the context of failed business ventures or the sale of securities. Like claims against attorneys under the Securities Act, RICO claims are usually coupled with more traditional claims such as fraud, breach of fiduciary duty and misrepresentation. Because RICO provides for an award of attorney fees and triple damages to successful litigants, RICO claims are extremely popular.

RICO claims are complex, and despite the fact that the law has been around over 25 years, it is still not clear how RICO should be interpreted and applied. Most RICO claims allege that the lawyer illegally was employed by or associated with an enterprise (business) "to conduct or participate, directly or indirectly, in the conduct of such enterprise's affairs through a pattern of racketeering activity or collection of an unlawful debt." In a RICO claim, you must show that:

- there is or was a business
- the lawyer participated in business matters
- the lawyer engaged in two criminal acts within a ten-year period, and
- you have suffered damages as a result—usually damage to your business.

Here are some examples of possible RICO claims against the lawyer for your former adversary:

- You may be able to sue the attorney who signed the offering memorandum in connection with the sale of a bogus security (or one where the facts were seriously misrepresented), if you relied on an attorney's opinion in the memorandum.
- You may be able to sue the attorney whose opinion you sought about whether to invest in a particular security, if the investment fails and the lawyer failed to disclose to you that he was involved in the running of the business.

- You are a stockholder. The company in which you own stock made a terrible business decision and the value of the stock plummeted. You could sue the attorney who advised the company to take the action if you could show that the attorney had a conflict of interest. (See Chapter 4.)
- You are a creditor. You may be able to sue the attorney who files a fraudulent bankruptcy action on behalf of the debtor who owes you money to frustrate your collection efforts.

 Tanya's Tip: Shop Carefully for the Lawyer to Bring Your RICO Claim

Not only should you get legal advice to bring a RICO claim, but be sure the lawyer knows what he is talking about. Most lawyers know little about RICO and know even less about suing a lawyer under the RICO Act. Most RICO claims against attorneys are part of complex business litigation matters against multiple defendants, meaning that if you have a RICO claim against a lawyer, it will usually be part of a much larger lawsuit, involving multiple claims, and involving multiple defendants.

To pursue a RICO claim against an attorney will be expensive. Unless a bundle of money is at stake, a RICO claim probably isn't economically justified. Further complicating the matter is the fact that many insurance companies won't pay the defense costs of any judgment for RICO claims under a lawyers' malpractice policy.

Specifically, beware of the lawyer who charges by the hour and encourages you to file a RICO claim against an attorney because you may be able to recover attorneys' fees and triple damages. The only one sure to benefit is the lawyer you are paying. You may get a huge bill for legal fees before you even get to trial—and by that time, you might not still be able to afford your lawyer.

Endnotes

[1] *Rutgers Casualty Insurance Co. v. Medical Inter-Insurance Exchange of N. J.*, 641 A.2d 1112 (1994).

[2] See, for example, *Haggerty v. Moyerman*, 184 A. 654 (N.J. 1936), where a lawyer was sued for malicious prosecution when he levied on and purchased property worth $13,000 to satisfy a $74 judgment.

[3] 15 U.S.C. § 77a & §78a and following.

[4] 18 U.S.C. §§ 1961-1968.

Chapter 11

Help Beyond the Book

This book gives you basic information on common problems you may have with your lawyer and suggests what to do about those problems. But the information in this book is limited, and you may need to do further research. Here are some places to go if you need more information or advice than this book provides:

Law library. In a law library, you can research in more depth a specific issue raised in this book.

Legal reform group. In many states or communities, consumers—often the victims of lawyer malpractice or unethical behavior—have established groups that work to reform laws such as those limiting access to lawyer discipline records. They also offer practical support to victims of lawyer misconduct and usually have lists of "good" lawyers whom they can refer you to.

Lawyer. A lawyer can provide you with information, legal advice or legal representation.

Online. A host of information is showing up on the Internet.

Before discussing each of these in more detail, here's a general piece of advice: After getting top-quality information, make key decisions yourself. By reading this book you've made a good start. If you decide to get help from others, apply this same self-empowerment principle—shop around until you find an advisor who values your competence and intelligence, and recognizes your right to have access to top-notch information necessary to make your own decisions.

A. Law Libraries

Often, you can find the answer to a legal question yourself if you're willing to do some research in a law library. The trick is in knowing the type of information you can find there. The library can help you find a law and any court interpretations of it. For example, in the library you can read your state's statute of limitations, find out the general rule for how long you have to sue your lawyer, and then read the court cases that have carved out exceptions to the general rule.

Here's what you should find in an average law library:

- your state's laws (often called "statutes" or the "legal code")
- the text of your state's Rules of Professional Conduct, as well as rules promulgated by the American Bar Association
- court cases interpreting the ethical rules that apply to lawyers in your state
- court cases from your state and other states interpreting the American Bar Association's ethical rules
- discussions and explanations by expert lawyer commentators as to what constitutes lawyer malpractice or violations of lawyer ethical rules, and
- forms and written guidance for filing a lawsuit in court.

RESEARCHING OUTSIDE OF THE LAW LIBRARY

Sometimes, what you need to know isn't written down and therefore won't be found in the law library. For instance, if you need to sue your former lawyer for failing to return your file and want to know whether your small claims court has evening hours, you probably won't find out by going to the law library. You'll need to call the small claims court clerk.

At the same time, some questions that can be answered at the law library may be answered more efficiently elsewhere. If, for example, you want to know what constitutes lawyer abandonment under your state's lawyer ethical rules, your state Rules of Professional Conduct, which your local law library would have a copy of, would have the answer. But making a telephone call to your state lawyer discipline agency is usually a better approach.

Here, briefly, are the basic steps to researching a legal question. For more detailed, but user-friendly, instructions on legal research, see *Legal Research: How to Find and Understand the Law*, by Stephen Elias and Susan Levinkind (Nolo Press) or watch the video, *Legal Research Made Easy: A Roadmap Through the Law Library Maze*, by Nolo Press and Robert Berring (Legal Star Video).

1. Find the Law Library

In some states, finding a well-stocked law library that is open to the public is no problem; at least one library will be at a principal courthouse in every metropolitan area. But in other states, courthouse libraries are nonexistent or inadequate, and the only decent law libraries open to the public are located at publicly funded law schools. Some private law schools also open their law libraries to the public, at least for limited hours.

State	Location of Lawyer Ethical Rules
Alabama	Rules of Alabama Supreme Court
Alaska	Alaska Rules of Professional Conduct
Arizona	Arizona Rules of the Supreme Court
Arkansas	Arkansas Court Rules—Model Rules of Professional Conduct
California	California Rules of Court—Professional Rules
	California Rules of Court—Rules of Professional Conduct
	California Business & Professions Code
Colorado	Colorado Rules of Professional Conduct
Connecticut	Connecticut Rules of Professional Conduct
Delaware	Delaware Rules Annotated—Rules of Professional Conduct
District of Columbia	District of Columbia Court Rules Annotated—Rules of Professional Conduct
Florida	Florida Statutes Annotated—Bar & Judiciary Rules (Rules of Professional Conduct)
Georgia	Code of Georgia—Title 9, Appendix (Attorneys at Law)
Hawaii	Hawaii Rules of Professional Conduct
Idaho	Idaho Rules of Professional Conduct
Illinois	Illinois Supreme Court Rules—Rules of Professional Conduct
Indiana	Indiana Court Rules—Rules of Professional Conduct

State	Location of Lawyer Ethical Rules
Iowa	Iowa Court Rules—Professional Responsibility
Kansas	Kansas Rules of Professional Conduct
Kentucky	Rules of the Kentucky Supreme Court
Louisiana	Louisiana Revised Statutes—Article 16 (Louisiana Rules of Professional Conduct)
Maine	Maine Bar Rules
Maryland	Maryland Rules—Appendix: Rules of Professional Conduct
Massachusetts	Massachusetts Rules of Professional Conduct
Michigan	Michigan Court Rules
Minnesota	Minnesota Rules of Professional Conduct
Mississippi	Mississippi Rules of Professional Conduct
Missouri	Supreme Court Rules—Bar & Judiciary, Rule 4 (Professional Conduct)
Montana	Montana Rules of Professional Conduct
Nebraska	Nebraska Supreme Court Rules Code of Professional Responsibility
Nevada	Nevada Supreme Court Rules—Rules of Professional Conduct
New Hampshire	New Hampshire Rules of Professional Conduct
New Jersey	Rules of General Application—Rules of Professional Conduct
New Mexico	Rules of Professional Conduct
New York	Code of Professional Responsibility Supreme Court, Appellate Division (Disciplinary Rules)

State	Location of Lawyer Ethical Rules
North Carolina	Rules of Professional Conduct
North Dakota	Rules of Professional Conduct
Ohio	Code of Professional Responsibility
Oklahoma	Rules of Professional Conduct
Oregon	Professional Responsibility
Pennsylvania	Rules of Professional Conduct
Rhode Island	Supreme Court Rules (Rules of Professional Conduct)
South Carolina	Appellate Court Rules
South Dakota	South Dakota Codified Law—Courts & Judiciary, Appendix (Rules of Professional Conduct)
Tennessee	Rules of the Supreme Court—Code of Professional Responsibility
Texas	Texas Rules of Court—State Bar Rules, Article 10 §9 (Professional Conduct)
Utah	Code of Judicial Administration—Rules of Professional Conduct
Vermont	Administrative Orders & Rules—Code of Professional Responsibility
Virginia	Rules of the Supreme Court of Virginia
Washington	Rules of General Application—Rules of Professional Conduct
West Virginia	Rules of Professional Conduct
Wisconsin	Supreme Court Rules—Professional Conduct
Wyoming	Rules of Professional Conduct

For simple legal research tasks, a public library can be a fine place to start. The main branch of your public library may have a small but helpful legal section where you can find your state's statutes as well as county and local ordinances. Another possibility is to ask for permission to use the law office library of any lawyer you consult (or know).

2. If You Want to Find a Relevant Statute or Regulation

Statutes and regulations passed by state legislatures govern several issues raised in this book, such as how much time you have to sue a lawyer for malpractice (the statute of limitations) and what circumstances extend that time, whether a lawyer-client fee agreement must be in writing and whether you must/may arbitrate any fee dispute you have with a lawyer. To find a statute, you need to look in a multivolume set of books known as your state code, which will probably be organized by subject matter. To find your state lawyer ethical rules, see the accompanying chart which gives the name of your state's ethical rules.

To read a statute or regulation, find it in your law library, locate the title you need, turn to the section number and read. If you already have a proper reference to the statute or regulation—called the citation—finding the correct one is straightforward. If you don't have a citation, you can find it by referring to the general index.

When you look up a statute or regulation, try to find an "annotated" version. These contain the actual language of an official statute or regulation, along with short summaries of the significant court cases (including their legal citation for easy reference) that have discussed each statute or regulation, and references to other resource books and articles.

⚠️ **Be Sure All Information Is Up to Date**
After you read the statute or regulation in the hardcover book, turn to the back of the book. There should be an insert pamphlet (called a pocket part) for the current or previous year. Look for the statute or regulation in the pocket part to see if it has been amended or if additional cases interpreting it have been decided since the hardcover volume was published. If the volume has no pocket part, look on the shelf for a separately-bound supplement before assuming there's no update. If the pocket part is six months or more out of date and you want to make sure you have the absolute most current version, ask the librarian to help you find something called the Advanced Legislative Sheets or to help you look up the law online.

If you have trouble locating any statute or regulation, ask a librarian for help.

3. Go Beyond the Statute or Regulation

If you want to find the answer to a legal question, rather than simply look up the text of a statute or regulation, or if you want to find, read and understand cases that interpret the statute or regulation or otherwise shed light on your problem, you will need some guidance in basic legal research techniques. Good resources—in addition to Nolo's *Legal Research* book and the *Legal Research Made Easy* video—

that may be available in your law library include:

- *The Legal Research Manual: A Game Plan for Legal Research and Analysis*, by Christopher and Jill Wren (A-R Editions)
- *Introduction to Legal Research: A Layperson's Guide to Finding the Law*, by Al Coco (Want Publishing Co.)
- *How to Find the Law*, by Morris Cohen, Robert Berring and Kent Olson (West Publishing Co.).

4. Read Court Cases

In cases that come before appellate courts, appellate judges review the record and decisions of trial courts. They interpret the meaning of statutes, regulations, constitutional provisions and other court cases, making what's known as "common law" (judge-made law). Sometimes, appellate courts write decisions (called opinions, case law or cases), in which they summarize the facts that the trial judge or jury found to be true and set forth the appellate court judges' legal reasoning and "holding" (decision).

Appellate court cases are collected and published in hardbound volumes called "reporters," "reports" or "case reports." There are many separate reporters for different courts and geographical areas. For example, a case from the New York Court of Appeals (the state's highest court) may be published in a series of state reporters called *New York Appeals* and also in a regional reporter series called the *Northeastern Reporter*, which includes cases from several other states.

Recent cases, not yet included in a hardbound reporter, are located in softbound supplements. And cases decided in the last few days or weeks may often only be available from the appellate court itself or an online reporting service. If you want to look up a new case you just read about in the newspaper, for example, ask the librarian to assist you; it won't yet be in the hardbound books.

Cases, like statutes and regulations, have citations that let you look them up easily. Let's say you want to read the case noted in Chapter 9 where the lawyer handling an adoption sent a copy of the adoption petition to the birth parents, thereby revealing the adoptive parents' identity and whereabouts. The name of the case is *Kohn v. Schiappa* and the citation is 281 N.J. Super. 235 (N.J. 1995). The names are the parties to the lawsuit. The first number means the case is located in volume 281. The abbreviation in the middle (N.J. Super.) is for New Jersey Superior Court Reports, the case reporter series where the case is published. The last number tells you the case begins at page 235. The parenthetical at the end tells you the state and year in which the case was decided.

5. Use Background Resources

If you want to research a legal question but don't know where to begin, an excellent resource is *Legal Malpractice (Fourth Edition)*, by Ronald E. Mallen and Jeffrey M. Smith (West Publishing Company). This four-volume treatise is the most comprehensive resource on legal malpractice and is often cited by courts in their written opinions. It is written for lawyers,

but the last volume has a list of legal malpractice cases for each state with citations so that you can find them in the law library. This treatise is in many, but not all, law libraries. Call around until you find a library that has it. It is possible that a larger public library carries it in the legal section, but call and ask first.

Other good resources that might be found in your local law library include:

Lawyers' Manual on Professional Conduct, published by the American Bar Association and Bureau of National Affairs. This loose-leaf, multivolume set contains information on many topics, including conflicts of interests, confidentiality, malpractice, attorneys' fees and attorneys' obligations when holding property or funds for a client. It is written for lawyers and not very user-friendly. Read the instructions at the beginning on how to use the book or ask the librarian for help. It includes the ABA Model Rules of Professional Conduct, ABA ethics opinions and state and local ethics opinions.

Professional Negligence Law Reporter, published by the Association of Trial Lawyers of America. It is written for lawyers, but is easy to read and is an excellent resource for finding cases on legal malpractice. It has short summaries of cases and verdicts in professional negligence cases. It names the lawyers who handled the case, which might help you find a lawyer.

How to Sue Your Lawyer: The Consumer Guide to Legal Malpractice, by Hilton Stein (Legal Malpractice Institute), was written in 1989 and includes an overview of common claims against lawyers. It contains an extensive discussion of insurance issues affecting legal malpractice matters, including coverage issues and claims procedures. If you can't find it at the library, contact the publisher at 103 Washington St., Morristown, NJ 07960.

A law or public library may carry the following books on attorneys' fees:

- *Attorneys' Fees (Second Edition)*, by Robert Rossi (Bancroft Whitney 1995).
- *Putting a Lid on Legal Fees: How to Deal Effectively with Lawyers*, by Raymond M. Klein (Interlink Press, Inc.) is a good guide on how to get cost-effective legal services, written mostly for the business client.
- *Beyond the Billable Hour: An Anthology of Alternative Billing Methods*, edited by Richard C. Reed (American Bar Association 1989). This is a collection of lawyer comments, thoughts and ideas on how to charge fair fees on an hourly basis. The collection is written by lawyers and for lawyers, but has creative ideas which you might use in negotiating an hourly fee arrangement.

B. Lawyers

As a general rule, you should get an attorney involved in your malpractice or breach of ethics dispute if it is potentially worth a lot of money. Only if the damages are small and the mistake is clear (such as failing to file a complaint on time or filing a bankruptcy case three days too early) should you consider handling the case on your own.

EXAMPLE 1: Your business lawyer advised you to sell your business because it was failing and ended up purchasing it himself for $500,000. You may have a claim against the lawyer for breach of fiduciary duty, legal malpractice and fraud if the business was worth a lot more than the lawyer paid for it. Although you will probably need an accountant to do a valuation of the business, you will want a lawyer to help you with this kind of case.

EXAMPLE 2: You want to sue your former divorce lawyer for malpractice. If the value of the estate is over $100,000 and the division was clearly unfair, you will probably need an attorney to help you. Causation and damages are complex in most malpractice cases against divorce lawyers because the value of all of the assets need to be reconsidered to determine fairness.

1. What Lawyers Can Do for You

There are three basic ways a lawyer can help you:

Consultation and advice. A lawyer can analyze your situation and advise you on your best plan of action. Ideally, the lawyer will describe all your alternatives so you can make your own choices—but keep on your toes. Many lawyers will subtly steer you in the direction the attorney wants you to go, often the one that nets the attorney the largest fee.

⚠ You May Need to Hire an Out-of-Town Lawyer
Lawyers often hesitate to sue one another, especially local lawyers who are likely to see each other at lawyer functions or professional meetings. Even though it may be inconvenient or cost more to have a lawyer from out of town handle your case, an out-of-town lawyer can at least give you an opinion or evaluate your case. If the case is strong, the out-of-town lawyer may be willing to travel to represent you. If not, the out-of-town lawyer can probably help you find a lawyer to handle your case.

Negotiation. The lawyer can help you negotiate—especially if you have a fee dispute or are trying to get your file from your first lawyer. Lawyers often possess negotiating skills, especially if they negotiate a lot in their practice. Your first attorney may be more apt to settle with a lawyer representing you than with you. Once you bring another lawyer into the dispute, your first lawyer may be eager to settle to avoid being sued for malpractice.

Representation. If you want to sue a lawyer for malpractice or you've been sued for failing to pay your bill, you may very well want (or need) a lawyer to represent you. This could get expensive, however (unless the lawyer will take the case on a contingency fee), so be sure you want to be represented by a lawyer before you hire one. You also may consider hiring a lawyer as a coach while you represent yourself. Although many lawyers are reluctant to only partially help you, a growing number will. But you'll have to call around to find someone.

When you look to hire an attorney, avoid those who know little about legal malpractice.

Many attorneys think that because they have sued a doctor, that they can sue a lawyer. Wrong! You will not get good advise or representation from a lawyer who has little experience with legal malpractice cases.

When a lawyer advises you about your case, a good test of the strength of the lawyer's convictions about your case is whether the lawyer will offer you alternative fee arrangements, such as a partial hourly, partial contingency or full contingency fee. If the lawyer is willing to take your case on a contingency fee or even a partial contingency fee, the lawyer thinks your claim is a good one. If the lawyer is willing to handle your matter only by the hour, then be cautious about proceeding.

Although you will probably have to pay for it ($2,000 or $3,000), if you have lost $25,000 or more, ask for an opinion letter from a lawyer with a summary of what she thinks about your cases, its strengths and weaknesses, your chances of success, how much it should cost to proceed and whether it is worthwhile to do so. This can be very useful in focusing you and the attorney on the strengths and weaknesses of your case and in helping keep communications clear.

2. How to Find a Lawyer

Finding a lawyer who is willing to sue (or defend someone sued by) another lawyer is not easy.

Most people who have been the victim of malpractice, fee gouging or other lawyer abuses are hesitant at best—petrified at worst—to hire another lawyer. There are many highly principled lawyers who do good legal work, but there are few lawyers who regularly handle legal malpractice cases against other lawyers. Expect your search to be a difficult one. You will need to be patient and persevere in your effort to find the right lawyer for your case. It is best to consult with a lawyer who regularly handles legal malpractice cases, if you can find one.

Here are a few suggestions on how to find a lawyer.

If You Want to Sue a Lawyer: A Directory of Legal Malpractice Attorneys. This book was written by Kay Ostberg and Theresa Meehan Rudy and published by HALT (a group of Americans for legal reform). A new edition came out in 1995, and it remains the only directory of lawyers who sue other lawyers. If you can't find it at your bookstore, public library or law library, call HALT directly at 202-347-9600 or write to HALT at 1319 F St. NW, Suite 300, Washington, DC 20004. Enclose $12 for the book plus shipping and handling.

To find a lawyer's new address and phone number, call your state bar association. A word of caution about the lawyers included in the book: many primarily defend lawyers sued for malpractice and work for insurance companies (and therefore will not represent plaintiffs); many others have limited experience handling legal malpractice cases. In spite of its shortcomings, this is still the most valuable place for you to begin your search for an attorney.

The lawyers listed in this directory are listed by state and city. Because many local lawyers won't sue lawyers in their community, it is good to talk to an out-of-town attorney if you can.

Personal referrals. In general, this is the most common approach to finding a lawyer. Often, if you know someone who was pleased with the services of a lawyer, it makes sense to call that lawyer first. But it rarely will be a help in this situation because so few lawyers take these cases and the likelihood that you know someone who hired a lawyer to sue another lawyer is slim.

But, a lawyer you talk to may know lawyers who defend lawyers for insurance companies, and you can call defense lawyers and ask for the names of good lawyers who represent plaintiffs in legal malpractice cases. They will know plaintiffs lawyers and usually will give you their names, if asked.

Yellow Pages. Generally, this is an unlikely place to find a good lawyer. But because so few lawyers regularly handle legal malpractice cases for plaintiffs, the phone directory may not be a bad resource. Turn to "Attorneys" and look for ads that say "legal malpractice," not just "malpractice," or ads stating that the attorney handles cases against attorneys. Some lawyers who are former state bar prosecutors advertise that they take legal malpractice cases, and although they occasionally do some work for plaintiffs, most defend lawyers in disciplinary proceedings or in malpractice cases.

When you find a name in the phone book, before making an appointment to meet with a lawyer, call to make sure that the office handles legal malpractice cases and does work for plaintiffs.

Professional Liability Reporter. This publication summarizes legal and other malpractice cases from all over the country. You may be able to find the *Reporter* at your local law library. Look for legal malpractice cases for your state—both in (or near) your town and out of the area. Call the lawyers who handled the cases and ask if they represent plaintiffs or for referrals.

Jury Verdicts. This publication summarizes civil cases from your state. You may be able to find *Jury Verdicts* at your local law library. Look for the legal malpractice cases—again, both in (or near) your town and out of the area. Call the lawyers who handled the cases and ask if they represent plaintiffs or for referrals.

Lawyer referral panels. Most county bar associations will give out the names of attorneys who practice in your area. But bar associations often fail to provide meaningful screening for the attorneys listed, which means those who participate may not be the most experienced or competent. Many new lawyers sign up with these referral panels to get business. When you

call a bar referral panel, you will be given the next lawyer on the list who includes "legal malpractice" as an area of work she does. The likelihood of getting a good lawyer this way isn't high.

Prepaid legal insurance. Prepaid legal insurance plans offer some services for a low monthly fee and charge more for additional or different work. Participating lawyers may belong to the plan as a way to get clients who are attracted by the low-cost, basic services and then sell them more expensive services. This is an unlikely place to get a lawyer with experience in suing other lawyers.

Group legal plans. Some unions, employers and consumer action organizations offer group plans to their members or employees, who can obtain legal assistance free or for low rates. If you're a member of such a plan, check with it for a lawyer. But it is unlikely that your group legal plan will cover suing another lawyer for malpractice.

Once you find a lawyer willing to talk to you or who indicates interest in your case, here are some questions to ask to satisfy yourself that you have the right lawyer for your case:

- How many cases has she handled against other lawyers?
- What percentage of her practice is legal malpractice?
- What other kind of work does she do?
- What percentage of her practice is representing plaintiffs and what percentage is representing defendants?
- Does she work for insurance companies?
- Which insurance companies does she regularly work for?

- What will she do if the lawyer you want to sue has insurance with an insurance company that she works for?
- Can she give you the names of clients or opposing counsel with whom you can talk?
- Has she handled cases similar to yours?
- In her office, who does what work, and whom will you be working with or talking to most frequently?
- What is her work load and how much time can she devote to your case?
- What is her fee? Do you have a choice of the fee arrangement?

3. What to Look for in a Lawyer

There are several levels of experience you should expect to find when you speak to a lawyer who sues other lawyers:

Lawyers who sue lawyers for malpractice a lot. There are few lawyers who fall into this category. If you can find one, your odds are best placed here. These lawyers are often not members of lawyer clubs. They get clients from other lawyers, speaking engagements and opposing attorneys, and by advertising in the phone book, legal directories and legal publications. Because there are so few of these lawyers, however, they are often very selective in the cases they take. If your case is rejected by such an attorney, call the next person on your list. Just because one lawyer won't take your case, doesn't mean another one won't.

Lawyers who sue lawyers for malpractice only in their area of specialty. Some lawyers specialize in a legal area, such as real estate, tax, divorce or bankruptcy. If your legal malpractice case is in such an area, you may find a lawyer specialist who also handles legal malpractice cases in his area of expertise. Although these lawyers are rare, such a lawyer could be a good choice for handling your legal malpractice case. Most of the time, however, the lawyers will give you an opinion about your malpractice claim, but won't take your case. Ask for a referral to another attorney who might.

Lawyers who handle some legal malpractice cases, but handle many other kinds of cases, usually for plaintiffs. These lawyers are often called "plaintiff's lawyers" or "trial lawyers," and are often members of a local, state or national trial lawyers association. These lawyers often handle malpractice cases against doctors, dentists, accountants and other professionals, and personal injury cases such as automobile accidents and defective products cases. These lawyers tend to have a large volume of cases and you may get little personal attention. But, generally—especially if your case isn't highly complex—these lawyers can be a good choice.

A lawyer who is willing to sue another lawyer for malpractice for the first time. Every lawyer who regularly or occasionally handles malpractice cases once fell into this category. A new and hardworking lawyer can be a good choice, and often is your only choice. A new lawyer may not have experience, but can often make up for it with extensive preparation, hours in the library and determination. A new lawyer will probably charge less per hour or be willing to take a case on a contingency fee.

No matter which type of lawyer you eventually hire, here are three suggestions on how to make sure you have the best possible working relationship. Given that you've already been burned once by a lawyer, you will want to take these suggestions to heart.

First, fight the urge you may have to surrender your will and be intimidated by a lawyer. You should be the one who decides what you feel comfortable doing about your problem. You are hiring the lawyer to perform a service for you; although your choice may be limited, don't hire someone if the price or personality isn't right.

Second, you must be as comfortable as possible with any lawyer you hire. When making an appointment, ask to talk directly to the lawyer. If you can't, are you at least able to talk to a paralegal?

If you do talk directly to the lawyer, ask some specific questions. Do you get clear, concise answers? If not, move on. If the lawyer says little except to suggest that he handle the problem— with a substantial fee—watch out. You're talking with someone who doesn't know the answer and won't admit it, or someone who pulls rank on the basis of professional standing. Don't be a passive client or hire a lawyer who wants you to be one. If the lawyer admits to not knowing an answer, that isn't necessarily bad. In most cases—particularly in lawyer malpractice cases—the lawyer must do some research.

Also, pay attention to how the lawyer responds to your having considerable information. If you've read this book, you're already better informed about your rights than most clients are. Many lawyers are threatened when the client knows too much—or, in some cases, anything.

Once you find a lawyer you like, make an hour-long appointment to discuss your situation fully. Your goal at the initial conference is to find out what the lawyer recommends and how much it will cost. Go home and think about the lawyer's suggestions. If they don't make complete sense or if you have other reservations, call someone else.

Finally, keep in mind that the lawyer works for you. Once you hire a lawyer, you have the absolute right to switch to another—or to just fire the lawyer and handle the matter yourself—at any time, for any reason.

All this being said, recognize that your ability to shop around for a lawyer willing to sue another lawyer will be limited, and more so in less populated states with fewer lawyers than in heavily populated states with many lawyers. Even if you find a lawyer who handles these cases, he may be too busy to talk to you or he may refuse to because of a conflict of interest.

If the lawyer can't talk to you because he has a conflict, he probably won't say more because to do so could disclose confidential information. But it usually means that the lawyer has represented the lawyer you want to sue, is representing the lawyer you want to sue or has a personal or business relationship with the lawyer which would either prevent him from taking the case or make it uncomfortable for him to do so.

4. How Much Legal Malpractice Lawyers Charge

Lawyers handling legal malpractice cases may work by the hour, on a contingency fee or in some combination of both. Whether they will advance costs will depend upon the case, the nature of the lawyer's practice and her personal finances. If the lawyer you want to sue for malpractice claims that you owe fees, a lawyer you hire may be reluctant to take your case on a contingency fee or will want a very large contingency fee.

Here are some general rules about how much legal malpractice lawyers charge.

Lawyers who charge by the hour. Although some malpractice lawyers work only on a contingency fee, most lawyers will work by the hour. The hourly rate charged depends on the lawyer's geographical location, overhead and experience. An experienced legal malpractice lawyer might charge between $150 and $300 per hour.

Lawyers who work on a contingency fee. Because legal malpractice cases require proof of two cases (see Chapter 9, Section E.3), the amount of work and expenses of litigation are more than in a regular civil case, and lawyers often charge a hefty percentage to take a case on a contingency fee. This is especially true if your damages are $100,000 or less. If your damages are more, you may be able to negotiate a lower fee. (See Chapter 3, Section D.)

Some lawyers have a set contingency fee which they charge for all cases, such as ⅓ or 40%. If your damages aren't very high, these offices will reject your case outright (because the office won't make enough money on your case) rather than raise their contingency fee percentage. If your case is rejected for this reason, you can offer another lawyer a higher percentage to handle your case. But in truth, if

your damages are $25,000 or less, it is unlikely that you'll find a lawyer with legal malpractice experience who will take your case.

Lawyers who charge a hybrid fee. Some lawyers will offer you a combined hourly and contingency fee, such as where you pay half of the hourly rate and half of a contingency fee. (See Chapter 3, Section E.)

Lawyers who offer options. Some lawyers will offer you a choice of fee arrangements which might look something like this:

- $200 per hour
- 40% contingency fee, or
- $100 per hour and a 20% contingency fee.

One final word: No matter what reason you hire a lawyer for, at whatever fee, be sure the lawyer puts the fee arrangement in writing and you sign it. If the lawyer doesn't mention a written fee agreement, ask about one. If you hire a new lawyer to help you with your problems with your former lawyer, you don't want the financial arrangement with your new lawyer to be misunderstood so that the new lawyer's fee becomes another lawyer problem.

C. Legal Reform Groups

For a number of years, Americans who have felt poorly treated or ripped-off by their lawyers have established nonprofit organizations with the goal of doing something about their anger. Often the focus has been to pressure state attorney regulatory agencies to do a better job at weeding out (disbarring) rotten apple lawyers. Reform groups have also targeted consumer unfriendly lawyer regulatory systems under which lawyer discipline is all too often lax, secret and slow.

In response to efforts to create efficient, public and accountable lawyer discipline systems, a few states have made some improvements, a number of which are discussed in Chapter 8. In California, for example, the state adopted a number of reforms, including establishing a state bar court. The result has been that lawyers are being given much tougher discipline when they are found to have abandoned, stolen from or sold out their clients.

But we have barely scratched the surface when it comes to regulating lawyers in the public interest. For example, because lawyer discipline agencies are very slow to investigate ethics complaints against lawyers—and even worse, the agencies won't look into general complaints of incompetence—your only real avenue of redress is to sue for malpractice.

For more information about how you can help reform the lawyer discipline system in your state, your best bet is to join HALT— Americans for Legal Reform, 1319 F Street, NW, Suite 300, Washington, DC 20004, 202-347-9600. Membership includes a subscription to HALT's quarterly newsletter.

Many excellent legal reform organizations also exist for individual states. HALT maintains a list of those and should be able to point you to any local organization.

D. Online Resources

By now, everyone has heard of the Internet and such popular commercial online services as CompuServe, America Online and Prodigy.

Every day more and more basic source materials are finding their way onto far more accessible online sites, referred to collectively here and elsewhere as "the Net."

The Internet is a worldwide network of computers that share common rules for access to and transfer of data. There are a number of different ways to use the Internet to search for relevant material, such as Gopher (a series of nested menus), FTP (a way to connect directly to another computer and download files) and Telenet (a way to actually use programs on remote computers to accomplish a particular task). But by far the most important tool for doing research on the Internet is something called the World Wide Web (WWW). This tool offers a point-and-click graphic interface that provides links among documents, and makes it easy to skip from one relevant resource to another. It promises to dominate the Internet for years to come.

It is also possible to find helpful legal information on the large commercial online services, such as CompuServe, America Online and Prodigy. In addition, each of these services provides a gateway to the Internet, including the WWW. For example, by subscribing to America Online, you not only get the services and content offered exclusively to America Online's subscribers—including the Nolo Press self-help law center and the Legal Information Network—but you also get full Internet access.

Through the Internet, you can contact the American Bar Association and possibly your state lawyer disciplinary agency for copies of ethics rules and opinions. In addition, lawyers are increasingly advertising their services—you may be able to find a lawyer in your state who handles legal malpractice cases.

⚠ This Is Only an Introduction

This section does not provide the basic instruction that some readers may need in order to understand and "get into" the services and information available on the Internet. There are several books that serve this purpose. For an exhaustive treatment of the subject, see Law on the Net, *by James Evans (Nolo Press);* Law on the Net *is available in hard copy or online through Nolo's site. Anywhere on the Internet you can reach Nolo at http://www.nolo.com. From America Online, choose keyword: Nolo.* ■

Index

Flat fees
   and firing of lawyer, 5/14-15
   lawyer's bills exceed amount quoted, 5/8
   and payment of costs, 3/31
   and retainers or advances, 3/28-29
Florida Statement of Client's Rights, 3/45-46
Fraud, suing lawyer for, 9/3, 9/5-6, 9/38-45
Fraud cases, and contingency fee arrangements, 3/16
Friendships between lawyers, and conflict of interest, 1/6
Frivolous lawsuits, by lawyer for other side, 10/3-4

G

Going rate, for certain types of legal work, 3/2
Group legal plans, 11/11-12

H

HALT—Americans for Legal Reform, 11/15
Hearings
   change of dates, 2/25
   lawyer failed to show up, 1/7, 8/2
   See also Court; Date changes; Trial
Hiring new lawyer, 5/20-21
   fees as damage in legal malpractice case, 9/17
   finding one, 5/2, 5/17, 5/20, 11/9-12
   to help with lawyer-client dispute, 11/2, 11/8-14
   payment of, 5/14
   personal referrals, 11/10
   Substitution of Attorney form, 6/3
   what to look for, 11/12-13
Hourly fee agreement
   lawyer wants to change, 1/6
   payment of bills, 7/4
Hourly fee arrangements, 3/10-16
Hourly fees, 1/2-3
   combined with contingency fees, 3/25-26
   and estimate of expenses, 8/20
   estimating expenses to help limit, 3/11
   and firing of lawyer, 5/11-12
   and lawyer's time, 2/8
   and legal malpractice lawyers, 11/14
   negotiation of, 3/10-11
   and new lawyer, 5/20
   and payment of bills, 7/4
   and payment of costs, 3/31
   and retainers or advances, 3/28-29
   setting a limit on, 3/10-11
Hybrid fees, 3/25-26, 11/14

I

Ignoring of case, by lawyer, 2/31, 2/34, 2/35
Impropriety, appearance of, 4/3, 4/20-22
Incompetence, 1/2, 1/7, 5/7. *See also* Malpractice

Independent counsel. *See* Second opinion
Information
   client's responsibility to provide to lawyer, 2/3-4, 2/8
   concealment by lawyer, lawsuit over, 9/38-40
   lawyer's failure to provide on possible outcomes, 1/8
   lawyer's responsibility to provide, 2/11-20, 5/2-4
Insurance coverage
   of lawyer or law firm, 9/24-25, 9/25-28
   and payment of fees, 3/42-43
Intentional misconduct, by lawyer , 9/3, 9/5-6, 9/40-45
Interest, on actual damages, 9/42
Interest On Attorney Trust Accounts (IOLTA), 3/42
Interference with economic advantage cases, 3/16
Internet, legal research on, 11/2, 11/15-16
Invasion of privacy, 10/3, 10/20-21
Investigation of case
   estimating expense of, 3/11
   lawyer didn't do, 1/14
     suing lawyer over, 9/3
IOLTA. *See* Interest On Attorney Trust Accounts (IOLTA)

J

Judges, approval of lawyer's fees, 7/8
Judgment
   adverse, as damage in legal malpractice case, 9/17
   against former lawyer, collection of, 9/25-28
   errors in, by lawyer, 9/46-47
   motion to set aside, and statutes of limitations on legal malpractice, 9/22
Junior lawyers
   hourly rate charged to client, 3/16
   naming as defendants in lawsuit, 9/24
Jury trials, right to, and arbitration, 7/17
Jury verdicts, 2/27-28

K

Knowledge by lawyer, element of fraud case, 9/38, 9/39

L

Law libraries
   background resources, 11/7-8
   finding statutes or regulations, 11/5-6
   legal research in, 11/2-8
   location of lawyer ethical rules, by state, 11/4-5
   reading court cases, 11/6-7
Lawsuit
   lawyer didn't file on time, 1/7-8, 9/3
   lawyer filed against wrong person or entity, 1/10, 9/3
Lawyer, to help with lawyer-client dispute, 11/2, 11/8-14. *See also* Hiring a new lawyer

CATALOG
...more from Nolo Press

		EDITION	PRICE	CODE

BUSINESS

	EDITION	PRICE	CODE
The California Nonprofit Corporation Handbook	7th	$29.95	NON
The California Professional Corporation Handbook	5th	$34.95	PROF
The Employer's Legal Handbook	1st	$29.95	EMPL
Form Your Own Limited Liability Company	1st	$24.95	LIAB
Hiring Indepedent Contractors: The Employer's Legal Guide	1st	$29.95	HICI
How to Form a CA Nonprofit Corp.—w/Corp. Records Binder & PC Disk	1st	$49.95	CNP
How to Form a Nonprofit Corp., Book w/Disk (PC)—National Edition	3rd	$39.95	NNP
How to Form Your Own Calif. Corp.—w/Corp. Records Binder & Disk—PC	1st	$39.95	CACI
How to Form Your Own California Corporation	8th	$29.95	CCOR
How to Form Your Own Florida Corporation, (Book w/Disk—PC)	3rd	$39.95	FLCO
How to Form Your Own New York Corporation, (Book w/Disk—PC)	3rd	$39.95	NYCO
How to Form Your Own Texas Corporation, (Book w/Disk—PC)	4th	$39.95	TCOR
How to Handle Your Workers' Compensation Claim (California Edition)	1st	$29.95	WORK
How to Mediate Your Dispute	1st	$18.95	MEDI
How to Write a Business Plan	4th	$21.95	SBS
The Independent Paralegal's Handbook	4th	$29.95	PARA
The Legal Guide for Starting & Running a Small Business	2nd	$24.95	RUNS
Marketing Without Advertising	1st	$14.00	MWAD
The Partnership Book: How to Write a Partnership Agreement	4th	$24.95	PART
Sexual Harassment on the Job	2nd	$18.95	HARS
Taking Care of Your Corporation, Vol. 1, (Book w/Disk—PC)	1st	$26.95	CORK
Taking Care of Your Corporation, Vol. 2, (Book w/Disk—PC)	1st	$39.95	CORK2
Tax Savvy for Small Business	1st	$26.95	SAVVY
Trademark: How to Name Your Business & Product	2nd	$29.95	TRD
Your Rights in the Workplace	3rd	$18.95	YRW

CONSUMER

	EDITION	PRICE	CODE
Fed Up With the Legal System: What's Wrong & How to Fix It	2nd	$9.95	LEG
How to Win Your Personal Injury Claim	2nd	$24.95	PICL
Nolo's Pocket Guide to California Law	4th	$10.95	CLAW
Nolo's Pocket Guide to Consumer Rights	2nd	$12.95	CAG
Trouble-Free Travel...And What to Do When Things Go Wrong	1st	$14.95	TRAV

ESTATE PLANNING & PROBATE

	EDITION	PRICE	CODE
How to Probate an Estate (California Edition)	8th	$34.95	PAE
Make Your Own Living Trust	2nd	$21.95	LITR
Nolo's Simple Will Book	2nd	$17.95	SWIL
Plan Your Estate	3rd	$24.95	NEST
The Quick and Legal Will Book	1st	$15.95	QUIC
Nolo's Law Form Kit: Wills	1st	$14.95	KWL

FAMILY MATTERS

	EDITION	PRICE	CODE
A Legal Guide for Lesbian and Gay Couples	9th	$24.95	LG
Child Custody: Building Agreements That Work	2nd	$24.95	CUST
Divorce & Money: How to Make the Best Financial Decisions During Divorce	3rd	$24.95	DIMO
Get A Life: You Don't Need a Million to Retire	1st	$18.95	LIFE
The Guardianship Book (California Edition)	2nd	$24.95	GB
How to Adopt Your Stepchild in California	4th	$22.95	ADOP
How to Do Your Own Divorce in California	21st	$24.95	CDIV
How to Do Your Own Divorce in Texas	6th	$19.95	TDIV
How to Raise or Lower Child Support in California	3rd	$18.95	CHLD
The Living Together Kit	7th	$24.95	LTK
Nolo's Pocket Guide to Family Law	4th	$14.95	FLD
Practical Divorce Solutions	1st	$14.95	PDS

GOING TO COURT

	EDITION	PRICE	CODE
Collect Your Court Judgment (California Edition	2nd	$19.95	JUDG
The Criminal Records Book (California Edition)	5th	$21.95	CRIM
How to Sue For Up to 25,000...and Win!	2nd	$29.95	MUNI
Everybody's Guide to Small Claims Court (California Edition)	12th	$18.95	CSCC
Everybody's Guide to Small Claims Court (National Edition)	6th	$18.95	NSCC
Fight Your Ticket ... and Win! (California Edition)	6th	$19.95	FYT
How to Change Your Name (California Edition)	6th	$24.95	NAME
Mad at Your Lawyer	1st	$21.95	MAD
Represent Yourself in Court: How to Prepare & Try a Winning Case	1st	$29.95	RYC
Taming the Lawyers	1st	$19.95	TAME

☐ **Book with disk**

		EDITION	PRICE	CODE

HOMEOWNERS, LANDLORDS & TENANTS

	EDITION	PRICE	CODE
The Deeds Book (California Edition)	3rd	$16.95	DEED
Dog Law	2nd	$12.95	DOG
▣ Every Landlord's Legal Guide (National Edition)	1st	$29.95	ELLI
For Sale by Owner (California Edition)	2nd	$24.95	FSBO
Homestead Your House (California Edition)	8th	$9.95	HOME
How to Buy a House in California	4th	$24.95	BHCA
The Landlord's Law Book, Vol. 1: Rights & Responsibilities (California Edition)	5th	$34.95	LBRT
The Landlord's Law Book, Vol. 2: Evictions (California Edition)	5th	$34.95	LBEV
Neighbor Law: Fences, Trees, Boundaries & Noise	2nd	$16.95	NEI
Safe Homes, Safe Neighborhoods: Stopping Crime Where You Live	1st	$14.95	SAFE
Tenants' Rights (California Edition)	12th	$18.95	CTEN

IMMIGRATION

	EDITION	PRICE	CODE
How to Become a United States Citizen	5th	$14.95	CIT
How to Get a Green Card: Legal Ways to Stay in the U.S.A.	2nd	$24.95	GRN
U.S. Immigration Made Easy	5th	$39.95	IMEZ

MONEY MATTERS

	EDITION	PRICE	CODE
Building Your Nest Egg With Your 401(k)	1st	$16.95	EGG
Chapter 13 Bankruptcy: Repay Your Debts	2nd	$29.95	CHI3
How to File for Bankruptcy	6th	$26.95	HFB
Money Troubles: Legal Strategies to Cope With Your Debts	4th	$19.95	MT
Nolo's Law Form Kit: Personal Bankruptcy	1st	$14.95	KBNK
Nolo's Law Form Kit: Rebuild Your Credit	1st	$14.95	KCRD
Simple Contracts for Personal Use	2nd	$16.95	CONT
Smart Ways to Save Money During and After Divorce	1st	$14.95	SAVMO
Stand Up to the IRS	3rd	$24.95	SIRS
The Under 40 Financial Planning Guide	1st	$19.95	UN40

PATENTS AND COPYRIGHTS

	EDITION	PRICE	CODE
The Copyright Handbook: How to Protect and Use Written Works	3rd	$24.95	COHA
Copyright Your Software	1st	$39.95	CYS
Patent, Copyright & Trademark: A Desk Reference to Intellectual Property Law	1st	$24.95	PCTM
Patent It Yourself	5th	$44.95	PAT
▣ Software Development: A Legal Guide (Book with disk—PC)	1st	$44.95	SFT
The Inventor's Notebook	1st	$19.95	INOT

RESEARCH & REFERENCE

	EDITION	PRICE	CODE
Law on the Net	1st	$39.95	LAWN
Legal Research: How to Find & Understand the Law	4th	$19.95	LRES
Legal Research Made Easy (Video)	1st	$89.95	LRME

SENIORS

	EDITION	PRICE	CODE
Beat the Nursing Home Trap: A Consumer's Guide	2nd	$18.95	ELD
Social Security, Medicare & Pensions	6th	$19.95	SOA
The Conservatorship Book (California Edition)	2nd	$29.95	CNSV

SOFTWARE

	EDITION	PRICE	CODE
California Incorporator 2.0—DOS	2.0	$47.97	INCI2
Living Trust Maker 2.0—Macintosh	2.0	$47.97	LTM2
Living Trust Maker 2.0—Windows	2.0	$47.97	LTWI2
Small Business Legal Pro—Macintosh	2.0	$25.97	SBM2
Small Business Legal Pro—Windows	2.0	$25.97	SBW2
Small Business Legal Pro Deluxe CD—Windows/Macintosh CD-ROM	2.0	$35.97	SBCD
Nolo's Partnership Maker 1.0—DOS	1.0	$47.97	PAGI1
Personal RecordKeeper 4.0—Macintosh	4.0	$29.97	RKM4
Personal RecordKeeper 4.0—Windows	4.0	$29.97	RKP4
Patent It Yourself 1.0—Windows	1.0	$149.97	PYWI
WillMaker 6.0—Macintosh	6.0	$41.97	WM6
WillMaker 6.0—Windows	6.0	$41.97	WIW6

▣ Book with disk

SPECIAL UPGRADE OFFER

Get 25% off the latest edition of your Nolo book

It's important to have the most current legal information. Because laws and legal procedures change often, we update our books regularly. To help keep you up-to-date we are extending this special upgrade offer. Cut out and mail the title portion of the cover of your old Nolo book and we'll give you 25% off the retail price of the NEW EDITION of that book when you purchase directly from us. For more information call us at 1-800-992-6656. This offer is to individuals only.

ORDER FORM

Name

Address (UPS to street address, Priority Mail to P.O. boxes)

Catalog Code	Quantity	Item	Unit Price	Total

Subtotal	
In California add appropriate Sales Tax	
Shipping & Handling: $5.50 for 1 item, $6.50 for 2-3 items $7.50 for 4 or more.	
UPS RUSH delivery $7.50-any size order*	
TOTAL	

UPS to street address, Priority mail to P.O. boxes

* Delivered in 3 business days from receipt of order.
S.F. Bay area use regular shipping.

METHOD OF PAYMENT

☐ Check enclosed   ☐ VISA   ☐ Mastercard   ☐ Discover Card   ☐ American Express

Account #   Expiration Date

Signature   Phone

FOR FASTER SERVICE, USE YOUR CREDIT CARD and OUR TOLL-FREE NUMBERS

ORDER 24 HOURS A DAY   1-800-992-6656
FAX US YOUR ORDER   1-800-645-0895
e-MAIL   cs@nolo.com
GENERAL INFORMATION   1-510-549-1976
CUSTOMER SERVICE   1-800-728-3555,
Mon.-Sat. 9am-5pm, PST

Or mail your order with a check or money order made payable to:
Nolo Press, 950 Parker St., Berkeley, CA 94710

VISIT OUR STORE

You'll find our complete line of books and software, all at a discount.
BERKELEY—950 Parker St., Berkeley, CA 94710
SAN JOSE—111 N. Market Street, #115, San Jose, CA 95113

VISIT US ONLINE   • **on AOL** — keyword: NOLO   • **on the INTERNET** — www.nolo.com

Take 2 minutes & Get a 2-year
NOLO *News* subscription free!*

With our quarterly magazine, the **NOLO** *News*, you'll

- **Learn** about important legal changes that affect you
- **Find out first** about new Nolo products
- **Keep current** with practical articles on everyday law
- **Get answers** to your legal questions in *Ask Auntie Nolo's* advice column
- **Save money** with special Subscriber Only discounts
- **Tickle your funny bone** with our famous *Lawyer Joke* column.

It only takes 2 minutes to reserve your free 2-year subscription or to extend your **NOLO** *News* subscription.

*U.S. ADDRESSES ONLY.
TWO YEAR INTERNATIONAL SUBSCRIPTIONS: CANADA & MEXICO $10.00;
ALL OTHER FOREIGN ADDRESSES $20.00.

NOLO *News* SPRING 1994

Legal & Consumer Information for Everyone

Work-place Rights

CATALOG INSIDE

call 1-800-992-6656

fax 1-800-645-0895

e-mail NOLOSUB@NOLOPRESS.com

or mail us this postage-paid registration card

R E G I S T R A T I O N   C A R D

NAME _____ DATE _____

ADDRESS _____

_____ PHONE NUMBER _____

CITY _____ STATE _____ ZIP _____

WHERE DID YOU HEAR ABOUT THIS BOOK? _____

WHERE DID YOU PURCHASE THIS PRODUCT? _____

DID YOU CONSULT A LAWYER? (PLEASE CIRCLE ONE)   YES   NO   NOT APPLICABLE

DID YOU FIND THIS BOOK HELPFUL?   (VERY)   5   4   3   2   1   (NOT AT ALL)

SUGGESTIONS FOR IMPROVING THIS PRODUCT

_____

WAS IT EASY TO USE?   (VERY EASY)   5   4   3   2   1   (VERY DIFFICULT)

DO YOU OWN A COMPUTER? IF SO, WHICH FORMAT? (PLEASE CIRCLE ONE)   WINDOWS   DOS   MAC

MAD 1.0

We occasionally make our mailing list available to carefully selected companies whose products may be of interest to you. If you do not wish to receive mailings from these companies, please check this box ❑

"**N**olo helps lay people perform legal tasks without the aid—or fees—of lawyers."—**USA Today**

Nolo books are ..."written in plain language, free of legal mumbo jumbo, and spiced with witty personal observations."—**Associated Press**

"...Nolo publications...guide people simply through the how, when, where and why of law."—**Washington Post**

"Increasingly, people who are not lawyers are performing tasks usually regarded as legal work... And consumers, using books like Nolo's, do routine legal work themselves."—**Washington Post**

"...All of [Nolo's] books are easy-to-understand, are updated regularly, provide pull-out forms...and are often quite moving in their sense of compassion for the struggles of the lay reader."—**San Francisco Chronicle**